This outstanding multi-method study of the evolving character of Hong Kong's repeated waves of protest lays forth a new understanding of how threats influence the organizational forms that movements assume. Masterfully researched and skilfully analysed, this study will be of great interest to scholars of both social movements and authoritarian politics.

Mark R. Beissinger, Henry W. Putnam Professor of Politics at Princeton University, author of *The Revolutionary City: Urbanization and the Global Transformation of Rebellion*

This valuable book, grounded in extensive empirical research, illuminates the characteristics of a 'leaderful' format. It explains how large numbers of protesters collectively exercise leadership simultaneously, as well as the relational mechanisms involved.

Donatella della Porta, Professor of Political Science at Scuola Normale Superiore, author of *Social Movements, Political Violence and the State*

How did Hong Kong people mobilize en masse without leaders to challenge a powerful authoritarian state? Drawing on eight years of on-the-ground research, this book theorizes a leaderful form of mass mobilization that challenges conventional understandings. The authors capture what it means for protestors to "be water" and its implications for contemporary leaderless social movements.

Diana Fu, Associate Professor of Political Science at the University of Toronto, author of *Mobilizing Without the Masses: Control and Contention in China*

Using quantitative and qualitative methods, Cheng and Yuen meticulously account for how spontaneous self-mobilization of citizens has generated several large-scale protests in Hong Kong in recent years. It is a book to be appreciated by social movement scholars around the world. Their pathbreaking discovery of the dynamics of leaderful mobilization helps us understand why massive protests could still erupt as they did under authoritarian regimes.

Ho-fung Hung, Henry M. and Elizabeth P. Wiesenfeld Professor in Political Economy at Johns Hopkins University, author of *Protest with Chinese Characteristics: Demonstrations, Riots, and Petitions in the Mid-Qing Dynasty* and *City on the Edge: Hong Kong under Chinese Rule*

In their capacious new book, Cheng and Yuen join a new transnational generation – including names like Benjamin Abrams, Santiago Anria, Philip Ayoub, Diana Fu, Neil Ketchley, and Dana Moss – whose work addresses fundamental theoretical issues through deeply place-based investigations. Their book advances a creative concept of movement leadership — "leaderful mobilization" — between the tired duality of spontaneity and elite control found in classical movement studies. They demonstrate how — through the capacity of informal leaders to motivate masses of citizens — the movement held the state at bay for months. It should have both a deep and a broad influence in the study of contentious politics.

Sidney Tarrow, Maxwell Upson Professor of Government
at Cornell University, author of *Power in Movement*
and *Movements and Parties*

The Making of Leaderful Mobilization is a great example of a widely anticipated volume that more than lives up to the very high expectations that many people in a field had for it. For years now, Cheng and Yuen have been steadily producing some insightful articles and book chapters on varied aspects of protest in Hong Kong. Their book not only pulls together the key strands from those pioneering publications in a beautifully clear way, but also brings in important new data and arguments. The result is a major contribution to both Hong Kong Studies and Social Movement Studies. I was eagerly awaiting this book – and it proves well worth the wait.

Jeffrey Wasserstrom, Chancellor's Professor of History
at UC Irvine, author of *Vigil: Hong Kong on the Brink*

The Making of Leaderful Mobilization

The past few decades have seen the transformation of Hong Kong from a liberal enclave to a revolutionary crucible on the edge of China. *The Making of Leaderful Mobilization* takes you through the evolution of protests in this restive city where ordinary citizens gradually emerged as the protagonists of contention in place of social movement organizations. The book presents a theory of mediated threat that illuminates how threat perceptions fuelled shifting forms of mobilization – from brokered mobilization where organizations played guiding roles to leaderful mobilization driven by peer collaboration among the masses. Bringing together event analysis, opinion polls, interviews, and social media data, this book provides a thorough and methodical anatomy of Hong Kong's contentious politics. It unveils the processes and mechanisms of collective action that likely prevailed in many contemporary social movements worldwide. Our temporal approach also uncovers the multiple pathways reshaping hybrid regimes, underscoring their resilience and fragility.

Edmund W. Cheng is Professor of Political Science at the City University of Hong Kong. His research spans contentious politics, political communication, and the sociology of knowledge. He co-edits *Social Movement Studies* and is a recipient of the Gordon White Prize.

Samson Yuen is Associate Professor of Political Science in the Department of Government and International Studies at Hong Kong Baptist University. His research interests include contentious politics, civil conflicts, public opinion, and civil society, focusing on East Asia. He is a recipient of the International Convention of Asia Scholars Best Article Prize.

Cambridge Studies in Contentious Politics

General Editor
David S. Meyer *University of California, Irvine*

Editors
Mark Beissinger *Princeton University*
Donatella della Porta *Scuola Normale Superiore*
Jack A. Goldstone *George Mason University*
Michael Hanagan *Vassar College*
Doug McAdam *Stanford University and Center for Advanced Study in the Behavioral Sciences Si*
Holly J. McCammon *Vanderbilt University*
Sarah Soule *Stanford University*
Suzanne Staggenborg *University of Pittsburgh*
Sidney Tarrow *Cornell University*
Charles Tilly (d. 2008) *Columbia University*
Elisabeth J. Wood *Yale University*
Deborah Yashar *Princeton University*

The Making of Leaderful Mobilization

Power and Contention in Hong Kong

EDMUND W. CHENG
City University of Hong Kong

SAMSON YUEN
Hong Kong Baptist University

CAMBRIDGE
UNIVERSITY PRESS

Shaftesbury Road, Cambridge CB2 8EA, United Kingdom

One Liberty Plaza, 20th Floor, New York, NY 10006, USA

477 Williamstown Road, Port Melbourne, VIC 3207, Australia

314–321, 3rd Floor, Plot 3, Splendor Forum, Jasola District Centre,
New Delhi – 110025, India

103 Penang Road, #05–06/07, Visioncrest Commercial, Singapore 238467

Cambridge University Press is part of Cambridge University Press & Assessment,
a department of the University of Cambridge.

We share the University's mission to contribute to society through the pursuit of
education, learning and research at the highest international levels of excellence.

www.cambridge.org
Information on this title: www.cambridge.org/9781009445856

DOI: 10.1017/9781009445832

When citing this work, please include a reference to the DOI 10.1017/9781009445832

First published 2025

A catalogue record for this publication is available from the British Library

Library of Congress Cataloging-in-Publication Data
NAMES: Cheng, Edmund W., author. | Yuen, Samson, 1986– author.
TITLE: The making of leaderful mobilization : power and contention in Hong Kong /
Edmund W. Cheng, City University of Hong Kong; Samson Yuen,
Hong Kong Baptist University.
DESCRIPTION: New York, NY : Cambridge University Press, 2025. | Series: Cambridge
studies in contentious politics | Includes bibliographical references and index.
IDENTIFIERS: LCCN 2024021477 | ISBN 9781009445856 (hardback) |
ISBN 9781009445832 (ebook)
SUBJECTS: LCSH: Hong Kong Protests, Hong Kong, China, 2019– | Protest
Movements – China – Hong Kong. | Civil disobedience – China – Hong Kong. |
Hong Kong (China) – Politics and government – 1997–
CLASSIFICATION: LCC JQ1539.5.A91 Z46 2025 | DDC 303.6095125–dc23/eng/20240716
LC record available at https://lccn.loc.gov/2024021477

ISBN 978-1-009-44585-6 Hardback
ISBN 978-1-009-44584-9 Paperback

To our loved ones

Contents

Figures

Tables

Preface

This book began its life as a casual conversation in early October 2014. Both of us were postgraduate students at that time, writing our doctoral theses and taking a break from our fieldwork in mainland China. We bumped into each other in Admiralty, a business district in downtown Hong Kong that was then occupied by angry protesters. Though we were no strangers to the spectacle of mass protests in our hometown, the Umbrella Movement truly surprised us with its sheer scale and burst of energy. As often happens in academic dialogues, we agreed that we should start studying these unfolding events; and we did. In the following days, we designed a survey, assembled a team, and distributed the surveys across the three protest camps. Time was of the essence as it seemed likely that the police would clear out these camps at any minute. Thanks to our team's efforts, we were able to complete the data collection. We never anticipated that the occupation would continue for another two months. Nor did we foresee that the movement would become a key turning point in Hong Kong's history and politics.

Since then, we closely followed protest events in what was known to international observers as the 'city of protests'. We dug into Hong Kong's history of protests and continued to conduct surveys and ground observations whenever there were major rallies or demonstrations. We interviewed politicians, activists, protest participants, government officials, and ordinary citizens. Our research deepened the conviction that this dynamic laboratory of protests could contribute important insights to the scholarship of contentious politics. As exemplified by the Umbrella Movement, the intensity and innovative forms of Hong Kong's popular contention have often resonated with mass mobilizations happening globally since the early 2010s, including the Arab Spring uprisings, the Global Occupy Movement, the Spanish Indignados, and the Maidan Revolution in Ukraine.

In 2019, the eruption of the Anti-Extradition Movement once again brought this liberal enclave on the fringe of China into the global limelight, making it arguably the most extensively reported protest event of the twenty-first century. As students of contentious politics, we readily deployed our research toolkits and studiously documented the unfolding events. This time, we were again surprised – not only by the scale of participation in the movement but also by its resilience, despite the lack of a centralized leadership. International observers would soon recognize similar dynamics in mass mobilizations emerging globally in the ensuing months in 2019 and 2020, from Belarus to Chile, France to Lebanon, Sudan to Iraq, Indonesia to Thailand, and even in the United States. Although these mobilizations were sparked by various causes, they shared a common thread of spontaneity and a conspicuous absence of leadership. The tactical repertoire on display also bore striking similarities, with many tactics evidently originating from Hong Kong. This is why we felt a compelling need to produce a comprehensive account of Hong Kong's protest trajectory and its gradual shift from organized contention to leaderful mobilization. We hope that this book will yield comparative insights for contentious politics scholars. For those interested in Hong Kong and China, we hope that this book offers a systematic account of the sociopolitical evolution of this semi-autonomous city, leading to the implementation of the National Security Law in 2020. While times and circumstances have undoubtedly shifted, our belief in the value of research and scholarship remains as strong as ever.

Academic research often feels like a solitary journey, but co-authoring this book has made it much less so. Being co-authors meant we were constantly exchanging our ideas and challenging each other. There were innumerable moments of intense debates and disagreements, but each time we were able to come to a consensus and ultimately refined our ideas. This book is a product of these intellectual dialogues and our friendship. Although we took the lead on different chapters, we spent a lot of time critiquing, cross-examining, and rewriting each other's work. Both of us equally contributed to this book and regard each other as co-first authors.

Acknowledgements

We are extremely grateful for the numerous informants and respondents to our surveys. Without their support and trust, this book would not have been possible. Their willingness to share their experiences and knowledge has been invaluable, and this book would not have been the same without their contributions. Some of our informants have either left Hong Kong or, for various reasons, are unable to read this book. We hope that it will live up to the rigorous standards of academic research while providing an informed analysis of the protest events and social changes in Hong Kong.

At Cambridge University Press, we extend our gratitude to our editor, Rachel Blaifeder, for her patience, flexibility, and guidance. We also appreciate the editorial assistance of Jadyn Fauconier-Herry, Chloe Quinn, and Santhamurthy Ramamoorthy. Our sincere thanks go to Jack Goldstone for his enthusiastic support in the early stages of the book project and for introducing this project to David Meyer. As the editor of the Cambridge Series in Contentious Politics, David assigned reviewers, offered encouraging and constructive feedback, and made it possible to include our study in this prestigious series. We are particularly grateful to Sid Tarrow, who read the full manuscript and generously offered chapter-by-chapter comments. Above all, we are deeply thankful to the two anonymous reviewers for providing penetrating and constructive comments on the first draft of the manuscript.

Our heartfelt gratitude also goes to scholars who generously gave their time, insights, and suggestions for early versions of the book. Ma Ngok has been a supportive mentor to both of us, always sharing his boundless knowledge of Hong Kong and offering insightful suggestions for the manuscript. Ming-sho Ho, Yao-tai Li, and Sebastian Veg read the entire manuscript and provided critical and constructive comments. Our long-term collaborators and friends Francis Lee and Gary Tang generously offered us suggestions, granted us access to our jointly owned data, and allowed us to use the articles we co-authored as the foundation for some of these chapters. Anita Chan and Jon Unger made us thoroughly enjoy our short stay in Canberra and always challenged us intellectually with the 'so what' question. Michael Biggs and Patricia Thornton kindly chaired our book seminar at the University of Oxford and provided insightful feedback. Eliza Lee and Ray Yep have provided us with endless inspiration, illuminating a path of how public intellectual life can be guided by empirical scholarship.

We would also like to extend our sincere gratitude to Benjamin Abrams, Mark Beissinger, Teri L. Caraway, Paul Chang, Killian Clarke, Priska Daphi, Diana Fu, Jean Hong, Hank Johnston, Yi Kang, Neil Ketchley, Yao-Tai Li, Dana Moss, Anthony Spires, Meredith Weiss, and Katherine Whitworth for kindly agreeing to participate in various book seminars or offering useful feedback on early versions of the book. Tetsuro Kobayashi, Debby Chan, Kitty Ho, King-wa Fu, Ho-fung Hung, Elvin Ong, Xi Chen, Ariel Hu, Wing-Kei Cheng, and See-Pok Loa, and Anthony Spires also provided timely suggestions at various phases of the project, for which we are immensely thankful.

This book is the result of significant contributions from numerous individuals. John Mok, Billy Tang, Anthony Cheng, Hiu-Fung Chung, Elgar Teo, Yuner Zhu, and Kin-Man Wan offered invaluable research assistance at different stages. A special shout-out goes to Billy Tong for his generous help during the crucial final stage of the book when we were up against the deadline. Mary Hui provided valuable stylistic guidance and editing advice, helping to make the book more approachable for non-academic readers. This book is truly a collective endeavour of our combined efforts.

We are immensely grateful to the numerous institutions, including the Australian National University; Academia Sinica; the University of British Columbia; the University of California, Santa Barbara; the University of New South Wales; the Berlin Social Sciences Centre; the University of Tokyo; Tohoku University; Aarhus University; and Oxford University, which graciously hosted us, allowing us to present chapters, receive feedback, and further refine our work. These intellectual environments have been pivotal in shaping this book. We also thank Jean-Pierre Cabestan, Anita Chan, Chris Chan, Jay Chen, Cristina Flesher-Fominaya, Thomas Gold, Masaaki Higashijima, Ben Hillman, Swen Hutter, Minhua Ling, Kevin O'Brien, Jack Qiu, Hyun Bang Shin, Leo Shin, Kurata Toru, Akiko Toru, Mariko Tanigaki, Sebastian Veg, Jon Unger and Jieh-min Wu for inviting us to various conferences and workshops held between 2019 and 2023.

We would also like to thank various publishers, journals, and co-authors for permitting us to incorporate parts of our previous publications into some of the chapters of this book. Chapter 3 is derived in part from 'Street Politics in a Hybrid Regime: The Diffusion of Political Activism in Post-colonial Hong Kong', published in the *China Quarterly*. Chapter 7 is derived in part from 'Instagram and Social Capital: Youth Activism in a Networked Movement', published in *Social Movement Studies*. Chapter 10 is derived in part from

'Dynamics of Tactical Radicalisation and Public Receptiveness in Hong Kong's Anti-Extradition Bill Movement', published in the *Journal of Contemporary Asia*.

To our families and friends, words cannot express how grateful we are for your support in our endeavours over the years. Edmund Cheng owes his steadfast source of love and encouragement to his wife, Sum. Her mindfulness, empathy, and artistic sense provide him with the compassion and strength needed to continue his work, despite the dramatic changes in the surrounding environment. The mentorship, friendship, and insights from Shu-yun Ma, Albert Weale, and Lin Chun have guided him through both old and new intellectual terrains. He is also grateful for the professional engagement and intellectual dialogue over the past few years with his friends and colleagues at various professional associations and academic journals. Their work exemplifies the pride and dedication inherent in scholarly pursuits.

Samson Yuen is thankful to his family for being an unwavering source of love and support. His parents have devoted their lives to raising him while granting him the freedom to pursue his dreams. He is also grateful to his wife, Phyllis, who has filled him with boundless love, care, and understanding. Her kindness, wisdom, and patience have made him a better person and helped him survive difficult moments in life. Their children are the best gifts he has ever received. Despite occasionally testing his patience, they have filled his life with abundant joy and laughter. He enjoys every moment of being with them and wishes that time would slow down. It is to his family that he dedicates this book.

Notes on Transliteration

In this book, important or noteworthy terms are transliterated into their Chinese Pinyin (included in the bracket following the terms). For terms that are specifically important in the Hong Kong context, Pinyin will also be followed by the *jyutping* transliteration, in which the characters are separated by a hyphen rather than a space.

Abbreviations

API	Application Programming Interface
CCP	Chinese Communist Party
CGLO	Liaison Office of the Central People's Government
CHRF	Civil Human Rights Front
CPPCC	Chinese People's Political Consultative Conference
ExCo	Executive Council
HKA	Hong Kong Alliance in Support of Patriotic Democratic Movements of China
HKCTU	Hong Kong Confederation of Trade Unions
HKD	Hong Kong Dollars
HKFS	Hong Kong Federation of Students
HKIAD	Hong Kong Higher Institutions International Affairs Delegation
HKPTU	Hong Kong Professional Teachers' Union
HKSAR	Hong Kong Special Administrative Region
HKSFF	Hong Kong Schools Sports Federation
HKUJMSC	Journalism and Media Studies Centre at the University of Hong Kong
HKUPOP	Hong Kong University Public Opinion Programme
KMT	Kuomintang
LegCo	Legislative Council
LSD	League of Social Democrats
NPC	National People's Congress
NPCSC	The Standing Committee of the National People's Congress
NSL	National Security Law
OCLP	Occupy Central with Love and Peace
OCTS	One Country, Two Systems

OLS	ordinary least squares
PLA	People's Liberation Army
PLG	Progressive Lawyers' Group
PRC	People's Republic of China
SAR	Special Administrative Region
SMOs	social movement organizations
SSStrike	Secondary School Strike

Introduction

At 7:30 am on 12 June 2019, it was already hot and sultry in Hong Kong. The early summer day had yet to reach rush hour, but a small group of protesters had already gathered, blocking Lung Wo Road near the Legislative Council (LegCo) where politicians were set to discuss a controversial bill that had sparked widespread opposition. Soon, more and more protesters arrived. They skilfully moved to stop the traffic on Harcourt Road, swiftly occupying the city's major highway that connects court buildings, government branches, financial institutions, and the garrison army. By 8:00 am, Admiralty was teeming with anxious protesters. They heeded the call to strike from work and surround both the LegCo and the adjacent Hong Kong government headquarters, a towering glass-clad structure. Equipped with face masks, goggles, helmets, and umbrellas, they were prepared for potential clashes with the police, ready to face the situation head-on.

Admiralty – once a navy dockyard during the British colonial era and now the political and economic heart of China's Special Administrative Region (SAR) – was an eventful place. Five years before the movement, in the autumn of 2014, a large section of it was occupied by protesters calling for democratic reforms to the city's electoral system. Known as the Umbrella Movement, the largely peaceful occupation persisted for over two months but ultimately fell short of its objectives, as the government dismantled the encampments. Half a decade later, it seemed as though history was repeating itself. This time, however, protesters appeared more equipped and resolute in their actions. Moreover, they were driven by a more pressing objective: to halt the advancement of an amendment to the city's extradition laws, which was scheduled for its second reading.

Several months earlier, the government put forth a controversial proposal to amend the city's extradition law, allowing for the extradition of fugitives to mainland China. Despite Hong Kong's status as an SAR of the People's

Republic of China (PRC) for the past two decades, there were no existing extradition agreements with the mainland. The amendment gradually ignited widespread public concern. Citizens feared that the law could be exploited to target political dissidents within the semi-autonomous city and erode the legal barrier that had traditionally distinguished Hong Kong from the mainland. Initial signs of dissent emerged in February 2019 as soon as the government tabled the amendment bill. However, it was not until May, after intense debates in the legislature and an online petition that garnered hundreds of thousands of signatures, that the opposition movement gained momentum and galvanized society.

June 9 marked a historic moment, as approximately one million people took to the streets in a peaceful demonstration against the imminent bill. The massive turnout made it the largest protest in Hong Kong's history.[1] Led by Civil Human Rights Front (CHRF), a coalition of prominent pro-democracy social movement organizations (SMOs), the June 9 rally was so massive that protesters found themselves stranded in Victoria Park for hours before they could commence the march. The rally officially ended at 10:00 pm – far later than typical marches. Many stayed on the streets for longer. But the Hong Kong government remained unmoved by the unprecedented turnout. It declared that it had no intention to suspend the bill and asserted that the second reading, the final step before the law's implementation, would proceed despite the opposition.

Outraged by the government's dismissal of public dissent, protesters once again assembled on June 12. This time, the demonstration unfolded quite differently. Unlike the organization-led rally on June 9, the day's protest was not initiated by any leaders or organizers. Numerous organizations and trade unions had urged citizens to strike but did not provide specific plans of action. Instead, individuals primarily relied on online platforms to disseminate the call to mobilize. One such call was started by two ordinary Facebook users, who created an event page to invite others to 'picnic alone' at the government headquarters. Remarkably, within hours, over 10,000 citizens expressed their intent to participate. As protesters arrived in Admiralty for their 'picnic' the next day, there were no leaders or organizers to provide guidance, nor was there any plan or timetable to be followed. The event was entirely improvised. No one knew what to do next and how it would end.

A decentralized yet implicitly 'organized' form of mobilization quickly emerged with a spontaneous division of labour. Protesters tacitly assumed various roles. Some positioned themselves on the frontlines, directly engaging with riot police. Others played crucial supporting roles that aligned with their existing expertise. Doctors and nurses established impromptu first-aid stations to provide essential medical care to injured protesters. Van drivers

---

[1] Activists suggested that the pro-democracy protest on 25 May 1989 drew around 1.5 million marchers in Hong Kong, but that figure is disputed (Lee and Chan 2010; Szeto 2011).

used their vehicles to transport vital supplies such as water, saline solution, and surgical masks. Christian groups formed choir lines, physically separating protesters from the police, filling the air with calming religious hymns. Meanwhile, students used the encrypted messaging app Telegram to create channels to disseminate verified information about the protest. This decentralized and spontaneous protest set the stage for what was to come for the Anti-Extradition Law Amendment Bill Movement (hereafter referred to as the Anti-Extradition Movement).

Under immense public pressure, the government suspended the bill three days later on June 15. But protesters were not satisfied. They continued their mobilization and built upon the unfulfilled demands of the 2014 Umbrella Movement to incorporate political reforms in their demands. Adopting a 'be water' strategy, protesters emulated the tactics employed on June 12 and orchestrated numerous protest actions citywide. In the following months, guided by this decentralized logic, protesters paralyzed traffic, staged wild-cat demonstrations and airport sit-ins, broke into LegCo, organized neighbourhood protests, and turned university campuses into fiery battlegrounds. They boycotted pro-government businesses and actively supported those aligned with the movement, leveraging their economic influence to exert political pressure. Some activists even pioneered an 'international front' to mobilize support overseas.

Despite intensifying momentum, the Hong Kong SAR government stood firm and refused to make further concessions. As the Chinese authorities signalled their disapproval of the protests, local authorities shifted to a more hard-line stance. Riot police escalated their use of crowd control measures to suppress the unrest. The situation quickly radicalized the protests. Faced with a hardened government, protesters felt compelled to use increasingly transgressive and violent tactics to hold their ground. Yet, the movement managed to maintain a surprising level of cohesion despite tactical radicalization. While some protesters resorted to using weapons such as bricks, bamboo poles, and Molotov cocktails to confront the police, moderate protesters remained tolerant of these transgressive actions. This exceptional level of cohesion extended beyond the streets and translated into a significant political victory at the ballot box. In the local District Council elections held in November 2019, the pro-democracy camp won a landslide victory, securing 388 out of 479 seats.

THE CITY OF PROTESTS

Despite the spectacle of 2019, mass protests were a familiar sight in Hong Kong. Since its handover to the PRC in 1997, the semi-autonomous city had earned a reputation as a 'city of protests' due to the regularity and scale of its protest activities (Dapiran 2017). Operating under the One Country, Two Systems (OCTS) principle, Hong Kong citizens enjoyed freedoms and rights not available to their counterparts on the mainland. Despite maintaining a closed political system dominated by business and state interests, the semi-autonomous city afforded citizens the freedoms of speech and assembly. Empowered by these rights, opposition activists successfully organized a series of protest movements over the past two decades. These movements were sparked by a range of issues comprising heritage preservation, infrastructural development, education, and constitutional reforms. Other protests were more routine. On every June 4, hundreds of thousands would assemble for a candlelight vigil to commemorate the victims of the 1989 Tiananmen Movement. On every July 1, the anniversary of the sovereignty handover, hundreds of thousands would again participate in an annual anti-government demonstration, demanding greater government accountability and the implementation of universal suffrage.

These protests shared a common feature, albeit one that would wane over time: the dominant role of SMOs. Both the annual July 1 rallies and the June 4 vigils were highly organized events, consistently led by pro-democracy parties or civil society organizations. They adhered to highly scripted and ritualistic formats – congregating in the same locations at the same times, marching the same routes, singing the same songs, chanting the same slogans, and following a familiar agenda. Participants in these demonstrations often engaged in a passive manner, following the familiar script laid out before them. The issue-driven movements, meanwhile, were less scripted and more improvised. They tended to be longer in duration and unpredictable in their evolution. For instance, the 2012 Anti-Moral and National Education Movement brewed for several months, eventually culminating in a week-long occupation of the government headquarters' forecourt. The 2014 Umbrella Movement originally started as a civil disobedience campaign and class boycott but exploded into a city-wide occupation for eleven weeks. However, even in these increasingly spontaneous movements, a form of centralized leadership often emerged, composed of SMOs, opposition parties, and prominent activists. This leadership played a vital role in coordinating protest actions, handling logistics, negotiating with the authorities, and directing the protesters.

The 2019 Anti-Extradition Movement stood out from the earlier movements in several ways. The most obvious was its duration and turnout. Unlike most previous movements that normally lasted a day or no more than a week, the Anti-Extradition Movement lasted for seven months, even significantly exceeding the duration of the Umbrella Movement. It challenged the expectation that urban revolutions are often 'limited in duration because they occur where the state's coercive power is strongest and its nerve centers are concentrated' (Beissinger 2022: 204). The movement comprised several hundreds of protest actions dispersed across the city, different from how previous movements tended to concentrate in a few locations. Its cumulative participation rate also dwarfed previous movements. According to a poll, an astonishing 45% of Hong Kong's population of seven million residents took part in at least one protest event during the movement, and 58% expressed support for its demands (Cheng et al. 2022). This level of involvement surpassed the city's largest protests after the handover – the 2003 July 1 rally and the Umbrella Movement – which reportedly mobilized 8% and 20% of the population, respectively (Cheng and Ma 2020). Compared with other notable mass mobilizations globally, the Anti-Extradition Movement also stood out. It surpassed the 12% participation rate in Ukraine's Euromaidan of 2014 (Chupryna 2021), the 16% in the Tunisian Revolution of 2011, the 8% in the Egyptian Revolution of 2011 (Beissinger, Jamal, and Mazur 2015: 3), and the 10% in the United States' Black Lives Matter protests of 2020 (Heaney 2022).

Perhaps the most distinctive feature of the Anti-Extradition Movement was its organizational form. In contrast to the routine and issue-driven protests, the movement did not have a centralized leadership. While it formally started with an organized rally led by a prominent SMO in early June, it swiftly became 'leaderless' as ordinary citizens, who were mostly unaffiliated with conventional organizations, planned and orchestrated protest actions in a decentralized and spontaneous manner, as described at the outset of the chapter. These protesters harnessed digital communication technologies and social networks to mobilize other fellow citizens and manage the intricacies of organizing. Instead of being passive participants following a pre-determined script, protesters became both the scriptwriters and the protagonists mobilizing on their own terms. While opposition parties and civil society organizations remained involved in organizing and coordinating some of the protest actions, they deliberately maintained a low profile and limited their role to resource provision and logistical support.

LEADERFUL MOBILIZATION

Many scholars and observers have characterized the 2019 protests as a 'leaderless' movement (BBC 2019; Lai and Sing 2020; Liang and Lee 2023) to underscore its departure from traditional movements with a clearly identifiable leadership structure. However, the label can be misleading in two ways. First, by merely defining the movement as *what it was not*, it fails to inform us about the movement's organizational structure and dynamics. Second, the term 'leaderless' could imply that leadership practices are absent, given that leadership is commonly understood as the defining quality of leaders. But this could misrepresent what occurred in the Anti-Extradition Movement. Leadership was certainly present, but it was not exercised by traditional leaders and organizations.

A new concept is needed to capture this unique organizational form. We argue that the 2019 Anti-Extradition Movement belongs to a class of movements that can be characterized as 'leaderful mobilization'. Leaderful mobilization is defined as *a form of mobilization where large numbers of protesters collectively and simultaneously exercise leadership without the traditional hierarchy that concentrates power in the hands of a few*. Under leaderful mobilization, leadership is distributed across a wide array of actors, including ordinary citizens, latent networks, and conventional SMOs. In this sense, protesters are actively engaging in organizing and coordinating protest actions rather than merely attending them. They take on different leadership roles and tasks (Earl 2007), such as planning, communication, information gathering, logistics, and advocacy, to sustain mobilization under a decentralized and horizontal structure. As such, leadership can be understood as a set of practices that are divided among participants and shared collaboratively, rather than as positions held by specific individuals or entities, or the attributes that they hold. In other words, the 'mass' in mass mobilization has developed a new life: they are no longer a collective entity *being* mobilized; instead, they are exercising agency and taking matters in their own hands. They are 'masses' of their own accord.

As leadership is distributed among participants, protesters who take leads can be considered to be informal leaders in these movements. These informal leaders do not necessarily have to reveal their identity to others. Moreover, they may not possess the same level of public profile or charisma as historical movement leaders like Mahatma Gandhi or Martin Luther King, and they usually do not wield the same authority over organizational bureaucracies and human resources as these traditional figures. Nonetheless, informal leaders have the capacity to develop strategic agency and make consequential decisions for the movement. For instance, they can craft and disseminate slogans, posters, or infographics via social media to frame issues and draw public attention. They can contribute ideas or devise innovative tactics that generate new political opportunities. Furthermore, they can utilize digital or latent social networks to mobilize their peers. To put ideas into action, they can assemble teams to strategize and execute specific initiatives. Although their leadership may be tied to specific actions and not be sustained over time, these informal leaders are capable of influencing and directing the movement through taking initiatives and collaborating with one another.

Another distinguishing feature of leaderful mobilizations is the intrinsic role of spontaneity. By spontaneity, we refer to events or happenings that are largely improvised without predetermined plans. David Snow and Dana Moss (2014: 1123) define spontaneity as a cover term for 'events, happenings, and lines of action, both verbal and nonverbal, which were not planned, intended, prearranged, or organized in advance of their occurrence'. Benjamin Abrams (2023: 3) further uses the term to characterize some of the recent protest movements, such as the Black Lives Matter Movement and the Arab Spring uprisings, as 'spontaneous mass mobilizations', which occurs when 'large numbers of people partake in contentious politics without reliance on social movement organizations and their networks'. This is similar to how we conceptualize leaderful mobilizations. But there are three reasons why we prefer not to use 'spontaneous' to define such mobilizations. First, spontaneity is inherent to protests. Even protests that are meticulously planned can exhibit a significant degree of spontaneity once they unfold. Protesters may deviate from predetermined plans or routes, or the situation may unexpectedly escalate due to police actions. Second, even though mass mobilizations are inherently unpredictable, structural conditions matter in conditioning their onset and outcomes. Grievances, previous acts of mobilization or political opportunities often create a structured set of choice for actors, contributing to what Mark Beissinger (2011) calls 'structure of contingency'. Third, elements of planning are often present within what appears to be spontaneous mobilization. For example, they still schedule and coordinate actions so that protesters can assemble at the same location and time, even though they might not have a detailed plan beyond that point. However, while we do not define such mobilizations primarily as 'spontaneous', it is still accurate to say that spontaneity is intricately woven into the fabric of leaderful mobilizations. Despite some form of planning, the absence of centralized leadership implies that protesters continually adapt and improvise their tactics according to the situation.

The term 'leaderful' was originally developed in organizational studies to address the evolving needs of the workplace and the inadequacies of the traditional leadership model, which typically revolves around a single leader. Joseph Raelin (2003, 2011) famously proposes the idea of creating 'leaderful organizations', in which he views leadership as a collective practice that can be distributed among members of an organization. The idea of leadership as a relational and distributive practice, rather than as a stable set of attributes inherent in individuals, has also been adopted by organizational scholars and applied to social movement settings (Sutherland, Land, and Böhm 2014; Western 2014). Sasha Costanza-Chock (2012: 9) described the Occupy Movement of the early 2010s as 'leaderful' to illustrate how any participant could learn to interact with the press without designating specific individuals as official spokespeople. While Costanza-Chock initially used the term in the context of the movement's media strategies, it is a fitting characterization of the Occupy Movement as a whole. Occupy protests around the world often adopted decentralized and horizontal structures with no identifiable leaders, with participants engaging in direct democracy and collective decision-making through participatory assemblies (Juris 2012; Smith and Glidden 2012). A similar characterization could be applied to the Arab Spring uprisings, which became a major inspiration for the Occupy Movement. These revolts saw civil society activists and ordinary citizens spontaneously mobilizing against authoritarian rulers without central leadership, relying heavily on social media for planning and coordination (Tufekci 2017). To an extent, one could also regard the New Social Movements – especially the feminist and environmental movements of the 1970s – and the anti-globalization movement of the 1990s and 2000s, as having leaderful elements, given how they rejected formal leaders and adopted horizontal organizational structures (Freeman 1972).

In other words, leaderful mobilization is not a completely new political phenomenon. However, there is something distinct and intriguing about Hong Kong's leaderful mobilization in 2019. First, even with an established political opposition, the Anti-Extradition Movement embraced a leaderful structure, eschewing the leadership of political parties and civil society organizations. This contrasts with other contexts where leaderful mobilizations emerged: in authoritarian regimes such as Egypt and Syria, the political opposition was either weak or non-existent before the uprisings. It was no surprise that protests had to take leaderful forms in such contests. But why did Hong Kong's opposition organizations, which were highly institutionalized with strong mass support base, *not* take a leading role in the Anti-Extradition Movement? Second, unlike leaderful movements elsewhere that often involved occupying public spaces or setting up protest encampments, the Anti-Extradition Movement adopted a more fluid and adaptable approach. Embracing Bruce Lee's 'be water' dictum, protest actions were spatially dispersed, eschewing fixed protest routes and avoiding the occupation of public spaces. Yet, even in the absence of a designated focal point – such as Tahrir Square during the Egyptian revolution, Zuccotti Park during Occupy Wall Street or Plaza Mayor during the Spanish Indignados Movement – the Anti-Extradition Movement maintained its resilience and carried on for more than six months. Furthermore, in contrast to other recent leaderful mobilizations that typically faced 'tactical freeze' (Tufekci 2017), where protesters found it difficult to develop new strategies after the initial stages, the Anti-Extradition Movement saw continuous innovation of strategies and tactics. Moreover, protesters also managed to keep themselves organized and maintain a high level of cohesion despite the lack of traditional organizational structures.

OUR PUZZLE

Hong Kong's evolution from organization-led and scripted protests to the 2019 Anti-Extradition Movement presents an intriguing puzzle. What contributed to the rise of leaderful mobilization in a semi-authoritarian context? What explains the waning influence of traditional organizations in its trajectory of mass mobilizations? What catalysed the transformation of ordinary citizens from passive adherents of established groups to engaged protesters motivated by convictions? How did this leaderful mobilization manage to attain such an extensive scale, sustain itself for months, and maintain a relative degree of organization and unity without centralized leadership or the occupation of a fixed space?

This book aims to explain the ascent of leaderful mobilization from a historically established paradigm of organization-led protests in post-handover Hong Kong. We present a theory of mediated threat to elucidate how perceived threats to civic freedoms and institutional autonomy gave rise to changing forms of mass mobilizations. Our central argument posits that threats do not instantly trigger protests; rather, they must be perceived and socially processed among citizens to spark mobilization. Different groups of citizens may perceive the same threat in different ways, resulting in a spectrum of mobilizational responses and the formation of new organizations, groups, and networks. This process gradually alters the relational dynamics of the opposition through which new threats are assessed, precipitating new mobilizing structures from which future mobilizations will arise, and ultimately altering their organizational forms.

EXISTING EXPLANATIONS

Existing social movement theories offer useful insights for some of these questions, yet they seem inadequate for addressing our broader puzzle. In what follows, we will explore three strands of literature, each centred on a concept that has significantly influenced the study of contentious politics and provides some degree of analytical leverage for our case.

Political Opportunity Structure

Political opportunity structure (POS) is one of the most influential and widely used frameworks in the field of contentious politics. In response to earlier theories that focus on the role of internal factors – such as resources, leadership, and strategy – in mobilization (Jenkins and Perrow 1977; McCarthy and Zald 1973, 1977), the POS framework highlights the political environment that provide opportunities for, or constraints on, social movements to arise, mobilize and achieve their objectives. The premise of the framework is that activists do not choose goals and tactics in a vacuum but do so within the contours of the political contexts (Meyer 2004). Key dimensions of POS include the openness of the political system, the stability of political alignments, the presence of elite allies, and the state's propensity for repression (Eisinger 1973; Kitschelt 1986; McAdam 1982, 1996; Tarrow 1989; Tilly 1978). When more political opportunities are available, social movements are expected to have greater likelihood of emergence or success.

The POS has served as a canonical framework for explaining why movements emerge and decline. Doug McAdam's seminal study of the civil rights movement in the United States (1982) has demonstrated its analytical power by showing how favourable changes in policy and the political environment – such as the collapse of the cotton economy, African American migration to the North, and Supreme Court rulings – allowed the movement to flourish, whereas diminishing policy responsiveness in 1970s led to its decline. The framework was also applied to other cases, such as the US women's movement (Costain 1992), the anti-nuclear movements (Kitschelt 1986), movements in Italy (Tarrow 1989), and the new social movements in Europe (Kriesi et al. 1992), to explain the rise and fall of movement activities both longitudinally and comparatively. The POS framework was subsequently challenged for its 'structural bias' (Gamson and Meyer 1996), with the primary charge being that the definition of political opportunities is too expansive, as it attempts to account for all potential factors that may contribute to movements (Goodwin and Jasper 1999). These challenges have led scholars working with the POS framework to moderate their structuralist orientation and focus more on the role of agency in engaging with structures (McAdam, Tarrow, and Tilly 1997; McAdam 2000). Meanwhile, they have also guided others to examine the cultural processes that shape movements, such as framing (Snow and Benford 2000), collective identities (Diani 1992; Gamson 1991; Melucci 1995), discourses (Polletta 2006), and emotions (Goodwin, Jasper, and Polletta 2001).

However, while the POS framework is widely used to explain movements in democratic contexts, it has limited analytical power for mobilizations occurring in authoritarian regimes, given that the conditions that facilitate movements are often missing in such contexts (Almeida 2003). In authoritarian settings, political opportunities may exist but they are often not easily accessible and may not be apparent to regime outsiders and ordinary citizens. Authoritarian incumbents also utilize various tools to eliminate political opportunities for protest (Fu 2018; Sika 2023). Furthermore, formal organizations that would typically serve as mobilizing structures are frequently banned or heavily restricted due to political repression in such contexts (Pfaff 1996; Spires 2011). This was roughly the case in Hong Kong. Although the city was not a full-fledged authoritarian regime, it did not witness increasing political openness in a structural sense like what facilitated the US civil rights movement. There were surely political opportunities emerging from time to time that enabled the occurrence of protests, such as elite division or legislative battles that bought time for activists to mobilize the public. However, these political opportunities were often contingent (Saunders 2009), fleeting or created by activists themselves (Gamson and Meyer 1996).

To explain mobilization in authoritarian contexts, some scholars have turned to the role of threats (Almeida 2003; Goldstone and Tilly 2001), which appear to be more prevalent and visible than opportunities. In fact, the importance of threats has already been highlighted (Tilly 1978). However, not only have scholars disproportionately focused on opportunity (Pinard 2011; Van Dyke 2013), they have also incorporated threat within the notion of opportunities (Almeida 2003), treating it as 'a negative measure of the same concept' (Goldstone and Tilly 2001: 181). Scholars interested in threats argue that the concept should be defined on its own terms. Jack Goldstone and Charles Tilly define threats as 'the costs that a social group will experience if it acts – or doesn't act' (2001: 183). As such, threats can provoke defensive mobilizations because they either undermine what individuals take for granted or cause further harm if they fail to resist. Paul Almeida masterfully illustrates the role of threats in triggering mobilization in El Salvador during its military dictatorship (2003, 2008). He argues that threats that emerged in the 1970s drove a second protest wave against the state when opportunities were not available; but this would not have happened without the opportunities in an early period, which enabled the formation of 'opportunity organizations'. Thus, as threats increased in the 1970s, these opportunity 'holdovers' provided the building blocks for mass mobilization.

A substantial amount of research has demonstrated how the presence of threats can ignite protests, especially in the absence of political opportunities (Andrews and Seguin 2015; Cunningham and Phillips 2007; Dodson 2016; Einwohner and Maher 2011; Inclán 2009; Johnson and Frickel 2011; Martin and Dixon 2010; Shriver, Adams, and Longo 2015; Simmons 2014; Snow et al. 1998; Van Dyke and Soule 2002). However, while these studies have highlighted the role of threats in sparking mobilization, they do not explain how threats influence the forms that mobilization takes. Why do some threats lead to organization-led protests, while others result in leaderful mobilizations? Furthermore, these studies often treat threats as objective and external conditions that trigger mobilization instantaneously, without thoroughly examining the processes by which threats are perceived, internalized, and socialized among citizens.

Social Networks

A second explanation for the rise of leaderful mobilization centres around the role of social networks. Social networks are essentially a web of individuals, groups, or organizations linked by various social relationships, such as friendship, kinship, coworking, exchanges, or trust. Scholarly attention on social networks in contentious politics primarily stems from resource mobilization theory, which highlights the significance of resources for movements and the capacity of organizations to amass and utilize these resources effectively. Similar to organizations, networks are pivotal in resource mobilization, acting as the conduits through which resources are acquired, allocated, and managed (Diani 2003, 2015). Networks are instrumental in recruiting participants (Clarke 2014; Snow, Zurcher, and Ekland-Olson 1980; Zhao 2001), fostering movement identities (Gould 1995; Pfaff 1996), coordinating protest actions (Wackenhut 2020), and inducing commitments to high-risk activism (della Porta 1988; McAdam 1986). Although these functions remain relevant in scenarios where organizations take the lead, the significance of social networks becomes particularly pronounced in contexts where organizations are absent or restricted from mobilization, which often happens in authoritarian contexts (Fu 2017; Glenn 1999; Pearlman 2021; Pfaff 1996; Zhao 2001).

Many scholars have demonstrated the pivotal role of social networks in protest movements that shared characteristics of leaderful mobilization. Karl-Dieter Opp and Christiane Gern (1993) find that personal networks of friends were instrumental mobilizing East German citizens to join the 1989 protests in the absence of opposition organizations. Focusing on the same case, Steven Pfaff (1996) highlights the significance of collective identities that emerged within small-scale social networks. Similarly, Asef Bayat (1997a, 2013) focuses on the 'passive networks' within Middle Eastern societies. These networks consisted of individuals such as squatters, the unemployed, street vendors, or immigrants from the same place of origin, who would come together on an ad hoc basis to discuss their issues or simply chat and socialize (1997a: 16). Such interactions fostered their collective identities and imagined solidarities. When these dispersed individuals encountered a shared threat, their passive networks had the potential to spontaneously evolve into active ones, propelled by 'interest recognition and latent communication' (1997a: 17).

The role of social networks remains significant in more recent leaderful mobilizations, as seen in the Arab Spring uprisings. In Egypt, Killian Clarke (2014) demonstrates how brokers played a critical role in activating ties and facilitating coordination among different social sectors, which led to the rapid and contingent reconfiguration of social networks. Katia Pilati and her coauthors (2019) observe how informal networks and established organizations collaborated to sustain mobilization efforts in both Egypt and Tunisia, highlighting the existence of intermediate mobilizing structures within authoritarian regimes. In a comparative study, Zachary C. Steinert-Threlkeld (2017) discovers that peripheral members of social networks were instrumental in catalysing spontaneous mass mobilizations throughout the Arab Spring. By providing credible signals about protest participation and information about the unfolding events, these peripheral networks were able to organize and coordinate protest actions in a decentralized fashion. In the case of Syria, where the authoritarian state banned political parties and independent associations, Wendy Pearlman (2021) underscores the essential role of social networks in driving mass mobilizations against the Assad regime. She described the 2011 uprising as a 'mobilization from scratch', emphasizing the absence of pre-established organizations and arguing that the first movers heavily depended on social ties and micro-solidarities, such as friends and neighbours, to recruit fellow protesters and coordinate actions. Nevertheless, due to the inherent risks, activists avoided replicating existing social networks; they instead formed what Pearlman terms 'unsocial social networks' (2021: 1805), wherein members remained anonymous to each other. These networks became the backbone of the uprising allowing participants to manage various functional tasks while maintaining their covert nature.

Social networks provide a compelling explanation for the emergence and persistence of mass protests in the absence of centralized leadership, thereby helping us to further understand how leaderful mobilizations occur. Indeed, social networks were crucial in the 2019 Anti-Extradition Movement, as well as in earlier mobilizations such as the Umbrella Movement (Cheng and Chan 2017). However, while social networks elucidate some of the mechanisms of mobilization, they do not fully account for why individuals choose to mobilize independently when established movement organizations are available to direct protest campaigns. This conundrum was particularly evident in Hong Kong, which had a political opposition with mobilizing structures and institutionalized bargaining power. The question remains: Why would protesters opt for networks over structured organizations? What drives them to forsake organization-led, predetermined protests in favour of mobilizing on their own terms, even if it means incurring greater personal risks?

Digital Communication Technologies

A third explanation focuses on the role of digital communication technologies, such as the Internet, smartphones, and various social media platforms (Earl and Kimport 2011), in enabling ordinary people to 'organize without organizations' (Shirky 2008). By allowing individuals to communicate and interact directly, these technologies are expected to function as 'organizational substitutes' (Buechler 2011: 221), dramatically reducing the costs associated with collective actions. Research has shown how digital technologies enable protesters to frame issues (Bonilla and Rosa 2015; Lim 2013), recruit participants (Clarke and Kocak 2020; Tufekci and Wilson 2012), and cultivate collective identities (Gerbaudo and Treré 2015; Khazraee and Novak 2018).

The power of digital communication technologies was demonstrated during the Arab Spring uprisings (Howard and Hussain 2013) and the global Occupy movement in the early 2010s (Juris 2012). Manuel Castells characterizes these mobilizations as 'networked social movements' to highlight the horizontal networking of participants in both online and physical spaces (Castells 2012). He sees networked movements as 'new forms of democratic movements' that can raise the possibility of re-learning how to live together '[i]n real democracy' (316). W. Lance Bennett and Alexandra Segerberg (2013) further theorize the decentralized nature of networked movements and characterized them as connective actions'. Unlike collective actions that rely on formal hierarchical organizations, connective actions emerge among individuals who share personalized action frames via social media networks, operating without the need for collective identity framing or organizational resources to respond effectively to opportunities. As a result, these self-organizing communication networks have supplanted formal organizations as the primary drivers of mobilization, serving as organizational hubs that allocate resources and respond to external events (Bennett and Segerberg 2013: 13). While organizations still play roles (Earl 2015; Pilati et al. 2019), they are often integrated within the networked structure, assuming less hierarchical forms and more coordinative and supportive roles (Bennett and Segerberg 2013; Bimber, Flanagin and Stohl 2012).

While the role of digital technologies may help explain the rise of leaderful mobilizations, it is less clear how such technologies help sustain protest momentum over time. Extant research focuses on how digital technologies enable activists to coordinate protest actions (Bennett, Segerberg, and Walker 2014; Gerbaudo 2017; Milan 2015). However, there is an assumption in the literature that digital technologies alone can handle all organizational tasks (Foust and Hoyt 2018). It remains unclear how protesters collaborate horizontally, handle logistics, and overcome tactical freeze. Indeed, scholars remain sceptical about the long-term viability of networked mobilizations. Jeffrey Juris (2012) observes that while digital technologies enable rapid aggregation of protesters, they do not necessarily ensure sustainability, as people can disperse as easily as they come together. As Juris states, 'it is only with the long-term occupation of public space that such 'mobs' are transformed from 'crowds' of individuals into an organized 'movement' with a collective subjectivity' (287).

Zeynep Tufekci further argues that networked movements are often guided by 'adhocracy', which means that tasks are accomplished in an ad hoc manner by those who are willing to contribute during the initial stages of movements (2017: 53). Although such movements can rapidly scale up and handle logistical tasks without substantial organizational capacity, they eventually encounter 'tactical freeze', where actors struggle to adapt strategies or negotiate demands due to a lack of cultural and infrastructural foundations for collective decision-making. Examining the Spanish 15-M Movement, Cristina Flesher Fominaya (2020) contends that online networks are insufficient for explaining the movement's emergence and organization. As she put it, '15-M does not reflect a connective logic whereby individual personal action frames are exchanged online, but rather a collective action logic whereby the connective capabilities and affordances of digital connectivity are strategically and effectively integrated into existing movement culture that rest primarily on face-to-face interactions' (71).

In short, while digital communication technologies provide protesters with the information to assemble at the right time and place, existing research has yet to explain how protesters handle the intricate planning and coordination tasks that require detailed discussions, specialized knowledge, and division of labour. Moreover, it remains unclear how digital technologies guide protesters in deciding which actions to undertake, where to protest, and who should be responsible for various tasks. The crux of the matter lies in identifying the mechanisms by which protesters organized and coordinated a continuous stream of protest actions.

A THEORY OF MEDIATED THREAT

To address these limitations, we present a theory of mediated threat that aims to explain the evolution of contentious politics and emphasizes how perceived threats mobilize political challengers while simultaneously influencing their relational dynamics. Our theory builds on the foundation of existing explanations, incorporating political opportunities, threats, social networks, and digital communication technologies as components. This approach is inspired by the seminal *Dynamics of Contention* (McAdam, Tarrow, and Tilly 2001), which critiques the political process model for analysing political contexts and actors as given. The dynamics of contention framework proposes to identify the recurring causal mechanisms that constitute, in different combinations and sequences, processes of mobilization and demobilization, through which different episodes of contention emerge. Additionally, it also aims to devote more attention to agency and incorporate mechanisms, such as threat attribution and identity shift, into structural approaches. The theory of mediated threat follows the guidance of this framework. On the one hand, it seeks to delineate the process through which mass mobilizations in Hong Kong emerged episodically but became gradually less reliant on organizations. On the other hand, it also seeks to identify the mechanisms that constitute the process – such as the mechanisms that changed the mobilizing structure and those that sustained leaderful mobilization.

At the centre of our theory is the concept of threat. In the contentious politics literature, threat is primarily conceptualized in two ways. The first approach, outlined by Goldstone and Tilly (2001: 183), defines threat as the cost of action or inaction – the 'costs that social groups will incur from protest or that it expects to suffer if it does not take action'. Based on rational choice theory, this definition portrays threats as negative rewards or what resource mobilization scholars refer to as negative selective incentives (Oliver 1980). Goldstone and Tilly further categorize threat into two types: 'current threat', which pertains to the costs incurred by not taking action to prevent the harms imposed by a regime; and 'repressive threat', which relates to the costs of facing repression when action is taken. Consequently, current threat can motivate individuals to engage in pre-emptive actions to avoid more severe outcomes, whereas repressive threat can deter mobilization that could otherwise be harmful. Individuals must then weigh these costs to determine the necessity of action. When the cost of inaction (current threats) outweighs the cost of action (repressive threats), collective action becomes more likely.

In contrast to the individual-level focus on incentives to join protests, Paul Almeida (2019) offers a structural approach. He suggests that despite a wealth of literature addressing structural political opportunities, such as elite conflict or institutional access, the concept of structural threats remains underdeveloped. Almeida defines structural threat as 'negative conditions intensifying existing grievances and creating new ones in stimulating collective action' (2019: 45). This definition differentiates threat from the well-established concept of grievances. In his view, grievances are pre-existing internal conditions experienced by aggrieved individuals, while threats denote external encroachments that aggravate these conditions or generate new ones. Almeida (2019) further identifies four forms of structural threats – (1) economic-related problems, (2) public health/environmental decline, (3) erosion of rights, and (4) state repression. He also demonstrates how they give rise to various types of mobilizations.

While these efforts have revived the concept of threat in contentious political research, the conceptualization of threat remains over-simplified. Viewing threats solely as costs implies an individualistic approach that considers protests as outcomes of individuals weighing costs and benefits. This individual-centric framework has been heavily critiqued by POS theorists. Moreover, it is unclear how individuals assign specific values to particular threats. This difficulty is especially evident in the evaluation of 'current threats' – gauging the cost of inaction is challenging since inaction tends to have a social rather than personal impact. Take, for instance, the case of Hong Kong's extradition bill. Most ordinary citizens are unlikely to be directly affected by the possibility of extradition. They only perceive the bill as personally costly when they can relate its social consequences to their individual lives. This process of connecting the collective impact to the personal level is not automatic. It requires individuals to see themselves as part of the collective even if they are not personally under threat.

Viewing threats as structural is also problematic. The structural view assumes that threats are objectively negative conditions that automatically prompt individuals to mobilize in protest. This view, however, ignores how structural threats also need to be perceived and understood as such by social actors (Leenders and Heydemann 2012). This distinction mirrors the difference between structural and perceived opportunities. Focusing on the 1979 Iranian Revolution, Charles Kurzman (1996) argues that structure and perception do not always align. People might fail to perceive opportunities, and they might sometimes perceive opportunities wrongly even when they do not exist. For Kurzman, Iranians protested not solely because they observed the weakening of the state (structural opportunities) but because they perceived the opposition as stronger (perceived opportunities). Similarly, in discussing the structural bias of political opportunity, William Gamson and David Meyer (1996: 276) assert that opportunities are 'subject to framing processes and often serve as a source of internal disagreements within movements regarding appropriate action strategies'. This is particularly evident when political opportunities are volatile or involve 'relative opportunities' between institutional and extra-institutional actions.

Like opportunities, threats must be framed or socially constructed as harmful to spur mobilization. This process typically necessitates the mediation of the social structures within which actors are embedded, which provide them with the interpretive frameworks and cultural resources to comprehend threats and offer responses (Shesterinina 2016). To illustrate, take the example of climate change. The increasing average temperatures of our planet, sea level rise, and the increasing frequency of extreme weather events are typically seen as structural threats. However, these climate phenomena themselves may not compel individuals or societies to act. They must be socially constructed as threats, and this process requires the mediation of existing social structures. For example, academic institutions may contribute by conducting research that scientifically validates climate change as a threat. The media then disseminates this information to the public, framing climate change in a way that highlights its catastrophic impact on human societies and ecosystems, thereby inducing a sense of urgency and danger. On the other hand, there are also groups that perceive climate change not as a threat, but as a conspiracy. These groups, leveraging their own media outlets and influential figures, construct an alternative reality where climate change is seen as a false threat propagated by vested interests. This shows that social structures and their interpretive frameworks do not always lead to a consensus on what constitutes a threat but instead create divergent or opposing perceptions.

In the context of Hong Kong, the perception of the extradition bill as a threat to Hong Kong's civic freedoms and autonomy did not emerge immediately. Rather, it required continuous learning and social interactions, as well as experiences with previous threats, for such a perception to coalesce among citizens. Moreover, it required persistent effort from opposition actors to frame the bill – initially seen as a legal matter – into a political issue with profound repercussions. In short, threats are not merely assessed individually or imposed structurally. They demand perception and mediation by social actors within their cultural context and relational configurations before they are viewed as harmful to well-being. This mediation process is crucial because it not only determines the possibility of protest mobilization but also shapes the organizational forms that the mobilization assumes.

RECONCEPTUALIZING THREATS

Before outlining the threat mediation process, we first propose our own conceptualization of threats to bridge individualistic and structuralist views. We define threats as both the *actual* and *potential* harm directed at either institutions or individuals. This definition goes beyond our everyday understanding of threats – the potentiality to cause harm – to encompass the actual harm being inflicted. By considering both institutions and individuals as potential victims, we aim to reconcile individualistic and structuralist perspectives.

We distinguish threats along two dimensions. The first concerns the scope of the harm. Threats can be either *generalized* or *particularistic*, a distinction similar to the one between generalized and particularistic trust (Luo 2005). Generalized threats pose harm to institutions, which encompass formal and informal rules and norms that organize social, political, and economic relations (North 1990). Examples of institutions include government accountability, protection of social rights and civic freedoms, elections, rule of law, and due process. The term 'generalized' refers to the non-targeted nature of these threats. They inflict harm not on specific individuals, but on the wider institutional structures, which affect individuals indirectly and non-specifically. On the contrary, particularistic threats are those that inflict harm on selected individuals, based on their actions or attributes. This targeted nature makes them particularistic. These threats often manifest as targeted repressive actions such as harassment, surveillance, spying, bans from public office, arrests, torture, and mass killings (Davenport 2007).

The second dimension is the temporality of harm. Threats can manifest in different temporalities. Some could be long-term, inflicting slow and gradual harm to institutions or individuals. For example, state actors could gradually

TABLE 1.1 *A typology of threats*

		Scope	
		Generalized	Particularized
Temporality	Recurrent	• Executive aggrandizement • Erosion of legislative and constitutional oversight • Manipulation of electoral rules, such as gerrymandering	• Prosecution, harassment, and surveillance of opposition activists • Oppression or restriction of independent and marginalized groups • Unregulated police powers
	Contingent	• Barring opposition candidacy • Electoral fraud • Introduction of policies or legislations that can bring fundamental changes	• Crackdown on mass protests • Detainment or arrests of high-profile politicians or activists • Use of emergency powers

expand executive powers and erode legislative or constitutional oversights; and they could harass opposition activists and prevent them from obtaining any positions of political power. These acts do not happen overnight but are slow, protracted, and gradual. We refer to them as 'recurrent threats'. Conversely, threats can also be imposed suddenly. State actors could introduce policies, legislations, or court rulings viewed as threatening to established institutions, or use coercive forces against individuals, such as violently repressing protesters or imprisoning activists. These threats occur in a much shorter time frame, often driven by events with a sense of urgency. Hence, we characterize them as 'contingent threats'. Table 1.1 presents a typology of threats based on these two dimensions.

Our conceptualization seeks to amend the distinction proposed by Goldstone and Tilly (2001). As discussed, Goldstone and Tilly differentiate between current threats and repressive threats: current threats pertain to the 'harms that are currently experienced or anticipated' (184), while repressive threats refer to the harm posed by repression. Although logical within their definition of threat, it fails to encompass the full spectrum of threats. Both current and repressive threats can exist in the background or emerge afresh, and both can be directed at institutions and individuals. By distinguishing between temporality and scope, our conceptualization aims to provide a more nuanced categorization of the threats that society and people could encounter. Furthermore, by moving away from a simplistic cost-based conceptualization, we diverge from Goldstone and Tilly's assertion that repressive threats deter people from mobilizing in protests. Indeed, extensive research has shown that repression can also increase mobilization (Francisco 1996; Khawaja 1993; Moore 2000; Olivier 1990; Rasler 1996; Schock 1999).

It is important to differentiate between types of threats with greater nuance because not every type of threat has the potential to catalyse protest mobilizations. We expect that contingent threats, whether generalized or particularized, are more likely to spur mass mobilizations because they create shocks and surprises. Meanwhile, recurrent threats seldom spark mobilization directly because citizens are more used to them; however, they are still prone to the accumulation of grievances, which raises the likelihood that contingent threats in the future will spark mobilization. Furthermore, it is important to note that the boundaries between these four types of threats are not rigid. Contingent threats can evolve into recurrent threats over time, losing their initial sense of urgency. Moreover, contingent threats can bring attention to the existence of underlying recurrent threats. For instance, a crackdown on mass protests can expose the unchecked nature of police powers. While particularistic threats primarily target individuals, they can also indirectly damage norms and procedures. For example, unchecked police powers on individual cases can create precedents to undermine due process and the rule of law. Conversely, generalized threats can also harm individuals indirectly. For instance, barring opposition candidacy not only restricts the freedom to run for election but also involves the exclusion of specific candidates.

RELATIONAL DYNAMICS OF THE OPPOSITION

After differentiating between various types of threats, our next step is to outline the threat mediation process through which threats result in mass mobilization. The previous section posits that contingent threats have greater mobilizing potential than recurrent threats. But how do contingent threats trigger mass mobilizations and shape different organizational forms? Figure 1.1 illustrates this process. A key component here is the relational dynamics of the political opposition, which conditions how threats are perceived, framed, and constructed. This component determines two outcomes: first, whether a threat can spark mobilization; and second, what kind of mobilizing structure from which protests will occur. By mobilizing structure, we refer to the 'collective vehicles, informal as well as formal, through which people mobilize and engage in collective action' (McAdam et al. 1996: 3). But before turning to that, let us focus on two key factors that shape the opposition's relational dynamics:

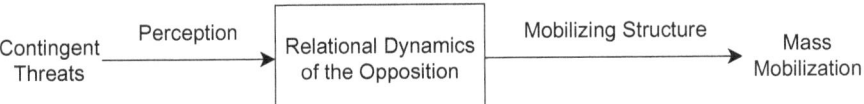

FIGURE 1.1 Mediation process of threat-induced mobilization.

(1) the relative strength of the institutionalized opposition to the state, and (2) the level of fractionalization within the opposition.

Relative Strength of the Institutionalized Opposition

Institutionalized opposition is defined here as formalized and organized dissent against existing political, social, or economic institutions within a society (Helms 2004). It typically involves the establishment of various formal organizational entities, such as political parties, interest groups, and activist organizations, which challenge the policies, practices, or ideologies of the dominant institutions and strive to compete for political power. Therefore, when assessing the strength of the institutionalized opposition, we are essentially evaluating its power relative to the state or ruling government, primarily in terms of its ability to secure political power.

A strong institutionalized opposition typically combines opposition parties with significant representation in political institutions and substantial popular support, along with civil society organizations that possess plentiful resources and extensive networks. Such organizational strength enables the opposition to position themselves as an alternative to the ruling government effectively and offer robust mobilizing structures, derived from their existing organizations and networks, to organize protests in response to opportunities and threats. An example is the Democratic Progressive Party in Taiwan, which successfully put an end to the Kuomintang's one-party rule in the early 1990s due to its increasing institutional representation and influential civil society networks (Rigger 1999). A similar case is El Salvador under military rule, where the opposition took advantage of the regime's liberalization in the 1960s to establish a robust organizational infrastructure characterized by substantial membership bases and extensive interorganizational linkages, despite lacking institutional representation at that time (Almeida 2003).

However, authoritarian regimes often obstruct or suppress opposition organizations (Ash 2015; Hostrup, Haugbølle, and Cavatorta 2011; Jiménez-Martínez 2021; Nugent 2020; Sika 2019; Trejo 2012) or attempt to co-opt them into political institutions, such as the legislature (Gandhi 2008; Lust-Okar 2005). These actions often serve to weaken or eliminate the opposition, rendering it less institutionalized. Even when autonomous organizations do exist, they are often subjected to stringent regulations and forced to focus on non-political activities (Fu 2018; Teets 2013). Additionally, citizens often deeply distrust organizations that are sanctioned by the regime, likely perceiving them as either co-opted by the state or lacking the capability to challenge state power (Abdelrahman 2013). As a result, when contingent threats loom large, mass protests are unlikely to be spearheaded by an institutionalized opposition.

Still, mass mobilizations do occur in oppressive contexts. But when they do, the mobilizing structures are usually constituted spontaneously by informal networks and loosely structured social groups, rather than an institutionalized opposition. The critical question is what enables individuals, whether they are isolated or connected through dense informal networks, to quickly respond to threats and recognize threats as threatening (Bayat 1997b). One explanation is that they have shared experiences with previous threats – either they have mobilized together against contingent threats before, or they have been experiencing recurrent threats. These experiences instilled grievances and created mutual understanding among them, enabling them to develop a rapid, reflexive response to new contingent threats. Because of that, pre-existing networks can quickly be galvanized into mobilizing structures, while individuals outside of such networks can also rapidly establish trust and create spontaneous entities to facilitate mobilization.

In summary, the strength of the institutionalized opposition significantly influences the organizational form of mobilization. When emerging threats are mediated by a strong institutionalized opposition, mass mobilizations tend to be brokered by mobilizing structures derived from opposition organizations. Conversely, when threats are mediated by a weak or non-existent institutionalized opposition, mass mobilizations are more likely to be guided by mobilizing structures formed by pre-existing networks or spontaneously created organizational entities. To illustrate the mediating role of opposition strength, consider, briefly, the differences between the Tunisian and Egyptian uprisings during the Arab Spring. In Tunisia, the relatively institutionalized and autonomous status of trade unions and other civil society organizations allowed them to broker the movement, lead the uprisings, and facilitate the power transition (Gerbaudo 2012). In contrast, in Egypt, widespread perceptions of civil society groups and opposition parties being co-opted by the state made protesters distrustful of formal organizations, leading them to mobilize independently through informal political groups and networks (Abdelrahman 2013; Gerbaudo 2012; Pilati et al. 2019).

Fractionalization within the Opposition

Fractionalization within the opposition refers to the degree of division or fragmentation of opposition groups or parties within a political system, regardless of whether they are institutionalized. Fractionalization can stem from a variety of factors, including ideological differences, strategic disagreements, divergent policy preferences, and personal rivalries. A fractionalized opposition often results in infighting and obstructs cooperation, thus reducing its capacity to effectively challenge the government or ruling party and bring about political change. In authoritarian regimes, the political opposition is often fractionalized by design. Autocrats may create 'divided structures of contestation' that include some opposition groups in electoral institutions while excluding others, leading to their fragmentation (Lust 2009). They may also co-opt opposition figures into the government, preventing them from joining opposition coalitions (Arriola, Devaro, and Meng 2021), or use repression to marginalize opposition figures, creating leadership vacuums for opposition groups (Ash 2015). Nevertheless, building an opposition coalition or alliance, while challenging (Haugbølle and Cavatorta 2011), is not impossible. Research shows that opposition groups can sometimes coordinate and overcome their differences under specific conditions (Armstrong, Reuter, and Robertson 2020; Ong 2022; Sato and Wahman 2019; Selçuk and Hekimci 2020). When they do, they are more likely to advocate for political change effectively (Bunce and Wolchik 2010).

Opposition fractionalization is consequential for contentious politics because it shapes people's perceptions of threats and their participation in protests. Opposition groups not only serve as mobilizing structures, but they also filter information and provide interpretive frames that influence how their supporters or sympathizers perceive threats and opportunities (Gould 1995; Shesterinina 2016; Wood 2003). When the opposition is highly fractionalized, a multitude of frames is likely to emerge, offering diverse and occasionally conflicting interpretations of the political situation. Consequently, the same threat can be interpreted differently by different factions of the opposition, leading to disparate collective identities. For instance, Ellen Lust (2009) observes that within 'divided structures of contestation', opposition figures co-opted into political institutions tend not to use protests to pressure the incumbent during an economic crisis, while those excluded would prefer otherwise.

Research has further illustrated how varying threat perceptions can produce distinct forms of collective action. For example, Thomas Maher (2010) investigates how different threat perceptions among prisoners in three Nazi death camps led to different mobilization outcomes. Although all camps had resistance groups, not all could mount resistance. Revolts and collective organization were more likely when prisoners perceived an immediate and lethal threat – what Maher termed 'total threat'. This was observed in the Sobibor and Treblinka camps, where a series of events contributed to the accumulation of total threat, unlike Auschwitz. Anastasia Shesterinina (2016)'s study of civil war mobilization during the 1992–1993 Georgian-Abkhaz conflict similarly explains individual decisions to fight or flee based on their differing threat perceptions. Shesterinina argues that individuals did not form threat perceptions in isolation; rather, they did so within social structures such as family, friendship networks, local relationships, and national authorities. These local and everyday structures play a crucial role in filtering national threat narratives and shaping collective notions of threat, thereby influencing mobilization decisions. Specifically, individuals who perceived the threat as directed towards themselves or their immediate family and friends were more inclined to flee, while those who perceived the threat as aimed at their larger groups were more likely to fight.

The degree of fractionalization within the opposition, similar to the strength of the institutionalized opposition, significantly influences the form of mobilization. When the opposition is united and cohesive, groups within it often share similar perceptions of threats and are more inclined to form a unified mobilizing structure for mass mobilization. However, when the opposition is fractionalized, different groups within it held divergent threat perceptions. These disparate perceptions of threat make cooperation more challenging, limiting the scope and scale of mobilization. Even when cooperation happens, such coalitions are likely to be fragile and prone to internal conflicts over protest tactics and goals, due to the differing threat perceptions among factions.

ORGANIZATIONAL FORMS OF MASS MOBILIZATION

Figure 1.2 illustrates four ideal-types of organizational forms in a 2x2 typology. The vertical axis represents the strength of the institutionalized opposition, defined as the opposition's capacity to contest political power. A strong opposition is more likely to trigger organization-led mobilization in response to a contingent threat, maximizing the opposition's challenge to the incumbents. Conversely, when the opposition is weak, threat likely gives rise to mass mobilizations guided by networks or non-hierarchical structures. Meanwhile, the horizontal axis represents the level of fractionalization within the opposition. When fractionalization is low, implying that opposition groups are more unified, their perceived threats would align more closely, leading to a more cohesive mobilizing structure. However, when fractionalization is high,

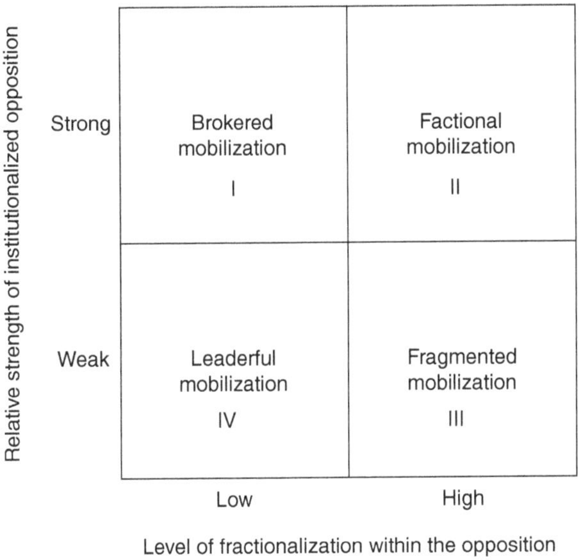

FIGURE 1.2 Relational dynamics of the opposition and the organizational forms of mobilizations.

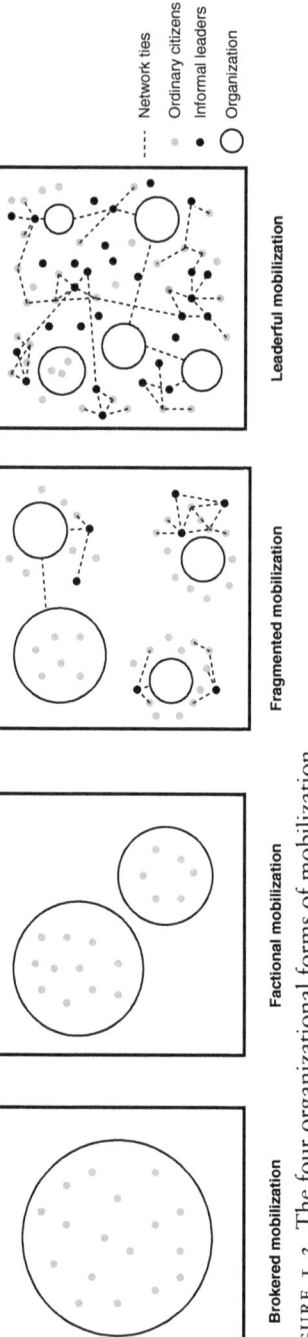

FIGURE 1.3 The four organizational forms of mobilization.

different opposition groups would perceive a threat differently and propose different tactical solutions, leading to a more fragmented mobilizing structure.

'Brokered mobilization' arises when the institutionalized opposition is strong and there is minimal fractionalization among opposition groups. In this scenario, mass mobilization is orchestrated by a primary SMO or a coalition of SMOs acting as brokers. On the other hand, 'factional mobilization' occurs when a strong institutionalized opposition is marred by significant internal divisions. Here, multiple opposition organizations or SMOs lead and organize movements concurrently, each with its distinct goals and tactics. 'Fragmented mobilization' emerges when the institutionalized opposition is weak and fractionalization is pronounced. Under these conditions, networks, informal groups, and individuals engage in spontaneous mobilization without formal organization, yet with low levels of cooperation and cohesion. Such mobilization is characterized by multiple centres of authority and action, which may not necessarily align around a unified goal. Lastly, 'leaderful mobilization' unfolds when the opposition is weak but exhibits low levels of fractionalization. In this situation, networks, informal groups, and ordinary citizens in the opposition camp can become united in response to a contingent threat. As a result, they can mobilize spontaneously but cohesively without centralized leadership. Although multiple centres of authority and action exist, protesters in leaderful mobilizations always collaborate towards a shared objective. Figure 1.3 provides the graphical representation for each organizational form: circles, dots and lines represent organizations, actors, and ties respectively.

THREAT-INDUCED CHANGES

It is important to note that the opposition's relational dynamics is by no means a static structure. It can evolve over time. While contingent threats are more likely to trigger mass mobilizations, recurrent threats can continuously reshape opposition's relational dynamics. First, recurrent threats can erode the strength of the institutionalized opposition. For example, executive aggrandizement and the erosion of legislative oversight present generalized threats that can isolate opposition figures or parties from political institutions, thereby weakening the opposition's standing against the incumbent (Thompson 2021). Similarly, restrictions on resources or curtailment of civil society organizations affiliated with the opposition can undermine their organizational infrastructure, hindering their ability to effectively organize dissent (Cavatorta and Durac 2010; Wiktorowicz 2000). Second, recurrent threats can foster fractionalization within the opposition. Selective repression targeting radical opposition figures or parties can deepen the chasm between them and their moderate counterparts, heightening fractionalization within the opposition (Ash 2015; Sika 2023). Conversely, undifferentiated repression may have the inverse effect, consolidating previously fractionalized opposition groups due to the shared experience of widespread repression (Nugent 2020).

Third, recurrent threats can stimulate the development of new organizations, groups, or networks, providing fresh mobilizing structures. For example, during the rule of General Hosni Mubarak in Egypt, longstanding grievances against the political and economic status quo, combined with the perceived ineffectiveness of the institutionalized opposition, led to the rise of a new opposition movement named the Kefaya in the 2000s. This movement served as a loosely structured umbrella for various opposition groups and activists (Clarke 2011). However, the emergence of new formal or informal structures can sometimes lead to increased division within the opposition. We see this in conflict-ridden regions like Northern Ireland during the Troubles or present-day Palestine, where ongoing repressive threats from British and Israeli authorities respectively led to the creation of radical offshoots from the opposition, further fractionalizing it (Alimi, Bosi, and Demetriou 2012; De Fazio 2013). Still, regardless of the degree of fractionalization, the rise of threat-induced groups introduces new relational dynamics within the opposition. The threats that prompt their creation also shape their structures, goals, and tactical preferences, making them more responsive to future threats.

Although recurrent threats have the potential to reshape the opposition's relational dynamics, the agency of opposition actors also plays a pivotal role. These actors can proactively establish new organizations, groups, or networks in response to threats. Without their willingness to collaborate and take risks, new mobilizing structures would not materialize. Additionally, opposition actors can strive to lessen intergroup fractionalization by setting aside their differences. While this is often challenging under normal circumstances, it becomes more achievable when the opposition faces immediate and critical threats, especially when these threats do not differentiate between opposition groups. Furthermore, opposition actors can endeavour to frame impending threats in a way that aligns their threat perceptions more closely. This framing can create collective identities based not on existing political divisions, but on more fundamental social identities, such as occupation. While fractionalization may not entirely vanish, it can be concealed or temporarily brushed aside.

SCOPE CONDITIONS

Our analysis focuses on the evolution of contentious politics in post-handover Hong Kong, which had been governed by a hybrid regime. This hybrid regime is distinctive in its blend of liberal and authoritarian elements. Governed by the OCTS principle, the city's historical legacy of civil liberties, coupled with the influence of capitalist elites, has fostered a degree of openness not found in mainland China's one-party socialist rule (Fu 2018). It is within this context that opposition movements and mass mobilizations had arisen. However, the structure of this regime was not predetermined; it evolved in response to shifting political circumstances and developed in tandem with contentious politics. Thus, our analysis adopts a within-case, temporal approach to trace the dynamics of contention from the late colonial period to the early post-handover years, spanning from the 1980s to the 2010s. Throughout this time, the hybrid regime's institutional openness, civil liberties, and media freedoms provided a space for opposition and dissent, albeit within an increasingly constrained political environment under a more assertive state.

The scope conditions of our theory should thus be set within the context of non-democracies or democracies experiencing backsliding. It is primarily relevant to competitive authoritarian regimes that maintain a certain level of political openness, allowing for the presence of opposition, though not necessarily its flourishing. There are many examples of such countries: Egypt, Tunisia, Algeria, Ukraine, Thailand, Myanmar, Malaysia, and Sri Lanka during the 2010s. In these places, mass protests often emerged as political negotiations and electoral processes were increasingly viewed as insufficient for preventing electoral fraud, enabling power-sharing among diverse social groups, or rectifying adverse injustice (Weiss and Aspinall 2012; Sidel 2021; Ketchley 2017; Moss 2022). Moreover, our theory could also be applicable to backsliding democracies, where recurring threats are undermining the representativeness and accountability of political institutions, thereby diminishing their capacity to respond to those threats effectively. Some recent examples include Hungary, Poland, Chile, India, Indonesia, and the Philippines, where debates surrounding immigration, identity, religion, and environmental sustainability have heightened politicization, undermining trust in established elites and respect for formal institutions.

Our theory is less applicable to consolidated and functional democracies, in which power can alternate between incumbents and the opposition, and where threats are typically managed through the judiciary, electoral competitions, or civic actions (Vanessa et al. 2021). In these regimes, the interplay between incumbent and opposition would allow the energies from the streets to be channelled into formal institutions. However, even in consolidated democracies, mass mobilizations do happen occasionally to counteract perceived threats. For example, Taiwan's Sunflower Movement of 2014 and South Korea's candlelight protests of 2016–2017 showcased how even democracies could experience threat-induced mobilizations (Ho 2018; Jung 2023). In the United States, despite having strong democratic institutions and an independent judiciary, threats associated with immigration, abortion, identity, and electoral procedures have sometimes triggered massive protests where rival political groups are pitted against one another (Tarrow 2021). Thus, our theory can shed light on such contexts, even though they have better institutional systems to address popular demands. Finally, our theory also does not apply to full-fledged autocracies, where there are scant political opportunities for intermediate associations to form, latent networks to develop, or leaderful structures to emerge. Nonetheless, some aspects of leaderful mobilization resonate with the Belarus protests in 2019–2020, the anti-Covid lockdown protests in mainland China in 2022, and the Iranian protests in 2021–2022.

The case of Hong Kong is distinguished by its liberal oligarchy structure, which does not conform to the conventional models of competitive authoritarianism or backsliding democracies. Nonetheless, it does share elements from both types of regimes, as evident in its power dynamics and contentious politics. Thus, despite being a single-case study, Hong Kong's distinctive political context, coupled with its changes along the spectrum between a backsliding democracy and a competitive authoritarian regime, enables us to conduct within-case comparisons and engage in inductive theory building (George and Bennett 2005; Pepinsky 2019).

CASE DESCRIPTION

To showcase the analytical power of our theory, let us place it in the context of Hong Kong. In the early post-handover years, the city has faced various recurrent and contingent threats across a spectrum of issues, including constitutional reforms, introduction of new legislations, plans for infrastructure development, and the impact of inbound tourism. Some of these issues originated domestically, while many others were a result of efforts to promote economic and political integration with mainland China. From the early 2000s to the latter half of the decade, the democratic opposition was relatively strong and cohesive. Pro-democracy parties and organizations adopted a two-pronged approach to counteract contingent threats. On the one hand, they leveraged their institutional power in the legislature and other advisory bodies to bargain with the authorities. On the other hand, they organized mass protests from time to time that were often well-ordered and ritualistic to showcase the popular support that they could mobilize. In such protests, these established organizations often formed the mobilizing structure and served as its leadership, providing both strategic guidance and logistical support. Mass mobilizations, in this sense, could be said to be 'brokered' by these organizations.

The anti-government demonstration on 1 July 2003, which mobilized half a million citizens, serves as a perfect example of what we call 'brokered mobilization'. The demonstration was sparked by a national security legislation, known as Article 23, which was framed by the opposition as a dire threat to the city's civic and political freedoms (Ma 2005). Threat perceptions among opposition groups were promptly coalesced under two demands: the retraction of the national security legislation and the resignation of the then Chief Executive, Tung Chee-hwa. With the presence of a robust institutionalized opposition, these groups united within a coalition spearheaded by the newly established CHRF. The coalition eventually orchestrated a centrally coordinated, meticulously scripted demonstration in which the CHRF was responsible for everything from the claims to picketing arrangements. Protesters simply attended the rally, adhering to the prearranged plan.

Entering the late 2000s, while contingent threats like Article 23 legislation diminished, recurrent threats persisted. These recurrent threats were arising from issues such as urban redevelopment and economic integration with the mainland. Viewing the established opposition as incapable of counteracting these threats, new opposition actors and groups began to emerge outside of the institutionalized opposition, advocating a more confrontational approach that gave emphasis to street protests. These actors, mostly consisting of young activists, gained inspiration from the anti-globalization movements abroad and promoted more spontaneous and disruptive forms of mobilizations. Meanwhile, the democratic opposition began to split. The emergence of new opposition parties, such as the Civic Party and the League of Social Democrats, led to intense competition for votes, ultimately eroding opposition unity. On the other hand, pro-government parties and organizations became increasingly strengthened under Beijing's intensified state-building efforts after the 2003 mass rally, gradually eroding the overall institutional power of the opposition.

What occurred during this phase was an amalgam of mass protests that coexisted with contrasting forms – what we term 'factional mobilizations'. The traditional opposition carried on with their routine mass protests, such as the annual July 1 rallies and the June 4 candlelight vigils, even as turn-outs dwindled. Despite continuing to call for a faster pace of democratization, these routine protests failed to address the emerging threats that citizens were facing. In response to these threats, new opposition groups staged protests that adopted more decentralized and spontaneous forms, such as the heritage preservation campaigns between 2006 and 2008, the Anti-Express Rail Link (Anti-XRL) Movement of 2009, and the Anti-Moral and National Education (Anti-MNE) Movement of 2012. They shared a similar group of participants as the routine protests, but these participants became much more involved in the mobilization process rather than simply show up as an attendee. Also, although conventional pro-democracy parties and organizations remained relevant in supporting these protests, they were often marginalized from the leadership core.

As the state continued to erode the institutional bargaining power of the opposition, pro-democracy supporters increasingly questioned its effectiveness as the primary broker for mass mobilization. Meanwhile, the rise of new opposition groups and networks, which differed in their perception of threats from the traditional democrats, further fragmented the opposition, leading to ongoing internal conflicts. This set the stage for 'fragmented mobilization', characterized by loosely organized, spontaneous protests that were often regarded as 'leaderless'. These movements were 'fragmented' because the opposition groups often disagreed on strategies to counteract perceived threats. One major point of contention was the role of political institutions: while moderates still considered parliamentary politics and electoral competition as viable means to counteract threat, radicals found these institutional approaches inadequate and leaned towards more assertive street mobilizations. The latter approach was promoted by a burgeoning faction within the pro-democracy camp, known as the localists. They viewed the increasing political and economic integration with the mainland – exemplified by the surge of Chinese tourists and immigrants – as a recurrent threat to Hong Kong's local identity. For the localists, the only recourse was to push for greater autonomy or even independence from China, employing more militant protest tactics to confront these challenges.

The anti-mainlandization protests that occurred between 2012 and 2014 were the precursors of 'fragmented mobilization', when localist protesters organized repeated actions against mainland tourists and parallel traders. But the Umbrella Movement of 2014 stood out as a perfect illustration of this mobilization form. During the movement, pro-democracy protesters occupied several city areas and called for universal suffrage. The movement's organizational structure was unique: it was led by a diverse coalition of civil society groups, traditional SMOs, and pro-democracy parties, while day-to-day activities were self-managed by regular protesters. Despite initial unity among the protesters in response to the police's use of tear gas, the movement saw a growing divide in threat perception across different groups and factions, notably between the localists and the traditional democrats. The traditional democrats were concerned that sustained, widespread occupation might trigger a violent crackdown by the authorities, whereas radical protesters viewed the occupation and the adoption of militant tactics as potent symbols of defiance against the state. The radical stance gained traction among the young student leaders, who felt pressured to heed the demands of the more committed occupiers. Such dynamics led to a split within the movement's formal leadership, crippling the pro-democracy movement as a whole.

This does not imply that the opposition remained perpetually fragmented. In the years following the Umbrella Movement, opposition groups began to see a greater alignment in their threat perception, spurred on by Beijing's state-building efforts (Lee 2025). These efforts were coupled with indiscriminate crackdown on pro-democracy activists, which shifted from targeting just the radicals to increasingly affecting the moderates as well. This shift led to a significant convergence in the threat perceptions among opposition groups, especially between localists and traditional democrats.

The proposed extradition bill in 2019 proved to be the tipping point that unified these factions. Although the bill initially garnered little attention, it soon mobilized significant opposition once the 'early risers', including activists and pro-democracy politicians, portrayed it as a severe threat to Hong Kong's political and legal autonomy. A massive online petition campaign in May 2019 further united a diverse array of alumni, professional, recreational, religious, and community networks against the bill. These threat attribution mechanisms synchronized the perceived threats among citizens, galvanizing numerous existing and newly established groups and networks. This gave rise to a leaderful mobilizing structure that encompassed SMOs, networks, and individual citizens, but without a singular figure or entity taking the lead. Leveraging both digital communication technologies and offline networks, informal leaders and protesters engaged in what we describe as 'peer collaboration' despite the

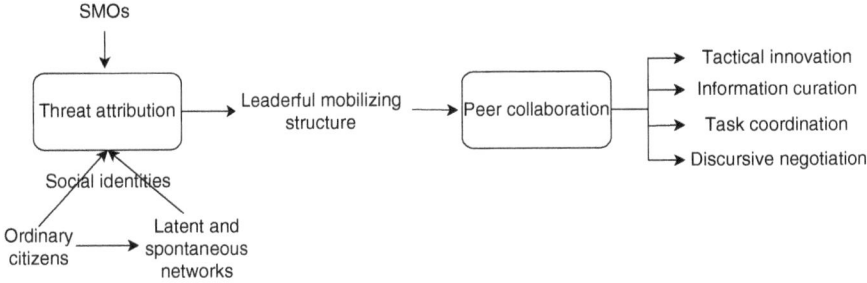

FIGURE 1.4 Mechanisms of leaderful mobilization

absence of centralized leadership. This overarching mechanism encompasses a range of micro-mechanisms, including tactical innovation, information curation, task coordination, and discursive negotiation – all of which were crucial in sustaining mobilization. Figure 1.4 outlines the relationship between different actors and the key mechanisms of 'leaderful mobilization'.

To summarize, the theory of mediated threat aims to illuminate the dynamics of contention that brought Hong Kong to the moment of leaderful mobilization. Instead of viewing threats as objective realities imposed externally, our theory conceptualizes them as socially constructed, requiring perception and interpretation by oppositional actors through specific cultural or political lenses. Moreover, threats do not merely trigger mobilizations; they also continually reshape the relational dynamics in the democratic opposition. This process gives rise to new forms of political agency and influences the mobilization strategies used by both actors and supporters involved in protests. In other words, threats shape not only the likelihood of mobilization, but also its organizational form. It is this dynamic process that contributed to the eventual rise of leaderful mobilization.

THEORETICAL AND EMPIRICAL CONTRIBUTIONS

This book aims to contribute to three spheres of knowledge: the conceptualization of threats; decentralized and spontaneous mobilizations; and hybrid regimes. First, our theory of mediated threat seeks to enrich how threats are conceptualized in the study of contentious politics by offering a more nuanced categorization of threats. While extant literature only offers broad categorizations of threats (Almeida 2019; Goldstone and Tilly 2001), we distinguish different types of threat based on their target (institutions or individuals) and temporality (recurrent or immediate) – a typology that we will elucidate in Chapter 2. This typology allows us to go beyond the predominant focus of the literature on the impact of immediate repressive threats on mobilization (Francisco 1995; Hess and Martin 2006; Lichbach 1987; Opp and Roehl 1990; Rasler 1996; Steinert-Threlkeld, Chan, and Joo 2022) and to also concentrate on non-repressive and longer-term threats. Moreover, we focus on the process through which threats are mediated before inciting potential mobilizations. Rather than presuming a direct mobilizing effect of threats, we consider how threats are perceived and interpreted by political actors, altering the relational dynamics of the opposition by fostering new political agencies and the emergence of new groups and networks. Lastly, while existing theories usually focus on how the source of discontent triggers the occurrence of mobilization, our theory further links it with the organizational form of the mobilization – not just in terms of its structure, but also its participatory nature. This bridges the gap between why people mobilize and how they mobilize – a connection that has been under-theorized in the current literature (Simmons 2016).

Second, our findings enrich the knowledge of decentralized, networked, and spontaneous mobilizations, which have become prevalent worldwide over the past decade. By conceptualizing them as *leaderful* rather than *leaderless*, we introduce a perspective that illuminates their inherent qualities, instead of defining them by what they lack. Moreover, while existing research often concentrates on the emergence and initial phases of mobilization (Abrams 2023; Castells 2012; Tufekci 2017; Pearlman 2021), our work delves into how such movements sustain themselves and maintain unity without central leadership, and how they innovate tactics and coordinate actions. Also, moving beyond the conventional focus on digital communication technologies, we stress the interplay between online and offline realms, examining how protesters leverage digital technologies and real-world social networks. Our analysis transcends a simplistic parallel view of online and offline networks, instead emphasizing their interplay, which shapes the overall organizational landscape of leaderful mobilizations. Furthermore, we explore the impact of contingent events and the absence of centralized leadership on protest radicalization, an aspect that existing scholarship has not thoroughly investigated. Our findings suggest that solidarity played a critical role in both propelling and restraining radicalization. This shows that although the dynamics of leaderful mobilizations are inherently unpredictable, they can generate endogenous mechanisms to regulate their development.

Third, our book contributes to the growing literature on hybrid regimes by examining how mass mobilizations can alter the political dynamics within such systems. Existing scholarship primarily focuses on how autocrats preserve their power by selectively incorporating democratic elements, which ostensibly creates a 'balance' that bolsters their rule (Gandhi 2008; Levitsky and Way 2010). Our findings from Hong Kong illustrate the inherent instability of such a 'balance' (Carothers 2018; Dresden and Howard 2016). While Hong Kong's liberal oligarchy, which limited citizens' suffrage but allowed a degree of contestation through alternate channels, maintained a delicate power balance between the ruling coalition and pro-democracy opposition, escalating mass protests gradually unsettled this balance. This prompted the Chinese party-state – the de facto patron of the liberal oligarchy – to expedite state-building efforts in the semi-autonomous region. Paradoxically, these state-building measures only served to further amplify mass protests and deepen the distrust of conventional pro-democracy organizations among their supporters, thereby further destabilizing the balance. Our findings thus emphasize the crucial role of contentious politics in disrupting and reshaping the dynamics of hybrid regimes. Even if elite and opposition actors may not intend to alter the balance, their interactions, coupled with mass mobilizations, could result in unforeseen and unintended consequences, undermining the hybridity that underpins hybrid regimes.

METHODS AND DATA

This book is the result of eight years of extensive and on-the-ground research. Our journey began with the 2014 Umbrella Movement, which sparked our curiosity to delve into the complex dynamics of Hong Kong's contentious politics. Initially, our focus was primarily on individual episodes of protest. However, as we witnessed successive events unfold, we recognized the limitations of this episodic approach and pivoted towards a broader examination of the spaces between these episodes and the historical contexts that gave rise to them. Our research scope expanded to include the evolution of the political landscape, mobilizing structures, and modes of organizing in post-handover Hong Kong. Adopting a long-term perspective on these dynamics (McAdam, Tarrow, and Tilly 2001), we shifted our analysis from focusing on the visible elements of social movements, such as prominent organizations and individual activists, towards examining the relational dynamics between various types of challengers, powerholders, and bystanders.

We employed a mixed method approach in this book, utilizing multiple types of data to address our research question. Here, 'mixed method' does not merely denote the juxtaposition of quantitative and qualitative data. It emphasizes the potential of both to complement and reinforce one another, thereby enhancing the overall validity and reliability of our findings (Ivankova and Wingo 2018). This approach allows us to explore diverse perspectives on the same issue, leading to a more holistic understanding. Our data sources include onsite protest surveys, in-depth interviews with key individuals, participant observations, and social media data. We also used secondary data, such as official statistics, newspaper articles, video footage, and other protest-related records. In the following section, we will provide an overview of our data sources and illustrate how their integration enabled a comprehensive study of contentious politics in Hong Kong and its broader implications.

Onsite Surveys and Public Opinion Polls

To understand the participants and motivations behind protests, social movement scholars have traditionally relied on onsite protest surveys. Unlike population surveys, which randomly sample citizens about their protest involvement, onsite protest surveys target individuals actively participating in contentious events. By generating real-time data, this approach allows researchers to contextualize findings and design specific questions that capture individual participation (Andretta and della Porta 2014). Although the use of onsite protest surveys has been prominent since the 1990s, it remains a specialized method within the field of social movement research (Walgrave and Verhulst 2011; Heaney and Rojas 2015; Fisher et al. 2019). In our study, we heavily relied on onsite surveys as they provide direct and immediate access to understanding unfolding protests.

Our analysis used three distinct sets of onsite surveys. The first set includes annual surveys conducted during the Tiananmen vigil at Victoria Park from 2013 to 2018, with sample sizes ranging from 444 to 861. The second set involves an onsite survey conducted during the 2014 Umbrella Movement, encompassing the three occupation zones in Admiralty, Causeway Bay, and Mongkok, with a sample size of 1,681. The third set includes twenty-six onsite surveys conducted during the 2019 Anti-Extradition Movement, capturing nearly every major protest event with a total sample size of 16,386. In these surveys, we used a mixed-mode sampling method that combined face-to-face surveys with smartphone-based online surveys to ensure large and representative samples. This method allowed us to gather data from a total of 16,386 respondents while maintaining the necessary representativeness of our sample (Yuen et al. 2022).

These surveys were conducted using a systematic approach. Supervised by field managers, interviewers were directed to approach every 10th person within a specified area or route, inviting them to participate in the survey. If an individual declined, the interviewers would proceed to approach the next 10th person, and so on. Due to the unique spatial dynamics of each protest, minor modifications were also made to the sampling method to ensure its suitability. This approach was generally applied to the traditional demonstrations and rallies, where protesters would gather in a set location or follow a particular route. However, in the 2019 Anti-Extradition Movement, many protests were fluid and spontaneous. Because of that, our team combined face-to-face surveys utilizing paper-based questionnaires and smartphone-based online surveys facilitated by a self-administered, Qualtrics-based questionnaire accessible via a QR code. The smartphone-based mode was introduced to obtain larger sample sizes, considering the size limitations of the survey team. Following the radicalization of the protests, a third mode of survey was introduced: post hoc online surveys self-administered via smartphones. For this, interviewers distributed flyers containing a QR code, which allowed protesters to access the online questionnaire on their smartphones.

In addition to the surveys conducted with protesters, we also carried out two opinion polls sampled randomly to capture popular sentiment and compare the views of protesters and non-protesters. The first poll was conducted in November 2019, during the height of the protests, with a sample size of

2,007 respondents. The second poll was conducted in May 2020, just before the implementation of the National Security Law, with a sample size of 1,574 respondents. These opinion polls offer unique and valuable insights into the protesters' identities, their motivations for participation, and their level of involvement in the protests. By incorporating a wider segment of the population, these surveys provide a comprehensive understanding of the dynamics of the protests.

Semi-structured Interviews

In addition to surveys, we conducted seventy-seven semi-structured interviews with a variety of individuals, including politicians, activists, and ordinary protesters. These interviews allowed us to delve deeper into the context of their participation, the factors influencing their decision-making, and the specific actions they took at a micro-level (Blee 2013: 96).

We targeted several categories of individuals to understand the roles played by different actors: (1) politicians (i.e., opposition legislators, district councillors, and election hopefuls), (2) activists (i.e., movement organizers, community and NGO activists, and student leaders), (3) ordinary protesters (i.e., protest participants who were actively involved in movement organizing but avoided using their real identity).

We used a snowball sampling method to identify our interviewees from the three categories. In the first two categories, our focus was on individuals affiliated with political institutions, professional associations, and movement organizations. We selected individuals from our personal and professional networks as seeds and expanded our sample through referrals from these initial interviewees. Our goal was to ensure a balanced representation of different political factions and movement groups, capturing diverse perspectives within the political landscape. For the third category, which included individuals who were not publicly known, we relied on our onsite fieldwork to establish connections. Through participant observations, we could engage with ordinary protesters and build rapport. Furthermore, we used our social networks and contacts gathered during our onsite surveys. This mix of methods allowed us to reach individuals who actively participated in the protests but chose to remain anonymous, thus widening the range of perspectives we captured in our interviews.

The selection process aimed to achieve a balance between more organized and less organized actors, given the increasing decentralization of the city's protests. In total, we conducted seventy-six interviews, comprising twenty-four politicians, twenty-two activists, and thirty ordinary protesters. We also engaged with numerous other informants to develop a comprehensive understanding of various aspects related to our research. Additionally, we conducted follow-up interviews with selected participants to validate and cross-reference their personal accounts with empirical evidence.

During the early stages of the research, many interviews were recorded and transcribed. However, as the political environment changed, we decided to rely more on notetaking during interviews. This approach created a more comfortable atmosphere for interviewees, enabling them to express their views and share their experiences freely. Apart from prominent politicians and activists whose views were already in the public domain, we took measures to anonymize all other interviewees or assigned them pseudonyms to protect their identities. For a complete list of interviewees, please refer to the appendix.

Onsite Ethnography

In addition, we leveraged ethnographic methods to gain first-hand and on-the-ground insights into the dynamic process of contention. By observing how individuals and groups experience processes of mobilization and ascribe meanings to such experiences, ethnographic methods are particularly well-suited to answer the 'what', 'how' and 'why' questions of mobilization, which provide the foundation for delineating the mechanisms of contention (Fu and Simmons 2021). Through ethnography, we are also able to access experiences and emotions that are fleeting and not easily discernible in other public spheres (Altheide and Johnson 1994). This method allowed us to capture nuanced aspects of the contentious process that would have escaped our attention if we only rely on personal or textual recollections.

We conducted ethnographic observations in most of the significant protests taking place since 2014, including the annual June 4 candlelight vigil, the July 1 rallies, the Umbrella Movement, and the Anti-Extradition Bill Movement. At the protest sites, we initiated informal conversations with protesters and recorded detailed observations in diary-like notes, continuously cross-checking with each other to ensure accuracy. In addition to these protest events, we actively participated in various meetings, workshops, seminars, and activities organized by civil society and community actors. To maintain impartiality, we regarded and identified ourselves as researchers and observers, rather than protest participants.

Overall, these ethnographic observations allowed us to not only understand how perceptions and decisions of different groups of actors were formed and altered during contentious episodes, but also comprehend why they adopted certain actions. For instance, while the media might portray militants in protests simply as people who espoused radical ideologies, participant observations taught us that these 'militants' were often pragmatic and non-ideological as they had to deal with many daily routines to maintain the defence lines.

Social Media Data

Finally, we collected protest-related social media data from a diverse range of online platforms. With the considerable influence of the internet and social media in Hong Kong's protests, it is necessary to analyse digital traces to understand the mobilization and organizational strategies of the protesters. However, we did not merely selectively read specific posts or comments. Instead, we used computational tools for systematic data collection, employing automatic web scrapers to extract pertinent data. This approach allowed us to gather a comprehensive dataset for analysis.

We constructed three distinct sets of social media data for our analysis. First, we utilized Facebook's application programming interface (API) to identify key actors within Hong Kong's political landscape, focusing particularly on pro-democracy civil society groups that were not prominently featured in the news but remained active on social media. Using network analysis, we initiated the snowballing process by selecting a set of seed Facebook pages (major political groups) and expanding our inclusion to encompass all the other pages they liked. Through this iterative process, we manually identified the relevant groups.

Second, we collected over 470 online petitions that emerged prior to the onset of the Anti-Extradition Movement, meticulously documenting their entire texts. This extensive corpus of texts enabled us to examine how various social groups framed the extradition bill through their unique identities, despite the absence of centralized movement leadership. Third, to analyse activism among secondary school students, we collected social media data on Instagram, focusing on accounts created by students in relation to the protests. These data allowed us to outline the network structure of the secondary school concern groups and to illustrate the potential role of social capital in information dissemination.

In addition, we gathered posts from LIHKG, one of Hong Kong's most popular discussion forums that evolved into a central communication platform during the Anti-Extradition Movement. Specifically, we collected posts between 1 June 2019 and 31 December 2019, from two prominent chatrooms: the 'Public Affairs Channel' and the 'Chit-chat Channel,' where discussions related to the movement were concentrated. This collection encompassed a large volume of data, including 626,919 threads and 22,159,533 comments. These posts were a crucial source for analysing protesters' online engagement and tracing the dynamics of contention. They also facilitated our practice of online ethnography (Hine 2020) by allowing us to observe and study the discussions taking place within the online community.

We also incorporated secondary social media data that had already been collected by other researchers. A notable dataset is a protest event database of the Anti-Extradition Movement, compiled from the 'action posts' on significant Telegram channels by a team of researchers from the Journalism and Media Studies Centre at The University of Hong Kong (HKUJMSC 2020). This dataset provides valuable information on the various protest events that occurred during the movement. In addition, we utilized a network dataset that encompasses all the key Telegram channels and groups active during the

Anti-Extradition Movement. This comprehensive dataset, consisting of over 58,000 nodes and 354,000 edges, was constructed by Aleksandra Urman, Justin Chun-ting Ho, and Stefan Katz (2021). It provides insights into the communication and coordination dynamics within the movement's online ecosystem.

ROADMAP

The rest of the book is structured into 10 chapters. Chapter 2 analyses the formation of Hong Kong's entrenched liberal oligarchy from a historical-institutional perspective. We trace the emergence of a tripartite coalition consisting of the Chinese party-state, civil servants, and business elites. We also delve into the complex dynamics between this coalition and the burgeoning opposition, examining how protests have been managed and contained since the 1980s, until shortly after the handover. Chapter 3 examines the emergence and evolution of a new cycle of contention during the mid-2000s. We highlight how the deepening threat perceptions resulting from the regime's state-building advances spurred mass mobilizations. Meanwhile, we underscore how the creation of new civil society groups and how the normalization of new repertoires of contention contributed to changes in the episodes and modes of protest mobilization.

Chapter 4 explores the dynamics and consequences of the 2014 Umbrella Movement. We illustrate how its spontaneous eruption led to a hybrid organizational structure comprising a formal leadership and self-mobilized protesters who saw themselves as leaderless, and how such dynamics eventually led to the division and fragmentation of the opposition. Chapter 5 elucidates how the 2019 Anti-Extradition Movement erupted despite the lack of political opportunities in the post-Umbrella period. We demonstrate how abeyance networks from previous mobilizations and an online petition campaign transformed the idea of extradition into a widely perceived existential threat, galvanizing popular support for the movement and leading to a leaderful mobilization.

Chapter 6 looks at how sectoral networks propelled the movement. By focusing on religious groups, legal professionals, and medical practitioners, we demonstrate how social identities informed protesters what roles to take up during a leaderful movement, and how these sectoral networks provided expertise and resources to facilitate the movement's organizing efforts. Chapter 7 examines how secondary school action groups, established by students in their respective schools, played a crucial role in mobilizing teenagers against the extradition bill by tapping into and leveraging their latent social capital. Utilizing Instagram as a platform, these groups facilitated connections among students within and across schools, often by capitalizing on their schools' identities and leveraging various sources of social capital tied to those identities. This enabled loose and fragmented social networks can be mobilized in social movements, provided that they can activate their latent social capital.

Chapter 8 explains how the Anti-Extradition Movement was organized and sustained in the absence of a centralized leadership. We illustrate how protesters, networked in both online and offline realms, collaborated on a spontaneous, horizontal, and many-to-many basis to generate a continuous stream of actions – a mechanism that we term 'peer collaboration'. Chapter 9 investigates the emergence of political consumption as a protest tactic in the later stage of the movement. We examine how this innovative tactic, encompassing boycotting and buycotting, emerged by utilizing the market logic. We also highlight the significance of political consumption as a movement consequence. Chapter 10 delves into the process of tactical radicalization observed in the 2019 movement. By adopting a relational approach, we analyse radicalization as a result of dynamic interactions across multiple arenas. We explore how discursive negotiations among protesters served as both the driving force and the limit to radicalization. It induced moderate protesters to extend tacit support to their more militant counterparts while acting as a restraint mechanism to curtail excessive measures.

Chapter 11 discusses the implications of Hong Kong's contentious politics within the global context of democratic backsliding and leaderful mobilizations. We highlight the contributions of our theoretical framework and the implications of Hong Kong's contentious pathways for hybrid regimes and beyond.

PART I

CONTEXT

2

The Making of a Liberal Oligarchy

On 1 July 1997, Hong Kong was handed over from the United Kingdom to the People's Republic of China (PRC), ending its 156 years of colonial rule. The transition was meticulously choreographed, impeccably ordered, and laden with symbolism. As the British Union Jack was lowered in the Hong Kong Convention and Exhibition Centre at Admiralty, the Chinese five-star red flag took its place. This act marked a peaceful transition of sovereignty between two nations previously at war and initiated one of the most significant political experiments at the dawn of the twenty-first century (Hung 2022). It also symbolized the end of the British Empire as it relinquished its last major overseas territory and represented the Chinese nation's rejuvenation after 'a century of humiliation' (Jiang 1997). Under the principle of 'One Country, Two Systems', Hong Kong, an Asian Tiger and one of the most globalized cities in the Asia-Pacific, would now be ruled as a Special Administrative Region, a capitalist enclave within a vast communist state (So 1999). It would be guaranteed a high degree of autonomy, with its own people governing the territory. In principle, Hong Kong was to remain unchanged despite the change of hands – for at least fifty years.

However, as the dust settled, concerns about the sustainability of this political arrangement would gradually re-emerge over the next two decades (Linz and Stepan 1996: 19; Wasserstrom 2020). For the better part, Hong Kong remained a liberal and capitalist society. It sustained a free economy with impressive economic growth and human development that outpaced many established economies. Press freedom and the rule of law were generally upheld, and its civil society remained diverse and vibrant. On the other hand, political and socioeconomic inequalities in the territory have arguably intensified (Forrest, La Grange, and Yip 2004; Piketty and Yang 2021). Despite some democratic reforms, the political system was still primarily oligarchic: the Chief Executive was chosen by a small election committee, and half of the

LegCo members were indirectly elected and dominated by business interests. Simultaneously, China's gradual state and nation-building efforts have heightened tensions with civil liberties and local identity (Bush 2016), leading to recurring waves of protests in the 2010s (Cheng 2016).

What led to the making of this 'liberal oligarchy' where freedoms and activism flourished despite the lack of democracy? How did the democratic opposition evolve into an institutionalized political force within this hybrid regime? This chapter examines the historical and institutional context that shaped and sustained this distinctive political order. We argue that the power equilibrium underpinning the liberal oligarchy originated from the late colonial state's consultative governance, which incorporated a diverse range of societal interests into the political system. This equilibrium was kept alive post-handover through the establishment of a tripartite ruling coalition that shared power among the Chinese party-state, local government technocrats, and business elites. The institutional openness provided under this coalition, albeit partial, initially facilitated the formation of a democratic opposition. This system provided the opposition with the political opportunities to pursue a dual strategy: institutional bargaining and ritualistic protests. Threats posed by sporadic state advancements could be mitigated through this strategy. The sequential combination of opportunities and threats elucidates how the institutionalized opposition acquired the legitimacy and capacity to lead Hong Kong's pro-democracy movement in the early post-handover years.

HYBRID REGIME WITH HONG KONG CHARACTERISTICS

Hong Kong's post-handover political system has been widely regarded as a hybrid regime (Case 2008; Fong 2017). However, unlike many hybrid regimes around the world which often employ democratic institutions such as elections and legislatures to co-opt political elites, distribute spoils and demonstrate invincibility (Brownlee 2007; Gandhi and Przeworski 2007; Gandhi 2008; Magaloni 2008; Svolik 2012), democratic institutions only played a limited role in Hong Kong until recently. Although the late colonial era saw the onset of democratic reforms, their extent and progression were limited due to the compromise between Britain and China (Yahuda 1993). Nevertheless, despite the lack of democratic institutions, the city has upheld the rule of law, protected civil liberties to some extent, and preserved a relatively impartial bureaucracy since the late colonial era (Ma 2007). Dissent and public assemblies were also increasingly tolerated by the colonial regime, a practice inherited by the post-handover regime. This system of 'liberalism without democracy' differs significantly from the conventional hybrid regimes that emerged globally after the Cold War (Diamond 2002; Levitsky and Way 2010). And it raises the critical question about its long-term viability (Plattner 1998): Can liberalism survive without democracy?

To answer this question, we need a deeper understanding of the nature and evolution of Hong Kong's political system. The classification of Hong Kong as a 'liberal autocracy', 'hybrid regime' and 'electoral authoritarianism' (Case 2008; Fong 2017; Kuan and Lau 2002) are overly broad and do not adequately capture what underpins the multifaceted components of the political system and its toleration of dissent. In this context, Robert Dahl's (1971) typology of political regimes, which categorizes regimes based on their level of liberalization and inclusiveness, provides a useful framework. According to this typology, post-handover Hong Kong can be described as a 'competitive oligarchy'. The semi-autonomous city features an oligarchic state that strongly represents the interests of the Chinese state and a wide array of economic elites. Meanwhile, while citizens experience a low level of inclusiveness due to their limited electoral rights, they are afforded a considerable degree of liberalization that allows them to express dissent through consultative mechanisms and peaceful protests. This model has facilitated the opposition movement's growth while preserving the ruling coalition's interests. Although the ruling elites and the opposition consistently vie for power, their competition is generally contained by institutional rules and norms.

This hybrid equilibrium, however, is not immutable. It evolved as the product of political compromises between Britain and China during the 1980s. It was further consolidated by the international order, characterized by harmonious US–China relations and the globalization of the world economy, as epitomized by China's accession to the World Trade Organization in 2001. However, the Chinese party-state's political ideologies and relationships with the Western world have changed gradually in the past two decades (Fewsmith 2021). After the 2008 Financial Crisis, Chinese political elites advocated for an alternative approach to the Washington Consensus. Since the mid-2010s, they have stressed China's unique developmental path and security concerns (Nathan and Scobell 2015). The new ideologies and priorities of the Beijing central government, taken together, have clashed with the functional values of the liberal enclave – global connectivity, local autonomy, and high degree of contestation (Hung 2022; Huang 2023).

Internally, the liberal oligarchy was constantly reshaped by the interplay between power and contention within the SAR. First, due to its executive-led structure, wherein representative institutions have limited oversight, the hybrid system relies heavily on the choices, perceptions, and alignment of political and business elites in exercising power. Its liberal character can only endure if the powerholders perceive that the benefits of preserving it outweigh the costs. Second, Hong Kong's hybrid regime enjoyed greater political space and intermediate networks compared with the authoritarian structure in mainland China (Cai 2010; Chen 2012). Civil society organizations could exist and thrive, while the opposition gained institutional representation without state endorsement (Ma 2007). The space enjoyed by the political and civil society allowed dissent to directly promote their claims and confront the legitimacy of the authorities, rather than relying on the logic of 'rightful resistance', that is, collective actions that employ the regime's laws, policies, and rhetoric to serve as acceptable means to express dissent (O'Brien and Li 2006). As a result, Hong Kong's overt and open challenges often introduced uncertainties, especially with the gradual erosion of the external constraints outlined earlier. In response, authorities might modify the system's rules or counter-mobilize against these overt challenges, potentially tilting the balance towards a more illiberal direction (Ong 2022; Slater and Smith 2016).

NEGOTIATED POLITICAL AUTONOMY

The roots of Hong Kong's liberal oligarchy can be traced back roughly half a century ago from a strategic compromise that emerged from the struggles among various political forces. Positioned at the edge of two empires during the Cold War, colonial Hong Kong found itself sandwiched between the influences of London's welfare reforms and Beijing's Cultural Revolution (Carroll 2005). However, neither of these political programs firmly took hold in the city. Instead of unequivocally aligning with either empire, the colonial administration strove to uphold its political autonomy through careful negotiation with the two sides, forming a ruling alliance with the capitalist class and striving to alleviate social conflicts (Miners 1986; Ngo 1999).

Colonial Hong Kong experienced two riots, one in 1956 and another in 1967. Each involved repeated strikes, boycotts, and rallies that led to significant economic loss and political turmoil. The 1956 riot was initiated by local pro-Kuomintang (KMT) forces, while the 1967 riot received backing from local pro-Chinese Communist Party (CCP) factions. In the aftermath of 1956 riots, the colonial administration suppressed local pro-KMT associations while maintaining unofficial contact with the Republic of China. It thus signalled that Hong Kong would not serve as a base for anti-communist activities. This strategy was designed to accommodate Cold War conflicts at the colony (Tsang 1997). During the 1967 riots, fearing that severe repression might provoke China's hostile takeover of the colony, the UK Foreign Office initially recommended a more conciliatory approach to deal with the pro-CCP supporters (Cheung 2009). However, the governor opposed the suggestion, persuading Downing Street to suppress the local communists firmly (Yep 2008). The ensuing crackdown resulted in hundreds of anti-colonial protesters jailed, trade union leaders expelled, and students from pro-Beijing schools being denied entry into the civil service. These extensive measures significantly marginalized pro-Beijing groups from mainstream society in the subsequent decades (Bickers and Yep 2009).

Despite their anti-imperial and anti-capitalist rhetoric, PRC leaders Mao Zedong and Zhou Enlai upheld the principle of 'long-term planning and full utilization' (*changqi dasuan chongfen liyong*) to guide policies regarding Hong Kong (Xu 1993). This guideline aimed to leverage Hong Kong's unique status to interact with the international community and facilitate China's modernization. Consequently, the Beijing and Hong Kong governments reached a consensus to allow party-state branches to operate within the territory, albeit maintaining a low profile (Ng 2022). Following the riots, the colonial government gained increased political autonomy from London and consolidated its control over the local society (Yep and Lui 2010). During the tenure of Governor Murray MacLehose in the 1970s, the colonial administration introduced reforms to boost sectoral representation and advance partial decolonization (Scott 1989), despite maintaining tight control of the media and public sphere (Ng 2022). Institutionally, the Executive Council (Exco) broadened the scope of consultative governance by establishing City District Offices, incorporating more business and professional elites into the power structure (King 1975). The number of statutory bodies and consultative committees advising on issues such as town planning, consumer rights, and public broadcasting surged from a mere few dozen in the 1960s to several hundred by the 2000s (Holliday and Wong 2003). Despite a lack of electoral franchises, the emerging middle class found representation through these institutional bodies.

To gauge public sentiments, the Home Affairs Department launched a comprehensive weekly public opinion survey in each district in 1970. Senior officials scrutinized the confidential reports every week, ensuring that policymaking aligned with shifting public sentiment (Mok 2019). To enhance local representation, the colonial administration increased the localization of the civil service. The proportion of foreign civil servants gradually diminished, whereas the number of local civil servants in directorate grades rose significantly (Garcia 1989; Lee and Huque 1995). This partial decolonization allowed Hong Kong citizens of Chinese descent to gain access to the public policy domain, transforming career civil servants into a distinct force embedded within a Weberian bureaucracy that prioritized procedural norms, administrative efficiency, and impartiality (Cheung 1996; Burns 2004).

This emerging liberal oligarchic order is widely acknowledged as the bedrock of its prosperity and stability. From 1970 to 1982, the city achieved an impressive annual GDP growth rate of 9.4 per cent, outpacing other Asian Tiger economies. By 1990, Hong Kong's GDP per capita already exceeded that of the UK, and its GDP accounted for a quarter of PRC's total (Hong Kong Yearbook 1991; World Bank 1991). Furthermore, its human development index increased from 0.837 in 1997 to 0.952 in 2019, on par with the Scandinavian countries (UNDP 2018). Throughout the late colonial and early post-handover periods, Hong Kong functioned as a hub linking the Asian 'archipelagos' (Hamashita 2008), hosting regional headquarters for international business and media organizations, facilitating international trade, and establishing itself as a global financial centre immediately behind London and New York (Chiu and Lui 2004). These socio-economic benefits incentivized the Beijing central government, foreign governments, and local business elites to reach a strategic compromise to protect their vested interests in the city.

ROOTS OF THE TRIPARTITE RULING COALITION

Unlike the developmental path followed by other Asian Tigers (Woo-Cumings 1999), Hong Kong's post-war economic miracle is attributed to its non-interventionist state (Friedman 1998; Haggard 1990). However, it is important to note that the colonial government actively co-opted business elites to expand its societal influence. This process of elite co-optation acted as an informal brokerage between the government and Chinese communities, enabling business interests to gain privileged access to political power and disproportionate sway in policymaking (Faure 2003; Law 2009). High-ranking executives from renowned British trading firms and banks such as Jardine, Swire, and HSBC often held default membership in the Exco, which served as the governor's de facto cabinet. Furthermore, leaders of commercial chambers, charitable organizations, and professional associations were frequently appointed to the Exco or LegCo. This close alignment of state and corporatist interests exemplified the dynamics of comprador politics (Ma 2016; Ngo 1999). It also established the roots of the tripartite ruling coalition in the post-handover years.

Even before assuming control over Hong Kong, Beijing tacitly acknowledged the importance of the state-business linkages in the territory. Following the signing of the Sino-British Joint Declaration in 1984, which outlined the terms of the handover, Hong Kong experienced a period of turmoil marked by a stock market crash, a property crisis, and a wave of mass emigration. Chinese leader Deng Xiaoping sought to stem the brain drain and capital flight by adopting a reassuring stance, famously declaring that 'horse racing will continue, and dancing parties will go on'. This conciliatory gesture was effective. By preserving the OCTS principle, the Chinese party-state successfully maintained the pre-handover system established in the 1980s, bolstering investor confidence and facilitating China's reform and opening up policy (Lui 2015). The preservation of the capitalist system and its associated way of life was beneficial to China.

However, the appointment of Chris Patten as the last governor presented a new challenge to Beijing's efforts to maintain the status quo. Unlike his predecessors, who were experienced diplomats trained in the Foreign and Commonwealth Office, Patten was a senior politician and an outsider to the Sino-British negotiations. After losing his seat in the 1992 general elections, he was selected by then Prime Minister John Major to oversee the final years of British administration in the colony. Rather than striking a delicate balance between serving the Crown's interests and appeasing the concerns of the CCP, Patten focused his efforts on advancing democratization and ensuring Britain's 'graceful withdrawal' (Dimbleby 1997). In 1992, Patten introduced performance pledges for all bureaus and departments responsible for public services (LegCo 1992). With Patten's political leadership, the LegCo, backed by the democratic opposition, passed a bill that granted 2.7 million new electorates the right to vote in functional constituencies. Moreover, all government-appointed seats in regional and district councils were abolished. Although the Beijing government later reversed these political reforms through the appointed provisional LegCo in 1997, it allowed the administrative reforms to remain in place after the handover. These reforms introduced elements of new public management, viewing citizens as clients and stakeholders while promoting a culture of political and administrative accountability to regulate elected representatives and civil servants (Lee and Haque 2006).

LIBERAL OLIGARCHY AFTER THE HANDOVER

There are, however, substantial differences between the liberal oligarchy before and after 1997, particularly in terms of the level of formalization of the corporatist structure and the extent of contestation during gradual democratization. Following the handover, Beijing swiftly implemented a set of institutional arrangements that formalized the tripartite ruling coalition in Hong Kong. This coalition consisted of the local government, business elites, and the central party-state, with the aim of circumscribing the areas of contestation and containing the growing democracy movement through both informal and formal means.[1]

Formally, the Basic Law institutionalized the corporatist structure to organize and distribute control between the party-state and business interests in the post-handover regime. The Chief Executive, elected by a 1,200-member electoral committee, is prohibited from having any political party affiliations. This rule allows the Chief Executive to claim impartial legitimacy, leading a Weberian civil service that upholds due procedures and maintains credibility through administrative efficiency (Tsang 2003). It also ensures that the Chief Executive remains accountable to and serves the interests of the Beijing central government and its local business alliance. Meanwhile, LegCo seats are divided into geographical and functional constituencies. While geographical constituencies are elected through suffrage and had its representation steadily increased from 33 per cent in 1998 to 50 per cent in 2008, the majority of seats in the functional constituencies are determined through organizational votes (Ma 2016).[2] This arrangement institutionalizes interest representation and articulation, securing the political dominance of the business elites. Although the pro-democracy camp consistently won between 55 and 60 per cent of the

---

[1] As early as 1985, Deng Xiaoping reassured the business elite that the OCTS 'would allow people in Hong Kong to criticize the CCP but reminded them that the Central Government would not allow the locals to turn their words into actions and convey Hong Kong into the base of subversion to the mainland' (Deng 1987: 215–222).

[2] Around one-third of the seats in Legco's Functional Constituencies were elected by individuals working in the respective industry or sector. The democratic opposition won more and more seats in these constituencies. The corporatist structure, though semi-democratic, had helped to develop sectoral networks and professional oversight (Ma 2009).

popular vote in geographical constituencies after the handover, they remained a minority in the legislature (Wong 2019). Given the paucity of objective measures for identifying the sectors worthy of representation, the designation of functional constituency status was very much a state licensing process, which allows the state to selectively acknowledge and award its allies.

Informally, the CCP conducted active but covert united front work in Hong Kong to rally support from the conservative capitalists as well as grassroots to check the democratic opposition. The united front is a practice rooted in Leninism and hailed by Mao Zedong as one of the CCP's 'three great magic weapons' (*sanda fabao*), initially aimed at uniting all workers from non-socialist parties against the capitalist class. While the CCP's united front had long existed in Hong Kong since the 1920s (Chan Lau 1999), it was debilitated and marginalized after the 1967 riots. In the late 1970s, as the handover negotiations began to emerge, the local party branch in Hong Kong began rebuilding its social networks.

Promises that Hong Kong would be reunited with China under 'democratic reunification' were also made to an emerging group of pro-democracy advocates and students to gain their support (Xu 1993: 59). New institutions, including drafting and consultative committees for the Basic Law, were established, recruiting major tycoons as well as representatives from business chambers, professional associations, and trade unions to facilitate a smooth transition (Pepper 2008). These arrangements co-opted social and business elites by granting state recognition, allocating market interests, and fostering working relationships (Loh 2010: 145–168). However, united front work remained clandestine as the CCP did not have a formal presence during the colonial and early post-handover period. Its operations were limited to maintaining a state-business coalition through which the party-state could achieve its strategic objectives in the post-handover period (So 1999).

INTERLOCKING INTERESTS

Figure 2.1 presents a visual representation of the intricate and multi-layered institutional arrangements within the tripartite coalition during the post-handover period. The first component, and perhaps the most powerful, is the Beijing central government, which exerts its control through various channels, including the central and local apparatuses, grassroots, and professional associations, as well as the mainland market and political appointments. The second component comprises the Hong Kong government, along with a bureaucracy that faces the challenge of balancing the interests of its sovereign and the local population, while upholding due procedures and administrative oversight (Scott 2022). The third component consists of business elites who maintain political influence and vested interests by preserving their access to both central and local authorities. This alliance between the Communist party-state, Weberian bureaucracy, and capitalist class formed an interlocking

FIGURE 2.1 The interlocking structure of the tripartite coalition.
Source: Compiled by the authors.

system of power and interests, allowing for a high degree of autonomy within the post-handover regime during the first two decades. However, while the hybrid system demonstrated overall cohesion, it lacked the determination and tools necessary to address the discontent and grievances brewing under a neoliberal environment, as well as emerging pro-democracy aspirations.

In the post-handover era, the Central Government's Liaison Office (CGLO) played a crucial role as the party secretariat of the Hong Kong Work Committee, the highest-level party organ in Hong Kong. It is also the administrative organ of the Hong Kong and Macao Affairs Office of the State Council, a central government agency. Past leaders of the CGLO, who were always members of the Central Committee with access to the Politburo, possessed extensive organizational and social connections within the local society. Additionally, the CGLO exercised direct control over the pro-Beijing groups that acted as affiliates or extensions of the party-state in Hong Kong society. Alongside these veteran patriots, the CGLO began co-opting many social organizations to expand its patron-client networks and counter the pro-democracy movement following the mass rallies in 2003 and 2004.

The Hong Kong government enjoyed significant autonomy during the first two decades of the SAR. Until 2022, two out of the four Chief Executives, Donald Tsang and Carrie Lam, were former civil servants, with the remaining two coming from the business and professional sectors. Administrative officers – the senior civil servants rotating between and leading various bureaus and departments – formed the backbone of the Hong Kong government. They headed hundreds of statutory bodies and consultative committees, co-opting pro-Beijing business leaders, opposition legislators and independent professional elites. Following the introduction of a political appointment system in 2008, many former administrative officers continued to be appointed as secretaries or undersecretaries of the Hong Kong government (Cheung 2012). While enjoying autonomy from the political appointees, civil servants were also subjected to checks and balances from a range of sociopolitical institutions, including highly independent quangos, the partially elected legislature, critical media outlets, judicial reviews, and the courts. The institutionalization of the Independent Commission Against Corruption in 1974, the Office of Ombudsman in 1989, and the implementation of performance pledges in 1992 were crucial public sector reforms that emphasized civil service's commitment to efficiency, impartiality, administrative accountability, and clean governance (Burns 2004; Cheung 1996; Scott 2022).

Local business elites, as part of the ruling coalition, continued to be Beijing's key allies. The state-business coalition that shared political power and preserved vested interests has been characterized by scholars as 'statist corporatism', (Lee 2005) 'government-business partnership', (Fong 2014) and 'eclectic corporatism' (Ma 2016). Their involvement helped expand the patriotic force and support electoral campaigns for pro-Beijing politicians. Co-opted business elites often gained representation in national political institutions such as the National People's Congress (NPC) and the Chinese People's Political Consultative Conference (CPPCC), as well as in the LegCo and various statutory bodies within the SAR. Through formalized consultation, the capitalist class utilized their standing and influence in professional and business sectors to maintain the limited franchise in the LegCo's functional constituencies and garner support for government policies. At the grassroots level, they contributed manpower and resources to a wide range of pro-Beijing social organizations. A survey of Hong Kong's major hometown associations, groups that bring together migrants with a common township or region, revealed that close to 70 per cent of their income, amounting to tens of millions per year, came from donations by tycoons or activity income from the local government (Yuen and Cheng 2020: 146).

In summary, post-handover Hong Kong emerged as a liberal oligarchy underpinned by a multi-level power-sharing coalition with heterogeneous and sometimes conflicting loyalties to national sovereignty, administrative efficiency, and business interests. Elite alignment was not only maintained, but also adapted to serve multifaceted and multi-level interests. Keeping the relatively autonomous status of Hong Kong, rather than making it 'just another mainland Chinese city', was its official doctrine (Chu 2013; Economy 2022). Under these constraints, state-building efforts by the CCP in this reclaimed territory must be operated discreetly through united front work, channelled by intermediaries such as the local government and business sectors (Loh 2010).

This is why we characterize Hong Kong as a 'liberal oligarchy', a term that distinguishes it from often-used classifications such as liberal autocracy, liberal authoritarianism, or competitive authoritarianism. This term, we believe, more accurately encapsulates the nature, characteristics, and operations of the regime (Case 2008; Cheng 2016; Fong 2017; Kuan and Lau 2002). It acknowledges the considerable degree of openness within the regime and the existence of contestation across multiple institutional arenas. However, it is important to note that being a coalition does not imply any inherent fracture in elite alignment, which is common in other hybrid regimes. While elites within the ruling coalition may have disagreements, they remained cohesive against the democratic opposition, which was effectively barred from becoming the incumbent in the sub-national context.

EMERGENT PRO-DEMOCRACY ORGANIZATIONS

Despite the relatively high degree of elite cohesion, a pro-democracy opposition gradually emerged and became more institutionalized in the late colonial era, thanks to the partial openness of the liberal oligarchy and its restrained approach to repressing dissent. To understand the rise of this opposition, it is useful to revisit Dahl's typology of contestation and inclusiveness. First, the consultative governance model expanded the institutional arenas for activists to engage in public contestation. In the wake of the crackdown on social movements in the 1960s, the 1970s saw the proliferation of grassroots networks and professional associations focusing on social justice, civil rights, women's rights, and refugees (Chiu and Lui 2000). This development was partly spurred by the colonial administration's effort to address the social issues stemming from rapid population growth. For example, the Neighbourhood Level Community Development Project was launched in the 1970s to support social work organizations tackling citizens' livelihood and housing problems. Many social workers leveraged these resources to organize residents and cultivate their sense of community (Lui and Kung 1985), occasionally leading to grassroots level protests pressuring the government for policy changes (Kuah-Pearce and Guiheux 2009).

Although comprehensive data about the growth of the civil society sector is unavailable, a 2003 survey provided a snapshot. It identified 16,662 NGOs across fourteen fields, including charity, education, social work, and labour.

These NGOs often enjoyed substantial autonomy and had huge influence in citizens' public life. They operated three fourths of primary and secondary schools, provided four-fifths of social services, and employed 7.9 per cent of the total workforce by that time (Central Policy Unit 2004). Even though many NGOs received funding and licensure from the government, they also substantially relied on membership fees and service income, enabling some extent of financial autonomy (Chan and Chan 2017).

Second, gradual democratization created opportunities for professional elites and the middle class to engage in politics. A pivotal juncture was the signing of the Sino-British Joint Declaration in 1984. That year, dozens of pressure groups, community organizers, and professional elites convened at the Koshan Theatre to discuss about their strategies to promote democracy in the years leading up to the handover. Participants collected over 220,000 signatures in support of implementing direct elections in the 1988 LegCo elections. These participants eventually evolved into the 'Group of 190', a loose alliance advocating for a faster pace of democratic reform. This contrasted with a more conservative yet resourceful 'Group of 89' which comprised business and professional elites. However, since the colonial government sided with the business elite, the proposal for direct elections was rejected; and pro-democracy force won only one-third of the indirectly elected seats in the LegCo elections of 1988. Despite this, this early network formed the backbone of the United Democrats and Meeting Points, two groups that later merged to form the Democratic Party in 1994. The party then went on to secure a resounding victory in the liberalized LegCo elections of 1995 (Ma and Choy 2003).

Table 2.1 overviews the ecosystem of Hong Kong's pro-democracy movement, spotlighting five key organizations that have served as vital pillars connecting various constituencies. The two trade unions, which focused on welfare provision and bargaining, had their origins traced to the social activism of the 1970s. The Hong Kong Professional Teachers' Union (HKPTU) was founded during the certified teachers' strike in 1973 and became a formidable force in challenging the colonial government on education matters. At its peak, HKPTU claimed membership from nine out of ten registered teachers (Luk 2016). The Hong Kong Confederation of Trade Unions (HKCTU) was founded officially in 1990 but had its roots in the Hong Kong Christian Industrial Committee, a church-sponsored labour organization which was involved in grassroots movements in the 1970s. HKCTU had over 160,000 members and 70 affiliates across various industries and sectors (Chan, Chan, and Tang 2019). After the handover, both HKPTU and HKCTU continued to be influential in the pro-democracy movement, with their leaders always elected as members of the LegCo. Even though their advocacy work largely revolved the concerns of their members and sectors, their sizeable membership and sprawling networks ensured that the emerging pro-democracy force represented the interests of both the middle class and grassroots communities.

TABLE 2.1 *The ecology of institutionalized opposition in Hong Kong, 1970s–2010s.*

	Hong Kong Professional Teachers' Union (HKPTU)	Hong Kong Confederation of Trade Unions (HKCTU)	The Democratic Party of Hong Kong (DPHK)	Hong Kong Alliance (HKA) in Support of Patriotic Democratic Movements of China	The Civil Human Rights Front (CHRF)
Years active	1973–2021	1971–2021	1983–present	1989–2021	2002–2021
Membership	100,000 members	160,000 members and 70 organizational affiliates	800 members	Below 300 volunteers and around 140 organizational affiliates	Maximum 70 organizational affiliates
Constituency	Professions	Grassroots	Catch-all political party	Cross-sectoral	Cross-sectoral
Function	Welfare	Welfare	Election	Activism	Activism

Note: Membership refers to the latest figures realized by the organizations.
Source: Data compiled and synthesized by the authors.

The other three organizations were born during the gradual democratization process, particularly spawned by two significant protest movements in the 1980s and 2000s. The Hong Kong Alliance (HKA) in Support of Patriotic Democratic Movements of China was established following the 1989 Tiananmen Movement and became the organizer of the annual Tiananmen candlelight vigils, advocating democracy in mainland China. The Civil Human Rights Front (CHRF) was formed in 2002 in response to the introduction of a national security legislation. It became the main organizer for the annual July 1 marches and other mass pro-democracy rallies. Both organizations were primarily centred around activism. They did not have individual members except their core organizers and volunteers; but they developed strong affiliation networks comprising civil society organizations, which they relied heavily on to organize the annual protests. Lastly, the Democratic Party was founded as a political party in 1994, primarily focusing on primarily on elections and using their institutional position to bargain with the authorities. While the leadership figures overlapped across the three organizations, these organizations maintained distinct boundaries in order to ensure division of labour and minimize political risks.

Collectively, these three organizations played a pivotal role in shaping the agenda for the pro-democracy movement. They gained their status as stakeholders for government engagement through their organizational reach and established their moral authority as leaders of the pro-democracy movement through various collective actions. They served as what Mario Diani (2003: 107) called 'brokers', which act as the intermediary between actors that are not directly linked, thus creating a new line of communication and exchange. Still, these organizations wielded limited formal political power. While some of them maintained an electoral foothold, their political influence remained limited. Their primary influence lay in their ability to shape policy choices rather than in the power to enact policies or determine the outcomes of protests. However, during critical junctures – when authorities were perceived to violate procedural norms – these organizations were capable of mobilizing citizens to participate in mass protests.

THREATS-INDUCED OPPOSITION MOVEMENT

The two aforementioned protest events that greatly amplified the influence and reach of Hong Kong's democratic opposition warrant further examination. These events – specifically the crackdown on the Tiananmen Movement in 1989 and the march against national security legislation in 2003 – served as pivotal moments that dramatically reshaped the pro-democracy movement. Both emerged in response to contingent threats to the existing liberal order.

The Tiananmen Movement in 1989 significantly heightened the perceived threat to Hong Kong's status and continuity as a liberal enclave. As the movement unfolded in April and May, many Hong Kong citizens held onto hope for China's imminent democratic transition. They donated essential resources to sustain the occupation at Tiananmen Square, organized massive rallies in Victoria Park, and disseminated live reports about the movement world-wide (Béja 2009). The most remarkable moment occurred on 28 May 1989, when 1.5 million people, equivalent to one-fourth of the population, swarmed Hong Kong Island in support of the students in Tiananmen Square. Both these protesters and many political elites failed to foresee the violent crackdown that occurred a week later, on June 4. This shocking turn of events not only destroyed the hopeful narrative of China's democratization but also strained the relationship between the burgeoning democratic opposition and Beijing (Link 2010). Before 1989, Szeto Wah, the founding President of HKPTU, and Martin Lee, the founding Chairman of the Democracy Party, were the only two pro-democracy figures represented in the Beijing-controlled Hong Kong Basic Law Drafting Committee. In the aftermath of the Tiananmen crackdown, both resigned from the committee in protest. Their resignation marked the onset of a more confrontational relationship between the pro-democracy and Beijing.

The pro-democracy leaders viewed themselves as first-hand witnesses to the Tiananmen crackdown. They saw the importance of democratic institutions in safeguarding the existing freedoms of the liberal enclave against the encroaching threats of authoritarianism (So and Kwitko 1990). They decided to leverage the Hong Kong Alliance (HKA) in Support of Patriotic Democratic Movements of China – a platform established a month prior to the crackdown – to cultivate ties between the pro-democracy movements in Hong Kong and mainland China. At the height of its influence, the HKA consisted of 146 affiliated organizations, including the Democratic Party, the Hong Kong Federation of Students, HKPTU, and HKCTU. However, the core membership was confined to a dozen leaders and several hundred volunteers. In other words, the strength of the organization was not in its formal membership, but rather in its moral legitimacy and its connections to other civil society organizations.

The Tiananmen Movement catalysed a tradition in Hong Kong that evolved into a ceremonious ritual of the pro-democracy movement. From 1990 to 2020, on every June 4, tens of thousands of protesters would gather at Victoria Park in downtown Hong Kong to light candles in remembrance of the victims of the 1989 Tiananmen crackdown. During the poignant ceremony, attendees would light candles, sing pro-democracy songs, listen to survivors' testimonies, and perform Chinese funeral rituals to mourn the victims. These ritualistic practices served as a stark reminder of the Tiananmen crackdown, reinforcing their resolve to pursue democracy in both Hong Kong and mainland China. Table 2.2 illustrates our onsite survey conducted during the 2018 vigil. It shows that, irrespective of how often participants had attended the ceremony in the past, the primary motivation of attending was the preservation of memory. Participants also acknowledged the importance of continuing the commemoration, with the most common motivation being 'preserving Hong Kong society's memory of June 4'. Moreover, the objectives of 'demanding that the

TABLE 2.2 *Perceived motivations and participation frequency in the Tiananmen vigils, 2018.*

Participants/ Motivation	Mourn the deaths from 4 June	Demand that the Chinese gov't vindicate 4 June	Preserve Hong Kong society's memory of 4 June	Struggle for democracy in China	Struggle for democracy in Hong Kong
Casual ($n = 193$)	59.6	55.7$_a$	72.3	34.5	47.2
Regular ($n = 146$)	63.0	50.3$_b$	77.4	31.7$_a$	44.1
Stalwart ($n = 320$)	66.6	71.2$_{ab}$	75.9	42.5$_a$	58.7
F-values	2.196	10.441***	1.702	3.582**	2.645

Notes: Entries are the percentages of respondents within each group who strongly agreed with the statement. The F-values were derived from a one-way ANOVA test of differences in the means of the three groups of participants (casual, regular and stalwart) with the perceived motivations. Entries in the same column sharing the same subscripts 'a' and 'b' differ from each other significantly in post hoc Bonferroni tests.** $p < 0.05$; *** $p < 0.001$.
Source: Authors' onsite survey, 2018.

Chinese government vindicate June 4' and 'struggling for democracy in China', as officially articulated by the HKA, were significantly correlated with the frequency of participation. This finding suggests that individuals who attended the vigil more frequently were more likely to support the stated objectives of the institutionalized opposition. Overall, the data suggests that the vigil participants held an anti-authoritarian orientation, but also harboured some degree of patriotic sentiments towards the nation state. It was not until the 2010s that the term 'vindication' (*pingfan*) began to receive criticism from the localists for perceived subservience to the Chinese authorities (Veg 2017).

Through repeated public gatherings, the three-decade-long vigil tradition cemented the memory of Tiananmen. It also underscored the unique space for dissent available in Hong Kong, contrasting sharply with mainland China (Cheng and Yuen 2019). These gatherings functioned as a platform to mobilize resources for pro-democracy organizations and legitimized the moral authority of the democratic opposition in public discourse (Esherick and Wasserstrom 1990), which laid the groundwork for the transformation of Hong Kong's elite-led pro-democracy movement into a mass movement (Lam 2004).

The 1989 Tiananmen Movement ignited widespread concerns about the impending handover, triggering a new wave of emigration after the one sparked by the signing of the 1984 Sino-British Joint Declaration (Béja 2009). However, it did not alter the scheduled timeline of the handover. The new ruling coalition that emerged after the handover also remained relatively unscathed during the early post-handover years. Protests occurred, but they were generally of limited scale. A turning point, however, came in 2002, when the government introduced a national security law, which was required as a constitutional duty under Article 23 of the Basic Law. The legislation ignited a historic march almost a year later on 1 July 2003, which saw half a million citizens taking to the streets. Mounting public pressure subsequently led members of the Liberal Party, which represents the business sector in the ruling coalition, to resign from the ExCo. Their 'defection' meant that the government would lack enough votes to pass the legislation.[3] This unprecedented show of dissent compelled the Hong Kong government to indefinitely shelve the bill. A subsequent march in 2004, similar in size and peacefulness to the 2003 protest, ultimately led to the resignation of the first Chief Executive, Tung Chee-hwa, who cited personal health reasons for his departure.

There are intrinsic connections between the two protest movements in 1989 and 2003. In fact, the national security law that sparked the 2003 march had its origins in 1989. Archives and memoirs revealed that the early drafts of the Basic Law in the late 1980s did not include specific national security offences (Szeto 2011). The seven offences in Article 23 were introduced by Beijing after the Tiananmen Movement because of concerns that Hong Kong would become a 'subversion base' (Tsang 2004). Pro-democracy leaders and supporters were worried that government critics would be silenced, and that the annual vigil would be banned if the Article 23 bill were passed in 2003 (Chu 2021). Their concerns about the generalized threat to Hong Kong's freedoms were heightened by the Hong Kong government's decision to table a Blue Bill to the LegCo to enact Article 23, limiting the consultation period to three months, instead of issuing a white bill that would allow ample time for public consultation.[4]

Convinced that legislative oversight would be ineffective in reversing the government's decisions, the democratic opposition turned to mobilize their civil society networks. A week before the Blue Bill was formally introduced in September 2002, fifty-five pro-democracy parties and groups formed the CHRF. Serving as an umbrella platform, the CHRF highlighted the procedural irregularities of the provisions and their inconsistency with existing protections of human rights, civil liberties, and fair trial principles (Ma 2007). Various non-partisan groups and professional associations echoed these worries (LegCo 2003). For example, eminent barristers, including four former chairpersons of the Hong Kong Bar Association and the representative of the legal sector in the LegCo, formed the 'Article 23 Concern Group'. They published opinion pieces, held seminars, and distributed pamphlets in residential neighbourhoods. Their participation, which was unusual for elite professionals in Hong Kong, lent

---

[3] As guardian of the capitalist order, the Liberal Party saw the tug of war upset business interests. But it declared that it was merely concerned with the consultation procedures, not the legislation per se, and remained a 'loyal member of the patriotic force'. The business elites had not switched their allegiances, nor could the opposition build a new alliance with them. This episode of 'elite defection' thus did not disrupt the power balance between the incumbent and opposition.

[4] A white bill is a statement of policy intention pending feedback and input from the public, whereas a blue paper specifies the ordinances to be enacted and leave the scrutiny to the LegCo.

credibility to the cause. Due to their mobilizing efforts, a petition and a demonstration in late December 2002 respectively attracted 190,000 signatories and 60,000 participants, marking the largest scale of mobilization since the handover (Lee and Chan 2010). On 1 July, an estimated 500,000 people peacefully marched along the designated route, carrying printed slogans along the way, and dispersing in an orderly manner upon reaching the finish line.

The 2003 march serves as an exemplary case of *brokered mobilization*, where SMOs acted as the agenda-setter to coordinate civil society networks and construct action frames. In contrast to the *fragmented* and *leaderful mobilizations* observed a decade later, protesters during this time followed a preplanned script and marched along a predetermined route, led by the organizers. They readily embraced the protest frames put forth by the pro-democracy leaders. For instance, during the march, many held aloft the front page of *Apple Daily*, the largest pro-democracy newspaper, emblazoned with the slogan 'Walk down the street; Rain or shine'. Protesters' role was to march along the route, endure the sweltering summer heat, and adhere to the principle of 'peaceful, rational, non-violent, and non-foul language' (*heli feifei; wo-lei-fei-fei*) promoted by the organizers. Showing up and role-playing civic pride was their primary means to support the pro-democracy movement.

Certainly, the reasons behind the massive turnout on July 1 were not solely political. The city had been grappling with a prolonged economic downturn after the Asian Financial Crisis in 1997. The SARS epidemic in 2003 resulted in hundreds of deaths and, combined with government plans for a significant expansion of public housing, led to a sharp decline in property prices. However, amidst numerous grievances against the government, the opposition focused on two main themes: 'Oppose Article 23' and 'Power to the People'. These frames stroke a chord among many citizens. They underscored the urgency and gravity of the situation and offered a quick solution to address it.

CONTENTION WITHIN BOUNDARIES

After the retraction of the Article 23 legislation, the contingent threat to Hong Kong's civic liberties considerably subsided. The June 4 vigils and July 1 marches continued, albeit with a decline in attendance. These protest events began to be seen more as routine, primarily staged to advance specific issues and to enhance the electoral influence of the pro-democracy opposition. Nevertheless, these mass protests periodically displayed the strength of the institutional opposition, bolstering the collective identity of pro-democracy supporters. Through these recurrent demonstrations, the pro-democracy movement sustained its momentum and gradually extended its influence among the populace.

Empirical evidence indicates the growth in democratic support among citizens. Figure 2.2 presents a comparison of democratic support among Hong Kong citizens and their counterparts in newly industrialized economies in East and Southeast Asia. Longitudinal and cross-national surveys from the

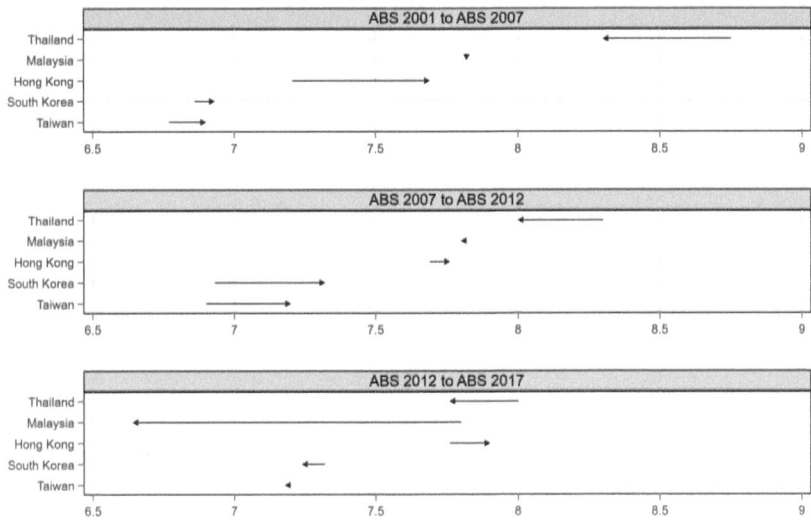

Whether you think democracy is suitable for your country/region

FIGURE 2.2 Support for democracy in newly industrialized economies, 2001–2016. Source: Asian Barometers Surveys, Waves 1–4. Scale 1 indicates completely unsuitable whereas 10 indicates perfectly suitable. Wave 1 data for Malaysia was unavailable.

Asian Barometers Surveys reveal that support for democracy was strongest in Hong Kong, steadily increasing from a mean of 7.2 in 2001 to 7.9 in 2016. Hong Kong consistently showed the highest level of support, and its growth trend remained positive. In contrast, countries with competitive authoritarian regimes such as Thailand and Malaysia saw a decline in support for democracy, raising concerns about the resilience of democratic institutions. Similarly, in new democracies such as South Korea and Taiwan, absolute support for democracy increased but at a slower pace compared to Hong Kong. These trends suggest that the democratic discourse of Hong Kong's institutionalized opposition was gaining ground.

The figure also demonstrates that the growth in support for democracy did not remain consistent over time. It witnessed acceleration after 2003, a slowdown in 2008, and a resurgence in 2016, with the accelerations seemingly coinciding with mass protests. It is also important to note that support for democracy did not automatically result in electoral victories for the pro-democracy opposition. The tripartite coalition did not sit passively; they actively strived to maintain their majority. In this extended tug of war, each side believed that time was in their favour, though for differing reasons. The institutionalized opposition was confident that threats to freedom, access to information, post-materialistic values, and demographic changes would ensure resilient support (Cheng, Chung, and Cheng 2022; Ma 2011a). On the other hand, the ruling coalition was confident that their efforts in nation-building, administrative efficiency, and economic development would contain the opposition and ultimately win over the populace (Jiang 2017).

These contrasting perceptions of the political situation prompted both the ruling coalition and the pro-democracy opposition to invest in the long game. Despite their growing rifts, they maintained a functional relationship within formal institutions to uphold stability, prosperity, and international expectations of preserving Hong Kong's special status and engagement with the liberal order (Wong 2022). For example, the Beijing government established the provisional LegCo before the handover and packed it with loyalists; yet it also decided to resume LegCo elections in 1998, allowing deposed democrats to run. Nevertheless, the government also opted to reinstate LegCo elections in 1998, permitting ousted democrats to participate. This action demonstrated the party-state's capacity to sideline the opposition, when necessary, as well as its readiness to accommodate them. The institutionalized opposition also demonstrated goodwill. Democratic Party leaders Martin Lee and Emily Lau, for example, lobbied the US government to grant the 'most favoured nation' status to the PRC in the post-1989 period. They also collaborated with the business sector to advocate for the PRC's membership in the World Trade Organization in 2001 (Du and Kong 2020). Furthermore, the institutionalized opposition consciously differentiated between its electoral and movement wings. Martin Lee, often referred to as the 'father of Hong Kong democracy', limited his role to elections and international lobbying (Overholt 2001), whereas Szeto Wah and other civil society actors took charge of organizing the annual vigils. Political parties, professional associations, and trade unions only joined the HKA as titular members.

The veteran democrats characterized their approach to democratization as 'contesting without decoupling' (*douer bupo; dau-ji-bat-po*) or 'negotiating amidst contending' (*youqing youqi; jau-king-jau-cai*) (Fung 2002; Szeto 2011). This middle ground approach recognized the opportunities and limitations faced by both the incumbent and opposition within the liberal oligarchy. By the 1980s, the institutionalized opposition had constructed its master frame of contention as 'democratic reunification' (*minzhu huigui; man-zyu-wui-gwai*), which referred to the reunion with China through democratization. However, after the Tiananmen crackdown, their master frame also integrated the concept of 'democratic resistance' (*minzhu kanggong; man-zyu-kong-gung*), which aimed to resist communism through democratization (Law 2009).

This strategy was guided by three principles designed to encourage institutional engagement and the expansion of supporter base, while mitigating the risks associated with political activism. First, the institutionalized opposition subtly endorsed a nationalistic discourse. Their role in the Tiananmen vigils and international lobbying both showcased their critical stance towards the party-state while displaying loyalty to the Chinese nation. Second, the institutionalized opposition prioritized electoral politics over protest politics, enabling them to gain institutional resources and recruit new members through elections and pork barrel services. They resorted to their civil society networks for mobilization only when institutional avenues were obstructed and perceived threats became more manifest. Third, the institutionalized opposition strictly adhered to a repertoire in line with the 'peaceful, rational, non-violent, and non-profane' principle. Instead of pressuring the government through confrontational means, the pro-democracy force sought policy concessions through electoral victories and large-scale protests. The choice of a moderate repertoire helped SMOs and their civil society networks to reduce political risks and minimize participation costs for activists as well as ordinary citizens. It aided in maintaining the power balance between the incumbent and the opposition within the liberal oligarchic order.

CONCLUSION

This chapter has examined the historical-institutional process through which contentious politics emerged and unfolded in Hong Kong. We have demonstrated how the formalization of consultative governance, alongside gradual democratization since the 1980s, shaped the contours of Hong Kong's political development. Unlike hybrid regimes in Southeast Asia and Latin America, Hong Kong's liberal oligarchy provided a window of regime openness that allowed for the growth of a democratic opposition. Within this context, the opposition could advocate for political reforms and policy changes, and mobilize whenever the city's freedoms and way of life were under perceived threat. This openness enabled the opposition to align electoral politics with street mobilizations. While the emergence of the pro-democracy movement illustrates the enduring relevance of the political opportunity structures, we also highlight how threat perceptions within a specific political context shapes the form of mobilization.

Under Hong Kong's liberal oligarchy, a tripartite ruling coalition consisting of the Communist party-state, Weberian-style bureaucracy, and business elites was formalized. While these parties might have had differing principles and interests, they aligned and compromised strategically to maintain prosperity and stability in the semi-autonomous region. This required the central government in Beijing to refrain from overt intervention, demonstrating its commitment to international obligations while preserving Hong Kong's unique value in national development (Krasner 2001). Under this arrangement, Beijing would delegate the Hong Kong government to focus on local governance, respecting procedural norms while offering tangible concessions to the opposition in times of crisis. It would also address business elites' concerns over pro-grassroots welfare policies and spending in exchange for their political support and economic investment. As sociologist Lui Tai-lok (2018) put it, the frozen status quo of the 1980s created a delicate equilibrium where 'every party gets something, but no one gets everything'.

The liberal oligarchic order also provided a platform for the veteran democrats to cultivate public support. While protests were becoming more frequent, they were often meticulously planned and routinized, making sure that political participation was neither too costly nor too risky, yet still offering a mechanism for checks and balances. These protests, over time, played a pivotal role in fostering a more active political agency among citizens, transforming them from the politically indifferent and family-centric individuals once depicted by scholars (Lau and Kuan 1988). In the ensuing years, apprehensions of autocratization, the expanding influence of professional ethos, and a heightened cosmopolitan identity would contribute to the expansion of civil society networks that would outgrow the institutionalized opposition. These networks stood poised to mobilize against new threats during critical times. Of course, perceptions over the nature and severity of threats would vary among different pro-democracy actors. After all, people held different ideals of the status quo they aimed to protect. While some championed the preservation of the liberal oligarchy, others sought a democratizing or a fully democratic Hong Kong.

3

A New Cycle of Protests

Following the landmark July 1 march in 2003, the scope of Hong Kong's contentious politics began to expand into broader arenas where recurrent and contingent threats emerged. The post-2003 period saw a series of critical events that challenged the traditional mode of brokered mobilization, putting its reformist frame and peaceful repertoire to test. Two heritage preservation campaigns were particularly significant in shifting the boundaries. The first began on 16 December 2006, when a group of students and young activists organized a sit-in, launching a campaign to protect the historic Star Ferry Pier, a modernist waterfront landmark that had stood for over half a century. Despite the authorities' rejection of their demands, protesters' actions struck a chord with the public. This led hundreds of thousands of people to pay their last respects to what many viewed as a symbol of Hong Kong's post-war socio-economic miracle. Several months later, young activists, self-labelling themselves as the 'post-1980s generation', occupied the nearby Queen's Pier, which was also slated for demolition to make room for land reclamation. Despite the disruption, the HKSAR government allowed the occupation to continue. Over the ensuing months, protesters camped in the pier. Writers, architects, singers, and artists took turns guarding the site and organized various activities, such as seminars, concerts, and hunger strikes.

These protests evoked collective nostalgia for a bygone era and profound critiques against crony capitalism under the city's corporatist governance (Lu 2009). Despite failing to preserve the piers, these protests ushered the city into a new protest cycle. They brought forth a new generation of movement actors to form new groups and networks. These newcomers promoted innovative claims and tactics that contrasted significantly with the ritualistic and routine protests that had previously prevailed. Initially, their motivations stemmed from grievances against pervasive social inequalities and urban redevelopment – issues common to cities in East Asian developmental states (Chiu and Lui 2004;

Shin, Lees and López-Morales 2016). However, after multiple unsuccessful attempts to challenge the ruling coalition, their objectives expanded to include post-materialist and identity-based claims. This shift occurred as they gradually developed a divergent perception of threats, which fragmented the pro-democracy opposition and led to a more factional mode of mobilization.

This chapter begins by examining how the Chinese state and nation-building efforts after 2003 effectively restricted the political space for the city's opposition, thereby weakening the veteran democrats' capacity to mediate threats through institutional contestation. It then explains how a series of protest episodes staged by young activists after the mid-2000s triggered a 'scale shift', normalizing certain claims and actions previously considered unwelcome and illegitimate (Tarrow 1993). Finally, this chapter also examines how fractionalization within the democratic opposition began. While the emergent activists advocated for a confrontational, direct action approach in their quest for democracy, the veteran democrats, who led the pro-democracy movement since the 1980s, adhered to their old playbook alternating between institutional bargaining and ritualistic protests. The latter chose to make a pact with the Chinese state by supporting the HKSAR government's constitutional reform proposal in 2010, a critical juncture that widened the chasm between the veteran democrats and the emergent opposition actors.

REGIME PROTEST RESPONSES

Existing research on how regimes respond to protests has primarily focused on protest policing and state repression during contentious episodes (Earl 2003; Gamson 1990; Tilly 1978). However, recent scholarship has shifted focus towards exploring the relational dynamics between political actors over extended periods (Cai 2010; della Porta 2008; Goldstone 2004). This relational perspective posits that regime responses encompass more than state coercion, extending to restrictions on institutional access for the opposition and civil society (Wiktorowicz 2000). Consequently, these limitations often prompt activist groups to explore alternative organizational forms and mobilization methods (Alimi, Bosi and Demetriou 2015; Slater and Smith 2016).

In semi-autonomous Hong Kong, these relational dynamics are best observed through the state and nation-building efforts that followed the mass protests of 2003–2004. State-building here refers to 'the creation of new governmental institutions and the strengthening of existing ones' (Fukuyama 2004: 17). When faced with profound challenges, incumbents may seek to enhance the capacity, role, and reach of their state apparatuses and grassroots networks, thereby acquiring authority and resources they previously lacked (Robertson 2010). This process involves recalibrating state infrastructures and redistributing power between multi-level governments and social elites (Tsai 2018; Wu 2016). In parallel, nation-building focuses on constructing or fostering a national identity, which often occurs in countries with diverse ethnic, religious, or linguistic groups or traditions. While state-building concentrates on the 'hardware' of political entities – their institutions, laws, and physical infrastructure, nation-building addresses the 'software', or the psychological, cultural, and social aspects that unite people. These two processes often go hand in hand, particularly in peripheral areas that are distant from the political centre (Linz 1993).

The large-scale rallies in 2003 and 2004 reinforced the party-state's belief that the 'hearts and minds' of the Hong Kong people had not returned to China, despite the change in sovereignty (Jiang 2017). Elite defections following the first July 1 march, although limited in scale, raised immediate concerns about the loyalty of the business sector to Beijing during political crises (Lau 2015). A mainland Chinese scholar, seconded to serve in the Central People's Government Liaison Office (CGLO) in the Hong Kong SAR, revealed that after 2003 the Beijing central government changed its policy from 'non-interventionist' to 'activism' (i.e., playing an active role in local governance) in an effort to regain the allegiance of the people in the former British colony (Cheng 2009). Despite being motivated by the protests, this policy shift was also the result of many ongoing structural developments and strategic considerations, including the increasing influence of pro-Beijing organizations in Hong Kong, the SAR's relative decline of economic significance to mainland China, and the waning appeal of the OCTS principle for Taiwan's unification with the PRC.

However, unlike in mainland China, where the party-state can fully harness its state apparatuses, political ideologies, and social organizations for political objectives, state-building efforts in Hong Kong faced limitations. The party was still not ready to openly operate in Hong Kong due to constraints imposed by the liberal oligarchy and the functional role of the OCTS (Loh 2010; Scott 2022). As a result, state-building had to be carried out in the name of the state, not the party. Despite the desire to expand its influence, the Chinese state had to engage with other stakeholders in the liberal oligarchy and communicate its intention to uphold the differences between the two systems. Therefore, state-building still necessitated the cooperation and compliance of the local government and business elites through united front work, rather than direct, top-down control (Cheng 2020).

STATE AND NATION-BUILDING IN THE SHADOWS

After the national security bill was shelved, the central government appointed career civil servant Donald Tsang as Chief Executive in 2005. Tsang, who notably declared his dual loyalties in 'serving two masters: the people of Hong Kong and the central government' (Ching 2005), was seen by the public as a concession by Beijing to fortify the partition between the two systems. Parallel to this, however, Beijing also began to enforce its proactive policy and accelerate its state-building efforts. Besides reorganizing the CGLO to enable a more active role in local politics (Lee 2020), a significant task for the party-state was to extend its influence at the grassroots level. This was achieved by enlarging the existing network of grassroots organizations, such as community groups, women and youth groups, and hometown associations. Some of these organizations were already functioning as a part of the united front work to 'work

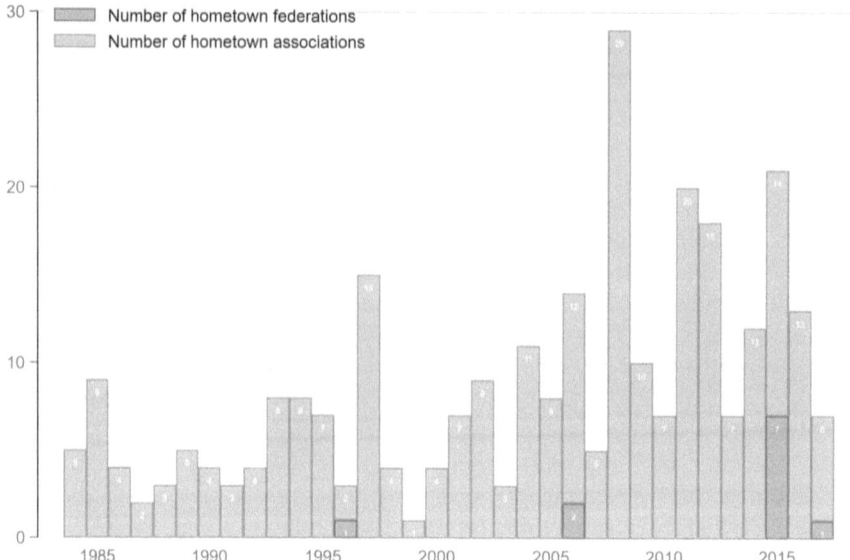

FIGURE 3.1 Number of hometown associations established by year, 1984–2017.
Source: Data compiled from Wisenews and official websites of hometown
associations.

on the masses' or 'rule by other means' (Ma 2007; Grzegorz, Perry and Yan
2020), while others were either newly established or newly incorporated into
the network. To illustrate the rapid growth of such organizations, Figure 3.1
shows the number of newly established hometown associations – associations
formed by Chinese migrants from the same places of origin in the mainland –
before and after the 1997 handover.

These organizations played a crucial role in mobilizing residents to vote
for pro-Beijing parties during elections (Lo, Hung and Loo 2019) and to partake in counter-protests against the pro-democracy movement (Cheng 2020).
Collectively, these efforts marked a gradual transition in the party-state's strategy
from elite co-optation, adopted well before the handover issue in the 1980s that
relied on a sense of partnership and mutual dependence, to a patron-clientelism
model that emphasized loyalty and exchange of interests (Kang 2020; Lee 2020).
This change was in line with a senior party official's public endorsement of constructing 'a second ruling team' to aid with local governance (Cao 2008).

The interactions between the tripartite ruling coalition and various grassroots organizations serve as a proxy to evaluate the extent and influence
of state-building over time. These grassroots organizations are not inherently governmental; they function as local intermediaries representing diverse
social interests. Although they were the tentacles of the state during the colonial government's state-corporatist structure, their significance waned briefly
in the 1990s due to the increasing number of elected representatives in the

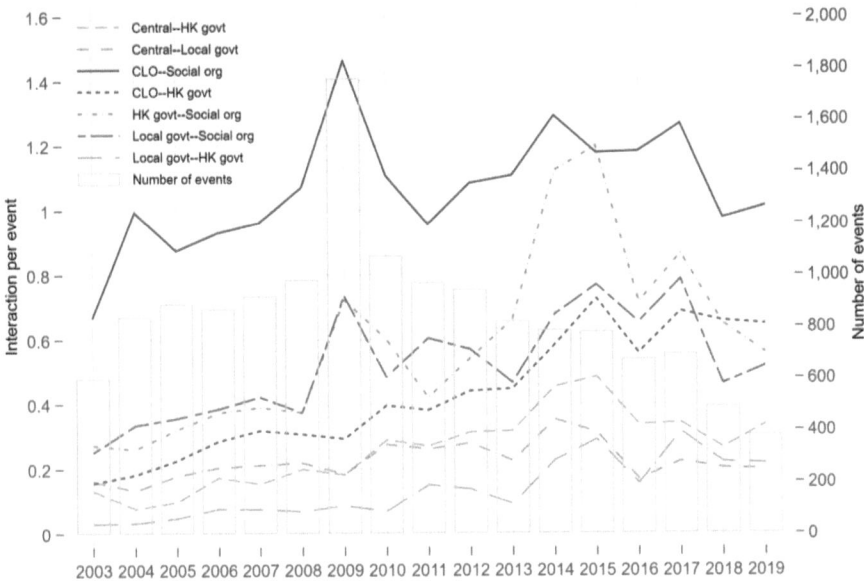

FIGURE 3.2 Interactions between state agencies and social organizations, 2003–2019.
Source: Data compiled by authors from Wenweipo.

LegCo and District Councils. By the 2000s, however, they were revived by the Chinese party-state as essential vehicles for extending patronage and enhancing penetration in society.

Figure 3.1 illustrates the co-occurrence of different types of organizational actors in events reported by the state-controlled newspaper *Wenweipo*.[1] Here, co-occurrence is defined by the presence of two types of actors in a single public event on average. For example, in 2004, the co-occurrence between the CGLO and any one social organization is 1.0, meaning that on average, every event that year would see one pair of interaction between a social organization and the CGLO. This figure becomes slightly higher than 1.4 in 2009, meaning that an average event that year would see around 1.4 pairs of interactions between a social organization and the CGLO.

Figure 3.2 depicts an increase in interactions between state agencies and various pro-Beijing grassroots organizations, such as hometown associations,

---

[1] The data is obtained from the social organization news section of *Wenweipo*, which is publicly available. We scraped the reports between 2003 and 2019. After data cleaning, we collected a total of 30,174 reports and identified 14,503 events (on average, 853 events per year) in total. We also identified the organizations present in each report, based on an organizational list that we have prepared alongside. The list consists of 3,869 organizations in total, spanning five different types: (1) central party agencies; (2) local government; (3) Hong Kong government agencies; (4) the CGLO; and (5) pro-Beijing grassroots organizations.

community organizations, and service-oriented NGOs, after 2003. The overall interactions remained steady but experienced a sudden surge in 2009, when numerous new grassroots organizations were established – likely in anticipation of the government's electoral reform package in 2010. Another significant spike from 2013 to 2015 was likely linked to the state's counter-mobilization against Occupy Central, a civil disobedience campaign initiated by the pro-democracy camp advocating for universal suffrage.

Several insights can be drawn from the figure. First, it underscores the significant role of the CGLO, as interactions between the CGLO and grassroots organizations were consistently present in nearly every event. Second, interactions between mainland local governments and Hong Kong grassroots organizations also increased over time. Here, the CGLO became the primary link between the mainland authorities and Hong Kong's community actors. Third, the Hong Kong government also played an active role in interacting with grassroots organizations, as demonstrated by the increased number and frequency of interactions, indicating strengthened connections within the tripartite ruling coalition. The state-building efforts effectively curtailed the institutional space for the democratic opposition. The expansion of patron-client networks increased the resource disparity between the tripartite coalition and the opposition, while the gerrymandering of electoral districts gave the pro-Beijing camp an institutional advantage (Wong 2019).

In addition to expanding grassroots influence, the party-state also actively promoted socioeconomic integration and cultural blending between mainland China and Hong Kong. Since 2003, central and local authorities have signed a series of bilateral agreements deregulating trade, investment, immigration, and tourism, binding Hong Kong's economy closer to the mainland's policies and market (Cheung 2015).[2] Large-scale infrastructural projects, such as the Guangzhou–Shenzhen–Hong Kong Express Rail Link and the Hong Kong-Zhuhai-Macau Bridge, were initiated to improve physical connectivity with the mainland and better integrate the SAR into national development schemes such as Guangdong-Hong Kong-Macao Greater Bay Area. Programs inviting high-skilled mainlanders to settle in Hong Kong were also introduced, adding to an existing immigration program for mainlanders focusing on family reunion. Concurrently, to foster cultural integration with the mainland, the local authorities implemented educational reforms to promote Putonghua as a language of instruction (Morris and Vickers 2015).

Initially, these state and nation-building efforts were met with public support. Opinion polls showed a significant increase in trust among Hong Kong

---

[2] The agreements increased Hong Kong's domestic exports to the mainland from 3% of total exports in 2004 to 38% in 2013 and the share of mainland companies' market capitalization in Hong Kong soared from 27 to 57% from 2003 to 2010. Since the introduction of the Individual Visit Scheme in 2003, the number of mainland tourists had grown exponentially from 6.8 million in 2003 to 54.3 million in 2013.

people in the local government, rising from 29.9 to 62.4 per cent, and in the central government, increasing from 37.7 to 54.9 per cent between July 2003 and July 2008. Respondents identifying as 'Chinese' and 'Chinese in Hong Kong' also increased from 52.8 to 65.2 per cent over the same period, peaking in 2008, the year China held its first Olympic Games (HKUPOP 2019a). Although apprehension towards the Chinese party-state still existed, cultural recognition of the Chinese nation consistently increased as people learned to 'belong to the nation' (Mathews, Ma and Liu 2007). This trend was reflected in the growing identification with a range of Chinese cultural symbols in successive identity surveys (Ma and Fung 2007). As a result, scholars predicted that the Hong Kong identity would eventually be replaced by a hybridized Hong Kong-Chinese identity (Ma and Fung 2007), which combines nationalist sentiments and liberal democratic values (Chan and Chan 2014).

However, around 2009, what seemed like an irreversible trend dramatically reversed, with opinion polls recording a sharp and continuous decline in institutional trust and national identity (HKUPOP 2019b; Steinhardt, Li and Jiang 2018). Exclusive Chinese identification dropped from 40% in 2008 to under 20% in 2015, and dual identification fell from around 45–40% during the same period. Concurrently, Hong Kong identification surged from under 20 per cent to over 40 per cent, mirroring the level in 1997. This shift is particularly pronounced among the younger generation: in the 18–30 age group, Chinese identification fell under 5 per cent, and Hong Kong identification increased to above 60 per cent by 2016.

To be sure, national-level political changes in late 2000s likely contributed to this dramatic shift in public opinion and political identification. For instance, events like the crackdown on Charter 08 signatories and the scandals concerning the alleged misallocation of HKD20 billion in donations to the 2008 Sichuan Earthquake relief effort received extensive coverage in Hong Kong. Although it is difficult to quantify their impact, these events likely played a significant role in reversing public optimism that China would embark on political reforms and embrace the rule of law (Béja, Fu and Pils 2012). These events also underscored the importance of the 'firewall' between the Two Systems, which could shield Hong Kong from their impact.

State and nation-building efforts in Hong Kong also played a significant role, although their effects were delayed. These efforts raised growing concerns about the erosion of local institutional checks and balances (Sing 2010; Yep 2018). Not only was the expanding role of the CGLO seen as having intersected with the autonomy of the HKSAR government, but their growing influence in elections was also perceived as tilting the playing field against the pro-democracy camp. Additionally, the proliferation of pro-regime grassroots organizations, along with increasing patron-clientelist practices, was perceived to be increasingly crowding out independent NGOs and civil society groups. Under a seemingly zero-sum game, these efforts reinforced the perception that recurring threats had become increasingly unmanageable within formal institutions. Although the presence of perceived threats alone would not necessarily result in collective actions, their increase prompted protest participants to seek alternative means to counteract the tide of change.

THE RISE OF STREET POLITICS

Mobilization fundamentally stems from the ability to popularize one's claims and inspire others to engage in collective action. This process is characterized by continuous interactions between those challenging the status quo and those in power, as well as innovative strategies to enlist bystanders as participants (Tilly 1999). Those who have successfully initiated and coordinated previous campaigns often earn implicit legitimacy to shape their struggles and the authority to guide future actions (Morris and Staggenborg 2004).

Doug McAdam, Sidney Tarrow, and Charles Tilly (2005: 331) identify 'upward scale shift' as an essential element of contentious politics, as it signifies 'a change in the number and level of coordinated contentious actions to a different focal point, involving a new range of actors, different objects, and broadened claims'. Asef Bayat (2013: 21) also underscores 'the power of big numbers,' where 'acting in common' can normalize and legitimize 'acts that are otherwise deemed illegitimate'. As the transgressive behaviour of new political actors gains popularity among the masses, these actors effectively challenge societal norms and establish a new boundary for collective actions. An upward scale shift certainly occurred in Hong Kong, but it was a process that unfolded over a decade. Even though a new cycle of protests began with the large-scale rallies in 2003 and 2004, this cycle did not fully scale up and shook off organizational influences of the veteran democrats and SMOs until the late 2000s.

Figure 3.3 presents the emergence and development of protests in Hong Kong from 1997 to 2014. Several trends can be observed here. First, the number of protests significantly increased. On average, there were three events per day starting in 2003, which increased to ten events per day in 2007 and twenty events per day in 2012. While the year 2003 was a pivotal moment showcasing the power of brokered mobilization, the figure suggests that there were two turning points when the number of collective actions sharply increased – in 2006 and 2009 respectively. Since then, the annual year-on-year change in the number of protests has been strongly correlated with the timing of mass events orchestrated by young activists. Compared to the organization-brokered protests, these direct actions were longer in duration and larger in attendance, contributing to the scale shift.

Second, the upward trend in the number of protest events indicates that the Hong Kong government would tolerate organizers and protesters as long as they were subject to administrative regulations. Between 1997 and 2014, an overwhelming 99.9 per cent of the 51,946 applications for public gatherings, including protests and other public events, were granted approval. Applications

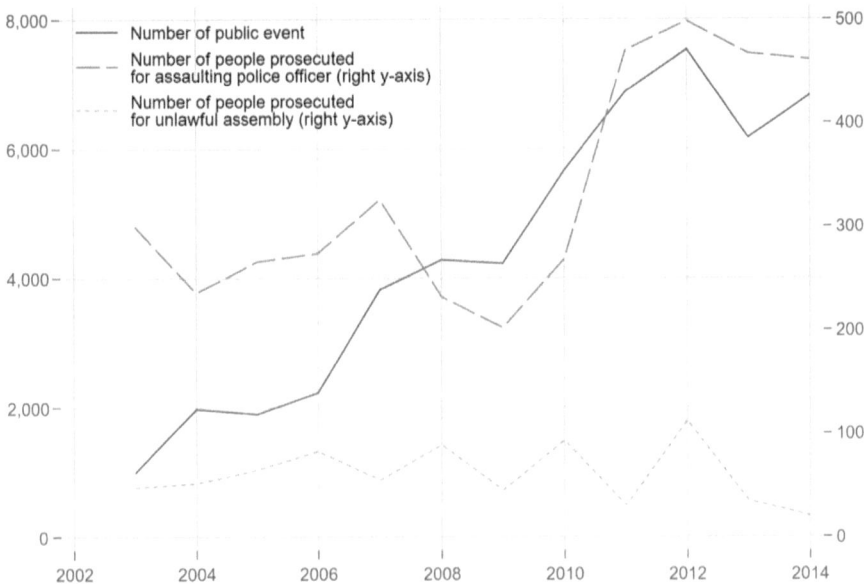

FIGURE 3.3 Number of public assemblies in Hong Kong, 2003–2014.
Note: Public events refer to public meetings with over fifty people or public processions with over thirty people who received a non-objection letter from the police under the Public Order Ordinance. Not all public assemblies are protest actions, but they serve as the best available proxies.
Source: Hong Kong Security Bureau 2016.

were typically rejected primarily due to procedural non-compliance. During the actual protests, the police and SMOs often cooperated under the principle of 'negotiated management' to ensure that protesters remained orderly (Ho 2020). Notably, while the agendas of the protests varied, they were chiefly formulated by a select group of individuals, predominantly politicians, unionists, their assistants, and stakeholders. Veteran activists typically devised and standardized the slogans and tactics used during these protests. The government accepted these ritualistic protests as they provided a controlled avenue to voice public grievances and interests.

Third, the government demonstrated less tolerance towards activists engaging in civil disobedience and confrontational actions, despite permitting peaceful protests. Over time, an increasing number of protesters were prosecuted for assaulting police officers, while the numbers charged with illegal assembly stayed relatively stable. Furthermore, those accused of assaulting police officers faced harsher punishment since around 2007.[3] These trends suggest that

---

[3] Before 2006, individuals charged with assaulting police officers were consistently prosecuted under the Police Ordinance (Cap 232 section 63), which allows for a suspended sentence if

while the authorities always possessed the legal tools to deter protest participation, they exercised restraint in their use, differentiating between protesters based on their tactical dispositions.

A SCALE SHIFT

This new cycle of contention can be further analysed through the lens of what William Sewell (2005) calls 'historical events'. Sewell characterized these events as 'a ramified sequence of occurrences that are recognized as notable by contemporaries, and that results in a durable transformation of structures' (2005: 228). While these events often reflect underlying structures and are dependent on past repertoires, they have the potential to reshape social relations and redefine the cultural implications of collective actions (Tarrow 2008; Tilly 2002). However, the events that Sewell refers to are not the commonplace occurrences usually considered in most protest event analyses. Rather, they refer to extraordinary and consequential happenings – akin to moments like the storming of the Bastille during the French Revolution in 1789 or the Montgomery Bus Boycott during the US Civil Rights Movement in 1955–1956.

In the context of Hong Kong's new cycle of protests, three events were particularly significant: the Queen's Pier Preservation Campaign in 2007, the Anti-XRL Movement in 2009–2010, and the Anti-MNE Movement in 2012. Table 3.1 provides an overview of these events. Collectively, they contributed to the 'upward scale shift' in Hong Kong's contentious politics. This shift represents the expanded involvement of diverse social actors in the pro-democracy movement – individuals who were previously on the sidelines of contentious politics – as well as issues that were once viewed as negotiable and manageable within formal institutions or through brokered mobilizations. By mobilizing alongside the organization-led protests like the July 1 rallies and June 4 vigils, these movements ushered the city into a period of 'factional mobilizations'.

The general trend reveals a remarkable increase in participant numbers. The Queen's Pier Preservation Campaign in 2007 saw a maximum of 450 participants in a single day. This number surged to 8,500 in the Anti-XRL movement in 2009–2010, marking a forty-fold increase in protest size over approximately two years. The Anti-MNE movement in 2012 saw participation surge even further to 120,000, representing an additional fourteen-fold increase over another two-year span.[4]

convicted. In contrast, after 2007, those charged were consistently prosecuted under the Offences against the Person Ordinance (Cap 212 section 36b), which mandates imprisonment for all convictions.

[4] Although official figures standardize the estimates among different events, the police only release headcounts for specific episodes, thereby hindering comparisons within an event spanning

TABLE 3.1 *Transgressive protest events in Hong Kong, 2006–2014.*

Event	Issue framing	Scale	Duration	Repertoire	Outcome
Queen's Pier Preservation Campaign, 2007	Cultural identity, mega development	30–450	122 days	Occupation, concert, petition	Pier demolished; pier relocated
Anti-Express Rail Link Movement, 2009–10	Integration, national development	800–8,500	89 days	Sit-in, siege, blockades, prostrating walk	Budget passed; village rebuilt
Anti-Moral and National Education Movement, 2012	Cultural identity, civic liberty	8,000–12,0000	51 days	Occupation, rally, bazaar, hunger strike	Curriculum retracted

Source: Data compiled and synthesized by authors based on newspaper reports.

These events significantly challenged traditional modes of protest organization. Unlike brokered mobilization that usually lasted within one day, these events became significantly extended in duration, with the longest lasting 122 days and the shortest 51 days. They often occupied public spaces, creating defensible territories held by devoted activists and awaiting mass participation after work or during holidays. They also managed to mobilize otherwise unavailable resources and address logistical challenges by collaborating with other professional and grassroots groups. This involved soliciting donations, recruiting volunteers, distributing goods and services, and liaising with the mass media. New and young activists, either independent from political parties or loosely linked to SMOs, often emerged as informal leaders on the ground (Interview A7).

These events also catalysed the emergence of new movement groups and networks with less hierarchical structures and favouring a more improvised forms of mobilizations (Ho 2018). Unlike traditional rallies that required months or weeks of planning and preparation, these events could attract hundreds of thousands of participants spontaneously or within a short time frame. Meanwhile, the newly formed protest groups often positioned themselves more as facilitators than traditional leaders of social movements. For example, the 2012 Anti-MNE Movement was initiated by Scholarism, an activist group established in May 2011 by several secondary school students, including the

several weeks or months. In contrast, organizers' figures are always highlighted in the mass and social media and catalyse further mobilization. This constructed reality aligns with our dynamic orientation and justifies reporting the organizers' figures.

fourteen-year-old Joshua Wong, who soon became the face of the movement. Scholarism began with distributing leaflets against the curriculum and attending major protests such as the July 1 rallies to rally for their cause. Within a year, the group expanded in size and influence, recruiting more than 300 members through Facebook and WhatsApp (Interview A3). By July 2012, this teenagers-led group, joined by traditional SMOs such as the CHRF, HKPTU, and Hong Kong Federation of Students organized a march that reportedly attracted over 90,000 protesters. A month later, Scholarism began occupying government headquarters, with several members starting a hunger strike. They invited citizens to bring their sleeping bags and floor mats to join the occupation. Many echoed the call, forcing the government to eventually withdraw the curriculum a week later.

This tactic of using non-routinized and more improvised forms of mass mobilizations to pressure the authorities for concession was not new. Two years earlier, the Anti-XRL Movement followed a similar playbook. Spearheaded by the same group of activists who started the heritage preservation campaigns, the movement staged frequent sit-ins and sieges in front of the LegCo in an attempt to stop the plan to build the railway. This movement failed to achieve its goals despite its sizable turnout, unlike in the Anti-MNE Movement. Regardless, both movements marked a significant shift from the brokered mobilizations modelled upon the July 1 rallies in 2003 and 2004. Activists still played a crucial role in leading these movements, but they relied more on mass participation to make their protests appear more organic and less scripted. Meanwhile, although the veteran democrats remained closely involved in these movements by mobilizing their supporters, providing logistic support, and negotiating with the authorities, they became less visible to the public. They recognized their diminished influence in mobilizing protesters, as evidenced by the low turnouts at the July 1 rallies or June 4 vigils during those years.

Despite the shift in mobilization strategies, protest participation continued to foster a strong sense of efficacy among protesters, reinforcing the belief that protests could compel the government to heed public demands. The new cycle of protests exerted significant public pressure, often putting the local government in a defensive position. For instance, during the Queen's Pier protests, then the Secretary for Development, Carrie Lam, was compelled to hold a public consultation at the protest site with casually dressed young protesters. Although she did not retract the reclamation project, she pledged to preserve the pier in some form. Similarly, the week-long occupation during the 2012 Anti-MNE Movement pressured then-Chief Executive Leung Chun-ying to ultimately shelve the curriculum. The only event that did not result in tangible policy concessions was the anti-railway protests. This was likely because the dispute was over a national project with significant investment that the local government had little leverage to reverse. However, this event prompted the Democratic Party to align with the emergent activists and revise its original position supporting the railway project. In this regard, protest participants partially achieved their demands either by restraining the government's plans or forcing veteran democrats to depart from institutional bargaining.

STRONG REPERTOIRES

Another salient feature of this new protest cycle was the adoption of 'direct actions' by activists as a repertoire of contention. This approach was in part inspired by the Global Justice Movement, a worldwide movement that emerged in the late 1990s to challenge neoliberal and corporate globalization. Activists in the Global Justice Movement often employed direct actions such as occupations, blockades, sabotage, and disruptions to confront and challenge the policies and practices of international organizations. Anthropologist David Graeber conceptualizes direct action as the act of 'insisting on acting as if one is already free' (2011: 207). Direct actions are 'direct' because they allow activists to manifest the changes they seek themselves, instead of relying on intermediaries such as politicians or bureaucrats. One frequently used direct action tactic, occupation, involves disrupting public spaces to challenge the existing order. This can be achieved by breaking away from organizational dependence, introducing transgressive claims and repertoire, and facilitating diverse situational responses during protests.

The young activists who subsequently initiated the heritage preservation campaigns had experienced first-hand the disruptive power of direct action tactics. In 2005, the World Trade Organization (WTO) held its Sixth Ministerial Conference in Hong Kong. Numerous South Korean farmers, led by their unions, travelled to Hong Kong to protest against the WTO's liberalization policy, which would open up their local markets to cheap foreign imports. They marched near the conference venue, kneeling and bowing along the way. Some even jumped into the Victoria Harbour, a narrow and busy waterway, attempting to swim to the conference venue. The protests evolved into fierce clashes with the police. These direct actions inspired local young activists who attended the protest in a show of support. One of them recounted:

The direct action of the South Korean farmers during the WTO in 2005 was eye-opening. Their bodily resistance and collective determination taught us that freedom has a price. [In contrast], the 1 July rally has become routinized. Constrained by precedent, we felt compelled to brief the authorities on complex operations and even help to disperse the crowd at endpoints. These are absurd. How can we defy the regime and then work with it with ease? Isn't protest supposed to be radical, or at least unpredictable? (Interview A5).

Partly motivated by these experiences, these young activists decided to apply some of these tactics themselves. They launched the heritage preservation campaigns by occupying the Star Ferry Pier and Queen's Pier. Surprise was a core element of their strategy. One activist recalled the initial moments of the occupation of Queen's Pier:

On the eve of 26 April 2007, we decided to act. A dozen of us marched towards Queen's Pier, already blockaded, waiting to be demolished. The guards tried to stop us, and the police arrived within minutes. When we thought our action would fail, the police suddenly retreated and secured a parameter. People from all walks of life joined. That parameter produced the city's most visible public space in the following months; the period was itself monumental (Interview A7).

To garner public acceptance, activists devised specific tactical innovations for each event. For instance, they organized heritage tours to memorialize the Star Ferry Pier and Queen's Pier as symbols of anti-colonial resistance and grassroots public space, with roots going back to the 1960s and 1970s. To protest against the express rail-link megaproject and express their support for Hong Kong's farming community, protesters performed a 'prostrating walk', reminiscent of Buddhist pilgrims. They held parcels of rice and moved across the city's five districts by kneeling and bowing, a tactic partially inspired by the Korean farmers. During the Anti-MNE Movement, teenage activists orchestrated the city's first-ever class boycott in the post-handover period, followed by a week-long occupation outside government headquarters.

These direct actions represented a sharp break from the highly scripted, routinized, and predictable rallies led by veteran democrats. While these new tactics remained predominantly non-violent, they often incorporated elements of surprise and created disruptions to social order. This challenged the existing 'strong repertoires' (Tilly 2008) – the favoured political performances deeply rooted in Hong Kong's pro-democracy movement since the 1980s. Reliance on frames and actions dictated by leading political parties and SMOs significantly diminished. However, even with the marginalization of centralized organizations, a protest leadership continued to exist, primarily consisting of amateur activists unaffiliated with political organizations. These activists developed new supportive networks during the spatial occupations by bringing together different groups and resources from civil society. In the process, the reach of the pro-democracy movement gradually expanded. But it also became more heterogeneous, spawning different groupings, each with their own preferred repertoire.

The HKSAR government was clearly not well-prepared for the shifting tactical repertoire. Not only did these events become more transgressive and confrontational, they sometimes also crossed legal boundaries by not seeking police approval. For instance, during the Queen's Pier occupation on 1 August 2007, around twenty activists chained themselves together in protest against state power (*InMediaHK*, 1 August 2007). Similarly, on 24 January 2011, more than seventy activists and villagers blocked workers and bulldozers to prevent the demolition of village buildings (*Ming Pao*, 25 January 2011). These events, fuelled by controversial issues and dramatized by disruptive tactics, attracted segments of society that might not otherwise have participated in illegal assemblies.

In response to the new protest cycle, the government mostly tolerated the disruptive protest actions and occasionally made limited policy concessions. During the campaign to preserve Queen's Pier in 2007, the government, in light of then-Chief Executive Donald Tsang's re-election bid that year, reportedly ordered the retreat of the police when protesters began to occupy the pier and allowed the occupation to continue for a few months (*South China Morning Post*, 23 April 2007). Even though the pier was eventually demolished, heritage preservation became a policy objective for the subsequent two administrations. Similarly, during the Anti-MNE Movement in 2012, the government withdrew the contested national education curriculum two weeks before that year's District Council elections. Although then-Chief Executive Leung Chun-ying was widely regarded as a Beijing loyalist, the pro-Beijing camp's electoral considerations took precedence. Despite not being a full democracy, budding democratic institutions constrained the regime's response, playing into the hands of the protesters.

The authorities tolerated this new protest cycle also because it did not pose a grave threat to the prevailing liberal oligarchic order. Despite their democratic undertones, these protests were primarily concerned with policy issues. As a result, the authorities could offer tangible concessions such as dialogues with officials and retraction of controversial policies. These measures helped to preserve the rules and norms of the liberal oligarchy, reinforcing the impression that the executive-led bureaucracy was capable of responding to dissent and alleviating grievances.

NEO-DEMOCRATS AND THE LOCALISTS

Another important legacy of this new protest cycle was the rise of a new generation of pro-democracy activists. Even though they were relatively new to the political scene, these young activists became the new faces of democracy owing to their prominent roles in the new protest cycle and their determination to bring a sense of dynamism and change. Their affiliated groups and networks – Local Action, Land Justice, and Scholarism – also gained increasing visibility and influence in the public domain. Born in the 1980s and 1990s, these activists shared the overarching pro-democracy goals of their predecessors; but they also espoused more post-materialist and redistributive conceptions of democracy that focus on issues such as urban redevelopment, environmental conservation, community engagement, heritage preservation and conglomerate dominance (Ku 2012; Lam-Knott 2020). Furthermore, they advocated for more radical actions to achieve these goals. While these activists were not yet prepared to challenge the veteran democrats in elections, they were critical of the older generation for their strategies of pursuing gradual reforms through institutional bargaining and ritualistic protests. As they garnered increasing support from young citizens through these protests, they saw it as an opportune moment to exert their influence on electoral politics. These emergent activists formed the backbone of a rising political force which we refer to as the 'neo-democrats', who shared broader goals of democratization with the veteran democrats but differed in terms of their tactical preferences and attitudes towards the authorities.

The rise of neo-democrats and their discourse were enabled by the growing significance of digital media. In early 2010s, several online media platforms including *InMediaHK*, *MyRadio*, *HouseNews*, and *Passion Times* were established. These platforms, which facilitated the instant sharing of personalized content (Bennett and Segerberg 2013), integrated activism into everyday life, thereby broadening the reach and longevity of contentious episodes. Internet traffic data reveals a dramatic increase in readership following the Anti-XRL Movement and Anti-MNE Movement. By 2014, *MyRadio* and *HouseNews* had surpassed most mass media outlets to become the most popular media sources in Hong Kong, trailing only the traditional pro-democracy newspaper, *Apple Daily*. These independent media not only injected new energy into the increasingly self-censoring mass media landscape (Tang and Lee 2013). They also constructed an alternative public sphere, enabling the neo-democrats to differentiate themselves from the veteran democrats.

Parallel to the rise of the neo-democrats was the emergence of an identity-oriented localist discourse. Different from the earlier 'progressive localism' that emphasized citizens' 'rights to the city' (Chen and Szeto 2015), this new strand of localism prioritized defending local autonomy, interests, and culture against perceived 'mainlandization'. These emerging localists advocated for a stronger and more exclusive Hong Kong identity. They posited that the objectives of Hong Kong's pro-democracy movement should encompass not only the preservation of political freedoms but also the protection of the unique identity of its people (Veg 2017). They argued that the peaceful rallies and moderate demands of the past decades had not yielded substantial results, necessitating alternative frames and methods (Kaeding 2017).

The localists began to mobilize in the early 2010s, initially focusing on the livelihood issues arising from increased interactions between Hong Kong and mainland China. Fuelled by anti-mainlandization sentiments, they frequently protested against the influx of tourists from the mainland and parallel trading at border crossings (Yuen and Chung 2018). Compared with other concurrent movements such as the Anti-XRL Movement and the Anti-MNE Movement, these protests were often smaller in scale and coordinated entirely through online platforms by netizens who had little or no experience in politics. Their repertoires also diverged significantly from traditional peaceful and nonviolent approaches (Ku 2004). Protesters often adopted militant and confrontational tactics, which they believed were more effective in achieving their objectives. For example, during the 'Liberate Sheung Shui' protests in September 2012, protesters insulted parallel traders – smugglers of high-demand goods like baby formula – as 'locusts'. They also engaged in physical clashes with the traders, aiming to garner public attention and prompt authorities to intervene.

While the localist discourse received extensive media coverage, the localists remained loosely organized and had yet to cement their standing as a potent political force. Nevertheless, these protests enabled them to distinguish themselves from the veteran and neo-democrats in the public domain. In their view, the stagnation of the pro-democracy movement was attributable to the dominance of these democratic factions. To undermine their leadership, the localists set their eyes on the annual June 4 candlelight vigil. They accused the organizer, the Hong Kong Alliance, of exploiting the vigil to garner votes and promote a pan-Chinese identity, an objective they said was manifested in the 2013 vigil's 'love the country, love the people' theme. Leaders and participants were dismissed as 'pan-Chinese idiots' (*dazhonghua jiao; daai-zung-waa-gaau*) for prioritizing China's democratization over the pursuit of Hong Kong's democracy and the protection of local interests. Beginning that year, localist groups began hosting parallel commemorations. Claiming that Hong Kong people had no obligation to build a democratic China, these parallel vigils discarded any rituals, symbols, or references that might evoke Chinese nationalist sentiments, as seen in the Victoria Park ceremony. The localists insisted that the commemoration should be grounded in universal values and should focus on the local significance of June 4th.

The rise of the neo-democrats and the identity-oriented localists significantly expanded the scope of the pro-democracy movement and altered the relational dynamics within the opposition. While these new actors had yet to directly contest elections, they influenced some of the existing democratic parties with elected seats in the legislature, pulling them into their ideological orbits. Specifically, the Civic Party and the League of Social Democrats (LSD), both established parties traditionally aligned with the veteran democrats, gravitated towards the neo-democrats. Despite representing markedly different constituencies, the two parties supported the neo-democrats' postmaterialist claims and progressive tactics. In contrast, People Power, which was established in 2011 as a spinoff from the LSD, leaned towards the localists – a shift characterized by their adoption of a more populist approach and frequent criticisms of the veteran democrats.

DIVERGING THREAT PERCEPTIONS

The emergence of new actors and their shifting mode of mobilization led to growing fragmentation within the opposition. Although these emerging actors shared the pro-democracy goals of veteran democrats, they perceived threats differently and advocated for different tactical approaches. A critical point of divergence was the 2010 electoral reform when the Hong Kong government sought the support of the veteran democrats for its reform proposal (Choi 2022). This presented the veteran democrats with a difficult decision: should they cooperate with the government and make incremental gains to expand suffrage?

The proposed 2010 electoral reform closely resembled the 2005 package that the veteran democrats had previously rejected because it ignored their demand for a roadmap to full universal suffrage for the Chief Executive and the LegCo. However, the new proposal introduced two amendments: (1) expanding the election committee for the Chief Executive from 600 to 1,200 members, and (2) increasing LegCo seats from 60 to 70, with five seats to be directly elected and the remaining five to be indirectly elected by district councillors. The veteran democrats, steadfast in their commitment to electoral participation and institutional bargaining, favoured a reformist approach to democratization. They believed that pact-making was crucial for cultivating mutual trust between the incumbent government and the opposition (Rigger 2001; Schmitter 2015). Ma Ngok provides a perspective for understanding the reasoning behind this strategy of pact-making:

> The 2010 deal was more symbolic than substantial. It marked the first time that representatives of the Beijing regime had sat down to talk face-to-face with local democrats about the democratization of Hong Kong. It was also the first time Beijing and the Hong Kong democrats had reached a deal, with both sides making concessions. (2011: 65)

The veteran democrats decided to make the bold political gamble of negotiating with the Chinese party-state. The stakes were high. On 24 May 2010, Democratic Party leaders entered the CGLO, where they were later photographed sitting side-by-side with central government officials.[5] They reached an agreement with representatives of the CGLO, endorsing the reform package while urging the central government to acknowledge universal suffrage as the ultimate goal. China's Politburo later approved the Chief Executive's revised proposal, allowing the five additional seats in the functional constituencies to be filled through popular elections.[6]

The results of these negotiations surprised and upset many within both the governing coalition and the democratic opposition. Many pro-Beijing politicians argued that the revised proposal violated the Basic Law and previous NPCSC decisions on electoral reforms. Pro-establishment political parties, including the DAB, Liberal Party, and New People's Party, expressed concerns that an expansion in suffrage could adversely impact their electoral performances. They feared that this could intensify competition among themselves, deplete resources for each party, and ultimately result in a decrease in the pro-establishment's overall strength in the LegCo (Choi, Ma and Chan 2021).

---

[5] ADPL followed suit. But since the party only had one LegCo vote, it was not decisive in securing the reform bill's passage.

[6] This effectively gained more than three million registered voters, who were only eligible to vote in the geographical constituencies, the right to vote in the functional constituencies.

Meanwhile, the democratic opposition – even including several veteran figures such as Martin Lee and Audrey Eu – openly opposed the deal, arguing that it would perpetuate the existence of sectoral interests and indirect elections. Along with the young activists who gained legitimacy through recent mobilizations, they viewed the proposal as a betrayal of their democratic aspirations and electoral promises. In May 2010, five legislators from the Civic Party and the LSD resigned, effectively triggering a by-election in every geographical constituency. This was intended to be a de facto 'referendum' (Civic Party 2010).

Despite a boycott by the pro-Beijing camp and non-cooperation from the Democratic Party, all five resigned legislators were re-elected to the LegCo. However, it only achieved a 17.1 per cent turnout, significantly lower than the figures observed in previous by-elections. Eventually, with backing from the Democratic Party, Hong Kong Association for Democracy and People's Livelihood (ADPL), independents, and pro-Beijing parties, the electoral reform proposal passed the LegCo and received endorsement from the NPC. In response, the neo-democrats, comprising both some of the elected legislators and protest activists, branded the Democratic Party as 'collaborators of the party-state' and 'betrayers of the pro-democracy movement' (Kwong 2016). They threatened to boycott the platform led by the Democratic Party to coordinate candidates in future elections, a strategy that had been employed to counter the pro-Beijing camp's political machinery and optimize electoral support under the proportional representation system.

The contrasting responses to the electoral reform between the veteran and neo-democrats underscored a widening chasm in their perception of threats presented by the state and nation-building efforts described earlier.[7] The veteran democrats believed that such threats could be mitigated through their existing strategy of combining institutional bargaining with ritualistic protests. They viewed the electoral reform, despite its limited scope, as an opportunity to strengthen their institutional leverage, as it was likely to increase their seat count. This cautious optimism was partly rooted in their better institutional access to the government and the ruling coalition. The veteran democrats had established working relationships with local authorities and regularly communicated with intermediaries of the central authorities. They also imagined that there were soft-liners within the party-state, who considered Hong Kong a testing ground for political reforms akin to the Singapore model (Thompson and Ortmann 2020).[8] Subsequently, they

---

[7] Most veteran parties such as DP and ADPL supported the reforms, whereas the neo-democrats such as LSD and CP opposed it. But divisions were presented within the pro-democracy parties and among different generations of their leaders and supporters.

[8] Insiders of the negotiation suggested that the final concession was endorsed by Vice President Xi Jinping, who was in charge of the leading small group on Hong Kong affairs and approved by President Hu Jintao.

viewed the electoral reform not as an ideological battle (Interview A21), but as a prerequisite for 'effective governance', as stressed by the Chief Executive Donald Tsang (Cheung 2010). The low turnout in the 2010 by-elections was interpreted by the veteran democrats as a signal that the majority of their middle class supporters aimed to minimize the cost of political participation and accept their role as brokers (Ho 2010). Despite the risk of diluting opposition unity, they felt obligated to counter the rise of radical politics (Interview A9).

In contrast, the neo-democrats were sceptical of the proposed reforms and the ruling coalition's intention to advance democracy (Interview A7). They viewed the proposal as a strategic ploy to split the opposition and legitimize a semi-democratic system, given its lack of clear timeline for implementing universal suffrage (Interview A22).[9] With a more distant relationship with the ruling coalition, they aligned more closely with the emergent activists, who increasingly viewed traditional methods of rallies, petitions, and deliberations as ineffective, routinized, and elitist (Interview A8). Encouraged by recent protests that often resulted in concessions from the authorities, they saw a growing sense of political awakening among the populace and viewed mass mobilization as a more effective strategy to promote democracy. Rejecting the reform presented an opportunity to delegitimize the entire system and stand with the masses.

The increasing fractionation of the opposition was reflected in the electoral outcomes. Figure 3.4 illustrates the share of seats and votes among different political camps from 2004 to 2016, from which two observations can be drawn. First, the gap between the vote and seat shares of the pro-Beijing and pro-democracy camps has gradually narrowed over time. This suggests that the ruling coalition's electoral success has expanded from the functional constituencies to the directly elected geographical constituencies. Between 2004 and 2012, the vote share between the pro-Beijing and pro-democracy camps shifted from an approximate 30–70 split to a 40–60 split in the 70-seat legislature. Second, from 2012 onward, the veteran democrats have faced increasing challenges from the neo-democrats and the localists in terms of vote and seat share. As the neo-democrats and localists secured more seats in the 2016 LegCo elections, the veteran democrats lost the one-third minority, which they considered crucial to securing their veto power on significant constitutional changes and thereby their leverage to pressure the government into accommodating the opposition. They needed to share the veto power with the emerging factions and count on their cooperation.

---

[9] Many veteran democrats' accounts and memoirs insisted that the post hoc engagement was part of the deal, whereas the pro-Beijing camp suggested that it was a wait-and-see condition (See Choi et al. 2021).

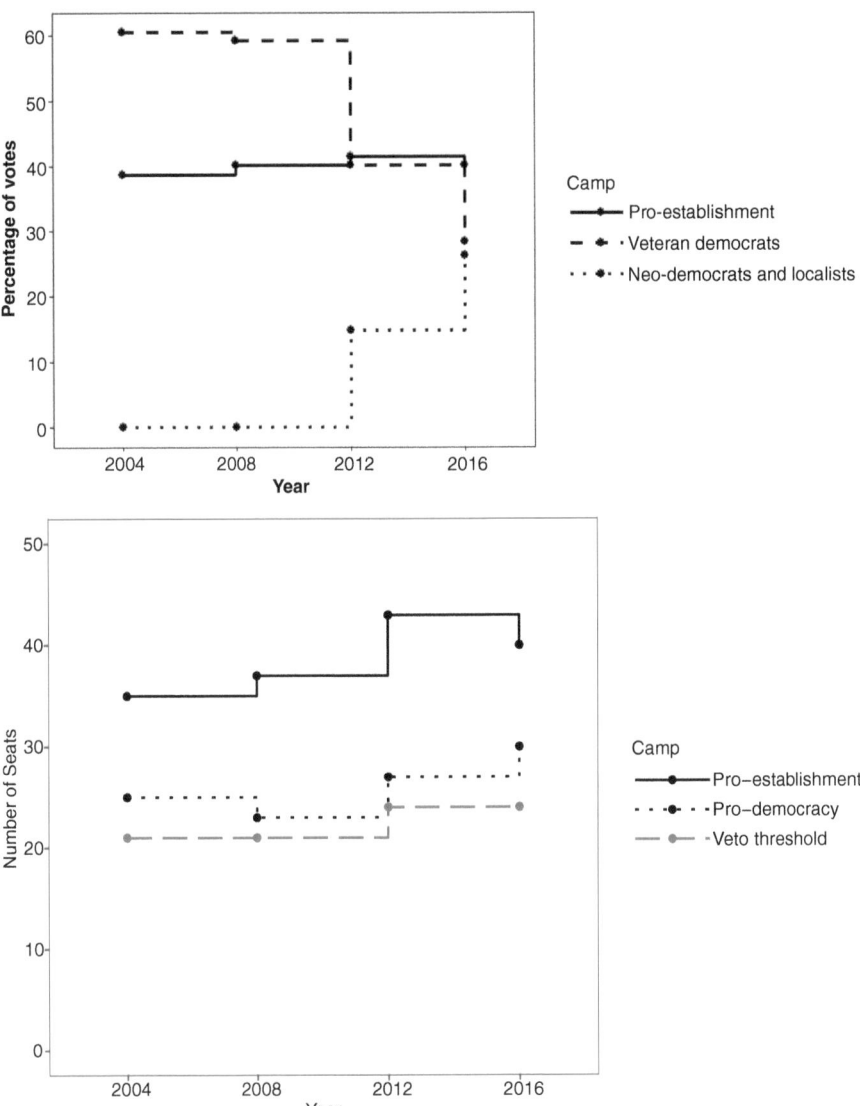

FIGURE 3.4 Share of votes and seats between political camps in LegCo elections, 2004–2016.
Source: Hong Kong Electoral Commission.

CONCLUSION

Between the mid-2000s and mid-2010s, Hong Kong witnessed an escalating cycle of contention that cemented its reputation as a city of protest. Popular protests during this period served as a means to exert pressure on the ruling coalition to make strategic concessions in response to public opinions that were inadequately represented in semi-democratic elections and public consultations. This protest cycle, which emerged partially to fill the institutional gaps in the liberal oligarchy, resulted in new strategies and the emergence of new political actors. This broadened the spectrum of the pro-democracy opposition but also led to its increased fragmentation.

The new protest cycle challenged not only the power dynamics between the regime and the opposition, but also within the democratic opposition itself. On the one hand, state and nation-building efforts curbed the growth of the democratic opposition in formal and grassroots institutions but were unable to suppress its ability to mobilize the masses. Meanwhile, the increasing practice of patron-clientelism in local politics and cultural blending with the mainland led to a growing sense of insecurity among citizens, as the perceived distinctions between the two systems became increasingly blurred. On the other hand, a new wave of protests reshaped the modes of mobilization as well as the relational dynamics within the opposition. The increasing public support for these issue-based protests indicated that brokered mobilization was insufficient for expressing citizens' demands and rallying mass support. Instead, the emergence of new groups and networks offered a new approach for safeguarding liberty and achieving universal suffrage, marking a significant shift towards *factional mobilization*.

The growing divide between the veteran democrats and the emergent activists in Hong Kong is not unusual for regimes undergoing prolonged political transitions. After more than two decades of unsuccessful efforts to achieve universal suffrage, Hong Kong's pro-democracy movement was experiencing what could be termed as 'transition fatigue', a phenomenon also observed in Latin America and Eastern Europe during the 1970s and 1980s (Diamond 2002). The veteran democrats saw that the power imbalance had increasingly tilted in favour of the incumbent, given that the regime's state-building efforts since 2008 had amassed a larger pool of economic resources and a stronger grassroots network, boosting the electoral performance of pro-Beijing parties. After voting down the government's electoral reform proposal in 2005, they were not sure whether another rejection would invigorate the pro-democracy movement or miss an opportunity to make elections more inclusive and competitive (Interviews A17, A19, and A21). Conversely, political stagnation drove the neo-democrats and localists to seek immediate changes. Unlike the veteran democrats who favoured institutional bargaining, these emergent activists preferred to experiment with a more decentralized, networked mode of activism. They saw it as the right time to move beyond electoral politics and seek a breakthrough through unscripted mobilizations (Interviews A3 and A5).

These dynamics resulted in a paradox from a resource mobilization perspective: while established SMOs and veteran democrats were increasingly marginalized, mass protests became more frequent and more likely to occur.

The weakening of balancing forces within the tripartite coalition and the institutionalized opposition pushed both the central authorities and the emergent pro-democracy forces to move beyond traditional strategies and adopt new approaches. In this context, we contend that a comprehensive explanation of the form and timing of mass mobilization must consider the relative strength of the institutionalized opposition against the incumbent, as well as the degree of fractionalization among opposition groups.

PART II

EPISODES

4

No Leaders, Only the Masses

On 16 January 2013, an op-ed titled 'The Most Lethal Weapon of Civil Disobedience' was published in the *Hong Kong Economic Journal* (Tai 2013). It was written by Benny Tai, a law professor at the University of Hong Kong. In the op-ed, Tai argued that previous protest strategies, such as large rallies and hunger strikes, were no longer effective in achieving genuine universal suffrage in Hong Kong. He proposed a non-violent civil disobedience movement called 'Occupy Central', in which protesters would occupy the streets of Central, the business district, for a prolonged period. The objective was to compel Beijing to change its stance. Despite mixed responses within the pro-democracy camp, the op-ed dropped a bombshell on the city's stalled democratic reforms. In March 2013, Tai, along with two other prominent figures, Chan Kin-man, a sociology professor, and Chu Yiu-ming, a pastor of the local Baptist Church, formed 'Occupy Central with Love and Peace' (OCLP). The trio became the leaders of the campaign, and a secretariat was established, recruiting hundreds of volunteers.

Unlike the Anti-XRL Movement and the Anti-MNE Movement, which were sparked by contingent threats, OCLP emerged in response to the chronic issue of universal suffrage. Although the Chinese government had promised universal suffrage by 2017, it introduced restrictions on candidacy and voting rights. Many pro-democracy activists and supporters viewed this as a violation of the Basic Law's promise to let 'Hong Kong people ruling Hong Kong', highlighting the perceived institutional threats against citizens' civic and political freedoms, including the right to choose their leaders (Ortmann 2015). Beijing disagreed: it considered its version of universal suffrage to be superior to what the British allowed for Hong Kong before the handover.

The OCLP proposed a new approach beyond the existing dual strategy of institutional bargaining and ritualistic protests. Its formation also showcased the involvement of actors beyond the institutionalized opposition.

Additionally, OCLP attracted volunteers primarily from professional, student, and ordinary citizen backgrounds, who supported democracy but mostly did not have organizational affiliations. Nevertheless, unlike other emerging opposition networks such as Local Action and Scholarism, OCLP styled itself as a formal, professionalized SMO, with the three co-founders serving as leaders and a secretariat overseeing daily operations. Those interested in joining the campaign had to sign a letter of intent pledging their commitment. This intention to formalize processes was evident in the drafting of an electoral proposal, which involved three rounds of participant deliberation guided by clear-cut rules (Yang 2020).

This chapter examines how generalized and particularized threats converged to shape the Umbrella Movement and give rise to a *fragmented mobilization*. It also discusses the consequences of the movement, particularly in terms of how ordinary citizens viewed their role in protests. While generalized threats initially prompted plans to stage an organization-led mobilization, particularized threats unintentionally transformed those plans into a mobilization characterized by a hybrid organizational structure comprising both formal leaders and self-mobilized protesters. Furthermore, we argue that divergent threat perceptions among protesters and their distrust of formal leaders sowed the seeds for the movement's eventual fragmentation. These differing interpretations of the repressive threat confronting the movement led to tactical divergence among actors. It also gave rise to an anti-leadership sentiment among protesters, which increasingly limited the decision-making capacity of both formal and informal leaders and resulted in tactical freeze.

THE ACCIDENTAL LEADERS

OCLP initially sparked mixed responses when it was introduced (Kan 2013). Pro-democracy parties and their supporters saw the concept of civil disobedience as groundbreaking, defying the traditional framework of institutional engagement. At the same time, younger democrats – including student activists, neo-democrats and localists – criticized OCLP's plan and the veterans for being too conservative. While these activists shared OCLP's goals, they believed the campaign to be overly limiting: the scale of occupation would be contained, and the intention was for participants to voluntarily surrender to the police afterwards (Ku 2019). To the young activists, this resembled the routine, highly choreographed mass rallies that deprived participants of their agency. From a strategic perspective, the top-down planning of OCLP implied that only older and more loyal pro-democracy supporters would join the campaign. Young people were unlikely to be interested. Indeed, before the summer of 2014, popular support for OCLP was lukewarm.

The opportunity for the younger activists to assert their role came when OCLP organized a civic referendum to determine their key demands for the occupation. The idea was to choose from proposals put forth by different groups through rounds of voting. However, the referendum ended up being a self-radicalizing process (Ku 2019). Beijing declared the referendum illegal, sparking a popular backlash that helped draw nearly 800,000 people to vote in June 2014 (Lee and Chan 2018). The three proposals that received the most votes all included the notion of 'civic nomination', which allowed all citizens to nominate chief executive candidates. Some of the veteran democrats considered this as a radical idea because of its significant deviation from Beijing's position (*BBC*, 10 January 2014). In fact, this idea was initially proposed by Scholarism and the Hong Kong Federation of Students (HKFS), the two major student groups advocating for democracy, and it gained popular support through public debates. Consequently, student activists emerged as leading voices, despite not being part of the OCLP campaign.

The surge in popular support for a more radical claim was a response to a high-level policy paper published by Beijing two weeks before the referendum. In the document, Beijing declared that 'as a unitary state, China's central government has comprehensive jurisdiction over all local administrative regions, including the Hong Kong Special Administrative Region' (State Council of the PRC 2014). The document stated that '[t]he high degree of autonomy of Hong Kong Special Administrative Region is not an inherent power, but one that comes solely from the authorization by the central leadership'. This marked the first-ever use of the phrase 'comprehensive jurisdiction' (*quanmian guanzhi*), deviating from previous emphases on 'high degree of autonomy' or 'Hong Kong people ruling Hong Kong'.

Another catalyst came on 31 August 2014, when China's National People's Congress (NPC) issued a decision outlining guidelines for the 2017 Chief Executive election. Beijing imposed three selection criteria: first, the Chief Executive's nominating committee must be formed 'in accordance with' the existing 1,200-strong four-sector election committee; second, the new committee could only nominate a maximum of three candidates for the final runoff; and third, each candidate must obtain support from more than half of the nominating committee members – four times the existing threshold, effectively excluding anyone not endorsed by Beijing. The NPC decision sparked outrage among pro-democracy supporters, who saw it as a violation of Beijing's promise of universal suffrage. Even moderate democrats were shocked. A political scientist, Brian Fong, declared it as 'the end of dialogue in the road towards democracy' and wrote a widely signed petition (*InmediaHK*, 31 August 2014). The shockwave revitalized the waning OCLP movement and provided the young activists with an opportunity to mobilize. On 22 September 2014, HKFS and Scholarism launched a weeklong class boycott at the government headquarters to demand the withdrawal of the NPC decision. The boycott served as an informal prelude to OCLP, which was scheduled to begin on 1 October, China's National Day.

The NPC decision came as a stark revelation for pro-democracy supporters, bringing into focus the recurrent threat to their civic and political freedoms.

It also marked the end of the discourse of 'democratic reunification', which had been put forward by liberal intellectuals in the 1980s to project a sense of political identity within a democratic and pan-Chinese, nationalist framework (Ku 2019). This discourse had been a central theme of Hong Kong's pro-democracy movement until then, fostering optimism that the city could eventually achieve democracy within the Chinese nation. The widespread feeling of futility brought about by the NPC decision prompted the young activists to proclaim a new vision: 'determining our own destiny' (*mingyun zizhu; ming-wan-zi-zyu*). This new master frame was reflected in the overwhelming support for civic nomination during the June referendum. It resonated with the rising localist sentiment in society, and the growing aspirations of the younger generation to assert their political subjectivity vis-à-vis Beijing and the older generation of democrats.

THE SPECTRE OF REPRESSION

Since the student boycott took place on weekdays during office hours, the turnout was disappointingly low. As the student activists desperately needed a catalyst was to mobilize the public, they decided to orchestrate a surprise action. Late in the evening of September 26, they stormed Civic Square, the forecourt of the government headquarters, scaling the metal fences that had been erected after the 2012 Anti-MNE Movement. Many activists were arrested, and it was broadcast live on television and widely shared on social media. The dramatic event prompted pro-democracy supporters to gather at the government headquarters, demanding the release of the detained activists. As more protesters arrived, OCLP was compelled to officially launch the civil disobedience campaign earlier than planned. While this decision was opposed by those who were not in favour of OCLP, an increasing number of protesters congregated at the headquarters on September 28.

In the late afternoon, the crowd spilled onto Harcourt Road, bringing the entire eight-lane highway to a standstill. Riot police were swiftly deployed. Around 6:00 pm, they fired multiple rounds of tear gas to disperse the protesters. At one point, a police officer unveiled a red flag that read 'disperse, or we fire', fuelling rumours that live ammunition would be used. Enshrouded by smoke, some protesters used plastic goggles, facemasks, and umbrellas as self-defence against the advancing police. The sight of protesters brandishing umbrellas quickly spread through social media and television, prompting even more citizens to join the demonstrations (Tang 2015).

This marked the second instance of tear gas being employed by the police to disperse a protest after the handover. The first time was during the demonstrations against the 2005 WTO Ministerial Conference when tear gas was used against militant South Korean farmers. Tear gas was also deployed on several occasions during riots in the colonial era. In all these prior instances, it was the protesters who instigated violence. However, although the September 28 protest was disruptive, it remained nonviolent and peaceful. The decision to employ tear gas against unarmed protesters generated widespread outrage among pro-democracy supporters. One protester expressed her feelings in a blog post:

Tear gas? Are you kidding me? We were just asking the police to make room for us. We were just supporting the students. We were just using umbrellas to protect ourselves from the pepper sprays. Was tear gas really needed? …I was angry. We did not charge at the police. Why did they do that? There was no broken glass, no cars that were stuck, no looting and no protesters using weapons. Hong Kong government, how dare you use pepper spray, tear gas and rubber bullets on us? Other than the truth, we have nothing! (Prestor 2014)

Confronted with repression, many protesters disregarded the calls of the OCLP trio and HKFS who urged them to disperse immediately. They viewed it as their moral obligation to remain steadfast. 'Protecting the students' was their paramount objective. To them, the use of tear gas by the police was disproportionate to protesters' actions and symbolized the institutional encroachment imposed on pro-democracy supporters in the context of the electoral reform.

To everyone's surprise, the area was re-occupied by protesters by late evening. Protesters also took control of the streets in other areas, including the bustling shopping district of Causeway Bay and Tsim Sha Tsui, and the working class neighbourhood of Mongkok.

A SPONTANEOUS OCCUPATION

The spontaneous occupation became known as the Umbrella Revolution, or more commonly referred to as the Umbrella Movement.[1] As protesters occupied different areas, the movement exceeded OCLP's original plan. The occupation attracted thousands of pro-democracy supporters who did not support OCLP. Over the following seventy-nine days, these protesters remained in the occupied zones and established tent villages, demanding universal suffrage. To sustain the mobilization, informal and self-organized groups emerged within the protest camps, assuming various roles such as supply sharing, medical assistance, frontline patrols, police negotiations, waste management, and volunteer recruitment (Cai 2016). Additionally, they utilized social media platforms, including Facebook, YouTube, discussion forums, and citizen-based media sites (Agur and Frisch 2019; Shen, Xia and Skoric 2020), to communicate, share information, and coordinate logistics.

---

[1] The usage between Umbrella Revolution and Umbrella Movement reflected people's different ideological positions towards it. Localists and young protesters tend to call it 'revolution' because it better captures their sentiments, whereas moderates prefer 'movement' to signify their intention of not wanting to be perceived as subversive.

The Umbrella Movement exhibited several characteristics of the sponta-neous, networked movements that had occurred in the early 2010s (Castells 2012), such as the anti-austerity movements and the global Occupy protests, which saw protesters occupying public spaces without formal leadership for extended durations. However, there was a marked distinction: despite its hori-zontally networked base, the Umbrella Movement had a centralized leadership. This leadership consisted of a broad coalition comprising both student activists and veteran pro-democracy advocates, with support from traditional political parties and SMOs. These leaders, encompassing a mix of new and established pro-democracy activists, were responsible for representing the movement pub-licly, making strategic decisions, and dealing with the government. However, their legitimacy and authority were persistently questioned, not only by pro-testers but also from within the leadership itself.

To characterize the Umbrella Movement's unique structure, Francis Lee and Joseph Chan (2018) draw upon the conceptual differentiation between connective and collective action (Bennett and Segerberg 2013). They viewed the Umbrella Movement as 'a case in which connective actions generated through bottom-up processes intervened into a collective action with cen-tral leadership' (Lee and Chan 2018: 19). According to their perspective, the logic of connective actions simply collided into the OCLP and triggered the Umbrella Movement, yet it did not displace the central organizers from their leadership roles. This characterization highlights the organizational tensions within the Umbrella Movement. While the presence of leaders as public fig-ures of the movement was recognized, many protesters viewed themselves primarily as 'self-mobilized' citizens who could not be represented by any-one but themselves. They had grown weary of the traditional top-down decision-making approach employed by conventional leaders and preferred to perceive themselves as independent agents rather than passive followers. This sentiment was epitomized by a popular slogan that emerged during the movement: 'No Leaders, Only the Masses' (*meiyou dahui zhiyou qunzhong; mu-tjau-daai-toi-zi-jau-kwan-zung*).

From this perspective, the Umbrella Movement can be understood as simul-taneously planned and spontaneous. It was planned in the sense that the lead-ers aimed to align it with their original plan, despite its initial deviation. It was also spontaneous in that many protesters considered themselves unbound by any specific leadership, preferring instead to act based on their own improvisa-tion (Ho 2019). As the movement progressed, this unique organizational struc-ture played a pivotal role in shaping its dynamics and outcomes, precipitating its eventual fragmentation.

ORGANIZATIONAL HYBRIDITY

The prominent involvement of various activist groups prior to the launch of the Umbrella Movement naturally positioned them as key players within the burgeoning movement. The two student organizations – HKFS and Scholarism – quickly emerged as leaders (Cheng and Chan 2017). Around two weeks into the occupation, approximately 57 and 29 per cent of respondents respectively recognized these two organizations as legitimate leaders, according to our survey. Both student groups had long been active and established pillars of Hong Kong's pro-democracy movement. The HKFS, established in 1958 by the student unions from local public universities, had played a pivotal role in defending civil rights and mobilizing university students before and after the handover. Scholarism, founded in 2011 by a group of teenagers including young activist Joshua Wong, had led the 2012 Anti-MNE Movement and had since then become a significant player in the pro-democracy movement.

OCLP, along with the student groups, was also swiftly recognized as one of the leading organizations. However, due to criticisms of 'hijacking the student movement' (Cheng and Chan 2017), OCLP enjoyed much less popularity compared to the student groups. According to our survey, only 18 per cent of the protesters considered OCLP as movement leaders. Consequently, despite their significant involvement in planning the campaign, the spontaneous nature of the occupation limited OCLP's influence. OCLP leader Chan Kin-man acknowledged that HKFS held the most influence and had veto power among the three leading organizations (*Citizen News*, 28 September 2017). As we will discuss, this power disparity would become a crucial factor in fuelling tensions within the leadership.

To bolster their legitimacy and mobilize additional resources, the three leading organizations established a 'Five Party Platform' by incorporating two additional actors – (1) major pro-democracy parties such as the Democratic Party, Civic Party, and Labour Party and (2) prominent SMOs like the Civil Human Rights Front. This expanded platform now functioned as what Marshall Ganz (2000) refers to as a 'leadership team'. The platform held occasional meetings to make decisions on higher-level matters, including framing, media engagement, strategic planning, and negotiations. It also took charge of forming a picket team, led by a seasoned unionist, consisting of around fifty individuals tasked to maintain 'law and order' within the camps (Interview A20). One of their responsibilities, for example, was controlling access to the central stage at the Admiralty camp, which leaders utilized to address protesters.

The process by which the leadership team emerged is illustrated in Figure 4.1. However, despite the general recognition of the formal leadership by the protesters, they did not adhere to the original plan of the campaign for a 'sit-in'. Across the three camps, protesters began taking their own initiatives to prepare for a long-term occupation. They formed self-organized groups to handle various logistical tasks, including defence teams, supply stations, and first aid stations. These groups set up makeshift facilities, recruited volunteers, and adorned the occupied areas with posters, banners, and artworks to express their democratic aspirations and assert their agency as a civic community (Pang 2020; Veg 2016). Barricades were constructed to demarcate the boundaries of

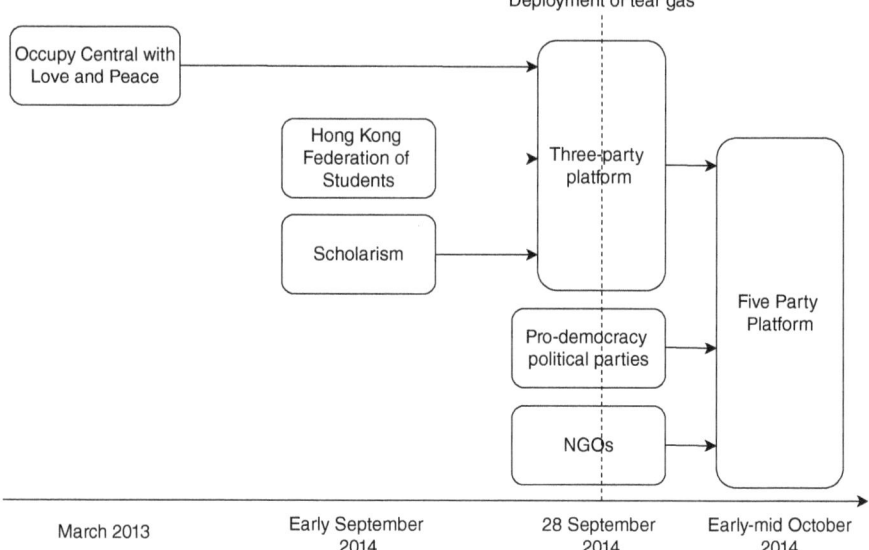

FIGURE 4.1 Origins of the five-party platform.
Source: Synthesized by the authors.

the occupied zones, and tents were erected for protesters to rest and sleep. At the Admiralty camp, protesters even created an open-air library and study area, equipped with electricity, LED lights, Wi-Fi, and a roof. According to a census conducted during the movement, there were as many as 51 major facilities and 695 tents in Admiralty alone at one point (See Figure 4.2 for an example).[2]

These self-organized groups emerged spontaneously. While some received support from political parties and SMOs, others were primarily initiated by the protesters themselves. The size of these groups ranged from a few people to dozens. Although they tended to adopt horizontal structures rather than bureaucratic hierarchies, they still had membership boundaries. Individuals seeking to join a group had to be trusted and accepted by existing members. While these groups lacked formal leaders, informal leaders often emerged within them. These leaders were not 'democratically elected' by group members, but were typically the founders or individuals who contributed more effort than others. For example, in the supply stations, a few informal leaders would represent the group and collaborate with other groups to handle practical matters such as supply reallocation, patrolling and frontline defence (Interview C14). These leaders sometimes engaged in negotiations with third parties,

[2] Umbrella Movement General Census. Retrieved on 25 August 2022. www.google.com/maps/d/u/o/viewer?mid=1f8aNWSCoVmRuNHQoUNaTnCK4_Vg&ll=22.28080262431846%2C11 4.16443475000003&z=17.

FIGURE 4.2 An occupied road in Admiralty, 2014.
Photo Credit: Ricci Yue.

such as negotiating with the tram operator about reopening blocked tram lines (Interview C15). However, decision-making within these self-organized groups was often ad hoc and informal, lacking formalized mechanisms or rules as seen in the anti-austerity movements and global Occupy protests.

Nevertheless, these self-organized groups played a vital role in managing the logistics of the occupation. One notable example was the allocation of supplies. As protests commenced, citizens donated various essentials such as water, food, and facemasks to the protest camps. In Admiralty, supply stations established a hub-and-spoke coordination network utilizing platforms such as Telegram and Google Sheets. Initially, supplies were centralized, after which volunteers would distribute them to smaller satellite stations based on the indicated needs in chat groups and online spreadsheets. Another example was the provision of mobile phone recharging facilities. To address the scarcity of electrical sockets within the protest camps, a group of university students procured cables, power banks, and generators, setting up a battery recharging station adjacent to the Admiralty metro exit. Initially, they relied on a simple registration logbook to record the entrusted phones, but eventually upgraded to a computerized registration system and enlisted trusted volunteers to safeguard the phones. Their free service gained immense popularity, with as many as 800 mobile phones passing through their station daily at the peak of the movement.

On an individual level, these self-organized groups served as avenues for protesters to exercise their voluntarism and autonomously participate in organizing the protests (Gold and Veg 2020; Pang 2020). This contrasted with conventional rallies and demonstrations, where participants were typically expected to just show up and adhere to a predetermined routine. When asked about their motivation for becoming volunteers, a protester at a recycling station said:

> Please don't call me a volunteer. I don't like this term. It reminds people of organizations. I am simply a passionate citizen. ...I have participated in many demonstrations before. July 1 rallies, June 4 candlelight vigils, all the big and small protests, I was there. But this is my first time occupying the streets and doing the actual groundwork. We recycled useful items from the rubbish so that they don't go to waste. This is something we ought to learn because democracy is not just about being able to vote. (Interview B22)

Protesters' handling of sanitation problems serves as another example of their high level of voluntarism. As public services were halted by the government within the occupation zone, rubbish accumulated, and public toilets became dirty. However, some protesters took it upon themselves to clean the toilets on a daily basis and replenish them with toiletry supplies crowdsourced from protesters and supporters. Others took charge of collecting and disposing garbage. Such voluntaristic acts played a crucial role in maintaining order within the occupation while enabling protesters to exercise their political agency. In many instances, protesters utilized their specific expertise to support the cause. Professional minivans and taxi drivers, for example, assisted in transporting supplies from donors to the protest camps, while construction workers helped erect makeshift furniture and barricades to make the protest camps more 'liveable'. These actions foreshadowed the significant role that social roles would play in the subsequent Anti-Extradition Movement, as we will explore in later chapters.

The mid-October onsite survey provides an indication of the high level of involvement among protesters: approximately 50% donated either money or supplies to the movement, 34% engaged in volunteer work, and 19% participated in defending the protest camps. However, while voluntarism was pivotal to sustaining the occupation, protesters' proactive participation inadvertently sowed the seeds of future disagreements with the formal leadership. Viewing themselves as self-mobilized actors, protesters felt no obligations to strictly adhere to the guidance of the Five-Party Platform. They considered the formal leaders as contingent and nominal figures: although leaders served as the public faces of the movement, their legitimacy came from the protesters, without whom the occupation could not have taken place.

The relationship between protesters and leaders was further complicated by differing perceptions among the leaders of the masses they were representing. The student leaders regarded themselves as representatives of those who remained in the protest camps and those who were more supportive of defending their territory. Being technologically adept and digitally connected, they keenly monitored the opinions regarding the movement on Facebook and major discussion forums, which they considered as indicators of popular support. Such opinions tended to be supportive of the occupation and militant tactics. On the contrary, the OCLP trio and veteran pro-democracy advocates were more concerned about moderate supporters who did not stay in the camps, as well as those who did not endorse long-term occupation. Their apprehension stemmed from worries that an extended occupation could prolong disruption and alienate conservative voters. Moreover, they feared that the occupation could provoke Beijing to violently suppress the protests, akin to the events of the 1989 Tiananmen Movement. Indeed, there were recurrent rumours that the police, and even the People's Liberation Army, would forcibly disperse the protest camps. Thus, in contrast to the younger activists, the older generation preferred to downscale the occupation and pressure the government into negotiation.

TWO VIEWS OF REPRESSION

As outlined by the Introduction, higher levels of opposition fractionalization weaken the cohesiveness of mass mobilizations. While the pro-democracy opposition was already fractionalized prior to the Umbrella Movement, the impact on mobilization soon became evident. Several events in October highlighted the differing perceptions of repressive threats among the formal leaders. On October 3, a group of masked individuals, widely believed to be triad members (Varese and Wong 2018), gathered at the Mongkok camp. Chanting anti-Occupy slogans, they dismantled barricades, destroyed tents, and violently attacked the protesters. In response, protesters who remained in the camp fought back against these intruders. As more gathered to reinforce the camp, they gradually outnumbered the thugs, eventually forcing them to retreat from Mongkok.

However, the attacks on the Mongkok protesters did not cease. In the early morning of October 17, when the camp had fewer protesters, police raided the camp and began clearing barricades and tents. By late morning, they had successfully reopened the occupied roads to traffic. However, by early evening, thousands of protesters once again returned to Mongkok to reclaim the streets. While some disrupted the resumed traffic, others tried to breach the police barricades. The police responded with shields, batons, and pepper spray, whereas the protesters resisted with umbrellas, and metal barriers. Many protesters sustained injuries during the clashes; but their actions led to the reoccupation of Mongkok within hours.

These two events strengthened the determination of the protesters to defend Mongkok. Following these violent confrontations, Mongkok was no longer viewed merely as an extension of Admiralty, but as a symbolic site of militant resistance against the government. A protester shared his experience of confronting the thugs:

I was shoved and beaten by them, and they were merciless. I couldn't say for sure the police were collaborating with the triads, but I felt that at least they were not taking a neutral stance. At that moment I felt that the police could no longer safeguard our freedom. We were in a 'state of nature' where we were obliged to defend ourselves militantly. (Interview C2)

The collective experience of standing against both the counter-protesters and the police generated a sense of place-based collective identity among the protesters in Mongkok, who saw themselves differently from their counterparts in Admiralty (Yuen 2018). To them, Admiralty was a safe haven without the imminent threat of repression and eviction, while Mongkok symbolized a battleground where protesters had to defend themselves constantly.

The more militant responses among Mongkok protesters presented a dilemma for the formal leaders. On the one hand, OCLP leaders and veteran pro-democracy figures viewed these actions as unnecessary provocations that went beyond the original plan of peaceful civil disobedience. While they publicly expressed support for the Mongkok protesters, they aimed to scale back the occupation due to concerns that violent confrontations could undermine the movement's legitimacy. As a pro-democracy LegCo member noted: 'We went to our constituencies and gathered feedback from the voters; and we had a strong feeling that ordinary citizens were increasingly fed up with the disruptions. It was the right move to urge protesters to return to Admiralty so that we could concentrate our mobilizational strength in one place.' (Interview A17)

On the other hand, the student leaders aligned themselves with the Mongkok protesters. They had already faced severe criticism for advising protesters to retreat on September 28 and were determined not to repeat the same mistake. This became particularly evident on October 5 when the HKFS released a statement stating: 'Let us reiterate: all occupation zones are important. They are the bargaining chips for the Hong Kong people to negotiate with the government. We urge all citizens who were staying in Mongkok to defend their positions firmly before substantive outcomes are achieved' (HKFS 2014a).

LEADING THE LEADERLESS

Exercising leadership within a self-mobilized protester base posed a significant challenge for the formal leaders within this hybrid organizational structure. The student leaders were acutely aware of this predicament and made efforts to address it from the start. On the second day of the occupation, HKFS and Scholarism jointly released a statement on their official Facebook pages (HKFS 2014b), expressing their commitment to 'continue to participate and support citizens' spontaneous occupation'. To enhance communication with the protesters and establish their presence on the ground, they set up makeshift booths within the protest camps. Despite their endeavours, establishing authority among the protesters proved to be more difficult than they could imagine. This was partly due to the fact that the student groups had not

TABLE 4.1 *Background and demands of the Umbrella Movement participants.*

	Mongkok	Admiralty	$\chi 2$ test
n	158	1,461	
Political affiliation			
Pro-establishment (including pro-government and pro-Beijing)	0%	0.3%	
Veteran democrat	20.4%	31.2%	
Localists/Neo-democrats	32.5%	26.9%	
Nil or unknown	47.1%	41.7%	8.551**
Demand (degree of importance)			
Calling for Universal Suffrage	91.1%	85.9%	
Agrees with the idea of civil disobedience	54.3%	45.5%	
Fighting for greater public participation in policymaking	32.9%	21.7%	
Dissatisfied with the Police's measures in dealing with protests	70.5%	51.1%	
Being resistant to the Central Government's interference in Hong Kong issues	45.9%	32.4%	
Fighting for better livelihood	15.7%	6.2%	
Defending Hong Kong's core values	66.7%	47.9%	N/A

Note: The survey collected a much smaller sample in Mongkok than in Admiralty because of the continued clashes and tensed environment in the latter, which made it difficult for researchers to interview protest participants. This question asked interviewees to rate the importance of different motivations, on a scale from 1 (very unimportant) to 5 (very important), in participating in the Umbrella Movement. The above graph shows the 'degree of importance', which is calculated by the following equation: Degree of importance = (% Very important + % Important) – (% Unimportant + % Very unimportant).
Source: Authors' onsite survey.
**p-value < 0.05.

enjoyed widespread societal support prior to the Umbrella Movement. For instance, even though the HKFS was formed by representatives of university student unions, its connection with both university students, and the broader society, remained weak. Before the occupation, protests initiated by the HKFS often garnered limited student participation (*InmediaHK*, 3 September 2015). Furthermore, the student leaders had not anticipated the movement's prolonged duration and thus had no preconceived plan for engaging with the protesters on the ground.

The challenge faced by formal leaders in gaining protesters' trust was further compounded by the pre-existing factional divisions within the pro-democracy movement (Table 4.1). In the early 2010s, the emergence of localism had sowed discord within the camp. Localists believed that veteran democrats were too moderate in their strategies and held implicit sympathies with pan-Chinese nationalism. Embracing identity politics as a new approach, localists advocated for preserving Hong Kong's local identity and strengthening the city's autonomy (Veg 2017). Through a series of small-scale anti-mainlandization protests, localists gained traction and promoted more militant tactics to assert their demands (Yuen and Chung 2018). The neo-democrats, represented by young activists such as Joshua Wong, also aligned themselves closely with the localist agenda, even if they did not actively endorse militant tactics.

The Umbrella Movement provided an opportunity for the localists to criticize the veteran democrats and the neo-democrats, whom they perceived as being embodied by the formal leaders. They cited the example of the formal leaders, including the OCLP, HKFS and Scholarism, calling for retreat on September 28 to question the latter's legitimacy. Notably, Chin Wan, an academic and prominent localist theorist, openly accused HKFS of being an 'agent of the United States' and 'spy of the (Chinese) communist'. Supporters of Chin put up posters in the Mongkok camp that depicted caricatures of HKFS leaders and veteran democratic activists, labelling as 'leftards' (*zuojiao; zo-gaau*), a derogatory term for individuals who adhered to the non-violent principle. The clashes in Mongkok on October 3 and 17, as depicted earlier, set the stage for Chan and the localists to advocate for their militant doctrine. When HKFS decided to hold discussion forums in the protest camps in mid-October, Chan criticized their actions as an attempt to reclaim leadership from the 'leaderless protest' and called on his supporters to disrupt the meeting in Mongkok. These actions eroded the credibility of the Five-Party Platform as the formal leadership.

Consequently, it became increasingly challenging for OCLP leaders to scale back the occupation. When the HKSAR government proposed resolving the deadlock through open dialogue, the formal leaders initially considered lifting the blockade of traffic lanes near the government headquarters as a gesture of goodwill. However, after the violent confrontations in Mongkok, many protesters regarded the occupied roads as non-negotiable. They argued that the formal leaders, who had not 'shed their blood', lacked the legitimacy to force them to leave.

The growing mistrust between the leaders and the masses eventually led to a split within the leadership. A significant moment leading to this was the televised dialogue between the HKFS and the Hong Kong government on October 21, arranged through the connections of the veteran democrats. The student leaders agreed to participate because they viewed the dialogue as a potential breakthrough. Watching the live broadcast, protesters in the camps applauded the performances of student leaders. Interpreting the enthusiastic response as a sign of victory, the student leaders returned to their Admiralty base and delivered passionate speeches condemning the government, urging protesters to persist in the occupation. This decision infuriated some of the veteran democrats. As an academic who played a role in brokering the dialogue said: 'Before the dialogue, there was a tacit agreement with the government that we would not escalate the situation, even though it was clear that we would not completely accept the government's proposal. The plan was to show the sincerity to negotiate. The student leaders have burned all the bridges.' (Interview B22) The student leaders, however, did not view the 'tacit agreement' as a binding promise. They considered the protesters on the ground as their constituents and were not willing to withdraw without significant concessions from the government. By this point, divisions within the leadership team became apparent. OCLP leaders eventually decided to step down from their positions in late October after attempting to organize a referendum among protesters.

However, the diminishing influence of OCLP did not improve the situation for the student leaders. Despite their dominant role in the leadership, they still needed to persuade the veteran democrats, who held most electoral seats within the institutionalized opposition, to support their plan for a LegCo by-election. They believed that if the democrats won the de facto referendum, it would exert pressure on the government to make concessions. Naturally, the plan collapsed given the lack of trust between the young activists and veteran democrats. Elected democrats viewed it as a risky move that could jeopardize their veto power in the legislature if they lost the by-election. They would only consider supporting the plan if the student leaders promised to end the occupation in return. Other strategic efforts by the student leaders also proved unsuccessful. Their attempts to invite government officials for a second dialogue were fruitless. They even wrote a letter to China's then Premier Li Keqiang in the hope of meeting him. This was a move reminiscent of the meeting between student leaders and Chinese leaders during the Tiananmen Movement. But before they could meet the Chinese leader, the student leaders were told that their travel permits had been revoked when they tried to board a flight to Beijing.

By early November, the Umbrella Movement had entered a phase of 'tactical freeze' (Tufekci 2017). While tents and makeshift booths still occupied the protest camps, many were abandoned as the weather grew chillier. The number of protesters at the camps dwindled, and confusion reigned regarding the next steps to take. The stalemate frustrated the radical faction, who increasingly blamed the student leaders for being too moderate and indecisive. Hoping to break the deadlock, some protesters began considering escalation as an option. On November 18, netizens spread a rumour that LegCo would be debating an Internet copyright law and called for a protest around the LegCo building that night. The proposed law had raised concerns among pro-democracy supporters as it could restrict online freedom of expression. The rumour, though proven to be a false alarm, generated thousands of responses online, with many expressing support for the action.

The radical faction seized on this opportunity to escalate the movement. On that night, masked black-bloc protesters gathered in front of LegCo. Some attempted to make an announcement on the main stage to invite other protesters to join, but they were stopped by the picket team, as the leaders did not want such radicalization. Undeterred, the masked protesters proceeded to break the front glass door of LegCo using metal rods and barricades. The police quickly arrived at the scene and arrested those attempting to break in. The radical protesters blamed the leaders for their inaction and criticized the picket team for preventing them from announcing their plans on stage. In the following days, hundreds of radical protesters continued to protest in front of the main stage, aiming to dismantle it. They emphasized the importance of adhering to the ethos of 'No Leaders, Only the Masses' and demanded further escalation.

The stalemate provided an opportunity for the government to undermine the movement through attrition (Yuen and Cheng 2017), without resorting to direct repression. The government mobilized business elites to file a series of civil court injunctions ordering the clearance of the occupied sites. However, the student leaders and veteran democrats became divided on whether to defy the court order, since the latter saw it as important to follow the principle of civil disobedience. This set the stage for the eviction of the Mongkok camp on November 25. For the radical protesters, this eviction once again highlighted the perceived incompetence of the student leaders. Pressured by the radical faction, the student leaders saw escalation as the only way to maintain their legitimacy, if any was still left. As Alex Chow, the Secretary General of HKFS, (*InmediaHK*, 3 September 2015) recalled, 'we had no more cards to play' when 'protesters had become increasingly anxious and there was no room for further dialogue (with the government)'.

On November 29, HKFS and Scholarism jointly called on the protesters to surround the Chief Executive Office the following night in a last-ditch effort to escalate the movement. The action, however, turned out to be a complete disaster. There were no concrete strategies other than surrounding the building, which was already heavily guarded by the police. When protesters gathered in front of the Chief Executive Office, the student leaders provided no instructions. As radical protesters attempted to break through the police lines, armed police intervened and dispersed them with batons and pepper spray. Many protesters were injured and at least forty were arrested by midnight. Student leader Alex Chow later explained that the action was launched not only to appease the radical faction, but also to demonstrate to them that further escalation at this late stage would be futile: 'We needed an 'action finale.' We need to let those who want to escalate see that escalation will not achieve its effect.' (*Cable TV*, 22 December 2014) However, radicals interpreted his statement as an indication that the escalation was merely a convenient stunt to shift blame.

BRINGING UMBRELLAS INDOOR

The failure of the planned escalation had a detrimental impact. The next day, angry protesters dismantled all barricades surrounding the main stage in Admiralty. This symbolized the complete disintegration of the movement.

In the hope of reigniting protest momentum, Joshua Wong and several other Scholarism activists embarked on a hunger strike, hoping to pressure the government into another dialogue. However, the effort had little impact. Taking note of the successful clearance of the Mongkok camp through a court injunction, the HKSAR government replicated the strategy for the remaining two protest camps. Ultimately, the Admiralty and Causeway Bay camps were evicted on December 11 and 15 respectively, with minimal resistance.

As a fragmented mobilization from the very start, the Umbrella Movement deepened internal divisions within the pro-democracy camp. Radical protesters were frustrated with the ineffective leadership of the student organizations. They were particularly offended by Alex Chow's remarks, which seemed to suggest that the November 30 escalation was intentionally poorly planned to demonstrate its ineffectiveness. For the radicals, the failure of the Umbrella Movement served as an indication that a more militant approach was necessary to rejuvenate the stagnant pro-democracy movement. In the following months, students in various public universities held referendums to withdraw their student unions from the HKFS. Four university student unions, including the University of Hong Kong, a founding member of the HKFS, voted to sever their ties. This withdrawal symbolized a significant moment, since the HKFS, once one of the most established pro-democracy organizations in Hong Kong, was dismissed by its very own constituents.

The Umbrella Movement also prompted Beijing to intensify its state-building efforts. Labelling the movement as a 'colour revolution' aimed at overthrowing the government, Beijing adopted a hard line stance and further tightened its control (*Wenweipo*, 13 October 2014). It focused on bolstering pro-Beijing grassroots organizations, such as hometown associations and community group, to counteract pro-democracy forces. Through formal political institutions such as the NPC and the CPPCC, Beijing incentivized local elites to establish and operate more grassroots organizations that could be mobilized against pro-democracy protests (Yuen 2023).

Beijing also began to exclude pro-democracy legislators and activists from local political institutions. These efforts became particularly pronounced after the democratic opposition rejected the government's electoral reform package in June 2015. The first sign of the change was the Hong Kong government's decision to ban six potential localist candidates from running in the 2016 LegCo election, the first such disqualifications since the handover. Following the LegCo election, an additional six members-elect, including both pro-democracy and localist figures, were disqualified for protesting during the oath-taking ceremony. While protesting during oath-taking had been a common practice since the early post-handover years, it was the first time democratically elected politicians faced disqualification. The expansion of repressive measures to include veteran pro-democracy figures, rather than just the localists, demonstrated Beijing's intent to reshape political institutions by excluding

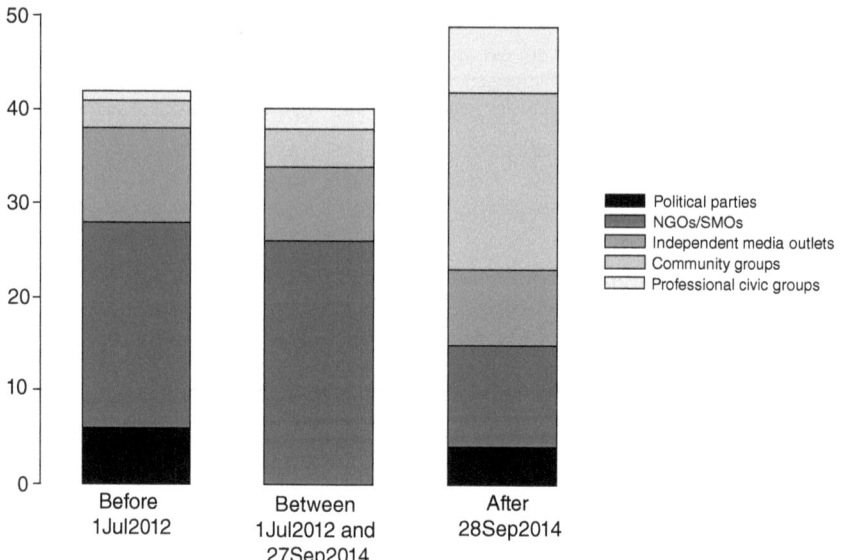

FIGURE 4.3 Establishment of major pro-democracy political groups.
Source: Data compiled by authors.

critical voices, irrespective of their tactical approaches. This indicated that moderate democrats were no longer seen as potential allies for co-optation by Beijing but became targets of exclusion and repression. In March 2017, the OCLP trio and six other pro-democracy activists were arrested and charged with 'conspiracy to commit public nuisance' (Kong 2019). Two years later, shortly before the emergence of the Anti-Extradition Movement, all of them, except for one student activist, were sentenced to prison. By this point, the institutionalized opposition had reached its lowest ebb.

In hindsight, due to its failure to achieve its goals, the Umbrella Movement significantly altered the trajectory of the pro-democracy movement. It spawned the 'Umbrella Generation', a politically engaged group of young people who developed a new political consciousness (Ku 2019; Mok 2020). The movement also transformed the organizational infrastructure of the pro-democracy movement, leading to the emergence of numerous opposition groups. Figure 4.3 illustrates the number and types of pro-democracy political groups established in three periods: before the 2012 Anti-MNE Movement; between the Anti-MNE Movement and the 2014 Umbrella Movement; and after the Umbrella Movement, until the end of 2017. The figure demonstrates that nearly fifty new political groups emerged after the Umbrella Movement.

Among these newly established groups were youth-led political parties such as Youngspiration, Hong Kong Indigenous, and Demosisto. Youngspiration and Hong Kong Indigenous, both founded in 2015 by young localists advocating Hong Kong's right to self-determination, actively organized anti-migrants and anti-parallel trading protests after the Umbrella Movement. Demosisto, launched in 2016 by former Scholarism and HKFS activists, pursued a similar but more moderate agenda, aligning with the neo-democrats. These youth parties sought to participate in elections while maintaining a more horizontal organizational structure and a stronger online presence, setting themselves apart from traditional pro-democracy parties. They aimed to be part of the political system while maintaining their protest group identity, recognizing that electoral legitimacy was crucial for supporting mass mobilizations.

In addition, numerous civil society groups with pro-democracy leanings emerged. Some of these groups represented a broad array of professional sectors, including lawyers, medical practitioners, architects, teachers, accountants, psychologists, cooks, IT workers, and cultural workers. One of the most notable was the Progressive Lawyers' Group (PLG), established in January 2015. Vowed to defend Hong Kong's rule of law, democracy, human rights, and freedoms, the PLG regularly commented on public affairs from a legal perspective and frequently organized talks, seminars, and even protests.

Others established themselves in various neighbourhoods. Unlike previous neighbourhood movements focusing mainly on urban redevelopment, these new community groups advocated for a bottom-up approach to involve residents in the pro-democracy movement. While these groups aimed to distance themselves from traditional clientelist practices of political parties, many kept a focus on local elections. This was especially true for groups formed under the district council initiative during the Umbrella Movement. These groups selected various geographical areas across the city as their bases. Core members typically consisted of movement participants who lived in the area and were political amateurs (*zhengzhi suren; zing-zi-sou-jan*) who had little experience or affiliation with existing political groups. Securing a seat in local representative bodies would give these political newcomers influence over district issues, such as infrastructural projects and budgetary matters, effectively challenging the pro-Beijing camp's dominance. It would also provide the financial resources needed for renting office space, hiring assistants, and supporting their community work. This was particularly crucial for community groups advocating localism. While these groups supported democracy, they differed from veteran democrats because they advocated more radical and less accommodative strategies to promote democratization. As these localists were not part of the mainstream pro-democracy camp, they needed a stronger presence in territorial communities to promote their unconventional political ideals.

There were also community groups that did not focus on elections but chose to promote democratic ideals through a localized and bottom-up approach. A prime example was Fixing Hong Kong, which emerged during the Umbrella Movement, founded by a diverse group of protesters, including students, white-collar workers, social workers, carpenters, and odd-job workers. Aware of criticism from working class citizens who viewed the occupation as a severe disruption, the group chose the low-income neighbourhood of To Kwa Wan as its base. Here, they began their work repairing furniture and appliances for residents who could not afford these services. This was the origin of its name, Fixing Hong Kong, which reflects its ultimate goal to fix the city's illiberal political system. Every week, volunteers worked in teams to visit residents' homes. Some would repair household items, while others would initiate conversations to build rapport. Once trust was forged, they would venture into discussing politics with their 'clients'. The primary aim was to convert these residents into pro-democracy supporters, or at least politically conscious individuals interested in current affairs. Although these efforts were not always successful, they often led to new relationships and the expansion of the group's network.

As subsequent chapters will illustrate, these civil society groups and networks played an essential role in expanding the pro-democracy movement's support base. Despite divisions in the aftermath of the Umbrella Movement, their increasing alignment in threat perception would gradually unify them.

Finally, the Umbrella Movement significantly impacted the tactical inclinations of pro-democracy citizens. Organized protests that were peaceful and nonviolent were no longer perceived as effective means of addressing the escalating systemic and repressive threats. In contrast, militant and leaderless protests became increasingly preferred as new tactics. After the Umbrella Movement, there were fewer large-scale protests, but those that occurred often adopted a more militant approach. A notable episode was the 'Fishball Revolution', which erupted on the first day of Lunar New Year in 2016. The unrest began after the government cracked down on unlicensed street hawkers, whom many localists viewed as symbols of the city's food culture. Hong Kong Indigenous, the young localist party, led a spontaneous and poorly coordinated protest in support of the hawkers, which quickly escalated into a violent clash with the police. Numerous localist leaders were arrested in the aftermath of the unrest. Veteran democrats, however, chose to maintain their distance. Some even issued statements criticizing the protesters' use of violence (*BBC*, 9 February 2016), an act that indicated the high level of fractionalization within the opposition.

CONCLUSION

This chapter has examined the emergence, dynamics, and consequences of the Umbrella Movement. We demonstrate the significant role played by repression in sparking a spontaneous movement, transforming the OCLP from a scripted campaign into the open-ended but fragmented mobilization. We elucidate how this spontaneous origin resulted in a hybrid organizational structure, characterized by a formal leadership coalition comprising various political organizations, and self-mobilized protesters who formed informal groups within the protest camps. While this structure sustained the occupation, divergent views towards repressive threats gradually divided the protesters and the formal leaders, leading to rifts within the leadership itself, specifically between moderate leaders seeking to scale back the occupation and student leaders aligning with the militants. Consequently, an anti-leadership sentiment emerged, constraining the authority of the student leaders and leading to the movement's fragmentation. Finally, we have delved into the consequences of the Umbrella Movement, emphasizing its impact on Beijing's policy towards Hong Kong and the fragmentation of the pro-democracy movement.

Our findings underscore the tensions and incompatibilities between a spontaneous protester base and a formal leadership that preferred adhering to plans. While the formal leaders aimed to shape the movement according to their own visions, the self-mobilized protesters saw themselves as active participants rather than mere followers. They actively exercised their agency through self-organized initiatives and militant actions to defend the protest camps from intrusions – all of which undermined the authority of the formal leaders. Moreover, diverging perceptions over the threat of repression widened the gap between the leaders and the protesters. To gain their authority, the student leaders had to align with the radical protesters and persist with the occupation, even in the face of protester fatigue and waning popular support. Ultimately, this led to a split within the formal leadership.

The Umbrella Movement marked the triumph of the anti-leadership ethos and the ascendance of the masses. This ethos quickly became a guiding principle for many pro-democracy supporters, particularly those with localist inclinations. Organized protests led by formal leaders were no longer seen as effective in advancing the pro-democracy agenda and countering the growing perceived threats. As the democratic opposition became increasingly fragmented, so did the mass mobilizations that accompanied.

5

Synchronizing Threats

On 15 December 2014, as authorities were clearing the final holdout of the Umbrella Movement, a large banner unfurled, displaying two slogans. One of them read 'It's just the beginning' and the other proclaimed 'We'll be back'. These slogans embodied protesters' determination to promote their pro-democracy cause. While both slogans may have appeared overly optimistic at the time, the events of 2019 Anti-Extradition Movement proved their foresight. Despite the regime's concerted efforts to extend its influence at the grassroots level and to penalize opposition activists after the Umbrella Movement, an unexpectedly vast number of people mobilized on 9 June 2019 to protest against the proposed amendments to the semi-autonomous city's extradition laws. This million-strong rally marked the onset of a long summer of protests, defying initial expectations that scant resistance would be met. How did the Anti-Extradition Movement erupt despite the lack of political opportunities on its eve? How did it evolve into a leaderful mobilization?

This chapter examines the origins and early dynamics of the Anti-Extradition Movement, focusing on why and how mass protests erupted within an unfavourable political context. We argue that the perception of the extradition bill as an existential threat galvanized the pro-democracy opposition and its networks. These networks, although increasingly marginalized over the years, became more unified in their objectives in response to heightened state repression and emerged from abeyance when the extradition bill was introduced. However, such a perception did not form immediately. When the government initially proposed the extradition bill in February 2019, few among the general public understood its far-reaching implications. The perception of the extradition bill as a threat to citizens' freedom and autonomy came into being only because it was being discursively constructed, partly by building on their long-standing apprehensions. As this perception was taking shape, numerous pre-existing and latent civil society networks were mobilized to oppose the extradition bill, alongside pro-democracy political parties and organizations. This set the stage for the June rallies, which witnessed a scale that exceeded the wildest imagination.

This chapter elucidates the role of civil society networks, pro-democracy organizations, and threat framing in catalysing the Anti-Extradition Movement and shaping its leaderful structure. First, we demonstrate how a diverse array of civil society networks, including professional, religious, recreational, and community groups, which entered a state of abeyance following the Umbrella Movement, emerged as 'early risers' of mobilization in conjunction with established activist organizations. Second, we explain how the democratic opposition, in collaboration with various civil society groups, leveraged the pre-mobilization period from February to June 2019 to attribute the extradition bill as a threat to their core values, norms, and identities. Drawing upon interviews, online observational data and surveys conducted during the protests, we illustrate how an online petition campaign played a pivotal role in framing the threat posed by the extradition bill and creating a strong collective identity, enabling the broader public to see a shared responsibility to act.

DEMOCRATIC BACKSLIDING AND ITS REPERCUSSIONS

In the years leading up to 2019, democratic activism in Hong Kong faced a shrinking space amidst an increasingly repressive political environment. Following the Umbrella Movement, the opposition found itself deeply fragmented. At the same time, under the administration of career civil servant and Chief Executive Carrie Lam, the Hong Kong government attempted to restore its performance legitimacy, achieving some success as evidenced by improved ratings (HKUPOP 2019c). Meanwhile, the Chinese party-state rapidly expanded its influence over the city. The CGLO, the party's branch in the city, took on a more conspicuous and expansive role in directing governance and broadening the state's influence (Lee 2020). This new strategy entailed the gradual increase of pro-regime social organizations and their intensifying interactions with the Hong Kong government (Yuen and Cheng 2020). The objective of this shift was to extend beyond simply securing the business elite's allegiance to Beijing and to actively engage in counter-mobilization against the pro-democracy movement.

For the institutionalized opposition, this period marked a decline in both political opportunities and organizational resources. Although the opposition as a whole won more seats in the 2016 LegCo elections compared to previous elections, the government seized an opportunity to disqualify six elected legislators based on their improper oaths of office. Notably, these disqualified legislators spanned the entire political spectrum, from moderates to radicals. In addition to these disqualifications, several prominent activists, including Benny Tai, Chan Kin-man, and Joshua Wong, were sentenced to prison for their leadership roles in protest movements. Simultaneously, the opposition

TABLE 5.1 *Regime repertoire targeted at the democratic opposition, 2014–2019.*

	Veteran democrats	Neo-democrats	Localists
Political platform	Universal suffrage	Self-determination or political autonomy	Pro-independence
Major parties	Democratic Party, Labor Party, ADLP	Demosisto, Land Justice League, LSD, Civic Party	Youngspiration, Hong Kong Indigenous, People's Power
Regime repertoire	No candidates banned from running in elections. Only one elected LegCo member disqualified. A few protest leaders prosecuted	All candidates banned from running in elections. All but one elected LegCo member disqualified; Majority of the protest leaders prosecuted and imprisoned	All candidates banned from running in elections. All elected LegCo members disqualified. All protest leaders prosecuted and imprisoned

Source: Compiled and synthesized by the authors.

struggled to rally public support against various controversial policies, such as the enforcement of mainland Chinese law within a section of a new high-speed rail station and the introduction of a massive HKD500 billion land reclamation project (Ng 2020). The CHRF, the umbrella platform for the pro-democracy movement, organized multiple rallies, all of which saw poor attendance. The group's financial reserves, typically sourced from citizen donations, dwindled to a mere HKD200,000, barely sufficient to cover the logistical requirements for organizing a large-scale rally (Interviews A16).

These developments illustrated how the liberal oligarchy appeared to have effectively subdued the opposition. Table 5.1 provides an overview of the regime's responses to the opposition in the post-Umbrella period. It highlights the extension of repressive actions to include the arresting of protest leaders, the banning of political parties, the disqualification of elected legislators, and efforts to undermine the opposition both within the legislature and on the streets. Although the localists were the primary targets of repression, veteran democrats also suffered indirectly from these measures. The broadening scope of repression suggests that the party-state was increasingly concerned not only about the radical factions but also the overall capacity of the pro-democracy camp to challenge the political order (Cheng 2020). While this increasingly indiscriminate repression led political actors to second-guess the state's intentions and engage in self-censorship, it also produced unintended consequences. As localists, neo-democrats, and veteran democrats all faced growing repressive threats, the once fragmented opposition found itself pushed closer together (Lee 2020).

Another unintended consequence of state repression was movement abeyance. Movement abeyance is 'a holding process by which movements sustain themselves in non-receptive political environments and provide continuity from one stage of mobilization to another' (Taylor 1989: 761). During abeyance, pockets of movement activity may continue to exist by forming abeyance structures, which serve as starting points of a new cycle of the same or a new movement later on. These structures allow a core group of activists to maintain their identity and ideals by developing distinct repertoires that are different from those during mobilization. In the context of undifferentiated repression in Hong Kong, movement abeyance played an important role in strengthening solidarity among pro-democracy activists and supporters. The post-Umbrella period witnessed the emergence of grassroots campaigns, industry-specific initiatives, and digital activism (Lee and Chan 2018), resulting in the formation of at least 100 new grassroots communities, trade unions, and professional groups, as detailed in Chapter 4.

These abeyance networks emphasized the reintegration of politics into everyday life and the importance of networking at the grassroots level (Pang 2020; Yuen and Mok 2023). The post-Umbrella groups developed a loose 'network of networks' through grassroots engagement and digital communication (Castells 2012). They often operated informally, lacking hierarchical structures and official memberships. Trust was built on personal, social, or professional connections, and actions were frequently coordinated through WhatsApp groups or Facebook pages (Interviews B11 and B22). These characteristics allowed them to navigate between advocacy and mobilization in a more repressive environment. Although these civil society networks alone cannot explain the unprecedented mobilization in the Anti-Extradition Movement, they played a crucial role in preserving a loose sense of collective identity among pro-democracy supporters, particularly at a time when traditional organizations became weakened and institutional channels contracted (Snow 2001).

THE EARLY RISERS

Just as opportunities need to be recognized before they can be leveraged for mobilizing collective actions, threats too must be perceived before they can be harnessed. In the initial months following the introduction of the extradition bill, formal organizations – despite their declining influence within political institutions and among pro-democracy supporters – remained the 'early risers' in framing the issue and organizing early protest actions (Clarke and Kocak 2020; Minkoff 1997; Tarrow 1989: 143–176).

The distant origins of the Anti-Extradition Movement can be traced back to a tragic incident that occurred in Taiwan in February 2018, when a young Hong Kong woman named Poon Hiu-wing was murdered by her boyfriend, Chan Tong-kai. Before being identified as a suspect by the police, Chan returned to Hong Kong and confessed to the local authorities. However, due to the lack of an extradition treaty between Hong Kong and Taiwan, Chan could not be extradited to Taiwan to face trial. In response, in February 2019, the HKSAR government proposed the establishment of a formal extradition mechanism that would allow for the transfer of fugitives to Taiwan. This proposed amendment, however, sparked controversy because it would also permit the extradition of fugitives to Macau and mainland China, with whom Hong Kong had no extradition agreements at the time.

The official justification for the proposed measure was to 'close legal loopholes' and prevent Hong Kong from becoming a 'haven for criminals' (LegCo 2019). Initially, the bill failed to garner significant public attention. For most citizens, the prospect of being subjected to extradition seemed a distant concern, as they were unlikely to commit crimes that would trigger extradition to other jurisdictions. Consequently, despite some opposition, the extradition bill was expected to pass in a manner similar to the controversial co-location arrangement approved a year earlier.[1] However, persistent opposition efforts led by lawmakers and civil society groups in April and May began to draw greater public scrutiny to the political and economic ramifications of the amendment. Intense filibustering in the LegCo in May heightened public awareness and concern. Citizens grew increasingly apprehensive that the amended law could be misused to target political dissidents for extradition from the semi-autonomous region, thereby blurring the legal boundary between Hong Kong and mainland China.

The introduction of the extradition bill also raised concerns among pro-government elites. Many local political elites, who had built their careers and proven their worth by leveraging the city's relative autonomy, were worried. Business elites, who operated transnational companies with dealings and legal interests spanning the border and subject to two distinct legal systems, were similarly apprehensive about the potential uncertainties introduced by the bill. Initially, a significant number of pro-government legislators backed the bill. However, as opposition gathered strength, divisions within their ranks emerged. In April 2019, a few pro-government business leaders openly expressed concerns about the bill. For example, media mogul Charles Ho remarked that he only truly appreciated the essence of freedom when he returned to Hong Kong from the mainland (*HK01*, 26 March 2019). Real estate tycoon Joseph Lau took a more assertive stance by initiating a judicial review to challenge the government's proposal (*South China Morning Post*, 1 April 2019). Despite these undercurrents of dissent, pro-government elites

---

[1] The co-location arrangement refers to an agreement between the HKSAR and mainland China that allows passengers to go through immigration and customs procedures for both Hong Kong and mainland China in a single location. This arrangement is associated with the Hong Kong section of a high-speed rail system that connects Hong Kong to several cities in mainland China. While the arrangement raised concerns among citizens who saw it as a compromise of city's autonomy, it was approved by the LegCo in June 2018.

continued to support the bill, particularly after being summoned by Beijing officials in May 2019. These fissures within the elite community, although present, remained largely hidden from the public eye.

Despite their diminishing influence, the opposition – particularly the neo-democrats – spearheaded the initial reactions. Immediately after the government's proposed amendment on 13 February 2019, pro-democracy political parties quickly voiced their concerns. Demosisto issued a strongly worded statement on February 17, unequivocally demanding the government to 'retract the changes'. Civil society groups and networks rallied behind the cause. For instance, in early March, nineteen professional networks, including the PLG, Médecins Inspirés and Frontline Tech Workers Concern Group, issued a statement urging the government to exclude Macau and mainland China from the amendment. The Hong Kong Bar Association (2019) issued a detailed twenty-two-page response and proposed an alternative resolution for the legal quagmire. Bolstered by these civil society and professional networks, the opposition took to the streets. On March 10, a small cohort of democrats, including legislators and leaders from the CHRF, held a demonstration outside the CGLO. On March 15, Demosisto organized a sit-in at the Admiralty government headquarters to protest against the bill's first reading. Although both protests attracted no more than a few dozen participants, they succeeded in capturing public attention and generating momentum for further actions. The CHRF organized two additional rallies on March 31 and April 28, claiming turnouts of 12,000 and 130,000 respectively. While these gatherings were not as large as some of Hong Kong's previous protests, they nonetheless stood out as some of the most impactful street mobilizations in the post-Umbrella Movement period.

As public support mounted, pro-democracy legislators gained confidence and began filibustering in the LegCo to stall the bill. The increasing public backlash, coupled with robust institutional pushback, prompted the government to revise the bill. These revisions aimed to appease concerns by narrowing the range of offences eligible for extradition to only the most serious ones, confining extradition requests to top authorities in mainland China, and improving the protections for human rights of the accused. Nevertheless, the changes failed to assuage public scepticism. Moreover, in an attempt to circumvent further challenges, the government also fast-tracked the bill for a second reading on June 12.

Perhaps the most crucial role played by leading activists was the crafting of the collective action frame 'no extradition to China' (*fansongzhong; faan-sung-zung*). This slogan resonated deeply due to its dual implications: in Cantonese, it was homonymous with both anti-extradition and anti-death. The latter meaning cast the extradition bill as an existential danger, representing it as a mortal threat to Hong Kong's rule of law, civil liberties, and its high degree of autonomy. While the exact origin of this slogan is unknown, it became prominent through the collective efforts of the pre-existing SMOs.

Opposition parties such as Demosisto and the LSD championed it, and it featured prominently on the front cover of *Apple Daily* during the April protests. It was also circulated widely across social media, amplified by opinion leaders and professional groups, and was embraced by the CHRF for the massive June rallies and thereafter. In the days leading up to the anticipated rally on June 9, *Apple Daily* released a trilogy of short films titled 'Animal Farm', 'On the Chopping Board', and 'Imprisoned Night'. These films collectively amassed over 1.5 million views on YouTube (*Next Film*, June 5–7 2019). The concerted framing of the threat, together with the subsequent rallies, effectively heightened public awareness about the extradition bill.

The presence of political opportunities alone does not fully account for the rise and extent of the resistance against the extradition bill, but they certainly influenced its timing and dynamics. Opportunities for activism are typically limited or less apparent in authoritarian or hybrid regimes. Nonetheless, activists and movement organizations can often forge new opportunities by taking on the risky roles of 'early risers' or 'first movers' (Clarke and Kocak 2020; Pearlman 2018). In the context of Hong Kong, the CHRF, a long-standing democratic alliance, assumed this role. The CHRF held a heated internal debate in late May regarding whether to organize a mass rally immediately following the annual Tiananmen vigil on June 4, considering the escalating opposition to the extradition bill. With the bill's second reading scheduled for June 12, there were concerns among some opposition leaders about the possibility of mobilization fatigue and a potentially subdued turnout if they were to organize another action on such short notice. Ultimately, the discussion concluded in favour of Leung Kwok-hung, the founder of the LSD:

Those who come to the June 4 rally would surely join the anti-extradition bill rally, not the other way around. They are the stalwart pro-democracy supporters who would always come out at critical times. So, we must let the former snowball into the latter rally and facilitate the committed protesters to spread the message [to the wider public] (Interview A1).

Subsequent events proved Leung's foresight. Even after the June 4 candlelight vigil drew 180,000 participants, the June 9 rally still saw an impressive turnout of one million. Mobilization fatigue did not happen. This shows that the democratic opposition's organizational experience remained influential, despite its weakened leadership in the pro-democracy movement. Because of that, after the violent clashes on June 12, Jimmy Sham, convenor of CHRF, decided to schedule another rally on June 16, even though several political parties raised concerns over possibly lower turnout. Sham explained his logic:

Only the Civil Human Rights Front has the credibility and manpower to organize a large rally. The rally will still happen even if we don't make the call. But it will surely take another form, probably with more confrontations and fewer participants. We should recognize our role and then search for our position as the movement unfolds.

The [frontline] protesters' suffering was clear and their message loud after June 12. After all, no one can convince the government to postpone the bill. So, we can only move forward (Interview A2).

These events highlighted two key dynamics in the formative phase of the Anti-Extradition Movement. First, despite their contested leadership status within the pro-democracy movement, veteran democrats continued to wield influence by setting the early agenda and spearheading mobilization. Their organizational prowess and well established credibility remained crucial from the standpoint of resource mobilization. Leveraging their institutional roles and media networks, they effectively crafted a strong narrative for the protests. Moreover, they demonstrated the ability to cultivate new political opportunities, even in the apparent absence of structural openings. The remarkable protest turnouts in June were a testament to their political acumen. Second, civil society groups and networks worked in close collaboration, and occasionally in tandem, with the opposition to fortify the resistance to the extradition bill. These actors had nurtured their own bases and ties across various sectors during movement abeyance, which allowed them to rapidly spread information about the bill to a wide audience.

ONLINE PETITIONS

Alongside the mobilization pursued by opposition parties and civil society groups, a wave of online petitions arose in late May, further galvanizing opposition to the bill. Petitions are considered one of the most traditional forms of protest (Tilly 1986). Due to their often low-cost and routinized occurrence in the digital era, petitions usually do not make a significant impact in mobilizing or exerting pressure on the authorities. However, the anti-extradition online petitions stood out from the norm. They played a significant role in engaging the masses in the opposition efforts and creating a leaderful structure for subsequent mobilizations.

The petition campaign began with the city's secondary schools and universities. Alumni, students, and teachers from various schools drafted and signed tailored petitions, leveraging the symbols and moral tenets of their schools to express their disapproval of the bill. The first petition was initiated by the teachers and alumni of St. Stephen's College, the alma mater of the murder victim, on May 17. It implored the government not to exploit Poon's murder as a pretext to revise the extradition law. This petition sparked a chain reaction, with other secondary schools following suit, including those attended by high-ranking officials. The swell of opposition quickly spread to various professional sectors. Lawyers, bankers, accountants, journalists, doctors, nurses, and tech workers each initiated their own petitions. Moreover, parents, housewives, immigrants, churches, residential communities, and various hobby groups also joined the effort. By early June 2019, more than 400 petitions were actively circulating on various social media platforms. Remarkably, by June 8, just a day before the first million-strong protest, these petitions had garnered over 270,000 signatures, reflecting the depth of public sentiment against the bill.

Most of these petitions originated from secondary schools – often initiated by their alumni but also signed by current students. The rest came from a diverse array of sources, including tertiary institutions, primary schools, professional sectors, community organizations, religious groups, and overseas diaspora networks. On average, each petition had around 560 signatures. Notably, most of the individuals initiating these petitions did not hold any leadership positions within political parties or activist organizations. Instead, they were predominantly ordinary citizens who relied on social media platforms and their personal networks to rally like-minded individuals and groups.

To enhance the credibility of these petitions, signatories often provided various personal details, such as their full names, years of graduation, professional titles, or places of residence, tailored to the context of the petition. For example, secondary school petitions organized signatories by their year of graduation, allowing signatories to identify classmates rallying for the same cause. Additionally, these personal details also contributed to a sense of authenticity and collective identity within their respective social groups.

Collective identity is a shared and interactive sense of 'we-ness' and agency that serves as a driving force behind collective actions (Melucci 1989). By explaining why collective actors become 'collective' in the first place, this concept emerged as a response to the dominant resource mobilization and political process models, which primarily focus on the structural factors facilitating mobilization. Although collective identity is often perceived as being constructed by SMOs or as arising from pre-existing social networks (Snow and McAdam 2000; Snow 2001; Tarrow 2022), the online petition campaign revealed a more bottom-up, decentralized process, through which collective identity was shaped through the lateral mobilization of intermediate 'social identities'. These social identities drew upon existing social connections and affiliations to foster commitment across diverse groups of individuals. In contrast to the encompassing nature of collective identity, social identities are 'grounded typically in established social roles […] or in broader and more inclusive social categories' (Snow and Corrigall Brown 2015: 174). They constitute a 'part of an individual's self-concept which derives from knowledge of membership in a social group (or groups) together with the value or emotional significance attached to that membership' (Tajfel 1978: 63). Therefore, unlike collective identity which operates at the group level, social identity is an individual characteristic (Klandermans 2014: 3). An individual can have multiple social identities concurrently, such as being a doctor, a parent, a Christian, an alumnus, and a community member. These social identities – which are 'closer' to individuals – provided the perspectives through which citizens perceived threats.

The text of the petitions vividly demonstrate how collective identity is shaped through various social identities. Despite sharing similar formats and dissemination networks, the petitions displayed remarkable originality in their content, tone, and phrasing. Each petition began with a political statement carefully composed by its initiators to resonate with their target audience. For instance, one person who authored a statement for her school recalled that 'drafted it quickly during a boat ride...using [her] experience as a policy researcher'. But she intentionally avoided borrowing from other statements because she wanted to create an original one that 'reflects the character of my school' (Interview C3). In another case, the authors of a petition consciously chose a more professional and neutral tone to connect with their audience, mainly composed of middle class professionals (Interview C4). They selectively highlighted a particular element of the bill – the possible seizure of private property – to garner support from fellow graduates, many of whom were middle class professionals. The petition initiated by information technology workers even opened with a statement reminiscent of computer programming language: 'if (law.pass) die'. In contrast, the petition aimed at homemakers was penned entirely in colloquial Cantonese, forsaking formal Chinese and using straightforward, everyday language to ensure clarity and approachability.

In addition to providing background information on the extradition bill and explaining the rationale for opposition, many petitions went further to include a call to action, specifically informing signatories about the planned June 9 rally. Of the 478 petitions collected, a significant 62 per cent, or 295 of them, contained details about the scheduled protest, including the date and location. With these petitions circulating online, expectations for a substantial turnout at the June 9 demonstration grew. This is because when groups of individuals observed a growing consensus among their families, teachers, friends, or colleagues opposing the bill, they were more inclined to align themselves with the prevailing majoritarian view and felt compelled to take a stance on the issue. These petitions can thus be seen as creating a positive feedback mechanism (Biggs 2003), setting off a revolutionary bandwagon effect (Kuran 1991). This mechanism led individuals from diverse social networks to become cognitively engaged and relationally persuaded that a distant legal amendment aimed at criminals could jeopardize their shared values and interests (Seferiades and Johnston 2016). Additionally, it also triggered an information cascade, wherein previously hidden information about the bill and the absence of checks and balances in formal institutions became widely disseminated (Lohmann 1994; Mekouar 2014). Ordinary citizens increasingly recognized the imperative of collective action as both generalized and particularized threats became contingent in this defining moment.

The significance of the petitions was further underscored by data from surveys conducted at the protest sites. Between June 16 and July 14, the surveys consistently found that over 70 per cent of respondents had signed the petitions. Figure 5.1 illustrates that consistently more than 40 per cent of respondents decided to participate in the protests during the online petition phase in late May, compared to other critical entry points into the movement. While other factors, such as the filibuster drama in the legislature and extensive media

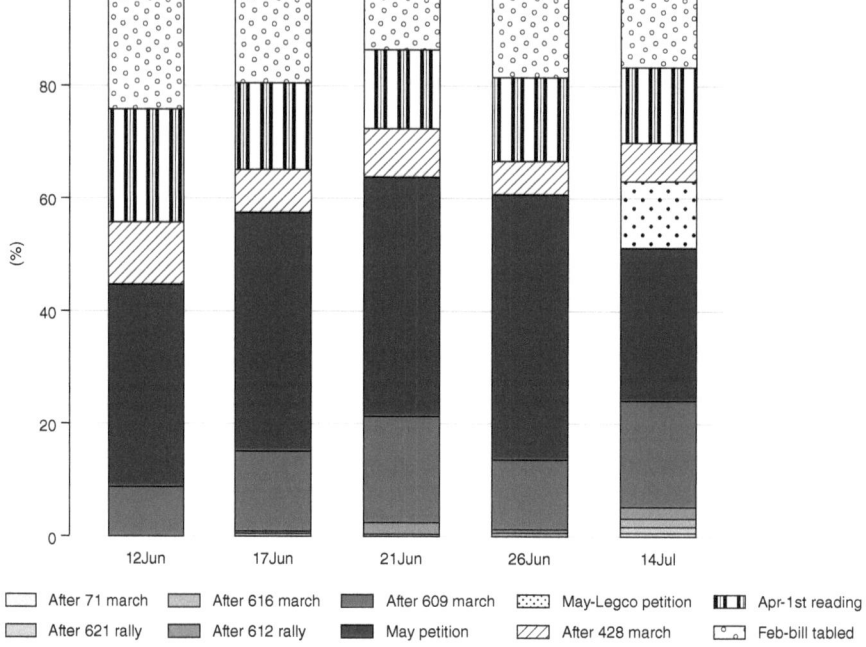

FIGURE 5.1 Time points when protesters decide to join the Anti-Extradition Movement, 2019.
Source: Authors' onsite surveys.

coverage of the extradition bill, also played crucial roles, the petition campaign made a substantial contribution by showcasing the extent of opposition and galvanizing various informal networks.

FRAMING EXTRADITION

In addition to making the extent of resistance visible, the online petition campaign also played a crucial role in framing the extradition bill as an existential threat from the perspective of various social identities. These identities, as manifested in the unique styles of the petitions, provided discursive resources for citizens to perceive the threat, acquire a sense of 'we-ness', and recognize the urgency to act (Gamson 1992). To illustrate how this occurred, it is useful to examine these petitions from a framing perspective. Frames are essential meaning-making devices to 'mobilize potential adherents and constituents, to garner bystander support, and to demobilize antagonists' (Snow and Benford 1988: 198). We analyse a subset of these petitions based on Snow and Benford's classification of three types of collective action frames: diagnostic, motivational, and prognostic.

Diagnostic Framing

Diagnostic framing serves to establish a common perception of a problem and to pinpoint accountability, thus providing potential participants with a cognitive basis for engaging in collective action. The most prevalent diagnostic frame in the petitions focused on the threat posed by the extradition bill to civil liberties and personal security. Some petitions succinctly referred to the bill as the 'send-to-China law', insinuating that it could lead to the transfer of Hong Kong citizens to the mainland.

In particular, professional sectors such as law, medicine, nursing, social work, and education tended to emphasize how the bill contradicted their commitment to preserving and practising their core principles. They held the Hong Kong government responsible for violating procedural justice and public consultation practices by bypassing the LegCo bill committee and refusing to withdraw the bill despite serious concerns expressed by the Hong Kong Bar Association and Hong Kong Law Society. Meanwhile, the arts, culture and journalism sectors highlighted the dependence of creativity, freedom of expression, and independent reporting on the presence of a firewall between the systems of Hong Kong and mainland China.

Other professional sectors, including accounting, information technology, architecture, surveying, and the environment, which have extensive interactions with the mainland, highlighted the economic repercussions of the bill. They expressed concerns that the comparative advantages and economic interests of Hong Kong would be compromised if their professions could no longer uphold internationally recognized principles, rules, and standards that were considered more rigorous than those on the mainland. Similarly, the religious sector expressed a profound distrust of the mainland's law enforcement system. They feared that the bill would bring Hong Kong's legal system closer to the mainland's socialist system, threatening their connections with underground churches there. Here are excerpts of some of these petitions:

[The bill] would expose the practitioners to legal risks, which will tarnish Hong Kong's image as an international financial centre and will bring about economic losses. (Finance sector)

From an economic perspective, if the bill is passed, there will be a new wave of mass emigration and divestment. The catering industry will certainly be affected, and the grassroots workers will of course suffer first. (Catering services sector)

Hong Kong people generally lack confidence in the mainland's law enforcement system. In the past, there were rumours that Hong Kong citizens were abducted back to the mainland. If the law passes, the risk of people being extradited will increase tremendously. (Legal sector)

In contrast, petitions originating from secondary schools, universities, and religious organizations placed greater emphasis on the threat to human rights, moral values, and civil liberties. These statements not only referred to the abstract values and principles that these groups cherished but also drew connections to their practical concerns:

At the hall on the first floor of our school hangs our school motto: 'When you know the truth, the truth will set you free.' Every year, when new students arrive, our principal always explains the meaning of these words and reminds us to remember them by heart. Hong Kong is now turning authoritarian. At this very moment, we especially need to defend truth and voice out for universal values such as human rights and freedom.' (High school A)

Can students be happy under this education system? Can teachers provide quality education under this restrictive environment? Can students develop their potential? If our next generation loses their freedom, can their lives still be fulfilling?' (High school B)

As Christians, we believe that God gives every government the duty to uphold peace, fairness, and freedom, such that the Church can obey God, serve Jesus Christ, and preach the gospel without hindrance...but given that the extradition lawld be applied retrospectively, Hong Kong church may infringe Mainland religious law without knowing it. (Church)

Motivational and Prognostic Framing

Motivational framing serves as the 'call to arms' to encourage potential participants to engage in collective action (Snow and Benford 1988). It involves making appeals that resonate with the emotional states and the cultural backgrounds of the targeted populations. In our case, motivational framing was particularly important for the petitions because their aim was not only to inform various social sectors about the bill but also to participate in the June 9 protest. Thus, petitions often appealed to symbols and collective memories to evoke a sense of belonging to the respective groups and to create a moral imperative to act. This was particularly the case for the petitions of secondary schools, which are a common experience for every citizen. For instance, the petition of a Christian girls' school and that of a Catholic boys' school wrote respectively:

We are in the midst of a raging storm. In the face of social injustice, we should scrupulously follow the motto of our alma mater: Brave, Gentle, Sincere. When it comes to being Good, we defer to no one and will actively voice out. (High School C)

[We] cherish freedom, human rights, critical thinking, and fraternity. The true spirit of fraternity is not about 'social harmony' on the surface; it means making decisions that can bring stability and justice to our society and the next generation. Some of our alumni have become key government officials. They should insist on what they have learnt in the alma mater and be the [people] that show commitment to our society. (High School D)

The petition initiated by a pro-Beijing school presented a unique example to demonstrate how motivation framing was employed to mobilize actions. In contrast to many other schools in Hong Kong that have religious affiliations, the school has a pro-Beijing background that could be dated back to its establishment in 1946. Given its background, one would expect that it would not openly oppose the extradition bill. Nevertheless, students from the school issued a critical statement:

Although our alma mater has long promoted the education of 'Love the Country, Love Hong Kong,' we understand that 'Love the Country' does not mean 'Love the [Communist] Party' and that 'Love Hong Kong' does not imply 'Love the ruler.' Students should follow our school motto to make China and Hong Kong better places with passion, honesty, truth-seeking and innovation. Let Hong Kong people enjoy freedom and democracy as well as preserve the legal system that we are proud of, so Hong Kong can become our cosy home where we can settle down. (High School E)

Apart from invoking a sense of belonging, the online petitions also sought to appeal to the cultural milieu of different social sectors by using specialized words or styles of writing. Apart from the IT workers' petition as mentioned earlier, another example was the petition started by a group of animation, comics, and games fans, which used a dramatic and imaginative style characteristic of these genres: 'Year 2020, the "send-to-China" extradition bill is implemented in Hong Kong. A "Dark Age" has arrived. Cartoonists are arrested, and people can only watch animation under surveillance.... Will this become the future? We need to stop it together'.

While petition authors could decide on the content, style, and tone of the statements, it is important not to neglect the bottom-up, participatory elements. The homemakers' petition, for instance, allowed signatories to leave messages regarding their feelings and attitudes towards the extradition bill, which would be updated on its Google Form page. Later are two examples of these comments:

Do not think that housewives don't care about worldly affairs and that you can do whatever you want. In critical moments, we will stand out to uphold justice.

Finally, there is a petition that fits who I am. I am already an old woman and may not have a long future, but how does the next generation continue? If this law passes, I will owe the younger generation a lot. I need to voice out when I still can and do as much as possible.

Finally, prognostic framing articulates a proposed solution to a problem. From this perspective, the main prognosis of the petitions was straightforward: the withdrawal of the extradition bill. During this phase of the movement, almost all of these petitions preferred institutional solutions that aligned with their diagnostic framing aiming to restore the accountability of the executive and legislative branches. Notably, none of these petitions called for radical changes to the political system. While they expressed concerns about Hong Kong's lack of democracy, their primary focus was on the withdrawal of the extradition bill, rather than electoral reforms or the removal of specific officials. The prognosis presented in these petitions was consistent and unified.

By drawing upon symbolic resources from various social identities, these movement frames engendered cognitive and moral imperatives to act collectively as group members. Our objective here is not merely to catalogue the participation of diverse social groups such as students, alumni, residents, professionals, churchgoers, or pet lovers in the early stages of mobilization.

Instead, our emphasis is on how these social identities served as an intermediary layer through which citizens became informed about the extradition bill. These intermediary identities anchored the rapid emergence of a collective identity at the onset of the Anti-Extradition Movement. Furthermore, their influence persisted beyond the early rallies. As Chapter 6 will show, social identities continued to significantly influence the trajectory of mobilization. Many protests were organized by distinct social groups specifically for their members, including those by mothers, lawyers, accountants, teachers, social workers, Christians, and secondary school students.

TAKING OVER THE STREETS

The online petition campaign foreshadowed the enormous scale of the June 9 protest. On that day, one million Hong Kong citizens took to the streets, participating in the rally organized by CHRF.[2] Many protesters adhered to the official dress code, wearing white as a symbol of mourning for their city's impending demise (Woneifei 2019; Figure 5.1). The march remained largely peaceful and orderly. Protesters held up posters with slogans, sang pro-democracy songs, picked up trash along the way, and made way for ambulances. The rally lasted for eight hours, concluding shortly before midnight. In response to the massive turnout, the Hong Kong government released a statement, saying it 'acknowledged and respected that people have different views on a wide range of issues'. However, it made no concessions and vowed to proceed with the second reading of the extradition bill on June 12 (Hong Kong Government 9 June 2019).

The government's unwavering response prompted some protesters to escalate their actions. On June 12, tens of thousands of protesters, mostly young activists and college students, gathered around the city's legislature and swiftly occupied the main road outside the building. As more protesters joined, riot police fired tear gas, rubber bullets, and bean bag rounds. Images of flames, smoke, and clashes were broadcast on live television and rapidly spread on social media. These violent clashes managed to stall the bill's second reading, but at the expense of altering the tradition of peaceful assembly. In a dramatic twist of events, the government announced the bill's 'suspension' on June 15– a layman term short of a formal withdrawal in legislative. Sources close to the government suggested that the concession had been planned after the first rally but was delayed due to the need to obtain endorsement from the central authorities (Interviews A12 and A13). A veteran democrat and an opinion leader recalled

---

[2] There are always significant differences between organizers and police estimates of the size of crowds. One alternative is to refer to a third-party assessment. The Public Opinion Programme at the University of Hong Kong estimated that 374,000 protesters participated in the 1 July 2019 rally, compared with the organizer's figure of 550,000 and the police's figure of 190,000. Here, we report organizer figures, as they were widely reported in the media and served as a catalyst for mobilization. In the subsequent sections, we will utilize various sources and data to substantiate the magnitude and intensity of the mobilization.

FIGURE 5.2 Mass rally on 16 June 2019.
Photo Credit: Eric Tsang.

that officials had reached out to them to explore if suspending the bill would be sufficient to call off the crowds (Interviews A23 and A24). Many protesters, however, viewed the concession as the result of the militant actions on June 12 (Lee et al. 2019). This public perception, whether accurate or not, significantly reshaped protest repertoires and the subsequent course of the movement.

The government's concession appeared to have little calming effect. Just hours after the announcement, a thirty-five-year-old man, named Marco Leung Ling-kit, tragically fell to his death while attempting to climb up a scaffolding structure and unfurling a banner scribbled with five political demands, including the complete withdrawal of the extradition bill. His death, widely perceived by protesters as a political suicide, heightened their commitment to their cause, which was not just the suspension of the bill but its formal withdrawal. On June 16, CHRF organized another rally (see Figure 5.2), which drew an even larger crowd. This time, protesters donned black attire, a dress code that would later become the defining colour of the movement. Organizers estimated a turnout of two million, making it easily the largest protest in Hong Kong's history. Leung's tragic death certainly influenced the mood of the protest and had a significant impact on its turnout. In the vicinity of the mall where he had fallen, a long queue of protesters carrying flowers gathered throughout the day, paying their respects to Leung. Leung's death also brought attention to the five demands written on the banner he unfurled just before his fall. These five demands would later evolve into the central claims of the protest movement.

High-ranking officials within the Hong Kong government at the time were taken aback by the significant increase in protest size during the June 16 rally (Interview A11). They interpreted the suspension of the extradition bill as a major concession, drawing an analogy with the Tung Chee-hwa administration's suspension of the Article 23 legislation in 2003. Nonetheless, it is essential to recognize that state-society relations had experienced profound shifts since that time. On the one hand, perceived threats were no longer seen as containable through institutional channels, as was the case between the tripartite coalition and the institutionalized opposition in 2003. In that era, the opposition still possessed the legitimacy to negotiate with the authorities and to determine protest demands. The defection of the Liberal Party also meant that the government lacked the necessary legislative support to reintroduce the bill, should it have wished to. By 2019, however, the ruling coalition's elites had lost such leverage with the state. Even with the bill nominally 'suspended', pro-democracy advocates still harboured concerns that the authorities might resurrect it once the immediacy of street protests diminished.

On the other hand, the post-Umbrella period saw a rising level of unity among the opposition, especially after the introduction of the extradition bill (Lee 2025). Therefore, many protesters viewed the minor concession as a strategy to divide the moderate and radical factions (Ho 2020). Some radicals even considered the movement to be a 'last stand' and were unwilling to tolerate any compromises (*Financial Times*, 15 August 2019; *New York Times*, 27 December 2019). In other words, it was unsurprising that the government's concession failed to quell the protest movement, unlike its success in containing the 2014 Umbrella Movement. The persistence of the protesters was fuelled by a deep-seated distrust in formal institutions and a high level of cohesion among opposition groups.

LEADERFUL MOBILIZATION

The early protests in June provided valuable insights into the organizational dynamics of the Anti-Extradition Movement, which blended both organized and spontaneous elements. On the one hand, both the June 9 and June 16 rallies were orchestrated by CHRF, mirroring the format of the annual July 1 rallies. Although civil society networks were crucial in mobilizing ordinary citizens, CHRF played an indispensable role in coordinating the schedules and logistics of these events. On the other hand, the June 12 protest stood in stark contrast. It emerged as a spontaneous, open-ended demonstration devoid of organizers and centralized leadership. There, protesters relied on their instincts to determine their next actions rather than adhering to a predetermined script. In the ensuing months, these two elements, organized and spontaneous, continued to coexist. CHRF, for instance, organized five more demonstrations until January 2020; but it did not assume the role of movement leadership. Instead, it simply operated within a decentralized and leaderful structure, where many other activists and civil society groups were actively mobilizing their own actions simultaneously. As CHRF's convenor Jimmy Sham emphasized in a speech during a protest on 12 December 2019:

> Before 9 June, the CHRF might really have been the 'main stage'. But as the evening of 9 June began, many frontline friends believed we could not just finish the rally and go home…When we arrived in Admiralty on the morning of 12 June, citizens have already taken the place of CHRF to surround the LegCo and government headquarters! CHRF is no longer the main stage, but a civic participant in the movement.[3]

This leaderful structure implied that neither individuals nor organizations held the legitimacy and authority to command the movement. The formulation of protest claims and action strategies required constant negotiation and fine-tuning to resonate with various audiences and maintain unity within the movement. Consider, for instance, the development of the protest claims. Process tracing indicates that the later widely recognized protest claims, known as the 'five demands', did not originate from specific leaders but rather emerged from symbolic events, evolving through discursive negotiations on digital platforms. Initially, during the June 9 and June 12 protests, the demand was straightforward: the withdrawal of the extradition bill. However, as the government announced the suspension of the bill, a broader set of democratic demands was presented. On June 15, an anonymous user using the pseudonym 'SaberA' posted on the LIHKG forum, which soon became the primary platform for movement discussion. The post listed four demands, including justice for protesters who had been beaten and arrested. This post rapidly gained popularity and became the most prominent thread on the forum.[4] It also spread to protest-related Telegram channels such as '612 Reminder' and 'Scout', each of which eventually amassed more than 200,000 subscribers.

These online claims found their way into the physical protests after the tragic death of Marco Leung, who had displayed a similar set of demands on a banner. Leung's tragic death triggered a public outcry and intensified the sense of solidarity among protesters during the massive June 16 rally. His final words were refined and formulated into concrete demands. Subsequently, several more instances of suspected suicides by young individuals occurred, and in each case, the deceased included the protest demands in their last messages. Amid these emotionally charged events, CHRF substituted the demand for the resignation of high-ranking officials with the introduction of genuine universal suffrage. This shift redirected the focus from political accountability to institutional reform. Although this modification initially faced criticism, protesters eventually accepted it tacitly, partly because universal suffrage was considered

---

[3] Civil Human Rights Front. 2019. 'Jimmy Sham: Civil Human Rights Front Will Never Retreat Because Hongkongers Have Sacrificed Too Much!' (In Chinese) December 19, *Facebook*. www.facebook.com/CivilHumanRightsFront/photos/a.517931904920872/2659128524134522/?type=3.

[4] SaberA. 2019 'Four Demands, Never Concede' (In Cantonese). LIHKG (online forum), Retrieved on June 15. https://lihkg.com/thread/1224111/page/1.

to be an institutional bulwark. This version of five demands received further endorsement after a short-lived occupation of the Legislative Council chamber on July 1, during which a protester took off his mask and read a manifesto proclaiming such demands. Ultimately, the following five demands gained widespread acceptance over the next several months:

1) Withdraw the extradition bill.
2) Retract the characterization of June 12 as a riot.
3) Establish an independent commission of inquiry.
4) Release all arrested protesters.
5) Implement universal suffrage.

As the prospects of realizing these demands grew increasingly uncertain, more radical slogans challenging the constitutional order began to surface, both online and in protest gatherings. Slogans such as 'Disband the police force' and 'Liberate Hong Kong, Revolution of our Times' emerged, reflecting a corresponding diversification and radicalization of protest actions within various sectors and communities. However, it is worth noting that the latter two slogans remained expressive and ambiguous, leaving room for multiple interpretations.[5] Protesters never reached a consensus to formally incorporate them as the sixth official protest demand. Instead, the original five demands continued to be the most commonly referenced in the calls for action, publicity materials and online discussions throughout the movement (Lee et al. 2020; Li and Whitworth 2022).

The scale of participation during the Anti-Extradition Movement was staggering. A representative population survey conducted in August 2019 revealed that 36.4 per cent of Hong Kong's seven million residents had participated in the movement, equating to two and a half million individuals. This figure increased to 45.6 per cent when we conducted another survey in May 2020. While it is possible that respondents may have over-reported their level of involvement (Wang and Soule 2016), a discounted turnout remained substantial. The May 2020 survey also highlighted that the movement drew significant participation from groups not typically associated with social movements: 49.3% were aged forty or older, 21.4% had secondary education or less, 31.9% were from upper-middle class and high-income households, 14.4% held centrist or pro-Beijing views, and 10.4% had no prior protest experiences.

This remarkable turnout can partly be attributed to the alignment between collective action frames and individual motivations. Table 5.2 summarizes the primary concerns of protesters during the two massive rallies on June 9 and June 16. Onsite surveys conducted on these days found that participants' most pressing concerns included the potential extradition of pro-democracy activists, politicians, and government critics to mainland China; the erosion of the rule of law; and the

---

[5] The Hong Kong government declared on 2 July 2020 that the slogan is pro-independence and secessionist, and thus criminalized under the national security law enacted in June 2020. HKSAR Government Statement, Retrieved on 2 July 2020, www.info.gov.hk/gia/general/202007/02/P2020070200869.htm.

TABLE 5.2 *Protesters' primary concerns regarding the Extradition Bill, June 2019.*

Date	June 9 285			June 16 875		
Number	%	Mean	SD	%	Mean	SD
How worried are you regarding the occurrence of the following if the extradition bill is passed?						
Property price drops significantly	34.3	2.94	1.338	46.6	3.39	1.212
Foreign capital leaves Hong Kong	76.2	4.00	1.113	78.0	4.14	1.014
International community imposes sanctions	75.0	3.99	1.061	75.2	4.07	1.021
Extradition of you, your family or friends	56.2	4.02	1.103	79.9	4.26	1.039
Extradition of pro-democracy leaders	90.1	3.52	1.420	95.6	4.71	0.636
Extradition of critical general public	90.7	4.48	0.862	95.9	4.75	0.613
To what extent do you agree or disagree with the following regarding the extradition bill?						
Turning Hong Kong into one country, one system	97.6	4.72	0.605	93.4	4.57	0.738
Destroying the rule of law in Hong Kong	96.8	4.76	0.537	96.7	4.72	0.581
Expressing Dissatisfaction with protest policing	–	–	–	98.5	4.89	0.378

Source: Authors' onsite surveys. Respondents were asked to rank their preferences on a five-point Likert scale. The percentages for extremely worried and worried responses were combined.

weakening of OCTS framework. Over 90 per cent of respondents indicated that the threats to dissenting voices and civil liberties were their primary motivations for joining the rallies. Concerns related to Hong Kong's financial status and global connectivity only ranked as their secondary concerns, whereas worries about personal safety and household wealth were the least motivating factors.

It is worth noting that the perceived threats significantly intensified between the two rallies held on June 9 and June 16. Concerns related to personal safety, including the fear of being extradited personally or having the same happen to friends or family, surged from 56.2 per cent to 79.9 per cent. Fear over the erosion of civil liberties and the rule of law also increased, even already at a high level. This is a stark indication of the impact of threat framing. Typically, as the size of a rally increases, the likelihood of attracting diverse participants with varying attitudes also rises. However, the results from June 16 indicated that fear and anxiety remained widely shared among participants, despite the expansion of the protest scale. Respondents' perceptions of threats did not diminish, even though the government had suspended the extradition bill one day before the second mass rally.

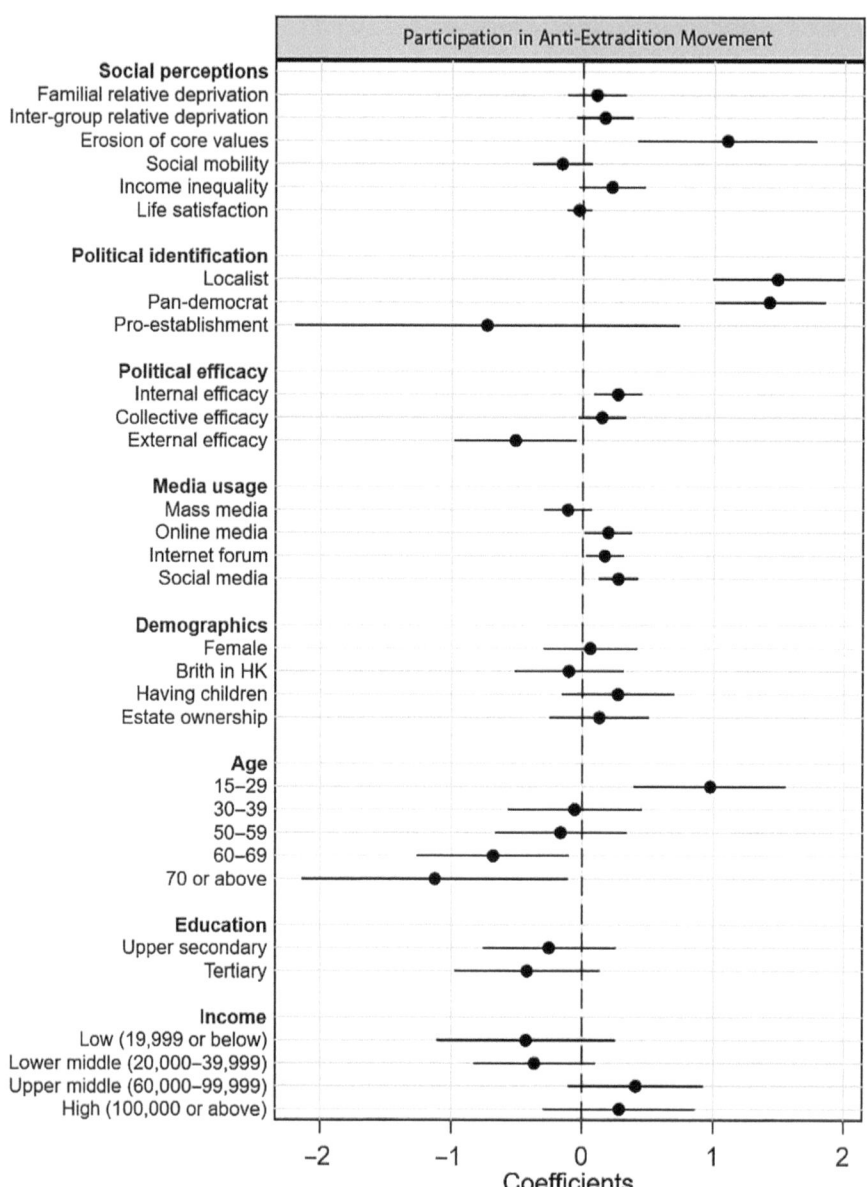

FIGURE 5.3 Protesters' primary concerns regarding the Extradition Bill, May 2020.
Note: Entries are logistic regression coefficients with 95% confidence interval.
N = 1,574. The McFadden's R^2 is 0.498.
Source: Authors' random population survey.

Figure 5.3 presents the data from the representative population survey conducted in May 2020, which corroborates the trends observed in the onsite
surveys. Among those who had participated in the movement, their foremost

concerns revolved around the erosion of fundamental values such as civil liberties and the rule of law, with other structural and economic grievances occupying a secondary position. Notably, individuals who accessed information through social media exhibited a higher degree of concern regarding threats compared to those who relied on traditional media sources. Meanwhile, while significant disparities in threat perception were evident between the pro-Beijing camp and the pro-democracy camp, the distinctions between respondents with a localist orientation and those with a veteran democratic orientation were minimal. This indicates a significant degree of alignment in threat perception among various segments of pro-democracy supporters.

CONCLUSION

The eruption of the Anti-Extradition Movement took nearly everyone by surprise. It unfolded in a political climate that was highly unfavourable to organized dissent, challenging the fundamental assumptions of conventional social movement theories that emphasize political opportunity and resource mobilization as prerequisites for mobilization. Despite this challenging context, what began as a small-scale opposition effort gradually gained widespread attention and transformed into a massive, resilient, and leaderful movement, mobilizing nearly half of the city's population in hundreds of protest actions. Its capacity to forge consensus, sustain momentum and maintain internal cohesion without a centralized leadership structure was truly exceptional among contemporary social movements.

This chapter has elucidated the emergence of this leaderful mobilization by examining the early mobilization efforts of established political groups and various kinds of civil society networks. These diverse initiatives played a crucial role in laying the groundwork and galvanizing public attention around the extradition bill, which initially seemed somewhat remote to the average citizen when it was first tabled. Of particular significance was the online petition campaign, which not only made the scale of resistance visible but also utilized a diverse range of social identities as intermediaries through which citizens became informed about the extradition bill. This leaderful structure attributed the extradition bill as an existential threat through the shared values, norms, and identities of ordinary citizens.

PART III

MECHANISMS

6

Sectoral Networks

The mass rally on June 9 failed to overturn the Hong Kong government's decision to proceed with the extradition bill. Three days later, young protesters escalated their actions by surrounding the LegCo and obstructing nearby roads. The protest on June 12, as briefly outlined in the Introduction, unfolded in a spontaneous fashion. Protesters simply followed their instincts to determine their course of action. Some adopted a more radical approach by directly confronting the police, while others took up supportive roles. Doctors and nurses quickly established makeshift first aid stations to assist injured protesters during the clashes. Van drivers delivered essential supplies such as water, saline solutions, and surgical masks. Christian groups conducted public prayers near the government headquarters, even amidst the skirmishes, hoping to reduce tensions through hymns, and by acting as human buffers between the police and protesters. Technically, all these civilians were participating in an illegal assembly. But they joined the protests anyway, despite the legal risks. Guided by their social roles, they sought to contribute in ways that aligned with their expertise, values, and identities, aiming to serve in the manner they knew best.

This early scene foreshadowed the ensuing developments. In the following months, various segments of civil society and social groups rallied within their respective sectors, leveraging their expertise and identities to orchestrate a range of protest actions. Lawyers provided legal assistance to secure the release of arrested protesters. Accountants offered guidance for crowdfunding campaigns to ensure compliance with money laundering rules. Designers produced thousands of pro-movement posters and infographics, disseminating them widely online. Social workers extended counselling services to distressed protesters and even attempted to mediate tensions on the protest frontlines. Computer programmers developed apps for crowdsourcing and sharing protest-related information. Mothers organized unity sit-ins, and students formed human chains outside schools in various neighbourhoods as a public display of support. Even football and basketball fans mobilized on several occasions, donning jerseys of their favourite teams to demonstrate their unity against the government, despite their usual rivalry.

This chapter delves into how a diverse array of sectoral networks fuelled the Anti-Extradition Movement. At first glance, it is not surprising to find that pre-existing networks played a considerable role in the protests. The existing literature on contentious politics has consistently underscored their role in drawing early supporters and protest participants (Clarke 2014; Leenders and Heydemann 2012; Wackenhut 2020; Zhao 2001), fostering movement identities and solidarities (Gould 1995; Pfaff 1996), and shaping protest norms (Opp 2001). Even in networked social movements where protesters are connected through digital communication tools, pre-existing social networks still matter significantly in recruiting and mobilizing participants (Mateo 2022; Onuch 2015). However, the intriguing difference with the Anti-Extradition Movement lies in how these sectoral networks extended their role beyond merely recruiting participants or generating movement identities. They also played a pivotal role in mobilizing sector-specific actions, often leveraging their unique social identities. These networks did not simply vanish under the blanket of the collective; they remained noticeable and active throughout the entire movement.

This chapter argues that sectoral networks served as mobilizing structures through which protesters organized and coordinated protest actions. The social identities that they cultivated provided guidance to protesters regarding how they could participate in the movement and contribute beyond merely adding to the headcount. This explains why doctors and nurses provided first aid assistance, van drivers transported supplies, and lawyers offered pro-bono legal aid during the June 12 protest – actions that seemed to spring forth as if from ingrained habit. Moreover, sectoral networks also facilitated the mobilization of specific expertise, norms, and resources. This enabled protesters to build trust in a high-risk environment and foster collaboration despite the lack of a centralized leadership structure.

In this chapter, we shed light on three sectoral networks: religious groups, medical practitioners, and legal professionals. These networks are rooted in Hong Kong's corporatist system, which organizes societal interests into a range of sectors and occupations. Despite being co-opted by the ruling coalition into various consultative bodies, these networks have maintained a relatively high degree of autonomy from the state since the colonial era thanks to their functional contributions to governance (Lee 2005). As long as they are recognized by the state, they are able to create organizations or professional bodies to advocate for their interests, organize their separate constituencies, and tap into new pools of resources (Ma 2016). For example, lawyers have established professional associations such as the Hong Kong Bar Association and the Law Society of Hong Kong, which practitioners are obliged to join, to regulate their conduct, norms, and practices. Meanwhile, religious groups, particularly

Christians, have been organized into different orders, such as Anglicans, Baptists, Methodists, and Lutherans, each developing its own elaborate church structures (Leung and Chan 2003). As a result, sectoral networks can be highly differentiated and are well-positioned to develop strong social identities among their constituencies. Because of their autonomy from the state and deep-rooted presence, they have formed the bedrock of Hong Kong's civil society.

That said, while many of their constituents might have participated in previous pro-democracy protests as individuals, they seldom mobilized collectively in the name of their sectoral networks. By mobilizing as distinct sectors, these networks brought together both people and resources, making significant contributions to the expansion and sustainability of the movement in the absence of centralized leadership.

PROTEST DIFFUSION

The involvement of sectoral networks was evident before the large-scale rallies in June 2019. As discussed in Chapter 5, the online petition campaign in May saw the mobilization of many social groups, including schools, professional networks, religious organizations, residential communities, and hobby groups, resulting in more than 400 petitions and hundreds of thousands of signatures. However, while these petitions contributed to the massive turnouts in the June rallies, sector-specific protests were not yet common. It was only after the storming of LegCo on July 1 that sectoral protests became more frequent. Following this incident, while public support for the movement remained high (Lee et al. 2022a), the level of police repression also increased significantly. Organizing another large-scale rally – such as those on June 9, June 16, and July 1 – was deemed increasingly ineffective in extracting concessions from the government. Alternative tactics were urgently needed to provide new direction to the movement and maintain pressure on the authorities (Li and Whitworth 2022). In this context, the protest motto 'be water' emerged as a guiding philosophy. It encouraged protesters to reject conventional forms of protest actions and instead experiment with innovative and adaptive tactics for navigating state repression.

This philosophy had a profound influence on the subsequent evolution of protests. As illustrated in Figure 6.1, which documents 528 protest events between March 2019 and February 2020, mass rallies were gradually replaced by two types of protests after July 2019 – one was the neighbourhood protests, initiated by residents within a neighbourhood precinct; and the other was the sectoral protests, initiated by various social sectors such as doctors, lawyers, churchgoers, and students. The neighbourhood protests began in early July, starting with the 'Kowloon Rally' on July 7 in Tsim Sha Tsui. This was the first mass rally that took place outside of Hong Kong Island since 1989, when Hong Kong citizens marched in support of the pro-democracy movement in mainland China. The July 7 protest, which attracted a massive turnout, inspired many other neighbourhood rallies across the city in places

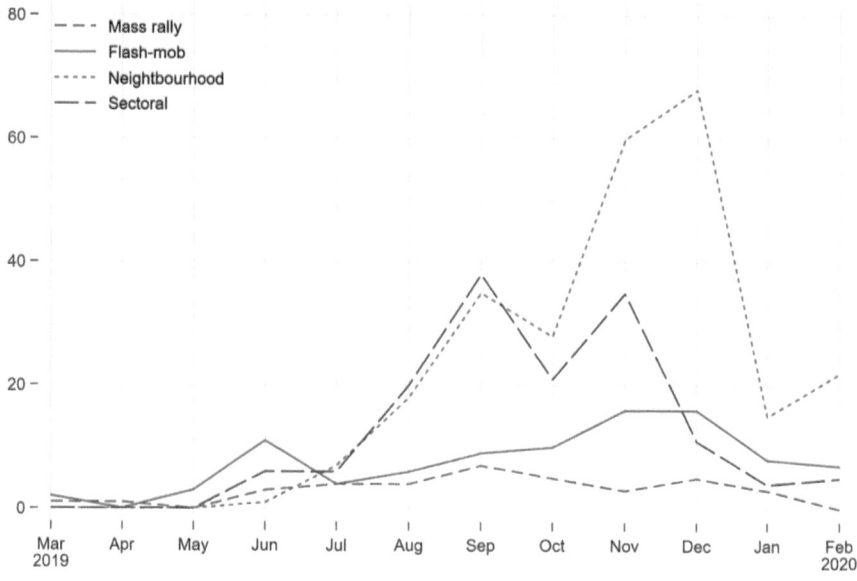

FIGURE 6.1 Diffusion of neighbourhood and sectoral mobilizations, 2019.
Note: The y-axis records the total number of protests of each type in a given month.
'Mass rally' = mass rally protests; 'Flash-mob' = flash mob protests; 'Community' =
community protests; Sectoral = sectoral protests.
Source: Protest event data compiled by the authors.

such as Sai Wan, Tseung Kwan O, Kwun Tong, Mongkok and Sham Shui
Po – many of them residential districts. These seemingly leaderless rallies were
often initiated and coordinated by activists connected to the post-Umbrella
civil society groups, whose roles were usually concealed to emphasize mass
participation.[1] But it is also important to emphasize that these activists did not
organize the neighbourhood protests solely by themselves. Instead, they relied
heavily on online networks, which provided access to a wide range of expertise
and social capital. According to two organizers of the neighbourhood rallies:

> Once the community rally was approved, we recruited helpers on LIHKG and other
> public Telegram groups. It only took us one evening to hire 200 pickets. A few of them
> were from our inner circle. But the majority were strangers (Interview B12).

> We pooled manpower from the well-known Telegram platforms. Then, we contrib-
> uted according to our expertise in small groups. Some of us took care of publicity;

---

[1] Based on the authors' calculation, out of the 120 approved public processions from July to
September, 65 per cent was applied for by veteran activists. These individuals negotiated with
the police over protest routes, identified the required number of pickets, and shouldered the lia-
bility for wrongdoing during the protests. This know-how determined why certain applications
were approved but others not – before the police banned all protests after August. The other 35
per cent of the applications were made by relative newcomers who connected with the veterans.

others arranged logistics. Once we decided on the next moves, we circulated the details back to the main groups. Our small Telegram groups continued to function after the protests, with members helping other groups to apply for a protest permit, defending Lennon Walls, or organizing video screenings (Interview B11)

The sectoral protests began even earlier. In mid-June, social workers and mothers staged their own sit-ins, both of which were in response to the police's excessive actions on June 12. Such sectoral protests became more frequent in late July, particularly following the Yuen Long attack on July 21. Numerous professional groups, including medical workers, lawyers, journalists, teachers, the elderly, finance professionals, flight attendants and even civil servants, organized their respective protests, mobilizing their own 'sectoral' constituencies. During these protests, these sectoral networks often exhibited their unique identities, either consciously or unconsciously. For instance, lawyers wore full suits even in sweltering summer heat; journalists put on safety vest and hard hat, their distinctive 'dress code' during the protests; doctors and nurses continued to wear their uniforms, despite not being on duty.

These sectoral protests also diffused to the workplace. Historically, due to the absence of robust legal protection, it has been difficult to organize strikes in Hong Kong (Chan, Chan, and Tang 2019). However, in late July 2019, protesters floated the idea of a general strike. Initially, pro-democracy trade unions consulted their members but received mixed responses. While they attempted to slow down the strike, the proposed schedule had already circulated on August 5, hundreds of thousands of workers effectively joined a citywide strike by calling in sick. Seven major assemblies were held across Hong Kong on that day. A few dozen schools declared it a holiday, citing traffic and security concerns. Thousands of shops closed for business, and even multinational companies allowed their employees to work from home in anticipation of the planned strikes. This widespread compliance and implicit endorsements across various sectors made the hastily proposed strikes possible. According to the Hong Kong Confederation of Trade Unions, more than 350,000 people from fifty different industrial sectors participated in the general strike, making it the largest labour action since the Canton–Hong Kong Strike in 1925. In the subsequent months, these pre-existing and newly established sectoral networks played a vital role in sustaining the movement. They continued to organize their own actions and facilitated the creation of over 450 new trade unions (Pringle 2021). They brought individuals with similar backgrounds together, creating platforms where they could collaborate and nurture a sense of belonging.

RELIGIOUS GROUPS

Among the various sectors actively engaged in the Anti-Extradition Movement, religious groups stood out as the most institutionalized and resourceful. With distant roots in the British colonial era, both the Catholic and Protestant missionaries and churches had wielded significant institutional influence and representation. The Christian churches functioned as intermediaries addressing medical, educational, welfare, and cultural needs in a rapidly modernizing Chinese society. In parallel, the British colonial government was supportive of their evangelical outreach efforts (Liu 2003). While the churches' influence in education had shrunk in the post-handover period, their organizational infrastructure and resources largely remained intact (Lee 2021). By 2019, there were as many as 800,000 Protestant Christians and 403,000 Catholics in Hong Kong (Hong Kong Yearbook 2019: 329). Moreover, the churches sponsored more than 60 per cent of primary and secondary schools, including some of the most prestigious ones (*HK01*, 17 February 2019).

However, the relationship between the state and religion in Hong Kong has not always been harmonious. Despite the fact that churches in Hong Kong depend heavily on state support (such as land leasing and granting of charity status), numerous religious groups and leaders have actively participated in pro-democracy movements and championed the cause of religious freedom (Chan 2015). Going as far back as the 1960s, the Hong Kong Christian Industrial Committee was a trailblazing advocate for labour unionism and human rights (Leung and Chiu 1991). One of its founding members, Chu Yiuming, was a member of the Hong Kong Alliance who played a key role in rescuing Tiananmen activists from the mainland and relocating them to Hong Kong and other overseas destinations after the events of 1989. He later became one of the leaders of the Occupy Central campaign in 2014. Cardinal Joseph Zen, the emeritus Catholic Diocese in Hong Kong, staunchly supported universal suffrage in Hong Kong. He consistently marched at the forefront of the July 1 rallies and June 4 vigils and was a vocal critic of the Sino-Vatican rapprochement, contending that sacred principles were more important than the church hierarchy.

The tension between the Christian faith and secular power extended well beyond a few isolated religious groups and leaders. Numerous religious organizations, originally based in mainland China and Hong Kong, had to abandon their churches and properties in Communist China and sought refuge in Hong Kong after 1949. Consequently, they became fervent critics of the atheist and authoritarian regime in the mainland. With the implementation of China's reform and opening up policies in the late 1970s, these groups began to establish extensive connections with Catholic underground churches and Protestant house churches on the mainland, engaging in activities such as smuggling millions of Bibles every year (Goh 2016). This historical context helps to explain why Christians were among the first to feel threatened by the extradition bill. Many priests and pastors expressed concerns that their connections and activities would be criminalized (Interviews B18 and B19). Ordinary Christians also feared that the churches would be compelled to cut ties with their fellow believers on the mainland who shared a common faith (Interview B19).

This prevailing perception of threat highlighted a unique ethos and sense of belonging within the religious sector. Rather than simply a network of churches and believers, this sector is also a faith-based community characterized by their shared ethos and beliefs towards Christianity (Wood 2002). Biblical stories, analogies, and symbols constitute their moral understanding of the world and serve as their common language. This explains why they could readily mobilize against a common perceived threat, despite belonging to different sects and orders. Faced with threats to their faith and community, the religious sector thus exhibited greater unity than during the 2014 Umbrella Movement. More specifically, Christians assumed three distinct roles in the Anti-Extradition Movement: organizing peaceful demonstrations, bolstering the movement's moral legitimacy, and contributing organizational resources.

The actions from the religious sector played a pivotal role, especially in the early stage of the movement. On May 9, after two months of intense public debate, including the April 28 march that drew approximately 130,000 participants, four Christian groups issued a joint statement highlighting the potential threats posed by the extradition bill to the civil and political rights of Hong Kong's residents (*Gospel Herald*, 23 May 2019). Among the signatories was the Pastoral Care Team, which had previously organized activities protesting the suppression of underground churches in China's Sichuan Province in December 2018. This petition campaign gained the support of at least nine other Christian groups from 12 May to 21 May, through public statements and prayer requests. In late May, as more local churches voiced concerns about the extradition bill's threat, an additional twenty-four churches signed petitions under the banner of 'groups of denominations'. To underscore the gravity of the issue, Cardinal Zen issued a strong warning that those who supported underground churches might 'disappear into thin air' and be extradited to a jurisdiction lacking fair trials (*Zen*, 1 April 2019). Even the Anglican Archbishop Paul Kwong, a pro-Beijing priest and a member of the CPPCC, issued a pastoral letter acknowledging the 'heated debates and deep-seated uneasiness' stirred by the bill (*Episcopal*, 11 June 2019). This unusual alignment between the liberal and conservative wings of the churches underscored the widespread concerns within the religious sector.

The involvement of churches significantly bolstered the moral legitimacy of the protests. Traditionally, religious groups often serve as a moral compass in society (Graham and Haidt 2010). This is also true in Hong Kong, where churches have long penetrated into education, medicine, and social welfare (Cheng 2004). The speeches and actions of the religious community thus lent credence to the protesters' claims. Following the June 9 march, hundreds of Protestant pastors and their followers conducted a seventy-two-hour prayer vigil outside the Government Headquarters and LegCo complex (Interview B18). During this extended prayer session, they repeatedly sang 'Sing Hallelujah to the Lord'. The song was broadcast live on nearly all local television channels and social media platforms (*The New York Times*, 19 June 2019), eventually becoming a familiar melody among protesters and sympathizers.

While the prayer sessions embodied the moral appeal of the religious sector, the peaceful demonstrations provided an avenue for connection between individuals with or without religious beliefs. On June 12, when violent clashes erupted between the police and protesters, churches not only engaged in what Ying Fuk-tsang (2021) characterized as 'spiritual resistance' but also served as a physical buffer between the protesters and the police. For instance, Pastor Roy Chan Hoi-Hing of the Good Neighbour North District Church co-founded the action group Protect Our Kids Campaign with parents and social workers. In the subsequent months, this group often positioned itself on the frontlines of protest sites to shield young protesters. Throughout June, numerous Catholic and Protestant churches organized hundreds of prayer sessions and masses, including a memorial ceremony for Marco Leung, the protester who tragically fell to his death.

In addition to leveraging their social capital, the religious sector also devoted organizational resources to support the movement. These resources were instrumental in protecting human rights and personal security. Starting in early to mid-June, some church buildings on Hong Kong Island made their facilities available to protesters for rest and shelter (Interview B17). As the protests expanded to other areas of Hong Kong, more churches opened their doors to those in need, providing crucial medical assistance, safe refuge, and counselling services. These facilities extended beyond church premises to encompass community centres and schools (Interviews B16 and B21). In the evening of July 1, when the police adopted more repressive means to disperse the protesters after some stormed the LegCo, several churches on Hong Kong Island opened their doors to provide respite for citizens. This decision stemmed not solely from the pastors' political stances but also from the faith and humanitarian concerns within their congregations (Interview B17). It is estimated that more than 150 Catholic and Protestant churches offered their spaces as rest stops for protesters from June to October (Ying 2021). One pastor articulated the motivations behind these decisions:

We did this [offering a shelter] in September 2014. When we opened our gates [after the firing of teargas], both student protesters and police officers entered. They were all exhausted and they simply lie down on the floor. We could claim that the church is open to all those in need... The situation was different in June 2019. We could only let one or the other in, take the risk of losing our trustworthiness or see them fighting with each other.

However, as the protests escalated, the religious sector encountered immense pressure from the pro-Beijing camp. In July, pro-Beijing newspapers accused a few religious branches and groups, such as the Chinese Methodist Church and the Salvation Army Education and Development Centre, of serving as 'warehouses for rioters' (*Takungpao*, 7 July 2019). By September, the Education Bureau had summoned the management of a Catholic primary school, which subsequently pledged not to accommodate protesters again (*Wenweipo*, 20 September 2019). Some pro-Beijing elites even threatened to withdraw donations from churches that supported the protesters.

These shifting dynamics over the course of the movement underscore the sectoral advantages and constraints faced by the Christian community. On one hand, the Christian churches' longstanding partnerships with the government provided them with extensive resources and internal cohesion. These formal networks could be readily mobilized in response to what they perceived as threats to their beliefs and communities. On the other hand, the Christian churches' structural dependency on state recognition and bureaucratic scrutiny influenced their level of involvement in the protests. They had to strike a delicate balance between their various social roles as a faith-based community and a provider of social welfare.

Consequently, the Christian churches were among the first to mobilize actively and collectively, but their visibility and collective action diminished over time. In contrast, the informal religious networks that took root following the post-Umbrella Movement positioned the established churches as supportive hubs of mobilization and organization in the later stages of the movement. While the religious sector's moral and instrumental roles in the movement continued to be significant, they became more decentralized and individualistic.

MEDICAL PRACTITIONERS

The extensive involvement of medical professionals serves as another example of how social identities drive sectoral mobilization in the Anti-Extradition Movement. Medical practitioners globally have a history of rallying together in support of activist causes, as evidenced in events like the 1964 Freedom Summer and the 1999 Anti-WTO protests (Dittmer 2009; Smith 2001). In Asia, doctors have also taken a leading role in protesting against human rights abuses during events such as the Nepalese revolution and Thailand's military coups (Adams 1998; Hewison and Kanchoochat 2018). However, in Hong Kong, the role of doctors in the pro-democracy movement has traditionally been minimal. Healthcare professionals, including nurses, therapists, pharmacists, and psychiatrists, have held stable, well-compensated jobs. Their professional interests have been adequately represented by quasi-governmental organizations and professional associations within the city's corporatist structure. For example, the Hong Kong Hospital Authority is responsible for managing resources and personnel for all public hospitals, while the Medical Council of Hong Kong oversees the licensing and conduct of all medical practitioners. The Hong Kong Medical Association, on the other hand, represents the interests of medical practitioners in various statutory and professional bodies. As a result, medical professionals have often been perceived as individualistic, with less engagement in social and political issues. They typically engage in collective actions in a personal capacity (Ma 2020), rather than as a cohesive group.

While medical professionals did not participate *en masse* until 2019, a loose network of medical professionals began to take shape during the 2014 Umbrella Movement. Initially, the organizers had planned for a medical team in preparation for a potential extended occupation. However, police's deployment of tear gas on September 28 and the looming threat of mob violence prompted the formation of voluntary first aid and medical teams at the three occupation sites. Additionally, a signature campaign involving 650 doctors in support of the occupation was published as a newspaper advertisement, marking the early stages of a nascent sectoral network among medical professionals (Interview B1). After the Umbrella Movement, many medical practitioners formed new groups with democratic leanings, such as Médecins Inspirés, HK Psychologists Concern, and Radiologist Conscience. These new groups and networks actively sought council memberships in formal professional bodies and effectively challenged the exclusive representation previously enjoyed by the established associations in their respective sub-sectors.

As these groups realized that achieving political reform through the streets was nearly impossible, they shifted their focus towards policy advocacy and network building. As one member expressed, 'The sentiment in my sector during that period was really low… personally, I was just waiting for another opportunity' (Interview B11). The medical sector experienced renewed vigour during the 2016 Chief Executive election campaigns, as pro-democracy professionals needed to assemble a thirty-person candidate list for each of the medical and healthcare subsectors of the electoral committee. To accomplish this, they reached out to supporters in various medical specialities and sub-fields. One member of the medical subsector noted, 'Without the Chief Executive election, we would not have found representatives and contacts in so many different sub-fields, specialties, and age groups' (Interview B14).

The institutional focus of these new groups and networks changed drastically with the emergence of the protests in 2019. The formal and informal networks they developed in the earlier period became the coordinating platforms for mobilization. In particular, some elected members of the electoral committee initiated the May petitions within their respective professional fields. As protest violence and police repression escalated after June, concern for personal well-being became an immediate issue, not only for protesters but also for the general public. In response, the medical sector promptly mobilized its specialized expertise to provide immediate treatment for those injured by rubber bullets, tear gas, and other weapons. Many medical professionals volunteered beyond their regular work hours, coordinating among peers on an ad hoc basis. WhatsApp groups and Telegram channels played pivotal roles in coordinating manpower, medical supplies, and treatment areas for these voluntary actions conducted outside of public hospitals. Two interviewees who served as administrators of the Telegram channels recalled that hundreds of doctors and nurses were involved in providing voluntary services. This number did not account for the additional medical professionals who only shared information or donated resources to support these efforts (Interview B5).

Several critical events played a pivotal role in galvanizing medical professionals and driving them to mobilize for action. The first significant turning point was the clashes on June 12. That day, as protesters attempted to storm LegCo, riot police responded with tear gas, rubber bullets, and batons. Dozens of injured protesters were transported to public hospitals, some of whom were placed under close police surveillance. In some instances, police officers entered hospital wards in an attempt to arrest protesters and requested patients' personal information. To some medical professionals, this was a violation of their core principle, which is to prioritize treating the injured and safeguard patient privacy. A doctor working in an emergency unit said, 'this crossed our bottom line; I don't care about your political position' (Interview B4). Following the events of June 12, Médecins Inspirés and six professional groups publicly criticized the police for interfering with their work and infringing on patients' privacy. The intensity of protest policing, witnessed by many through live broadcasts, further fuelled anger and elicited sympathy: We saw the beatings live on television. We are trained medical professionals. We know what kind of damage they can cause to the human body, and that is not acceptable (Interview B6).

August 11 marked another significant turning point. That day, a first aider was struck by a bean bag round, resulting in permanent damage to her right eye (*Reuters*, 12 August 2019). This incident triggered public outcry (Zhu et al. 2022). That same day, some 30 arrested protesters were brought to hospitals with severe bruises and broken bones. Amid suspicions that these injuries were the result of severe police beatings, nurses, doctors, and other healthcare workers in hospitals began organizing lunchtime sit-in protests. For instance, the sit-ins held on August 2 and October 26 respectively attracted protest crowds of more than 10,000 participants. These actions were voluntary and loosely networked, often triggered by key protest events. As one physician recalled:

There wasn't a coordinated effort to deliver the [first aid] services. Those who signed the early petitions were more likely to get involved, but many others joined spontaneously after the clashes on the street. The number of first aiders may have been as high as a few dozen, but there were probably more outside my circle (Interview B5)

On the frontline, first aid teams were exposed to threats of injury and arrest, as some police officers displayed hostile attitudes towards medics, perceiving them as sympathetic to protesters and obstructing law enforcement. These first aiders not only endured verbal abuse but were also not spared from tear gas, bullets, or water cannons. For instance, during the conflicts at Hong Kong Polytechnic University on November 17, some first-aid helpers were handcuffed and arrested on the protest site. Despite the growing tensions with authorities, the medical teams made efforts to maintain political neutrality, providing medical assistance to police officers and counter-protesters alike.

Medical workers' voluntary interventions became increasingly vital as some protesters lost confidence in the public health system over reports of police entry into public hospitals. As one volunteer medic recalled, 'many injured protesters refused to be sent to public hospitals after receiving immediate treatments, leading to a significant increase in the number of potential patients seeking care at private clinics'. (Interview B11). Another volunteer shared the dilemma they faced:

At the beginning [June], many injured protesters were admitted to public hospitals. Some came to the emergency rooms by themselves; others were referred by private doctors or social workers. But the police, without a court order, began to request the records of those with physical injuries. We don't know how long the Hospital Authority can protect the privacy of our patients. We are witnessing the mounting distrust of our system. We need to do something. (Interview B2)

Medical professionals also played a unique and indispensable role in the movement by harnessing their professional expertise and authority. They exposed how protesters sustained serious injuries from protests by presenting detailed medical evidence. They also ensured that injured protesters could receive fair and adequate treatment in hospitals, with their rights and privacy being protected. Meanwhile, they also dealt with the mental health of protesters, many of whom suffered from post-traumatic stress disorder following their exposure to violence (Interview B4).

Coordinating and administering volunteer medical services on such a large scale was no easy task. This challenge was compounded by limited resources and the absence of a hierarchical structure typically found in regular hospital settings, where standard procedures and chains of command help resolve potential disagreements over patient treatment. In this organizational void, medical volunteers had to rely on horizontal cooperation with one another to deliver the best possible care. This organic process, as one interviewee noted, was only possible by setting aside professional hierarchies and connecting over certain universal principles.

A similar pattern of collaboration emerged when medical voluntarism extended from Western to Chinese medicine. In Hong Kong, medical doctors often harbour doubts about the scientific basis of Chinese herbal medicine, whereas Chinese medicine practitioners believe they face discrimination within the licensing system. Chinese medicine practitioners also tend to be less vocal, as their practices require regular interactions with mainland China (Chung et al. 2011). Nevertheless, numerous Chinese medicine practitioners overcame structural and institutional barriers to address the immediate needs of protesters. Two of our informants estimated that approximately one-fourth of Chinese medicine practitioners from the younger generation were involved:

Many of them dosed medical powder tended to treat those exposed to tear gas and pepper spray. A few offered first aid on the frontline. Some treated fractures and sprains. Unlike western medical doctors, we don't have the skills and resources to treat emergency medical needs, but we could offer our expertise to relieve their burdens (Interview B9).

The medical practitioners effectively leveraged their social capital and expertise within their professional networks to provide comprehensive healthcare services, which sustained the mass mobilization. However, while their institutional positions and professional authority enabled them to play a crucial role in the movement, professional ethics also placed constraints on their engagement. For instance, despite frequently and openly criticizing police violence, Arisina Ma, then president of the Hong Kong Public Doctors' Association, chose to provide medical support in her own church during mass rallies rather than at the frontlines due to concerns about arrest. She believed that getting arrested would jeopardize the independence and credibility of the association.

One frontline medic, who had served in the medical teams during the Umbrella Movement, consistently reminded her team members to remain neutral, avoiding slogan chanting or confrontations with the police (Interview B6). Another doctor mentioned that her peers refrained from discussing protests or political matters within hospitals (Interview B4). During the August 5 general strike, participation of doctors and nurses remained limited, as their professional training emphasized prioritizing patients' interests. They also feared that injured protesters' access hospital care would be compromised if all sympathetic medical workers went on strike (Interview B12 and B13).

Much like their Christian counterparts, the organizational networks of doctors, nurses, and other medical practitioners enabled them to perceive the influences of the extradition bill on their professions and communities. These formal networks played a pivotal role in fostering moral agency and initiating mobilization. However, as the conflicts escalated and repression rose, these networks began to experience increased restrictions due to their relationship with the authorities. Compared with pastors and priests, medical practitioners bore a significantly higher risk of losing their licenses and jobs if they continued to protest in defiance of warnings from government authorities and regulatory bodies.

Still, many medical professionals continued to participate in the movement in a personal capacity. They continued to provide medical aid to protesters, while maintaining a facade of neutrality in hospitals to fulfil their professional obligations. Even though numerous medical practitioners may not view themselves as protesters, the services they provided effectively formed the 'supportive networks' that bolstered the protest movement (Parkinson 2022).

LEGAL PROFESSIONALS

Compared to medical practitioners, lawyers traditionally played a more important role in Hong Kong's pro-democracy movement. Since the late colonial period, a subset of Hong Kong's lawyers has been actively advocating for constitutional reforms and safeguarding the human rights of dissidents (Tam 2012). The legal functional constituency seat has consistently been won by members of veteran democrats since the inception of Hong Kong's pro-democracy movement. Leaders of the Democratic Party and the Civic Party, including barristers Martin Lee, Margaret Ng, and Dennis Kwok, successively held this seat from 1985 to 2020, until the electoral system was overhauled. This contrasts sharply with the medical functional constituency, which has traditionally been represented by doctors who tend to adopt more centrist positions.

The legal sector was among the first to voice reservations about the extradition bill in public. Following the July 1 march in 2003, the Hong Kong Bar Association, a professional regulatory body for barristers, became increasingly vocal in scrutinizing government policies. However, a more organized effort within the legal sector did not materialize until the 2014 Umbrella Movement. The organizers of the OCLP, the initial civil disobedience campaign, promptly assembled a team of pro-democracy barristers and lawyers to prepare for the anticipated mass arrests at the end of the campaign. When the spontaneous occupation movement began, this team established a hotline to provide legal support to those arrested during the early stages of the protests. As the Umbrella Movement drew to a close, approximately fifty lawyers came together to form a legal support team, taking on the responsibility of handling most of the following protest-related trials (Interview B1).

Some of these legal support teams evolved into more organized networks after the Umbrella Movement. One prominent group, the PLG, took a more proactive approach compared to the two existing professional bodies – the Hong Kong Bar Association and the Law Society of Hong Kong. Whenever controversial legal cases or issues arose, they would simplify complex legal concepts and prosecution procedures for better public understanding. They also collaborated with volunteer lawyers to secure bail for arrested activists and protesters. By early 2019, their membership grew to over 100 members, comprising barristers, solicitors, paralegals, and law students. In the summer of 2019, they gave more than 300 interviews, sharing their legal analysis of the extradition bill with local and international media outlets. A convenor of the group expressed how managing differences within the group helped foster solidarity:

We believe that our legal expertise can serve society better. While some colleagues stress advocacy, others contest boundaries [adopted by the professional associations]. We value these differences as they are deliberative. Regardless of our rank and politics, we have been more committed. We make ourselves available for countless bails, court trials, commentaries, and media interviews [Interview B11].

The Anti-Extradition Movement spurred even greater participation among lawyers. On 6 June 2019, three days prior to the first million-strong march, lawyers, including solicitors and barristers, staged a silent march from the city's Court of Final Appeal to the Admiralty government headquarters to voice their concerns about the extradition bill (Figure 6.2). Despite temperatures soaring to 33 degrees Celsius and heat warning issued by the observatory, most of the 2,500 participating lawyers were dressed in their black suits, with many of the men donning black ties as well. The march unfolded with impeccable orderliness, finely tuned to underscore their professional identity. Banners were conspicuously absent, and no slogans were chanted. Upon reaching their destination, they stood in silence for three minutes before dispersing. This marked the fifth instance of silent marches by Hong Kong lawyers, but it was undoubtedly the largest. Two months later, in August, lawyers organized another silent procession, with an even larger estimated turnout of 3,000 participants. Assuming they all were practicing lawyers, this amounts to nearly a quarter of the 12,700 registered lawyers in Hong Kong (Hong Kong Trade and Development Council 2022).

As the movement continued to evolve and the government's crackdown on protesters intensified, lawyers assumed a different role. With dozens of protesters being arrested daily, there was significant demand for legal representation. Unlike during the Umbrella Movement when the legal support

FIGURE 6.2 The lawyers' march on 6 June 2019.
Photo Credit: Lam Chun Tung.

team remained relatively small, hundreds of lawyers who had not previously been involved in human rights practice or pro-democracy advocacy stepped forward to volunteer for the legal assistance network (Interview B8). With the assistance of volunteers and technical experts, a few hotlines were established to provide legal support to those who had been arrested. Whenever legal representation was required, lawyers were dispatched to the respective police stations, even during late hours. These lawyers played a crucial role in overseeing the legal procedures, ensuring that the rights of the arrestees, including the right to remain silent, personal security, and effective communication with family members and witnesses, were upheld. Many of the arrestees were young and inexperienced with legal processes, so the presence of lawyers was essential. In some cases, lawyers had to wait for hours or even days at the police station, whereas others encountered chaotic situations such as unverified client lists and ad hoc charges they had never experienced in their legal practices (Interview B9). Nevertheless, they were supported by a well-organized sectoral network. According to an interviewee:

Compared with the Umbrella Movement, the division of labour and specialization were much more effective this time. The entire process, from an individual's arrest to lawyers visiting them in the police station and following up on their cases, including whether they would be charged, was more well-organized. The roles and responsibilities were clearly defined, and there was better coordination among lawyers. (Interview B1).

The rapid expansion of the legal network gave rise to new challenges. In addition to the typical coordination issues, such as determining the most suitable lawyer for a case, financial burdens were a pressing problem. While many lawyers were already charging minimal fees or offering pro bono services, legal proceedings incurred substantial administrative fees, bail expenses, and court-related costs. The need to raise funds from the public to cover these legal expenses became an urgent matter. To address the challenge, the lawyers' volunteer network initiated a crowdfunding campaign, which proved to be highly effective. The campaign drew lessons from previous initiatives that followed the Umbrella Movement, all of which emphasized transparency and procedural fairness (Interview B10). These initiatives included the Justice Defence Fund, established in 2016, which raised HKD 1 million to support the legal battles of young activists, and the Imprisoned Activists Support Fund, established in 2017, which raised an additional HKD 2 million to assist imprisoned activists and their families.

The 612 Humanitarian Relief Fund was established following the clashes on 12 June 2019, when many protesters were arrested. It was named to commemorate its date of foundation. During the June 16 march alone, the fund received HKD 12 million in public donations. Operationally, the fund was designed to cover three types of expenses: medical costs, legal fees, and emergency economic assistance for those in need. By 31 May 2020, the fund had accumulated a total of HKD 113 million, with 73 per cent of this sum coming from small donations. It responded to over 14,000 requests for support and allocated funds to cover more than 80 per cent of its reserve. This remarkable level of support was made possible through the voluntary efforts of legal teams and support from various sectors.

The legal activism in the Anti-Extradition Movement faced its own share of constraints. Primarily, the formalization of such efforts made them vulnerable to legal repression from the state. The government could exert pressure on registration bodies to revoke lawyers' practicing licenses if they were found to have committed any 'misconduct'. Aware of this vulnerability, figures such as ex-legislator and barrister Margaret Ng, one of the trustees of the 612 Fund, meticulously attended to procedural and legal details to avoid exposing the fund to danger. The 612 Fund maintained a detailed record of donations and expenditures and restricted the use of funds to its three designated purposes. This caution was well founded, considering what had happened to another major legal support fund, the Spark Alliance Fund. In December 2019, its HKD 70 million in donations was frozen by the police on suspicion of money laundering.[2]

Other than legal risks, lawyers also had to cope with the internal struggle between professional ethics and their protest commitment. A barrister reflected on her team's struggle:

We are under a lot of stress. In this movement, what we see is very different from what we studied in law school. For example, the police should not do this or that, but they keep doing it. We are in a kind of existential crisis. A lot of lawyers are quite young. It is like they just finish training, and you throw them into fighting in the Vietnam War (Interview B7)

Others thought that their intervention effectively demonstrated the importance of robust institutions and procedures at a time when public confidence in the rule of law was eroding (Interview B8).

You feel that you are in the midst of a turbulence. In this turbulence you see some fireflies; we are like those fireflies that give a little light and warmth (Interview B10).

Balancing their involvement in the movement with workplace pressures was a significant challenge for volunteer lawyers, especially those employed by commercial law firms. These firms often had major clients with close ties to the authorities or the Chinese market and were unwilling to be associated with the pro-democracy movement. As a result, many volunteer lawyers had to maintain a low profile to protect their careers and avoid conflicts with their employers. Some chose to contribute to the movement through less public

---

[2] Despite precautions, the 612 Fund was not spared from the post-protest crackdown. It eventually ended operations in August 2021 after the introduction of the National Security Law (NSL) in July 2020. Furthermore, the five trustees, including Margaret Ng, were arrested in May 2022 under the NSL, even though they were later charged with a lesser offense.

roles, such as legal research or backend administrative work, allowing them to support the cause anonymously while navigating the challenges posed by their workplace environment. This compromise enabled them to use their professional expertise to sustain the movement while minimizing the risk of unwanted pressure at work.

PROACTIVE ENGAGEMENT

Other social sectors also made their own contributions to mobilize and sustain the Anti-Extradition Movement, showcasing the intersectionality of sectoral networks. Professional journalists often found themselves on the protest frontline, doing on-the-ground reporting and live broadcasts during tense confrontations. They also challenged government officials and police spokespersons in press conferences on their accounts of events and sometimes staged protests during press conferences (Luqiu and Lu 2021). From June 2019 to March 2020, journalist groups issued thirty-nine statements condemning police violence against reporters, obstruction of reporting, verbal abuse, exposure of personal information and other violations against the press.

Social workers took up two main roles during the movement: frontline liaison and off-site counselling. A group of progressive social workers formed the Battlefield Social Workers group, which attempted to minimize violent confrontation on the frontlines. One veteran social worker, Chan Hung Sau, who was later charged with a count of riot for her participation, even refused to wear protective gear on the frontline so that the team would not be confused with the protesters. Similar to the medical professionals, they kept a deliberate distance from the protests: while they were physically in the protests, they refrained from participating in the actions and using offensive language against the police.

The campaign for international support at the 2019 G20 summit also demonstrated how sectoral networks and their respective expertise were mobilized in tandem without centralized leadership. A major part of the campaign was to place advertisements about the Hong Kong protests in nineteen major newspapers in more than ten countries. The effort, which will be examined in Chapter 8, required a broad range of knowledge and expertise. Many sectoral networks were mobilized: accountants took care of financial matters, lawyers attended to legal issues, media, and business professionals contacted the respective newspapers, and designers handled the graphics, with the linguists translating the scripts into different languages.

Although sectoral networks played a key role in mobilizing expertise and resources, the movement would not have been sustained without protesters engaging in a diverse set of repertoires. This multitudinous nature of participation, akin to the mobilization of religious groups, medical practitioners, and legal professionals, was shaped by the differing social identities within the movement. Simultaneously, it was also propelled by variations in the

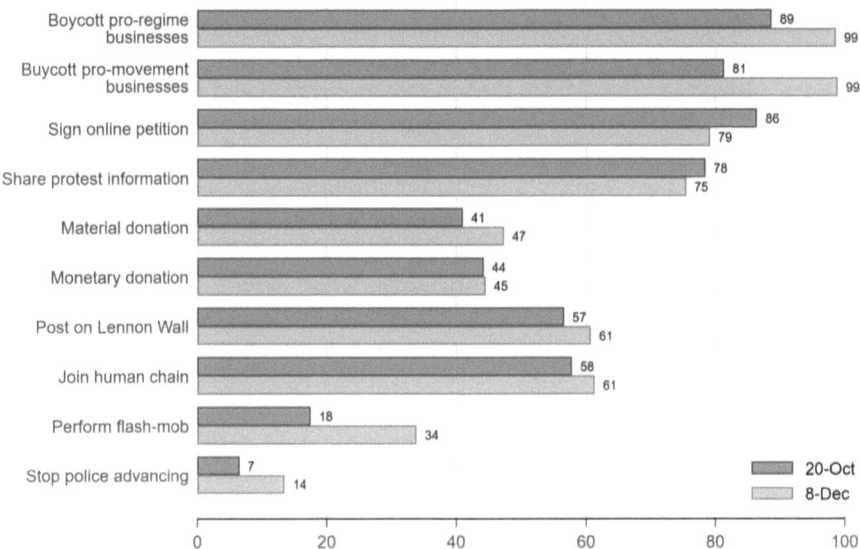

FIGURE 6.3 The diversity and resilience of protest repertoires.
Source: Authors' on-site surveys on October 20 (N = 921) and December 8 (N = 902).
Notes: Entries are the percentages of respondents who participated in the action. The
two data points were large rallies involving participants from across the territory and
served as a representative sample of the movement.

protesters' risk assessments and personal capacities. These differences inevita-
bly led to a broad spectrum of actions within the movement.

As Figure 6.3 shows, the majority, or around two-thirds of protesters
engaged in 'low-risk activism,' such as donations, forming human chains
outside schools, and posting messages on Lennon Walls, which were spread
across the city's eighteen districts and often present at public transport
interchanges. The city wide human chain protest on August 23was particularly noteworthy. With little preparation, an estimated crowd of 300,000
citizens formed a fifty-mile human chain along three main metro lines in a
recreation of the Baltic Way, a peaceful demonstration in the Soviet-ruled
Baltic nations that took place on the same day in 1989. The idea was floated
on LIHKG only four days before the event, but once it received majority
approval, participants in Telegram groups and other social media platforms
created maps, brainstormed routes, and deployed volunteers to ensure that
the chain would connect.

In contrast, up to one-third of protesters were willing to adopt 'high-
risk activism', such as stopping police from advancing and engaging in flash
mob actions in shopping malls or outside police stations. While the number
of arrests highlighted the risks of frontline actions, many young protesters

persisted. Even on the frontlines, the division of labour continued and intensified. Some wore full tactical gear, donning black clothes, goggles, gas masks, and helmets to hide their identities and formed makeshift barricades within minutes. Others benefited from informants on LIHKG and thousands of public and private Telegram groups. Messages were shared about police deployment and supply chains so protesters could adjust routes and arrange safe shelters. Despite their radical actions, the militants were not alienated from the peaceful protesters. On the afternoon of September 1, the police besieged thousands of frontline protesters rallying at the airport. The police suspended all public transport connecting to the airport, but scores of private vehicles rushed to the airport to rescue those left behind by the evening.

CONCLUSION

This chapter shows how sectoral networks formed the early mobilizing structure and precipitated a leaderful mobilization. Specifically, we focus on three sectors characterized by robust organizational foundations and pre-existing networks: religious groups, medical practitioners, and legal professionals. Our aim is to illustrate how these sectors were galvanized by the contingent threats posed by the extradition bill and how their informal networks sustained the movement despite the absence of centralized leadership. The challenges to their faith, professional principles, and judicial procedures served as the impetus behind the extensive involvement and mutual dependence among these unexpected protesters. Consequently, individuals who were previously strangers within these sectors, lacking formal affiliations or prior protest experience, were able to be recruited into various protest actions. This spontaneously emerging 'organic solidarity' (Durkheim 1984) allowed both groups and individuals to circumvent hierarchical commands and organizational obligations within their respective sectors.

However, it is crucial to recognize that their mobilization had its limitations. These sectoral networks were often constrained by their bureaucratic roles, obliging them to adhere to various institutional constraints and professional ethics. As a result, their participation remained ambiguous: while they were a part of the mobilized masses, their roles differed significantly from those of activists or ordinary protesters. From their perspective, they did not view themselves as typical protesters; instead, they saw their participation as a means to fulfil their professional ethos or social responsibilities. This ambiguity constrained their mobilization, particularly towards the later stage of the Anti-Extradition Movement.

7

Loss of Innocence

Sectoral networks such as religious groups, medical practitioners, and legal professionals are well-positioned to mobilize swiftly in spontaneous movements, thanks to their social status and pre-existing networks. What about social groups that lack status and networks to represent their collective interests? The extensive participation of secondary school students during the Anti-Extradition Movement raises precisely this question. Although secondary school students did not play a prominent role in the first few months of the movement, they began to mobilize intensely as a group once the new academic semester commenced in September 2019. Aside from protesting within their campuses, students staged numerous protest actions, including a citywide human chain protest where they gathered outside their campuses. This was unusual because secondary school students in Hong Kong seldom participated collectively in protests, except briefly during the 2014 Umbrella Movement (Chu 2018). Although there are inter-school connections developed through extracurricular activities, these students lacked established organizations and networks capable of providing resources and representing their collective interests like the legal and medical professionals. How did these teenagers mobilize en masse?

This chapter argues that school action groups, established by students in their respective schools in opposition to the extradition bill, played a pivotal role in mobilizing these teenagers by tapping into and leveraging the social capital associated with their schools. Utilizing Instagram as a platform, these action groups – formally known as 'concern groups' – facilitated connections among students within and across schools, often through capitalizing on their schools' unique identities and leveraging various sources of social capital tied to those identities, including school reputation, alumni influence and inter-school connections. By activating and harnessing their latent social capital, students managed to overcome their resource limitations and orchestrated a wide range of protest actions.[1] However, despite extensive inter-school collaborations, these action groups remained unequal in terms of their mobilization power. Schools with prestigious reputations, strong alumni networks, and extensive inter-school connections were more capable of shaping movement narratives and organizing territory-wide protest actions. Conversely, schools with less social capital tended to coordinate actions with neighbouring schools within local districts and relied more on external support. Our findings suggest that informal hierarchies can emerge in decentralized and seemingly non-hierarchical movements, corroborating insights from classic and recent research (Freeman 1972; Gerbaudo 2017; Leach 2013; Michels 1962). Even in the absence of an overarching leadership, these emergent structures prove essential in providing both material and symbolic resources for mobilization and enabling the division of labour.

STUDENT ACTIVISM

Students play a crucial role in contentious politics. However, while there is extensive research on student activism, the spotlight has predominantly fallen upon university students (Dahlum and Wig 2021; della Porta, Cini, and Guzman-Concha 2020; Ho and Wan 2023; Van Dyke 1998; Zhao 2001). This disproportionate emphasis is understandable, given that university students are older, more socially visible, and often more resourceful in organizing dissent. However, although generally less politically active than their university counterparts, secondary school or high school students are not entirely absent from political activism (Gordon and Taft 2011); in some contexts, they are active participants (Lertchoosakul 2021; Weiss and Aspinall 2012). This disparity in attention thus raises the question of the role and influence of these teenage students in contentious politics.

Historically, secondary school students in Hong Kong were not prominently visible as participants in mass protests. Despite the city's history of student activism during the 1960s and 1970s, secondary school students rarely took part in social movements before the 2010s. This was partly due to the city's depoliticized education system, established during the British colonial era. To encounter the influence of the CCP and KMT in the education sector, the colonial administration, from the 1920s onward, founded numerous government schools and encouraged religious organizations to sponsor schools. It also strictly regulated and depoliticized the curriculum

---

[1] Social capital refers to 'the aggregate of the actual or potential resources which are linked to possession of a durable network of more or less institutionalized relationships of mutual acquaintance or recognition' (Bourdieu 1986: 21). This definition constitutes two conceptual layers. The first is the networks of social connections that people can effectively mobilize, focusing on the ties between individuals and groups (Coleman 1988). The second comprises trust, shared norms and sentiments of solidarity that arise from such ties, which facilitate the cooperation among actors (Putnam 1993, 1995).

to prevent schools from becoming breeding grounds for communist ideology (Leung and Ng 2014). For instance, the curriculum of civic education in the 1960s heavily emphasized the importance of obeying the law and the government and not taking part in any political activities. Although social issues were discussed, they were not scrutinized, and the focus was on government efforts to solve the problems. However, aside from controlling the curriculum and funding, the colonial administration granted significant autonomy to the schools and their sponsoring bodies, allowing them to develop their own image, culture, and networks. To compete for students and funding, secondary schools often prioritized an examination-oriented teaching approach and heavily emphasized students' performance in public examinations (Tsao, Hardy and Lingard 2018).

This led to a highly competitive and hierarchical school system that endured beyond the 1997 handover. Under this system, secondary schools are categorized into 'bands'. By the 2000s, a three-band system was established: band 1 schools are considered top-tier, whereas band 3 schools are at the lower end of the spectrum. Schools are also characterized by whether they are single-sex or co-educational, private or government-funded, and whether they have specific religious affiliations, primarily Catholic or Protestant. After completing primary school, students are assigned to different schools by the Education Bureau based on internal assessments. As a result, this system has led to the emergence of a group of elite schools. These elite schools are not only characterized by their better band scores; they also have longer histories that can often be traced back to the early colonial era and notable alumnus in various sectors, while playing an important role in the colony's development as well as China's modernization. Moreover, these schools often have distinctive cultures and more extensive inter-school connections. For students, these attributes can provide social capital to be leveraged for later professional development. For schools, these social capitals are vital for attracting students and establishing unique identities.

A new wave of student activism emerged with the founding of Scholarism by the fourteen-year-old Joshua Wong in 2011. During the Anti-MNE Movement which Scholarism led in the following year, many secondary students participated in the protests. In 2014, shortly before the Umbrella Movement, hundreds of secondary students participated in a class boycott led by Scholarism to protest against the NPC's decision on universal suffrage. The political awakening of secondary school students can be attributed to two structural developments. First, the introduction of Liberal Studies into the school curriculum in 2009 played an important role in fostering students' awareness of social and political issues (Fung and Su 2016). Although the subject did not directly motivate students to engage in social movements, it did equip them with the knowledge and awareness to comprehend ongoing political developments. Second, the rise of mass mobilization since the early 2000s drew sustained attention to a wide range of social and political issues

(Cheng 2016). Recurrent mobilizations also brought new protest actors and participants into the fold. For instance, Joshua Wong attended his first protest during the 2010 Anti-XRL Movement, an experience that would later inspire his activism.

When the Anti-Extradition Movement officially began in June 2019, secondary school students did not assume a prominent role – at least not as a collective actor. However, some did participate on an individual basis. This was partly due to the online petition campaign in late May 2019, which began with petitions initiated in the name of secondary schools. Even though these petitions were mostly initiated by graduates, many current students were among the signatories. Data from our onsite surveys reveal that among those who attended the protest organized by secondary school students on September 30, many had actually participated in protests between June and September 2019. However, when they returned to school for the new semester after the summer break, they began to organize more collectively. Among our respondents, 91% said that they had participated in human chain protests near their schools, whereas 85% and 75% participated in singing protests and school strikes respectively. More than half of them organized action groups. Campuses became their main sites of protests.

INSTAGRAM NETWORK

From the early stages of the movement, digital platforms such as Telegram and LIHKG had been widely utilized by protesters to coordinate their actions (Lee, Francis 2020). However, for secondary school students, Instagram played a more important role. As indicated in Table 7.1, 85 per cent of secondary school student protesters reported being highly dependent on Instagram for accessing protest-related information, far more than the 18 per cent of general protesters who stated the same.[2] This discrepancy highlights the disproportionate importance of Instagram for teenagers in comparison to older protesters.

To gain insight into how teenage protesters utilized Instagram for disseminating protest-related information, we searched for secondary school action groups present on the platform. We utilized several keywords associated with the movement to identify the initial batch of action groups. After filtering out irrelevant groups, we scraped the list of Instagram accounts that each account followed. We then eliminated duplicates and unrelated groups from the second batch before merging it with the initial set of groups. This two-step process identified a total of 365 such action groups as of 1 October 2020, all

---

[2] The respondents for the first column of Table 1 were extracted from a survey conducted from April to May 2020 that targeted the Hong Kong citizens who participated in the Anti-ELAB protests.

TABLE 7.1 *Information sources for protesters.*

	All protesters (N = 6,017) (%)	Student protesters (N = 229) (%)
Online news media	63.7	85.4
Online forum	23.6	75.4
Facebook	49.2	47.1
Instagram	18.4	85.4
WhatsApp	31.5	41.8
Telegram	18.7	72.5

Source: Authors' onsite survey.

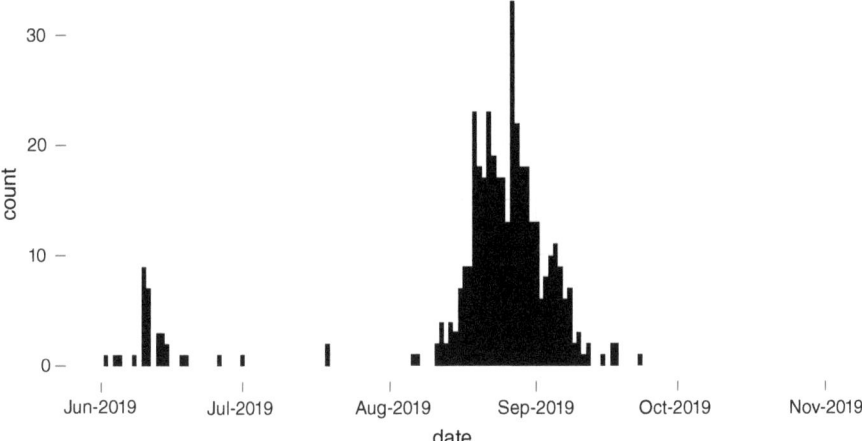

FIGURE 7.1 Publication dates of action groups' first Instagram posts, 2019.
Source: Data compiled from Instagram.

of which were public accounts.[3] Out of these, 327 were specific to secondary schools, representing 305 unique schools. The remaining thirty-eight accounts encompassed student-led SMOs and online news media. Subsequently, we compiled data on the number of followers for these accounts and the accounts they followed. As Instagram did not provide information about the account creation date, we used the date of the first post as a proxy.

Figure 7.1 illustrates when these Instagram accounts published their first posts. Only a small number of schools initiated their accounts in late May or early June, coinciding with the emergence of the online petition campaign. However, it was not until mid-August, as the new school year was approaching, that students began to organize on campuses. The data clearly indicate

---

[3] It is important to note that this keyword search may not be exhaustive. However, it still helps to identify accounts that are relatively more *identifiable* on Instagram for the public.

that the creation of new Instagram accounts peaked in early September. According to our informants, these action groups were established primarily to facilitate the organization of a territory-wide school strike. They served as formal platforms for students to engage in negotiations with school authorities regarding the strike's logistics. The Instagram accounts associated with these action groups became the primary means to mobilize their fellow students and peers. In addition to sharing images of the protests, these action groups frequently disseminated information that was particularly useful for teenagers who were new to participating in protests. This information included templates of consent letters from parents for students to join school strikes, lyrics for movement songs, and posters for sharing online.

Our initial puzzle revolves around the types of secondary schools that tend to establish action group accounts on Instagram. Of the 465 secondary schools in Hong Kong in 2019, our data reveal that 305 had established one or more action group accounts on Instagram. We conducted a logistic regression to understand the factors that make certain schools more likely to have such accounts. The results, as presented in Table 7.2, indicate that schools with higher prestige (higher band scores) and boys' schools are more likely to have an Instagram action group account. This finding aligns with our expectations, as it suggests that schools with greater reputational capital are more inclined to engage in online mobilization efforts.

Next, we shift our focus to the action group network. Figure 7.2 illustrates the network structure that disseminated movement-related information

TABLE 7.2 *Logistic regression of school action groups on Instagram.*

	Does a school have an Instagram action group account? (1 = Yes; 0 = No)	
Band score (Lowest = 1 to Highest = 9)^	0.354***	(0.050)
Boys' schools (No = 0)	1.405**	(0.653)
Girls' schools (No = 0)	0.460	(0.500)
Private schools (No = 0)	−0.281	(0.324)
Protestant/Catholic schools (No = 0)	−0.262	(0.239)
Schools of the other religions (No = 0)	−0.204	(0.415)
Constant	−0.874***	(0.273)
N	447	
Log likelihood	−244.432	
Akaike Inf. Crit.	502.864	

Note: The entries are unstandardized coefficients. Standard errors in parentheses.
Source: Data collected from Instagram.
*p < 0.05, **p < 0.01, ***p < 0.001.
^Band 1 = 7–9, Band 2 = 4–6, Band 3 = 1–3.

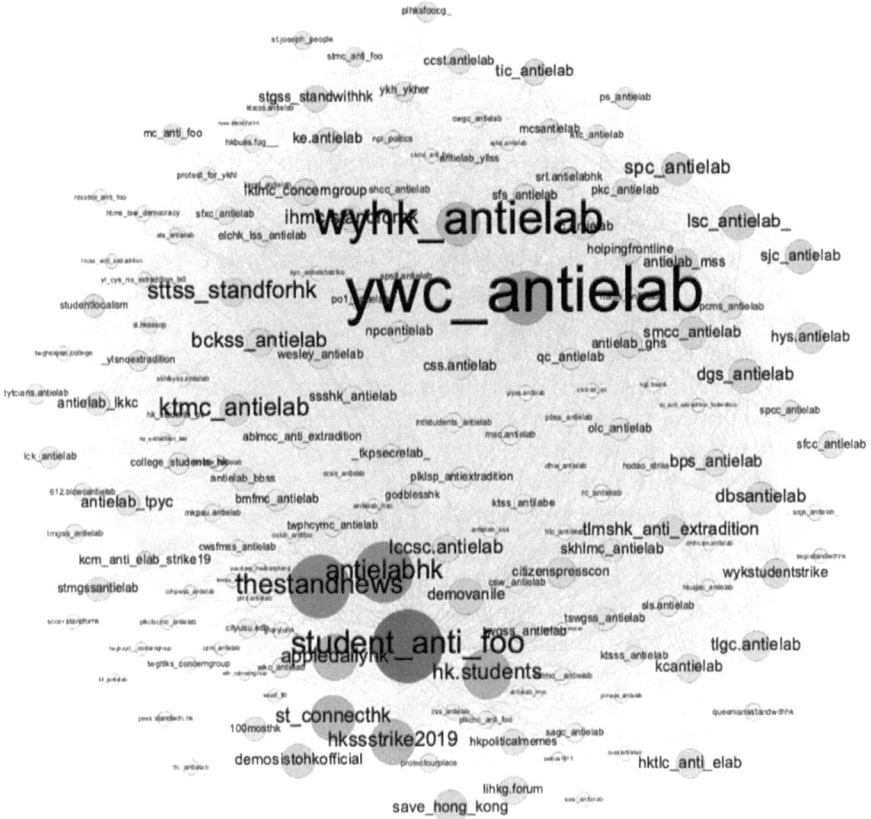

FIGURE 7.2 The Instagram follower network of school action groups, 2019.[4]
Source: Data compiled from Instagram.

on Instagram during the protests. In addition to student action groups, the network also encompasses the Instagram accounts of major movement organizations and online news media, as they serve as information sources for the action groups. Despite forming an extensive network, these action groups

[4] The network graph is a snapshot taken on 1 November 2019, during the height of the protests. For simplicity, it only displays nodes with in-degree >30 (i.e., more than thirty accounts follow them within the given network). The size of each node is proportional to its in-degree, or its number of followers. The more followers it has, the bigger it is. Finally, the size of the label is proportional to the eigenvector centrality of each node, which is a measurement of its influence within the network. The colour of each node reflects its betweenness. The higher the betweenness, the bluer a node is. Betweenness centrality measures the extent to which a node lies on the shortest path between other nodes in the network. It reflects the frequency at which a node acts as a bridge along the shortest path between two other nodes.

exhibit disparities in terms of their 'popularity'. Notably, the two most 'followed' nodes – 'wyhk_antielab' and 'ywc_antielab' – are the action groups of two elite schools with long histories: Wah Yan College, Hong Kong and Ying Wa College. Wah Yan College is a Catholic boys' school founded in 1919 and run by the Society of Jesus, a religious order of the Roman Catholic. Ying Wa College, a Protestant boys' school, was founded in Malacca of Malaysia in 1818 but moved to Hong Kong in 1843. It is Hong Kong's oldest school and the first that adopted Western education. The action groups of the two schools were highly active during the movement, which explains their significance within the network. Their centrality in the network, measured by their betweenness centrality and eigenvector centrality,[5] is even higher than the Instagram accounts of online news media (e.g., 'thestandnews') and student-led SMOs (e.g., 'demosistohkofficial', 'hkssstrike2019', and 'student_anti_foo'). This suggests that the two action groups were more interconnected with other influential accounts.

Among the action group accounts, elite schools held more central positions, even though none were formally regarded as protest leaders. This suggests that elite schools might be assuming a quasi-leadership role by attracting more attention from peers and the public. To corroborate this observation, we conduct an ordinary least squares regression on schools with Instagram accounts to assess the impact of school prestige on their network positions. The results are presented in Table 7.3. Model 1 illustrates how school prestige influences the number of followers of an action group account within the secondary school network, or the in-degree. Model 2 depicts how school prestige affects the number of followers outside the network, that is, the general public.

The results support our assumptions. The more prestigious a school, the greater the number of followers it garners both within and outside the network. Instagram accounts that are more proactive in following other accounts also accumulate more followers. However, being more active in posting images only attracts more followers outside the school network, not those inside. Regarding school attributes, girls' schools have more followers both inside and outside the network, whereas boys' schools have more followers solely from within. This underscores the gender dynamic in the social media realm and also suggests that action groups of single-sex schools generally have higher in-degree, likely because single-sex schools are more engaged in organizing joint-school activities. Finally, Catholic or Protestant schools can draw more followers from

---

[5] Betweenness centrality measures the extent to which a node lies on the shortest path between other nodes in the network. It reflects the frequency at which a node acts as a bridge along the shortest path between two other nodes. Eigenvector centrality assigns relative scores to all nodes in the network based on the principle that connections to high-scoring nodes contribute more to the score of the node in question than equal connections to low-scoring nodes. In other words, a node is considered important if it is connected to other important nodes.

TABLE 7.3 *OLS regression on action group followers.*

	Number of followers inside network of secondary schools		Number of followers outside network of secondary schools	
Number of posts	−.009	(.027)	0.765**	(0.251)
Out-degree	.190***	(.023)	0.746***	(0.210)
Band score (Lowest = 1 to Highest = 9)^	4.171***	(.660)	83.996***	(6.049)
Boys' schools (No = 0)	23.269***	(5.693)	20.044	(52.172)
Girls' schools (No = 0)	16.536**	(5.169)	251.129***	(47.371)
Private schools (No = 0)	7.368	(4.497)	31.535	(41.211)
Protestant/Catholic schools (No = 0)	0.524	(3.368)	67.089*	(30.866)
Schools of the other religions (No = 0)	−5.328	(6.546)	8.205	(59.996)
Constant	19.293***	(4.723)	4.119	(43.290)
N	321		319	
Adjusted R	35.5%		51.0%	

Note: The entries are unstandardized coefficients. Standard errors in parentheses.
Source: Data compiled from Instagram.
*p < 0.05, **p < 0.01, ***p < 0.001.
^Band 1 = 7–9, Band 2 = 4–6, Band 3 = 1–3.

outside the network. This suggests that religious schools may have broader public reach due to their religious network or perceived moral legitimacy.

LATENT SOCIAL CAPITAL

This emerging network of student action groups injected fresh momentum into the movement, which by then was facing increased government repression. From September onwards, the movement saw a surge in protest actions initiated by secondary school students, accompanied by increasing arrests of teenage protesters. This upsurge can be attributed in part to the decentralized nature of the network, which enabled the extensive student mobilization. However, as the analysis earlier reveals, the network did not adopt a purely leaderless, horizontal structure. Rather, it developed a leaderful structure, shaped and structured by the social capital available to the action groups. Specifically, schools with greater social capital held more central positions in the network, enabling them to shape movement narratives and mobilize territory-wide protest actions. In contrast, schools with less social capital were more peripheral in the network and more likely to be followers. They were more likely to organize local protest actions, often relying on student-led SMOs. We illustrate this contrast in the following sections. Drawing from in-depth interviews with student activists, we discuss three forms of social capital that proved essential for the extensive mobilization of secondary school students but were unevenly distributed across schools.

ALUMNI'S INFLUENCE

Alumni networks serve as vital channels through which students and graduates interact, seek guidance, and fundraise. Previous research has highlighted the role of alumni networks in fostering trust-based relationships, especially in the business world (Hall 2010). Here, we argue that alumni networks can also be utilized for political purposes. As secondary school students began to mobilize during the Anti-Extradition Movement, graduates from their schools became a critical source of support. As mentioned earlier, these graduates were already active in the petition campaign that emerged in late May. After action groups surfaced in August, graduates and current students established connections in the digital space, bridging the generational divide. Instagram emerged as a key platform for alumni to follow updates about the action groups. Additionally, alumni-initiated petitions enabled student activists to reach out to graduates who shared concerns about the extradition bill. One activist explained, 'Alumni knew our school well and could advise us on how to deal with the teachers; most importantly, they could raise money for the action group to print out flyers and posters' (Interview D3).

Connecting with alumni was crucial. Besides providing financial support, alumni also acted as intermediaries between student activists and their schools. Many schools consider their alumni network to be a valuable asset, as alumni often become potential donors and employers for their graduates. The significance of the alumni network is particularly pronounced among elite schools, where many alumni hold influential social positions. Thus, whenever alumni were involved, school management tended to avoid confronting them. This was evident during the territory-wide school strikes held in September when action groups called on students to boycott classes in opposition to the bill. A member of an action group from an elite Catholic girls' school recalled how her senior alumni served as intermediaries between student activists and the teachers:

On the day of the school strike, some teachers were harsh on us. They had us stay in a room so that we could not demonstrate out loud in the open space. But many old girls came back. We were touched. When they arrived, the teachers suddenly became more lenient on us and allowed us to move around. Their presence was very important for us because there were moments when we did not know what to do. (Interview D5)

The case of one of Hong Kong's oldest and most prestigious schools offers a revealing example. The school's old boys' association was established in the 1920s, comprising nearly 3,000 members. On September 3, when the school's action group urged students to boycott classes, the association collaborated with the student council to organize a series of 'civic learning classes'. These special classes featured guest lectures by numerous notable alumni. Students had the option to participate in the strike by attending these impromptu classes instead of their regular ones. As one activist explained,

Old boys are the backup for us to deal with the school. Some of them are prominent figures so the school has to give them 'face'. Because of their involvement, the strike was tacitly endorsed by the school. This gave assurance to the students and the parents, many of which are conservative and fearful of the consequences of us skipping classes. Many classmates joined the strike as a result. (Interview D8)

The human chain protests that followed the school strike also drew heavily on alumni networks. After a citywide human chain protest was held on August 23, which physically linked participants along most of the city's metro stations, many action group activists decided to organize their own human chain protests in collaboration with neighbouring schools. In early September, shortly after the school strike, these activists contacted their counterparts from other schools, primarily through Instagram, to organize these human chain demonstrations. Coordinating these efforts proved to be a massive logistical challenge due to the difficulty of mobilizing a sufficient number of participants. In this context, the alumni network played a crucial role. Using Instagram, action groups posted details about the date and time of these protests and extended invitations to alumni to participate. For schools with robust alumni networks, mobilizing participants was not too challenging. However, the situation differed for schools with weaker alumni networks. Such was the case for a Protestant co-educational school that had only been established a decade ago. As explained by one of their activists, 'only around a dozen alumni returned, and we didn't have enough people to form the human chain' (Interview D4).

SCHOOL REPUTATION

If alumni networks served as a counterbalance against the school authorities, then school reputation provided the symbolic resource for magnifying students' visibility and forming alliances. In Hong Kong, a school's reputation often hinges on its academic performance and extracurricular achievements. As such, school reputation not only represents cultural capital and self-identification (Bourdieu 1986), but also shapes students' action preference in choosing who to connect and collaborate with. The impact of school reputation on public attention is evident in the earlier regression analysis, which reveals that more prestigious schools can attract a larger following beyond the school network. This suggests that school reputation itself serves as a form of capital for influencing a protest movement, as the public is more interested in knowing the perspectives of their students.

A second wave of online petitions, this time organized by school action groups, illustrated the impact of school reputation. Starting in late August, secondary school students began initiating online petitions to advocate further actions, following the earlier petition campaign as a model. Utilizing Instagram, they connected with student activists from other schools to collaborate on petition drafts. We identified a total of thirty-nine petitions with schools as signatories throughout the movement. Among these, eighteen were district-based, involving schools from the same district, whereas nine were territory-wide petitions, often garnering support from dozens or sometimes more than a hundred schools. Additionally, seven petitions involved schools from across the territory but with fewer initiators, predominantly elite schools known for their high reputation and academic excellence. Counting the frequency of schools appearing as a signatory, we find that more reputable schools tended to sign a greater number of petitions than others. On average, Band 1 schools signed 1.37 petitions, whereas Band 2 and 3 schools signed 1.05 and 0.60 petitions, respectively.

The data suggest that while action groups predominantly co-initiated petitions in collaboration with neighbouring schools, there was a distinct cluster of elite schools that consistently partnered with one another. The presence of these multiple petition communities implies that school reputation not only facilitated connections among action groups but also influenced whether and how they collaborate in organizing offline, physical protests. A group of activists from an elite Catholic boys' school elaborated on their strategy:

If you initiate a petition and include as many schools as possible, it cannot stand out. The media will only find it interesting and report it if you have a limited number of elite schools. And after all, it is actually difficult to work with those [non-elite] schools... sometimes you have to admit, they couldn't draft a proper statement! (Interview D6)

A Form 4 activist from a top-tier Protestant boys' school echoed this rationale:

Our main task outside campus is to initiate petitions to draw attention because secondary school students deserve a voice. Usually, one person will draft the statement and will circulate it with the rest. We seldom argue about the wordings. [Researcher: Why?] I guess it is because the quality of the first draft is often good, and we trust one another. Interestingly, after we posted our petition, the district schools often followed suit. Even though the wordings might be different, the visual design of their Instagram posts is surprisingly similar to ours. That made me realize that as 'elite schools', we have some sort of agenda-setting power. (Interview D12)

The writing style of elite schools' petitions also stands out. In contrast to the straightforward and accessible language often used in territory-wide and district-based petitions, elite-school petitions were often well-crafted and had literary and historical references. For instance, all their petition titles referenced Chinese poems, those of other schools typically bore functional titles (e.g., 'An Open Letter from Shatin Schools Concerning the Emergency Regulation'). Additionally, these elite-school petitions frequently incorporated references to Confucian literary texts that were relevant to the principles of education. In their December petition, they even included a Latin phrase, 'caelum non animum muto', at the end of the statement. This phrase, which translates to 'our heavens may change but not our spirit', served as a motto of the Royal Hong Kong Auxiliary Air Force, a pivotal force in defending colonial Hong Kong against Japanese invasion during the Second World War.

JOINT-SCHOOL TIES

In addition to school reputation, pre-existing ties among schools also generated valuable social capital for student mobilization. Secondary school students in Hong Kong frequently engage in joint-school extracurricular activities, such as sports competitions, debates, speech festivals, science exhibitions and high table dinners. These activities fostered strong inter-school ties and numerous inter-school communities, inadvertently facilitating student mobilization during times of protest. As expected, the bonds among elite schools were particularly robust. For instance, the first protest organized by secondary school students, held at Edinburgh Place on September 2, was organized by twelve elite schools located on Hong Kong Island. One activist who played a key role in orchestrating the event mentioned that he was initially invited by an acquaintance from a Protestant girls' school. Subsequently, he extended invitations to his friends from various other schools and reached out to other action groups through Instagram. A similar demonstration took place on October 18 at the University of Hong Kong, organized by a similar group of elite schools. A Form 4 activist from a Catholic girls' school shared her perspective:

> Organizing a protest is not too different from organizing joint-school events, which I do a lot. Just like protests, joint-school events involve many logistical problems, like bringing together people and booking a venue. Protests may be different in that they carry more risk. So, we are glad to have the help of my seniors who are now in university. That is why we chose to hold our protest at the University of Hong Kong. It is safer for the participants because the police and counter-protesters would have reservations about coming in. (Interview D5)

Ties among elite schools are not the only form of joint-school connections. Sports competitions, for instance, also fostered relationships that student activists leveraged. One notable example was the Inter-school Swimming Competition, a prominent annual event held in late October bringing together twenty schools. Although the official organizer, Hong Kong Schools Sports Federation (HKSSF), imposed restrictions on the number of spectators for each participating school due to the ongoing protests, the event transformed into a protest gathering. Throughout the competition, spectators chanted slogans, brandished flags, and sang protest songs; some activists even coordinated a human chain protest during the lunch break. Many students who could not attend the competition in person also joined the protests. The aforementioned Form 4 activist, who was an organizer of that day's protests, attributed the smooth organization to the involvement of athletes:

Our school has been in Division 1 for many years and so are many others. That's why the athletes know one another well. In fact, it wasn't us – it was the athletes who contacted one another and coordinated our actions. You know, athletes are like celebrities in every school. They are popular and it is not hard for them to mobilize other students. (Interview D12)

Four days after the swimming gala, a follow up protest took place at the headquarters of the HKSSF. This protest emerged in response to the organization's decision to suspend all sports competitions following the swimming event. Infuriated by this sudden move, student activists and athletes rallied to voice their opposition. Despite an urgent call to action posted on Instagram shortly before the event, several hundred protesters turned up, forming an impressive human chain in front of the Federation. Many of them were still dressed in their school uniforms, and numerous student athletes also joined the demonstration.[6] The remarkable turnout effectively compelled HKSSF to reverse its decision.

Secondary schools that did not fall within either the elite or sports clusters faced greater challenges. With limited joint-school connections, action group activists from these schools tended to focus on their respective districts and cultivate relationships with neighbouring schools. As described by a sixteen-year-old activist,

It is hard for us to look for partners because we are not as well-known as the elite schools. To be honest, elite schools may not want to work with us. That's why we had to turn to neighbouring schools. You know, it is interesting because some of my childhood friends went to these neighbouring schools. We grew up in the same district together but ended up in different places. The protest somehow gave me an opportunity to reconnect with them. (Interview D6)

Coordinating protests with neighbouring schools proved difficult. An activist from a non-elite school recounted his experience of hosting a meeting for action group activists from various schools in Yuen Long, a suburb in the city's northwest: 'There were forty people crammed into a party room that we rented. The meeting was so noisy that we couldn't talk about anything. There was also a lot of mistrust because we have never met one another. And people kept on arguing, and in the end, we took the blame' (Interview D15). The planned protest was eventually cancelled because too few schools agreed to participate.

Lacking joint-school ties and facing challenges in coordinating with neighbouring schools, non-elite schools typically sought assistance from student-led SMOs, such as Secondary School Strike (SSS). Many regional assemblies were organized through these SMOs. In these protests, the role of SMOs proved to be pivotal: they determined the event schedule, provided audiovisual equipment, arranged the stage setup, invited guest speakers,

---

[6] Participant observation on 29 October 2019.

promoted the event on social media, and sent out press invitations. Perhaps the most critical task was securing a Letter of No Objection from the police, without which a protest would be deemed illegal. The spokesperson for SSStrike described his experience:

Protests in different districts differ from one another. If they involved students from elite schools, they were likely to have better execution. Take the Tsim Sha Tsui protest for example: as there were a few elite schools among the organizers, they tended to have more opinions on the run-down and did not want us to interfere too much. They were also more confident about their ability to invite guests. But for non-elite schools, the organizers often did not have many ideas for how to organize a protest. For instance, in the Kwai Tsing protest, the schools told us two days before the event that they couldn't find guest speakers. So, we had to step in and take charge of the whole thing. (Interview D11)

During these district protests, demonstrators often donned their school uniforms while concealing their school badges to protect their identities. These peaceful gatherings typically commenced with a series of speeches and songs delivered by young activists. Subsequently, participants were encouraged to take the stage to share their thoughts. In one of these protests, student participants were also provided with papers and crayons to illustrate their feelings about the protests. These repertoires were uncommon in a typical adult-led protest in Hong Kong. The entire arrangement was carefully crafted to foster a youthful and participatory atmosphere, aiming to amplify the voices of teenagers that had long been disregarded.

CONCLUSION

This chapter has examined the role secondary school students in the Anti-Extradition Movement. Unlike established sectoral networks such as legal and medical professionals, secondary school students lacked the resources and organizational structures that would readily unite them as a collective force. In this chapter, we have demonstrated how student-led action groups enabled these teenage activists to harness the latent social capital associated with their school identities. Through the utilization of alumni influence, school reputation and joint-school ties, these action groups became key mobilizing structures enabling secondary students to participate actively in a political environment that traditionally discouraged their involvement. By collaborating within various clusters, they successfully overcame their inherent limitations and organized numerous protest actions.

However, not all action groups enjoyed equal influence. Those with greater social capital were more proficient in shaping movement narratives in the online sphere and were more independent in organizing protest actions. In contrast, those with less social capital often played more passive roles. While having more social capital did not necessarily bestow these action groups the status of formal movement leaders, it provided them with more material and symbolic resources to influence movement narratives and coordinate offline protest actions. This suggests that informal hierarchies can naturally emerge in decentralized and seemingly non-hierarchical movements, simply because of the characteristics of the actors participating in them. Additionally, this underscores the pivotal role of social capital as a resource (Ling 2006), complementing mainstream resource mobilization theories that emphasize tangible resources such as manpower and money (McCarthy and Zald 1977), as well as leadership qualities such as skills and charismas (Morris 1986).

The active participation of secondary school students demonstrates that fragmented social networks, even those lacking established organizational structures, can be mobilized in social movements, provided that actors can activate their latent social capital. These actors do not necessarily need to share stronger pre-existing ties and identities, such as doctors, nurses, or lawyers. The case of secondary school students may shed light on why loosely organized social sectors, such as information technology workers, cultural workers, graphic designers, or marketing professionals, also actively mobilized during the movement. Like secondary school students, these sectors may have developed some pre-existing intra-sectoral networks but are certainly not as organized and resourceful as the medical and legal professionals. However, similar to the teenage students, these sectors possess latent but abundant social capital that can be harnessed for leaderful mobilization.

8

Peer Collaboration

The global wave of ''leaderless' mobilizations poses a crucial question for students of contentious politics: how do protesters organize their actions without organizations or any centralized leadership? While the terms 'organizing' and 'mobilizing' are often used interchangeably by social movement scholars, they carry nuanced differences. Mobilizing refers to the act of rallying and motivating individuals or groups to participate in a specific action or event. Organizing, however, involves a more protracted and complex process of coordinating individuals, groups, and resources to work effectively towards common objectives. Unlike mobilizing, which emphasizes visibility and immediate action, organizing is a logistically demanding process that mainly occurs behind the scenes, involving mundane and laborious tasks. These tasks include deciding on key claims and actions, determining a meeting time and location, setting a dress code, selecting communication channels, deciding on a name for the action, devising contingency plans for inclement weather, and ensuring adequate food, water, and medical supplies for participants.

The process of organizing has piqued interest among scholars of conflict studies (Loken 2022; Parkinson 2013). For instance, Sarah Parkinson (2022) examines what she terms 'backstage labour' in civil conflicts, which includes logistics, intelligence, medical, financial, human resources, and publicity work that facilitates organizational continuity, resilience, and survival. However, this dimension remains under-researched in protest studies. This is primarily because SMOs were assumed to handle all the backstage labour of protests. Besides handling high-level tasks such as framing, strategizing, and media engagement, SMOs also serve as key organizers, providing the necessary resources, manpower, infrastructure, and logistics for protest actions (Earl 2015). However, the rise of 'leaderless' mobilizations has significantly reduced the prominence of organizations in this role. In such mobilizations, even though organizations are not entirely absent, protesters often relegate them to the sidelines (Gerbaudo 2017). Instead, protesters depend heavily on digital communication technologies as coordinating platforms, enabling them to 'organize without organizations' (Shirky 2008).

This chapter explores how protesters organized and sustained protest activities in the Anti-Extradition Movement. We argue that 'peer collaboration' – an overarching process in which they work together on a horizontal, decentralized, and many-to-many basis – played a pivotal role in making the movement a sustained leaderful mobilization. It enabled protesters to devise, plan, and stage a continuous stream of protest actions. This process is partly enabled by digital communication technologies, such as online discussion boards, encrypted messaging apps, and online collaborative tools. But other than being a technologically determined process, we argue that peer collaboration involves a significant degree of human agency. First, peer collaboration necessitates strategic agency from protesters to leverage the capabilities of digital technologies for various purposes, especially translating ideas into actionable agendas and sharing mobilization information. Second, peer collaboration requires a substantial degree of offline relationships and interactions, superimposed on these online activities. Protesters often need pre-existing social networks and face to face interactions to facilitate complex organizational routines involving team building, division of labour, and coordination. These offline relationships serve as the relational infrastructures for accessing resources and specialized skills, and building trust among protesters, particularly in high-risk environments where they may not know each other.

We explore how peer collaboration was evident through three constituent mechanisms that supported various organizational routines in the Anti-Extradition Movement: (1) *tactical innovation*, wherein protesters devise new strategies and tactics; (2) *information curation*, wherein they collect, organize,

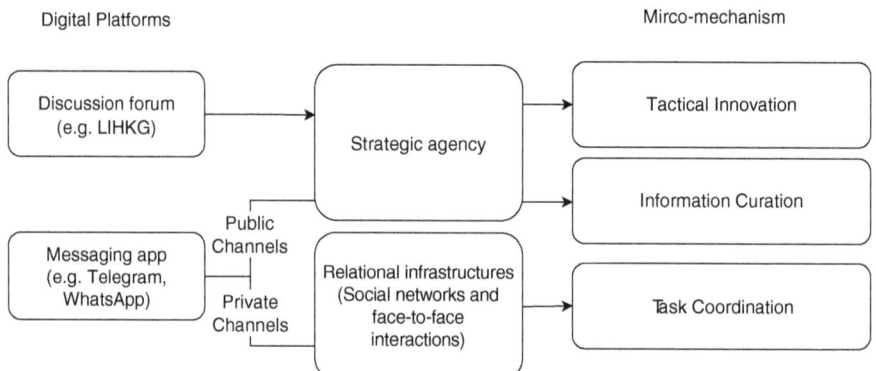

FIGURE 8.1 Conceptual relationship between digital platforms and micro-mechanisms.
Source: Synthesized by the authors.

and disseminate crucial movement and action-specific information; and (3) *task coordination*, wherein they break down action planning into concrete tasks and assemble teams to execute them. These mechanisms each involved peer collaboration in distinct ways. Tactical innovation and information curation were largely dependent on online platforms, but they also demanded protesters to skilfully leverage platform-specific features in order to be effective. In contrast, task coordination depended on both online platforms and offline ties. Without real-world connections and interactions, it would have been challenging for protesters to form teams and build trust to facilitate actions. Figure 8.1 provided a graphical illustration to summarize these components.

TACTICAL INNOVATION

Tactical innovation is crucial for the success of social movements. Defined as 'the creativity of insurgents in devising new tactical forms' (McAdam 1983: 736), it empowers challengers to gain bargaining leverage over their opponents (McCammon 2012). Traditionally, organizational leaders are tasked with devising tactics, carefully selecting those that resonate with movement actors and the general public. As Charles Tilly argues, '[repertoire] resembles an elementary language: familiar as the day to its users, for all its possible quaintness or incomprehensibility to an outsider' (1978: 156). Consequently, tactical repertoire often comprises only 'a handful of alternatives' and evolves slowly, usually 'at the margins of inherited forms' (Tarrow 1998: 101). However, in the context of leaderful mobilizations, the responsibility of devising tactics is shifted from organizations to ordinary protesters. Anyone can propose new tactics in the digital realm. But at the same time, this democratization of tactical discussions can complicate the decision-making process for selecting tactics. As a result, these mobilizations often experience a 'tactical freeze' following rapid expansion due to the lack of a collective decision-making culture and infrastructure, leaving little room for the development and agreement on new strategies (Tufekci 2017).

The need for innovative tactics was also apparent during the early stages of the Anti-Extradition Movement. Despite the million-strong demonstration on June 9, protesters were unsure about their future course of actions. The HKSAR government seemed unfazed by the opposition's scale and was determined to pass the extradition bill. Furthermore, CHRF, the main organizer of the two rallies, did not provide a clear roadmap for future actions. Concerned that the bill would pass in the legislature, protesters called for a siege of LegCo on June 12. Unlike the June 9 rally, the June 12 protest was spontaneous and leaderless. The protest was proposed by two ordinary protesters on Facebook who held no prominent positions within any SMOs. Despite the ensuing chaotic and violent confrontation with the police, this protest fostered a strong sense among the protesters that they had to take initiative rather than rely on established organizations for mobilization.

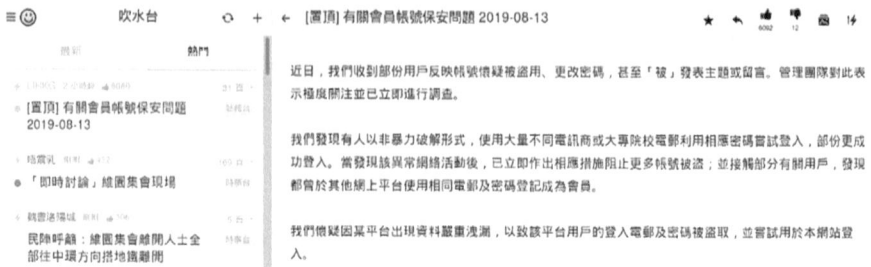

FIGURE 8.2 A sample screenshot of LIHKG, 2019.
Source: LIHKG.

Around this time, numerous tactical discussions started appearing on an online forum called LIHKG. Often likened to Reddit, LIHKG boasts over forty chatrooms where users engage in discussions on a range of topics, from pets to current affairs (see Figure 8.2). By allowing users to remain anonymous, the forum promoted an environment of open expression. Moreover, its upvoting and downvoting system essentially allows real time 'voting' on posts. Popular posts, indicated by more upvotes and comments, are showcased in a separate list, drawing attention to trending discussions. Furthermore, unlike Facebook or Twitter, LIHKG users do not 'follow' one another. This feature prevents the formation of individual follower-based spaces (Lee et al. 2022b); it also prompts users to compete for attention on specific topics, leading to a centralization of discussions and preventing their dispersion into separate silos (Liang and Lee 2023). These attributes contributed to LIHKG's popularity among protesters as a platform for discussing matters pertinent to the movement.

In June 2019, LIHKG saw an impressive influx of almost 10,000 newly registered users, a stark increase compared to the monthly average of around 3,400 newly registered users between January 2017 and May 2019. This upward trend continued, with around 14,500 and 11,800 new users in July and August 2019, respectively (Lee et al. 2022b). Additionally, there was a significant surge in the volume of discussions (see Figure 8.3). Between April and May 2019, the average number of posts and comments in two primary channels – 'Public Affairs Channel' and 'Chit-Chat Channel' – was around 47,000 and 402,400, respectively. However, in June 2019, those numbers skyrocketed to 89,500 and 1,951,100. Notably, a content analysis conducted by Francis Lee and his co-authors (2022b) reveal that 34.9 per cent of the posts proposed actions for protesters or public figures, and 5.2 per cent discussed movement strategies or the justification of specific actions. Nevertheless, not every idea gained attention, as the majority failed to make it to the popular lists.

A crucial question concerns how certain tactical ideas rose above the vast ocean of discussions, gained traction, and ultimately became actionable. Given the extensive volume of conversations on LIHKG, users adopted

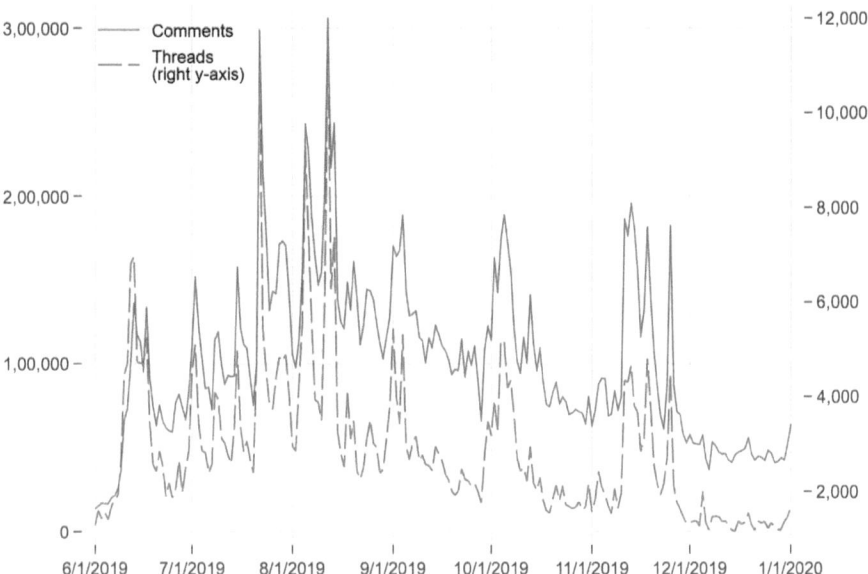

FIGURE 8.3 Daily number of comments and posts on LIHKG, 2019.
Source: Data collected from LIHKG.

several strategies to compete for attention and make their ideas noticed. First, users would post multiple short comments under their authored post in an attempt to make it a trending topic, as more comments imply greater engagement. Second, they would share the post's link on other social media platforms, aiming to reach a wider audience. Third, if a post failed to gain traction, they would repost the same message in hopes that the new post would attract more attention. These strategies primarily aimed at two goals: first, to 'exploit' the forum's algorithm (Kwok and Chan 2024) – which remained unknown to the end users – in order to promote a particular post to the popular list, which guarantee more viewership, and second, to gather more upvotes and supportive comments from others.

These strategies provide insight into how protesters used LIHKG to generate and highlight selected tactical ideas. However, they do not explain how ideas were converted into action. To illuminate this dynamic, let us examine the emergence of the so-called 'international front', a protest tactic that sought to gain international support for the movement. The idea's earliest form emerged in May 2019, prior to the June protests, when protesters mobilized others to sign a White House-run online petition on LIHKG, hoping it would prompt the US government to exert pressure on the Chinese and Hong Kong authorities. The idea of creating an 'international front' gained momentum after the June 9 rally. Concerned about the potential decline in protest momentum, some protesters proposed demonstrating at the upcoming

G20 meeting in Japan. Others continued to disseminate various petitions addressing foreign governments. Among these, a user named 'I want mutual destruction' (*woyao lanchao; ngo-yiu-laam-chaau*) was notably prominent. His posts often received thousands of upvotes and replies, making them highly visible on the popular lists. His first post appeared on June 10, where he mobilized protesters to lobby foreign governments to revoke the foreign passports of local government officials and pro-Beijing politicians. This post alone received over 7,000 upvotes, with many users offering their Telegram handles to join the Telegram work group. Subsequent posts by the same user even provided letter templates directed at various foreign governments and international organizations, which others could conveniently download and send out. The emergence of this innovative tactic catalysed a shift in the movement's direction.

This tactic quickly diffused into the offline world. On June 26, hundreds of protesters, responding to a call on the discussion forum, held a rally to deliver petitions to various foreign consulates. This event was followed by a demonstration directly addressing foreign leaders at the G20 summit. Innovative ideas on how to expand the 'international front' continued to emerge on LIHKG. About a week before the G20 summit, some protesters proposed launching a global advertising campaign with the goal of placing pro-movement advertisements in major newspapers worldwide. The idea was initially posted on LIHKG on June 23 in a brief text:

Some 'brothers' mentioned that one of the turning points of Taiwan's Sunflower Movement was that protesters placed an ad in the New York Times. Since the government now ignores our demands, what about crowdfunding to post ads in every major newspaper around the world? How's the idea? [...] Can brothers in different countries ask about the fee? See if we can make the deadline?[1]

The post swiftly gathered thousands of upvotes and a deluge of supportive comments, many offering practical suggestions on targeting specific newspapers and fundraising for the campaign. However, a concrete plan remained absent. This only changed when another user compiled all the suggestions into a new post, detailing which newspapers to target, the optimal timing for publishing the advertisements, the content to include in the advertisements, and an initial division of labour plan. The user also provided a Telegram group link to encourage interested individuals to join a public chat group for further discussions and brainstorming. This same user then encouraged others to copy the post and make necessary edits. The online discussion proceeded for another day and amassed 864 comments in total, culminating in the formation of a basic plan for the campaign.

---

[1] Caca Siu. 2019 'What if Open Letters Appear in Newspapers Worldwide on June 28?' (In Cantonese). *LIHKG* (online forum). Retrieved on 23 June. https://lihkg.com/thread/1252292/page/1.

As the thread's activity began to slow, a new post about the campaign surfaced on June 25, penned by a user going by the pseudonym 'Knorr macaroni' (*jialepai tongxinfen; gaa-lok-paai-tung-sam-fan*), later revealed to be an overseas university student.[2] In the post, 'Knorr macaroni' reported that the Financial Times had agreed to collaborate with them, but funding was necessary as advertising in such prominent newspapers was expensive. She shared a link to a crowdfunding page where supporters could donate to the campaign. This post also gained enormous popularity, amassing over 5,000 upvotes and spreading rapidly on Facebook and Telegram groups. Fellow users even shared it multiple times in the comments on other popular posts to increase its visibility. Thanks to these collective efforts, the campaign managed to raise an astonishing HKD 6.7 million within a day, consisting of over 22,000 donations, mostly small contributions of HKD 100. This overwhelming support enabled the team to publish advertisements in major newspapers in more than ten countries (Hong Kong Public Opinion Research Institute 2021).

The emergence of the 'international front' thus highlighted the pivotal role of LIHKG as a platform for fostering tactical innovation. Serving as a centralized communication platform, LIHKG offered various affordances that enabled protesters to propose, select, and refine innovative action ideas. The concept of affordances is often used by communication scholars to refer to the ways in which the material and design features of a technology request, demand, allow, encourage, discourage, or refuse certain actions over others (Davis and Chouinard 2016). While technological affordances are important, the transformation of ideas into actions depended heavily on the strategic agency of protesters in utilizing the platform's affordances. Since most strategic discussions often went unnoticed, users had to strategize to capture others' attention. They achieved this by skilfully employing features such as upvotes, comments, and cross-platform sharing. These manoeuvres were crucial for gaining visibility and traction for their ideas. Once ideas garnered sufficient attention, strategic and tactical consensus could then be developed and solidified.

Importantly, this process was not leaderless. Similar to what Pablo Gerbaudo (2017) observed in Egypt's Arab Spring uprising concerning the administrators of activist Facebook pages, informal leaders also emerged on LIHKG, playing a significant role in shaping the protest agenda. However, the structure of influence of LIHKG's informal leaders differed from that of Facebook page administrators. As mentioned earlier, informal leaders on LIHKG had to constantly compete for attention since users do not subscribe to specific individuals or groups, unlike on Facebook. To stand out, these leaders often used

---

[2] Knorr Macroni. 2019. 'Don't Stop the Offense! Passport-Holding Hongkongers Jointly Issue an Open Letter to Request Consulates around the World to Issue Travel Warnings for Hong Kong.' (In Cantonese), *LIHKG* (online forum). Retrieved on 14 June. https://lihkg.com/thread/1220737/page/1.

eye-catching words and grammar that conveyed a sense of urgency. Popular posts often read like a vernacular speech mixed with vulgar language more than a proper essay. Furthermore, the influence of leaders on LIHKG was not stable over time. According to Hai Liang and Francis Lee's research (2023), while influence on LIHKG tended to concentrate heavily on particular users, it also experienced fluctuations. Notably, this instability was more pronounced in movement-related discussions compared to non-movement ones. This suggests that users were less inclined to recognize specific groups or individuals as central leaders and remained open to shifting their attention to other influencers as the movement evolved. Collectively, these characteristics indicate that tactical innovation can continuously occur on LIHKG, as long as the platform maintains a substantial flow of traffic.

INFORMATION CURATION

While digital communication technologies have expedited the flow and exchange of content, they also lead to information overload (Bawden and Robinson 2020) and the propagation of misinformation (Kaufhold et al. 2019; Laato et al. 2020). In leaderful mobilizations, where protesters heavily rely on digital tools to disseminate information and resources, acquiring accurate and useful information can pose a challenge (Earl and Garrett 2017; Gillan 2009). To facilitate action organization, information about the movement must first undergo several steps: collection, selection, processing, categorization, filtering, and repackaging before being 'consumed' by protesters. We refer to this mechanism as information curation. The term 'curation' is borrowed from the work of W. Lance Bennett, Alexandra Segerberg and Shawn Walker (2014), which highlights Twitter's role in the Occupy Wall Street movement, not only in generating digital content but also in curating them – a process they define as the 'preservation, maintenance, and sorting of digital assets'.

Unlike in the Occupy movement, Twitter was not extensively used among protesters during the Anti-Extradition Movement, except for the purpose of garnering international support (Cheng, Lui and Fu 2023; Luqiu and Lu 2021). An arguably more important platform for protesters to gather information was Telegram, a free, cloud-based instant messaging app that enables users to generate content publicly and to communicate privately (Urman et al. 2021). Launched in August 2013 by privacy-focused programmers who founded the Russian social network Vkontakte, Telegram had already amassed 700 million monthly active users by 2022, thanks to its diverse range of affordances.

Telegram allows users to create public (searchable) or private (unsearchable) 'channels', through which creators and/or administrators can send messages to an unlimited number of subscribers. Messages are signed by the channel's name, and subscribers cannot see who created or administers the channel. This helps create large online communities without identifiable opinion leaders.

In addition to channels, users can also create public (open to all) or private (by invitation only) groups, akin to group chats on other instant messaging platforms. While the former functions like a public channel, the latter enables more private or secretive communication.

Telegram also offers a variety of privacy-enhancing features (Urman and Katz 2022). First, although Telegram accounts are linked to phone numbers, users have the option to set up a username alias, allowing them to stay anonymous when participating in online communities. They can also change the associated phone numbers and alias at any time to enhance their privacy. Second, all messages are encrypted, either on the platform's servers or through end-to-end encryption, providing an additional layer of privacy and security in their communications. Third, the absence of algorithmic filtering and advertising on Telegram means users have better control over their content consumption (Urman, Ho, and Katz 2021). They can easily unsubscribe from channels or leave groups, or simply mute them, whenever they wish to stop viewing their content. Lastly, Telegram allows users to forward messages anonymously or unsend messages, offering them better protection from law enforcement agencies seeking to use their chat history as incriminating evidence (Urman and Katz 2022).

By offering enhanced privacy and opportunities to gain publicity, Telegram has become a favoured digital platform for contemporary protests (Mateo 2022; Su, Chan and Paik 2022; Wijermars and Lokot 2022). Indeed, during the early stages of the Anti-Extradition Movement, Telegram quickly rose to prominence as an information broadcaster (Fu 2023). A notable example was a public channel named '612 Reminder', established on 10 June 2019. Its purpose was to consolidate information for protesters in preparation for the planned protest on June 12. Over time, the channel developed into a comprehensive information provider offering instant updates about protest sites, exit plans, and protest event details. Within the first month, the channel attracted 20,000 subscribers, and, by the end of 2019, it had grown to over 180,000 subscribers.

As the movement progressed, the number of Telegram channels disseminating movement-related information surged. According to Aleksandra Urman, Justin Ho and Stefan Katz (2021), around fifty movement-related public channels and groups were established in June, with the number reaching its peak in November when over 160 new channels created. In total, they identified more than 1,800 public channels and groups related to the movement through snowballing. These channels specialized in providing various types of information regarding the movement, such as news, event updates, on-site reports, and regional information. Such information was vital for protesters to organize and participate in actions, including knowing when and where protest actions were scheduled, what supplies and funding were needed, whether there was a heavy police presence in specific areas, and which number to call for legal support when arrested.

Beyond merely disseminating information, these channels also played a pivotal role in *curating* raw information. Different channels often specialized in curating specific types of information. Some channels focused on fact-checking: '@antiextraditionverifiednews', established by a group of protesters during the June twelve protest, aimed to debunk rumours and provide accurate updates about the movement. Within a week, it attracted nearly 70,000 subscribers. Others focused on organizing information about future protest events: '@hk_schedule' collected upcoming protest events from various sources and published easily shareable infographics of protest event schedules, as shown in Figure 8.4. These schedules played a crucial role in reminding protesters of the time and venue of upcoming events and generating a sense of rhythm and momentum. Additionally, there were reconnaissance channels that focused on providing real time and on-the-ground information about the protests, some of which were crowdsourced from protesters on the frontlines.

These channels were managed by dedicated volunteers who often worked in teams. Handling the large volume of raw information received by the channels daily was a time-consuming business. Extensive teamwork and division of labour were often required. In many cases, collaboration from fellow protesters was also essential. For instance, fact-checking channels frequently called on fellow protesters to report any information they found suspicious or were unsure about, which volunteers would then verify. Similarly, reconnaissance

FIGURE 8.4 Protest schedule in infographics, 2019.
Source: Data collected from Telegram channel.

channels often heavily relied on reports from protesters concerning real time situations on the ground. These collaborative efforts among protesters played a pivotal role in producing shareable information.

To better curate information, channel administrators skilfully utilized Telegram's affordances. One notable example was the use of hashtags. Similar to Twitter, hashtags in Telegram could 'stitch' related posts together, making them searchable within a channel or even the entire chat history of users. This allowed individuals interested in a specific topic to gather all relevant content (Bennett, Segerberg and Walker 2014). During the Anti-Extradition Movement, hashtags were widely employed by channels to curate various types of information. Chris Su, Michael Chan and Sejin Paik (2022) identified five primary categories of movement-related hashtags: geolocations, movement slogans, priming keywords, events, and mobilization form. Thanks to these hashtags, protesters could swiftly access specific types of information, thus fostering synchronous information-sharing among them. Among these hashtags, geolocations were the most frequently utilized, especially in reconnaissance channels. Geotags enabled protesters to stay updated about activities at specific locations and times, such as active protests or the presence of law enforcement officers and vehicles. This real time, on-the-ground information was invaluable to protesters, aiding them in better assessing situations during protests. This partly explains why the occurrence of geotags was highly correlated with protest events (Su, Chan, and Paik 2022).

Information curation extended beyond individual channels; it also transpired through cross-channel sharing, where protest-related information was disseminated among various Telegram channels. Given the large number of channels broadcasting protest information, there was a possibility of fragmentation into distinct online communities, similar to the 'cyberbalkanization' phenomenon observed on Facebook (Chan, Chow and Fu 2019). However, during the peak of the movement, the Telegram channel network did not experience fragmentation. Contrarily, the Telegram network became increasingly cohesive from June 2019 to December 2019 (Urman, Ho and Katz 2021). A plausible explanation for this phenomenon is that specific public channels gained significant authority due to their ability to address specific movement needs. As a result, other channels began sharing their content more frequently. Our analysis of the monthly top ten channels with the highest in-degree scores, as indicated in Figure 8.5, revealed that the nature of these channels closely aligned with the developmental stage of the movement.[3] For instance, action-oriented Telegram channels that provided frontline information and played a key role in organizing actions gained importance over time. Conversely, channels associated with political

---

[3] In social network analysis, in-degree score refers to the number of edges coming into a node within a directed graph. In our case, Telegram public groups with high in-degree score are groups whose messages are highly shared by other groups.

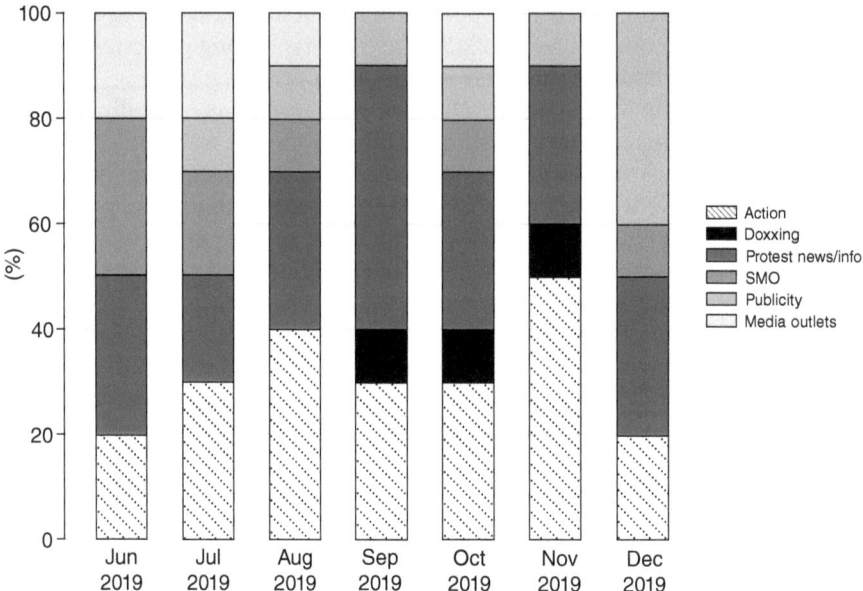

FIGURE 8.5 Top ten Telegram channels/groups with the highest inward connections (measured by in-degree scores).
Source: Data obtained from Urman, Ho and Katz (2021).

organizations became relatively less influential. This shift in influence among channels likely contributed to the network's increasing cohesion and collaborative nature during the height of the movement.

TASK COORDINATION

While tactical innovation and information curation explain the genesis of tactical ideas and the gathering and dissemination of movement information, they still do not explain how protest actions are organized. This necessitates task coordination, a mechanism that involves the division of labour. Unlike the first two mechanisms, which heavily rely on digital technologies, task coordination requires more than just digital connections. While networking online, protesters must leverage their pre-existing social networks and face to face interactions to enable complex coordinative efforts. We refer to these networks and interactions as relational infrastructures that connect individuals within their social lives. In this section, we explore how these relational infrastructures enable protesters to access resources and essential expertise when organizing specific actions, and to build trust within a high-risk environment.

This is not to downplay the importance of digital communication technologies. Undoubtedly, they remained the fundamental tools through which protesters coordinated and communicated. However, instead of using LIHKG and Telegram's public channels, protesters used private Telegram groups for task coordination due to the often-sensitive nature of discussions. The choice to use Telegram – rather than other messaging apps, such as the more popular WhatsApp – was deliberate, given that many people in Hong Kong had downloaded Telegram and activated accounts during the movement. As David Karpf noted (2012: 118), these private groups function as 'network backchannels', which 'delineate a space for off-the-record, private conversations among self-constructed on-groups'. Unlike Telegram public channels, Twitter, or public forums, network backchannels leave no public digital trace, ensuring confidentiality and enabling protesters to distinguish trusted participants from untrusted observers.

The global advertising campaign provides a vivid example of how task coordination was facilitated by the interaction between online and offline networks. The campaign's transition from LIHKG and public Telegram groups to more private 'network backchannels' was not immediate. In the early stages, as the campaign garnered popularity on the forum and millions of Hong Kong dollars were raised through crowdfunding, a public Telegram group was established to host preliminary discussions. However, this open forum quickly descended into chaos. As one core member, Kevin, recalled:

I first saw the idea on LIHKG. At first, I thought this was just another idea. But when I saw there were a few million [dollars] raised from crowdfunding, I knew that this was going to be serious. So many people have donated, and you can't afford to mess this up since that's public money. So, I traced all the related posts and found a Telegram link. It was an invite to a Telegram public group. When I joined it, I was really shocked. There were already more than 2000 people in the group. People discussed all sorts of things, and it was extremely chaotic. (Interview C5)

Kevin's participation in the group reminded him of his experience playing real time strategy games during his primary school days. Now a computer programmer in his twenties, he was once deeply immersed in a multiplayer online game called 'Travian: Legends', which enjoyed worldwide popularity in the 2000s. In the game, players communicated with each other using in-game messages, formed alliances, and collaborated on various tasks. From this experience, Kevin learned that coordinating through online text communication could be challenging, as people often interrupted each other, leading to disagreements and divisions. When he joined the campaign group, he felt compelled to take action.

Kevin spent a day to review all the previous messages – a distinctive feature of Telegram that allows users to view past posts in a group before joining, a feature absent in WhatsApp. He consolidated all the discussions into key points, which he then shared with the group. He continued to update this 'dashboard' based on subsequent discussions and sent out reminders about crucial decisions that had to be made. Gradually, a few others in the group joined him in this consolidation work. For Kevin, this work was essential to focus people's attention on critical matters and filter out unnecessary ones, drawing from the lessons he learned from his gaming experience. His experience provided a vivid illustration of how gaming literacy among the protesters facilitated protest communication and mobilization (Lin and Sun 2022).

As the global advertising campaign became more concrete, smaller public groups with specific functions were created, such as those for legal matters, country-specific concerns, and design. Simultaneously, the core members formed a private Telegram group, inviting active contributors from the initial discussions. Kevin, who was not part of the original 'founders', was invited to this core group, too. Their goal was to devise a comprehensive action plan. One immediate task for the group was to utilize the raised funds without violating money laundering laws. To achieve this, they asked the lawyers and accountants within their personal networks to join the team.

As the workload increased, there was a practical need to expand the group and divide its members into specialized teams. It was also decided that these teams should become private, with restricted membership to enhance collaboration. Several types of teams were formed based on the smaller public groups: country-specific teams (comprising individuals familiar with the target country's language and culture, where ads would be published), professional teams (comprising lawyers, accountants, and designers), deal teams (negotiating with newspapers for quotes and prices), public relations teams (managing external relations), and a secretariat (overseeing and managing the entire process). The formation of these teams further solidified the collaborative efforts behind the campaign.

The core members took on the responsibility of selecting the members for various teams. They not only included those who had actively contributed to the initial efforts but also leveraged their own personal networks to bring in new teammates. This approach was driven by the need for specific expertise, trust, and commitment, especially given the limited timeframe and the need for reliable volunteers. Consequently, approximately 15–20 teams were formed, each with its private Telegram group. These teams consisted of around 20–30 members, often with two designated persons-in-charge serving as group administrator to ensure around-the-clock collaboration. In addition to the work teams, two other groups played a crucial role in making high-level decisions. The first was a smaller group consisting solely of the core members. The second was a larger group that included the group administrators from the work teams. around 250 individuals were collaborating at the height of the campaign, many of whom hardly knew one another. Telegram private groups facilitated direct communication while maintaining anonymity.

This arrangement underscores how division of labour resulted from the interplay between digital platforms and social networks. The digital platforms served as virtual meeting spaces, enabling teams to collaborate. Simultaneously, social networks facilitated team formation. After teams were established, smaller circles of trust organically emerged among them. At the heart of these circles were the core members, who made the key strategic decisions. Following them were the group administrators, responsible for managing individual teams. On the periphery were the rank and file volunteers, solely focused on implementation tasks. This informal hierarchy emerged naturally, in which positions reflected both the stage at which individuals joined the campaign and the amount of effort they contributed.

The core team had to make numerous strategic decisions. For example, in the early stages, they had to decide which country and which newspapers to approach, and whether the quoted amount was affordable given the limited funding. Another critical decision involved how to frame the ads effectively. The decision-making process was often recorded in detail, with agendas, secretaries to take notes, and specific procedures for passing decisions. When making decisions, the ideal approach was to reach a consensus, but if that proved challenging, a vote would be called. The least preferred method was making decisions based on the input of those 'present' in the online discussion – but this did happen on many occasions.

Once decisions were made, the secretariat would announce them in the larger decision group. Such information would then be passed on to individual work teams through the group administrators. Lower-level tasks were subsequently devised and assigned to the volunteers. The secretariat would send a summary and pinned it in the bigger decision group. Telegram's features, such as hashtags and links, proved invaluable in summarizing all necessary information, including work progress, task assignments, existing drafts, and instructions for filling out claim forms. Their role was indispensable because of the impossibility of remembering all the minute details. Just as Kevin's 'summaries' had done in the public group, these digital summaries played a vital role in facilitating task coordination, serving as a crucial directory for implementing the campaign's efforts.

The campaign successfully leveraged both the affordances of the Telegram platform and the protesters' social networks to coordinate tasks, even without a pre-existing organizational structure. However, despite framing itself as leaderless, the global advertising campaign developed its own hierarchy to handle different kinds of decisions. Core members played a particularly significant role as the earliest and most proactive contributors, functioning essentially as the 'informal leaders'. This was similar to the 'social media teams' observed in the Arab Spring (Gerbaudo 2017). Although volunteers played a crucial role in the campaign by contributing their time and expertise, they had minimal involvement in making the most important strategic decisions. Their roles mainly revolved around operational tasks.

In other words, despite the absence of centralized leadership in leaderful mobilization, informal hierarchies remain relevant for getting the job done. This echoed our findings on secondary school students in Chapter 7. Interestingly, the majority of volunteers accepted, or at least did not contest, the implicit hierarchy. One volunteer, Kay, explained that the urgency of meeting deadlines left little time to question the informal power structures. Moreover, the anonymity of the campaign organizers made it difficult to attribute blame and responsibility, as volunteers often did not know their real identities and rarely encountered them in the groups that they were part of (Interview C6).

The dynamics of task coordination can be further understood through the case of another group known as the Hong Kong Higher Institutions International Affairs Delegation (HKIAD). Formed in July 2019 by university student activists, its aim was to lobby for international support of the pro-democracy movement. Many of these activists, who were student union leaders with localist leanings, had been previously involved in activism and knew each other prior to the summer of 2019.

To support this mission, they established a research arm led by a twenty-one-year-old student activist named Annie. According to her, the research team recruited volunteers online through a simple vetting process before adding them to a separate Telegram private group distinct from the one hosting core activists. Annie did not personally know most volunteers. Whenever new research tasks emerged, Annie would seek help from this volunteer group, assessing who had capacity and interest to contribute. Typically, tasks were generated top-down from the core activists. For instance, when HKIAD scheduled meetings, core activists would request a 'policy brief' from the research team. In this manner, the research team functioned as 'contractors' taking on projects on an ad hoc basis. Once volunteers expressed interest, Annie would create a new Telegram private chat for task-specific work groups consisting of herself, core activists, and interested volunteers.

This decentralized approach bore similarities to the global advertising campaign. In both cases, the core activists were responsible for making strategic decisions and defining high-level objectives, which then led to the generation of specific tasks. The volunteers, on the other hand, were solely tasked with implementing these assigned tasks. A critical role in this informal hierarchy was the person acting as a mediator between the core activists and the volunteers – similar to the secretariat's role in the global advertising campaign.

Annie took up this pivotal position in HKIAD, allocating tasks and supervising their completion. To manage the workflow efficiently, Annie maintained a project document on Google Sheets listing all ongoing tasks, the respective volunteers assigned to handle them, and deadlines for completion. Volunteers communicated directly with her and were only informed about the tasks they were specifically responsible for. The most crucial aspect of Annie's role was making each task as specific as possible and setting clear deadlines for completion. As she noted,

Since I don't know the volunteers personally, I have to think of ways to make people do their work, especially when you have a tight timeline... When people were simply volunteering, and when you didn't know their identity, you couldn't afford to be rude to them, because they could simply stop replying to you and remove their [Telegram] account. You need to encourage and incentivize them. (Interview C7)

Because of this, Annie found Telegram less useful for real time coordination because 'once you forgot to look at your Telegram chats for a while, you would miss a lot of messages and have no idea what was going on'. To address this, she utilized voice calls to communicate with volunteers in real time. Additionally, she also used Discord, a VoIP social media platform commonly used in gaming, to schedule real time voice call meetings with the task groups. Making voice calls allowed her to also 'assess the commitment of the person on the other end of the phone, since you could tell from a person's voice if he or she was genuinely helpful or not'.

These examples demonstrate how the task coordination relied on pre-existing social relationships or real time interactions for team building. However, this was not always the case, as groups and teams could also form spontaneously among strangers who simply met during the movement online or at protest sites. This raises the obvious question of trust: How could strangers establish trust within a high-risk environment? Ming-sho Ho (2023) finds that protesters during the Anti-Extradition Movement used three 'relational tactics' to collaborate and maintain trust – anonymity, pre-existing ties, and bonding. This chapter has so far provided corroborating evidence for anonymity and pre-existing ties. The following example, based on a Telegram 'publicity' (*wenxuan*; *man-suen*) channel, sheds light on bonding – the investment of personal feelings and sentiments. It shows how bonding played an important role in building trust among strangers.

The channel was established in late June 2019. With over 100,000 subscribers, it became one of the most popular channels, sharing infographics, posters, photos, and memes providing practical information, boosting morale, and criticizing authorities. The channel's 'owner', who went by the moniker Ice, was a high school student during the time of the movement. He did not establish the channel but was invited by a fellow protester to manage it. After accepting the role, he invited several other protestors he had encountered during the protests to assist him in managing the channel. Their primary responsibility was to create and disseminate diverse infographics about the movement, which were then distributed across other channels and networks of fellow protestors. During late June and early July, they also collaborated closely with the global advertising campaign to boost their efforts.

By August, the core team had expanded to over twenty members. In contrast to HKIAD, where team members were acquainted prior to the movement, his team comprised individuals who connected only once the movement had begun. Reflecting on his experience, Ice mentioned that the team often met in person, as solely relying on online interactions proved challenging. He said,

'There was a lot going on online, many strangers, many people talking. It is hard to discuss things. When you started to discuss a topic, only those who were online could participate'. (Interview C8) They discovered that face to face meetings promoted more effective collaboration and trust-building among team members. To facilitate this, the team secured a studio space where they could work collectively, which served as a 'safe house' for protesters following street actions. It became a meeting space where the group bonded and built personal relationships.

According to Ice, one of the challenges was ensuring new members were not police informants or spies infiltrating into them. To mitigate this risk, the team developed a vetting process: they would initially inspect the Instagram profiles of newcomers to glean insights into their personal lives. Ice stated that Instagram offered a window into individuals' real-life activities, which helped them assess if the person appeared trustworthy. An empty or inactive Instagram profile raised suspicion, whereas profiles rich with personal activities provided a degree of reassurance about the individual's authenticity and intentions.

As the chief administrator of the channel, Ice wielded significant influence over major decisions, such as the channel's content, posting schedule, and the selection of individuals to assist with the channel's operations. To effectively manage his responsibilities, he delegated several individuals from the core group as deputy administrators. These deputies aided in the daily running of the channel, which encompassed monitoring social media activities and disseminating information around the clock. They also held the authority to add or remove channel members. This structure, akin to that of HKIAD, placed the administrators as pivotal figures in team building and task coordination within the channel.

For Ice, acting as an administrator not only gave him with a sense of identity within the movement but also granted him the capability to expand the team and recruit new talent. After delegating routine tasks to other core group members, his primary responsibility became collaborating with graphic designers to produce innovative infographics. He actively followed various Telegram channels and Instagram profiles in search of potential graphic designers or photographers. Once he located suitable candidates, he would form small groups, usually comprising 5–6 people, and engage them in discussions to gauge their interest in specific tasks. Operating in these smaller groups proved to be the most efficient method for achieving their objectives.

CONCLUSION

This chapter has detailed how protesters in the Anti-Extradition Movement managed to organize protest activities effectively despite lacking centralized organizations and leaders. We attribute this capability to a process that we call 'peer collaboration', where ordinary protesters work together in a horizontal and decentralized manner to conceive, shape, and plan actions.

This overarching process was largely facilitated by digital communication technologies. Our findings show how these technologies facilitated three mechanisms of action organization, namely tactical innovation, information curation, and task coordination. At the same time, these mechanisms also depended heavily on the protesters' skill in using platform-specific features and their offline social connections. First, while tactical innovation and information curation predominantly occurred online, they were driven by protesters' strategic navigation within the platforms. Second, while digital technologies provided the platforms for facilitating task coordination, this routine necessitated a significant reliance on real-world relational infrastructures, which enabled team formation and trust-building.

It is crucial to stress that peer collaboration is not a leaderless and non-hierarchical process. Although the movement had no central leaders, informal leaders emerged throughout its course. The three mechanisms all underscored the critical role these informal leaders played in peer collaboration. They were among the prominent users on LIHKG who proposed tactical ideas that gained traction, influential Telegram public channels that became hubs for movement-related information, and administrators of Telegram private groups who assigned tasks to volunteers. They undertook tasks fundamental to action organization, which helped to maintain a continuous stream of protest actions.

In essence, peer collaboration is just like improvisation in a jazz ensemble. Although the musicians may not know one another personally or stylistically, they can listen attentively to each other's play and respond to their musical ideas, creating a dynamic and interactive conversation. They might start with familiar tunes, but once they familiarize themselves musically, they take turns soloing, while the accompanists provide the harmonic and rhythmic foundation. Mistakes are common and unavoidable during their improvisation; but jazz musicians are often adept at turning these into opportunities to steer their music in new directions.

9

Money Matters

Street protests were not the only tactical repertoire used in the Anti-Extradition Movement. As mass demonstrations continued through June, protesters turned to the economic front. They began by actively debating the political stances of various businesses and restaurants on the online forum LIHKG. Some proposed actions such as withdrawing money from Chinese banks or divesting from stocks of Chinese companies as forms of protest. Others closely monitored comments from business owners who expressed support for the government. For instance, when a co-owner of ZStore, an online grocery shop, posted pro-extradition bill comments on Facebook, protesters promptly initiated a boycott campaign against the company. The mounting pressure prompted the company to retract its earlier view, clarifying that the co-owner's opinions did not represent the company's official stance.

These actions paved the way for the rise of a new tactical repertoire in the movement: political consumption. Political consumption is defined as the practice of using consumer choices to express policy preferences and challenge undesirable institutional or market practices (Micheletti 2003: 2; Newman and Bartels 2011; Schudson 2007; Shah et al. 2007). The concept encompasses four key action forms: (1) boycotting, which means abstaining from buying certain products and services for sociopolitical reasons; (2) buycotting, which means deliberately purchasing specific products and services for similar reasons; (3) discursive and communicative actions; and (4) lifestyle changes (Boström, Micheletti, and Oosterveer 2019). The Anti-Extradition Movement heavily featured the first two action forms. Apart from boycotting, protesters also called for buycotting pro-movement businesses. They even promoted what they termed a 'yellow economic circle' (thereafter called yellow economy) – a reference to the symbolic colour of the pro-democracy protests – which encompassed a network of retailers, restaurants and consumers united by shared political and ideological values (Li and Whitworth 2023). The tactic gained prominence after a citywide strike on August 5, when protesters called on others to support shops that had participated in the strike. Consequently, several online platforms compiled lists of 'yellow shops' (pro-movement businesses) and 'blue shops' (pro-government businesses). Online directories and maps were also created to list and geo-locate these businesses.

This chapter explains the rise and impact of political consumption in the Anti-Extradition Movement. We demonstrate how the mechanism of peer collaboration, as outlined in Chapter 8, precipitated the emergence of boycotting and buycotting as tactical repertoires during the movement. We then show how the two action forms had disparate impacts, despite being used to achieve the same protest goals. Boycotting, as a punitive tactic, deterred businesspersons from openly supporting the government during the movement. Meanwhile, buycotting, as a reward-oriented tactic, promoted mutual assistance and network building among protesters, bolstering their solidarity in the absence of centralized leadership. Our findings shed light on the micro-dynamics of leaderful mobilization and highlight its potential to innovate tactically. They also demonstrate the social and political meaning of money (Zelizer 2017), as well as the role of the market in contentious politics.

BOYCOTTING IN A CAPITALISTIC CITY

With its robust capitalist roots, Hong Kong has long been governed under the substantial influence of the business elites. During the colonial era, the British ruled in the absence of democracy by securing support from representatives of the local business elites, including tycoons, leading professionals, and senior executives (Goodstadt 2000; Ngo 2018). This explicit state-business alliance persisted, and arguably strengthened, following the handover to China. Business elites continued to wield considerable influence through consultative bodies and functional constituencies in the legislature, forming a ruling coalition that exchanged specific interests for political support (Lee 2005; Ma 2016). Over time, business elites, particularly those with mainland China ties, were incorporated into China's top legislative and advisory bodies, which reinforced their loyalty to Beijing (Cheng 2020; Fong 2014). This powerful alliance allowed business elites to maintain economic dominance while staunchly defending government policies in return. The extradition bill was no exception: despite reservations, most had no choice but to fall in line.

It is against this backdrop that political consumption emerged as a tactical repertoire in the Anti-Extradition Movement. Given the economic elites' role in the ruling coalition, it was predictable that initial protests targeted pro-government businesses for boycotts. Following the actions against Ztore, several other major businesses were boycotted for various reasons. For example, Maxim's Group, a food-and-beverage conglomerate with over 1,000 outlets citywide, became a prominent target after a major shareholder criticized the protests. Best Mart 360, a grocery chain, was targeted due to the executive's alleged connections with vigilantes attacking protesters.[1]

However, while highlighting the political role of business actors and the longstanding economic foundation of Hong Kong's liberal oligarchy, these boycotts failed to pressure the government into addressing protest demands. As discussed earlier, Hong Kong's capitalist system grants business elites an entrenched, pervasive presence in the economy, which hampered pro-democracy protesters' efforts to single out specific targets. As predicted, the boycotts had a minor impact. The selection of targets was sporadic and lacked a systematic approach. Most boycott calls were based on flimsy allegations or the business owners' comments; and while they disrupted targeted companies, the overall economic dominance remained unaffected.

The limited impact of boycotting led protesters to adopt a more proactive tactic: buycotting. In late July, protest supporters on LIHKG began advocating not only for boycotting pro-government businesses but also rewarding businesses supporting the movement. The idea of supporting pro-movement businesses quickly gained traction through tactical innovation, as outlined in the Chapter 8. On July 31, an LIHKG user proposed a consumer campaign to support yellow businesses.[2] This was followed by a post calling for volunteers to create a digital platform to collect related information, which received over 1,000 upvotes.[3] The concept of buycotting gained momentum after a citywide strike on August 5 prompted many shops and restaurants to close in solidarity. Calls to reward these businesses evolved into the idea of creating a 'yellow economy' to unite pro-democracy businesses and consumers, sparking extensive discussions on LIHKG by early October. The ultimate goal was to create a self-sufficient marketplace independent of pro-government economic elites. This innovative concept quickly gained popularity, providing a new, safer avenue for people to continue their activism amidst increasingly repressive police responses to the protests.

FROM BOYCOTTING TO BUYCOTTING

Digital platforms played an instrumental role in materializing the idea of forming the so-called 'yellow economy'. They enabled information curation, another mechanism of peer collaboration. More specifically, they facilitated the mapping of relevant businesses, the crowdsourcing of information, and the creation of searchable databases (Poon and Tse 2022). On August 22,

---

[1] Debate database, 'Why decorate Best Mart 360,' https://debate.fandom.com/zh-hk/wiki/%E9%BB%9
E%E8%A7%A3%E8%A6%81%E8%A3%9D%E4%BF%AE%E5%84%AA%E5%93%81360.
[2] LIHKG post, Retrieved on 31 July 2019, https://lihkg.com/thread/1389825/page/1.
[3] LIHKG post, Retrieved on 4 August 2019, https://lihkg.com/thread/1404942/page/1.

an anonymous app developer and active LIHKG user repurposed his smartphone app, WhatsGap – originally designed to show the locations of the city's claw machines – into a map pinpointing 'yellow shop'.[4] The initial list featured around 200 such businesses, a number that quickly expanded to include thousands more. Around the same time, similar smartphone apps and websites such as NeoGuideHK, HKShopList, and YellowBlue Map (a Facebook page) emerged. Notably, all these platforms were founded by ordinary citizens without any affiliations with political parties or SMOs, who simply used their coding skills to contribute to the movement. There was no centralized leadership guiding their efforts. The platform creators were not protest leaders, and their identities remained unknown to the public. However, these platforms profoundly impacted the movement by offering an alternative avenue for low-cost activism.

Ordinary protesters were not simply users of these platforms. They were also content creators. For instance, YellowBlue Map maintained a Google Form for protesters to submit information and justifications for categorizing certain businesses as 'yellow' or 'blue'. Volunteers then fact-checked the information before publishing it on the platform and categorizing businesses accordingly. This process often involved subjective and arbitrary judgments, which the volunteers acknowledged and tried to mitigate through research and cross-checking (Interview C9 and C10). The result was a vast collection of businesses categorized by their political leanings and sectors. Figure 9.1 depicts the vast amount of information received by YellowBlue Map. Between August 2019 and June 2020, the platform received an average of seventy reports per day. Reporting activity peaked in December 2019 and January 2020, when most protests were banned by the police, with the average number of reports surging to 122 per day. Figure 9.2 further illustrates the number of 'yellow' and 'blue' shops digitized by the three major platforms. By November 2020, YellowBlue Map had documented 5,209 yellow businesses in its database.

Yellow businesses primarily consist of small and medium-sized enterprises that do not operate in mainland China, contrasting with most conglomerates (Chan and Pun 2020). NeoGuideHK's database provides a detailed breakdown of these businesses by type. Of the 3,442 yellow businesses catalogued by the platform, the majority (52 per cent) are food and beverage providers, including restaurants, cafes, bars, and beverage shops. The prevalence of food and beverage businesses is likely due to their customer-facing nature and their exclusive focus on the local market. The remaining share of yellow businesses are distributed across other service and retail sectors: grocery businesses (19 per cent), clothing businesses (5 per cent), hair and beauty services (3 per cent), and food products (2 per cent). The YellowBlue Map

---

[4] Official website of WhatsGap, https://appadvice.com/app/whatsgap-e7-99-bc-e5-a4-a2-e5-9c-b0-e5-9c-96/1475004773.

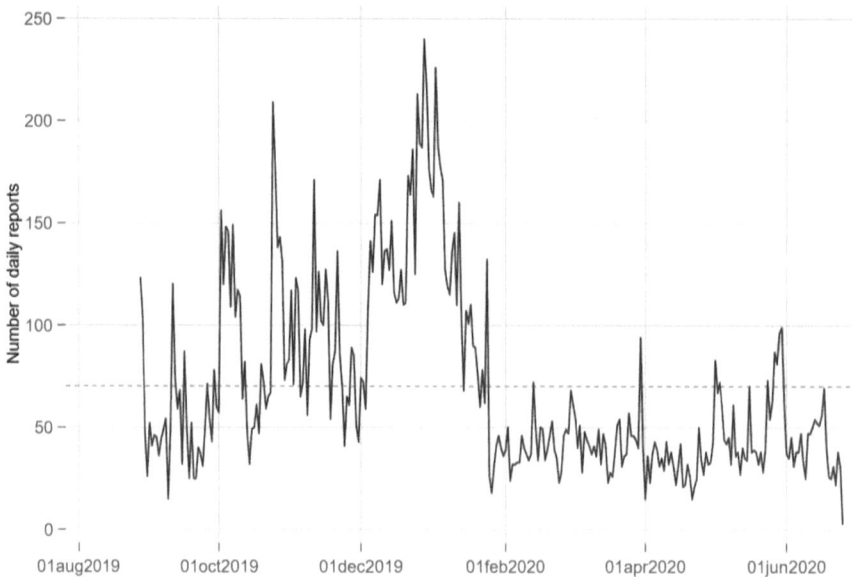

FIGURE 9.1 Daily number of netizens' reports received by YellowBlue Map, 2019.
Source: Data provided by volunteers from YellowBlue Map.

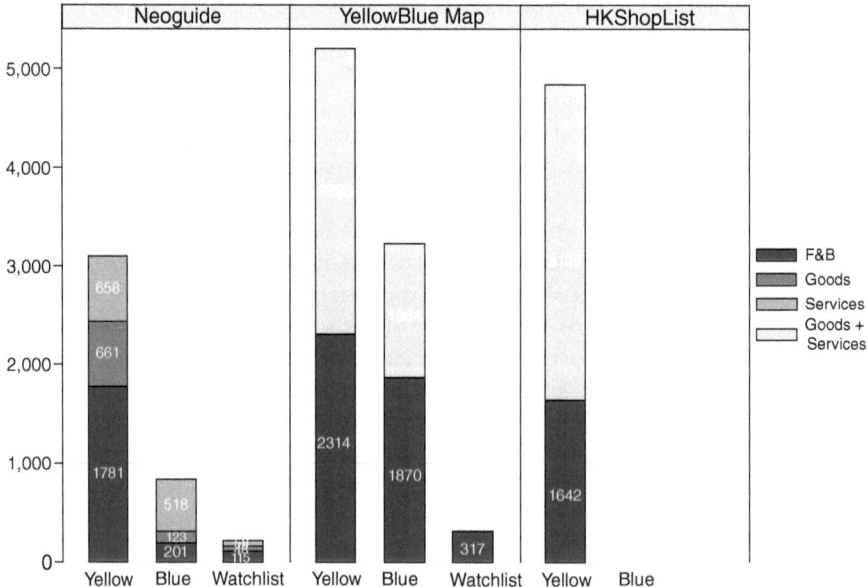

FIGURE 9.2 Distribution of yellow and blue businesses, 2019.
Source: Official websites of the three major platforms.

database reflects a similar pattern: of its 5,209 yellow businesses, 44 per cent are food and beverage providers, with the rest being retail shops.

MUTUAL ASSISTANCE

By serving as directories for protest supporters to make informed decisions about where to eat and shop, these online platforms provided a digital infrastructure for the yellow economy. Furthermore, they facilitated the transformation of thousands of businesses into spatially decentralized nodes of mutual assistance. At the height of the movement, many yellow businesses, particularly restaurants, offered free meals to young protesters who lacked the means to support themselves. These businesses also made donations to activist groups and foundations providing legal aid to those facing police charges. Some yellow businesses even employed protesters who had left their jobs or studies to fully commit to the movement. On protest days, some businesses provided shelter to protesters in need. Although hard to quantify, this support was crucial at a time when the movement lacked centralized leadership. These resources, garnered through crowdsourcing and distributed through a vast network of pro-movement businesses, provided vital support to many protesters, especially young and underprivileged ones, ultimately enhancing the movement's resilience.

Simon Chan, the owner of a 'yellow' noodle shop, embodied this role of mutual assistance (Interview C11). Initially politically indifferent, he was spurred to join the Anti-Extradition Movement after witnessing thugs attacking protesters and citizens in Yuen Long on 21 July. Traumatized by the incident, Chan used his restaurant's Facebook page to express support for the protests and allowed protesters to rest in his shop during the August and September strike actions. Every Wednesday, he provided free meals to university students involved in the protests. As the intensity of the protests escalated, Chan expanded his free meal offerings to secondary school students, journalists, first aiders, and medical workers, offering them both material and moral support. He also hired protesters who had lost their jobs due to their active involvement, giving them leaves to join the protests. On several occasions, Chan even advanced salaries to his politically active employees to help them with financial challenges such as bail and legal fees.

Some yellow businesses utilized their business model to foster mutual assistance among protesters (Li and Whitworth 2023). Agile Van, an app-based moving van-hailing service openly pro-democracy since the Umbrella Movement, is a notable example. During that time, the company coordinated some of its freelance drivers to deliver essential supplies to occupied protest sites. When the anti-extradition protests broke out in June, the company saw an influx of hundreds of new freelance drivers eager to join their cause. These drivers effectively used the app as a coordination platform to transport crucial supplies, including water, first aid kits, and protective gear, straight to the protest frontlines. Additionally, they undertook the task of providing safe transportation for activists fleeing from protest sites to evade police arrest. The automated app platform proved instrumental in efficiently coordinating these frontline requests and matching them with available vehicles. The owner of Agile Van described his role as that of a 'matchmaker', attributing the success of their efforts to the dedication of their freelance drivers. As he emphasized, 'many of our drivers don't work for us merely for monetary gain... because we don't have much business anyway. They are here because they support our vision. When they took their vehicles to the frontlines, they did not charge a single dime and were taking a lot of risks' (Interview C12).

From the protesters' viewpoint, visiting yellow businesses provided a unique and immersive protest experience. Many yellow businesses incorporated elements of the protests into their products and services. This was particularly evident in restaurants, local eateries, and coffee shops. Throughout the movement, many such establishments decorated their shop spaces with pro-movement posters, established Lennon Walls for customers to leave supportive messages, and creatively renamed menu items to reflect movement slogans or demands. Others played protest songs or printed slogans on customer receipts. These gestures transformed the act of dining or shopping at yellow businesses into an extraordinary protest experience. As thousands of shops transformed into sites of protest, they effectively spread contention across the city in spatial terms.

While these experiences may not have directly influenced the demands of the protest, they effectively transformed consumption into acts of protest and solidarity (Chan 2022). In this context, political consumption activated what Randall Collins (2004) refers to as 'interaction ritual chains'. Collins describes interaction rituals as mechanisms that generate a momentarily shared reality through mutually focused emotion and attention. This shared reality then cultivates solidarity and symbols of group membership (2004: 70). Successful rituals generate emotional energy, motivating individuals to seek similar experiences, thus creating a chain of interaction rituals. These rituals not only invigorate individuals but also endow symbols and objects with meaning, which then circulates in subsequent rituals. Viewed in this light, political consumption at yellow businesses can be viewed as an interaction ritual. It provides protest supporters emotional energy through their consumer experiences, even without directly participating in street protests. Through repeated acts of consumption, supporters foster a sense of belonging to the movement and actively contribute to its cause, creating a chain of experiences that fortifies movement solidarity.

Political consumption is often considered an individualized form of participation (Micheletti 2003), yet the buycotting in the Anti-Extradition Movement exhibited a collective dimension. People frequently dine at yellow restaurants with friends or family, recommend their favourite yellow businesses to others, and share their experiences on social media. These social interactions imbue buycotting with a collective quality, distinguishing it from boycotting, which involves individual refusal to purchase certain products or services and does not inherently require social interaction.

A quintessential example of buycotting as collective action is the buycott campaigns supporting yellow businesses. In early October 2019, LIHKG users proposed a buycott campaign, encouraging others to patronize at least one yellow shop on October 10 and to share their experience on social media using the hashtag #standwithhk. This date held historical significance, as it marked the commencement of the 1911 Wuchang Uprising that led to the establishment of the Republic of China. The campaign was rather success-ful and provided a respite from the escalating protest violence. Long queues formed outside many yellow shops on that day, with some businesses report-ing a notable revenue increase of 30–40 per cent (*Ming Pao*, 9 August 2019). Similar buycotting campaigns were organized in subsequent months, urging protest supporters to patronize yellow businesses across different districts. These campaigns continued even after the movement, with a week-long buy-cott campaign launched during the May 1 Golden Week in 2020. Coinciding with the traditional surge in mainland tourists, movement supporters pledged to support yellow businesses that had been heavily impacted by the COVID-19 pandemic. Prominent activists and newly elected district councillors amplified the impact of the campaign by using their social media platforms to recom-mend yellow businesses.

NETWORK BUILDING

As buycott campaigns galvanized political consumers, yellow businesses pro-actively formed networks and initiatives for mutual support and collabora-tion. These networks often emerged within geographically clustered regions. A prominent example is Central and Western District, where dozens of yellow restaurants established an alliance named HKEconRim. Taking inspiration from two local eateries in Yuen Long that offered mutual discounts, this alli-ance issued discount coupons to returning customers who made purchases at partner shops. HKEconRim aimed primarily at fostering collaboration and encouraging patronage of neighbourhood yellow businesses. The alliance experienced significant growth, launching with thirteen members in December 2019 and expanding to fifty-one members by May 2020. Later, it extended to the nearby Eastern District, attracting thirty-nine shop members. Besides formal alliances such as HKEconRim, numerous neighbourhood-based social media groups were established to focus on promoting specific local yellow businesses. By October 2020, we identified approximately ninety such social media groups – sixty on Facebook, twenty-three on Instagram, and seven on Telegram.[5] These community groups proved invaluable during the peak of the COVID-19 pandemic when businesses encountered severe disruptions. Many of these groups served as platforms for arranging takeout orders or

---

[5] Data was collected in October 2020 through online search and snowballing on different social media platforms.

bulk purchases from impacted restaurants, effectively helping some businesses weather the economic downturn.

Yellow businesses also endeavoured to form vertical networks along the production chain, addressing a crucial weakness in the fledgling yellow economy – the lack of similarly pro-movement suppliers or manufacturers. As a result, the yellow economy was restricted to service providers and businesses at the lower end of the production chain, such as restaurants, cafes, hair salons, and grocery stores. Restaurants, in particular, sourced most of their ingredients from mainland China – Hong Kong's main supplier of fresh produce – or from suppliers reluctant to speak out against the government due to their mainland business connections. This dearth of suppliers presented a fundamental challenge to the yellow economy, impeding businesses from achieving genuine self-sufficiency and sustainability.

In October 2019, a group of activists responded to a call on the LIHKG forum to create an online shopping site – HKongs Mall. After months of preparation, the platform launched with the primary goal of sourcing products locally, ideally from politically aligned suppliers. HKongs Mall aimed to serve as a one-stop platform for protest supporters and other yellow businesses to purchase groceries and provide employment opportunities for protesters who had lost their jobs due to their involvement in the movement. A few months later, a similar platform – Our Hong Kong Mall – was established with the same goals but expanded to include product selections from around the world. The platform's mission statement describes itself as the 'Noah's Ark' for protesters – a gathering place for mutual support. These initiatives quickly gained support from protesters. However, their operational scale remained limited, partly due to reliance on volunteers for running the platforms and partly due to the difficulty of finding pro-democracy suppliers. For example, some of HKongs Mall's most popular products were still sourced from a food conglomerate whose owner held staunchly pro-government views.

CONSUMER POWER

Political consumption showed remarkable resilience in the Anti-Extradition Movement despite growing restrictions on other forms of protest. From a participation perspective, political consumption offered anti-extradition protesters a critical way to maintain their activism at a comparatively low cost. In a two-wave panel survey conducted by us to follow up with 2019 protest participants, a notable percentage continued to engage in boycotting and buycotting even a year after the protests.[6] In May 2020, 98.6 and 98.7 per cent reported

---

[6] The panel survey was conducted online through Qualtrics. The first survey was conducted between 23 April 2020 and 5 May 2020 and collected a sample of 6,090 respondents. The second survey was conducted between 21 October 2020 and 1 November 2020 and collected a sample of 3,411 respondents.

participating in boycotting and buycotting respectively, either somewhat frequently or frequently. By November 2020, these figures remained steady, even as other forms of participation, such as signing petitions and making donations, declined. Furthermore, 98.9 per cent of respondents in the November survey stated they would endeavour to determine a business's political stance before patronizing it. When asked about the frequency of visiting yellow shops, 91.9 per cent reported doing so between one and ten times a week, whereas 5.7 per cent said more than ten times.

Political consumption also became considerably common among the populace, as demonstrated by a representative population survey in August 2020 with a sample size of 817. The results revealed that 59.7 and 61.4 per cent of respondents had participated in boycotting and buycotting respectively. Among these individuals, 76.6 and 79.5 per cent had persuaded others to boycott and to buycott, whereas 72.1 and 72.7 per cent had shared information about boycotting and buycotting on their social media accounts. Respondents cited multiple reasons for engaging in political consumption. In addition to fighting for protest demands, they viewed it as a means to achieve economic justice. Hence, while political consumption was initially perceived as a short-term protest tactic, supporters also saw it as a longer-term strategy to reform what they perceived as an economically unjust society.

The growing impact of political consumption was further reflected in the state's response. Initially, the HKSAR government dismissed the idea of a yellow economy, but it changed its stance when Beijing intervened. On 2 January 2020, *People's Daily*, the flagship state newspaper, published a commentary criticizing the yellow economy as 'the shame of Hong Kong's economic civilization' (*People's Daily* 2020). The commentary likened the idea to German Nazism and American Southern slavery, characterizing it as a means for protesters to purge those with differing opinions. This high-level state response sparked a series of attacks from local pro-Beijing elites on the yellow economy. On the second day of the May 1 Golden Week shopping campaign, the Central Government Liaison Office, the top local party branch in Hong Kong, openly criticized the yellow economy, accusing it of 'kidnapping the economy with politics' and striving to achieve 'political mutual destruction' (CGLO 2020).

Measuring the economic impact of political consumption is challenging due to the lack of available financial data. However, existing data suggests that boycotting significantly impacted targeted businesses. For example, Maxim's Group saw a 22 per cent profit decline in 2019, with a 34 per cent decline during the protests' second half (*HKNet*, 5 March 2020). Fulum Group, another targeted restaurant chain, recorded a 29 per cent decrease in revenue in 2019 (Fulum Group 2020). Best Mart 360 reported a 19 per cent decline in same-store sales and an 80 per cent drop in profit for the 2019 financial year, leading to a profit warning to investors (Best Mart 360, 7 May 2020). The company's stores were not only boycotted but also became targets of vandalism. By November 2019, 75 out of 102 of its stores had been vandalized by protesters (*South China Morning Post*, 28 November 2019). HeyTea, a rapidly expanding tea shop from mainland China, also saw its business decline significantly, reducing its number of stores in Hong Kong from eight before the protests to just one by mid-2020 after it became a target of boycotting.

Although anecdotal evidence supports the correlation between boycotting and economic losses, establishing a causal relationship remains challenging. Many businesses, not targeted for boycotting, also experienced declines in revenue and profit due to social unrest and the ensuing COVID-19 outbreak. Nevertheless, boycotting did influence the behaviour of pro-government business elites during the protests, with many choosing not to publicly support the government. For example, Maxim's Group stressed that the shareholder who criticized the protests was not a key company executive. The chairman of Best Mart 360 repeatedly clarified that he had no connection with the thugs who attacked protesters. He even openly supported one of the protest demands – calling for an independent inquiry into the cause of the protests. Still, the boycotts posed no real challenge to the economic structure that underpins Hong Kong's political system. Throughout the movement, protesters focused on a limited number of businesses for boycotting. Many pro-government businesses managed to avoid attention by maintaining a low profile.

Buycotting, in contrast, had a more direct and noticeable impact on the protest movement. First, it offered a new path for sustained political participation. Unlike boycotting, which depends on negative emotions (Lindenmeier, Schleer and Pricl 2012) and specific targets that may diminish in relevance over time, buycotting can be more easily maintained and made routine through basic human desires and market-based incentives aligning producers and consumers. In consumerist societies, the act of purchasing is more habitual than abstaining from buying, and the producers' profit-driven motivations lead them to meet customer demands. This dynamic establishes a self-sustaining cycle in which buycotting can persist within the market order. Furthermore, buycotting correlates strongly with engaged citizenship norms (Copeland 2014), offering a low-cost method for individuals to collaborate and contribute to social and political causes. This is particularly advantageous for social movements lacking centralized leadership, as it fosters a sense of community and engagement.

Secondly, buycotting functioned as a mutual aid mechanism and, to an extent, a means of resource mobilization among protesters, particularly in the absence of centralized leadership. Yellow businesses served as network nodes, enabling resources to be drawn from movement supporters through their consumption. While market logic dictates that profit-making remains crucial, some earnings are channelled back into the movement via donations or hiring protesters. This system allows resources to be reallocated to protesters in need, even in the absence of traditional SMOs. Thirdly, the establishment of the yellow economy led to the formation of new networks, initiatives, and platforms. These included shopping campaigns, neighbourhood alliances, and social media pages that connected yellow businesses and pro-democracy advocates.

These networks cultivated social capital among protest actors (Diani 1997), promoting solidarity within the movement even after the protests waned and entered a dormant phase (Geha 2019; Taylor 1989).

However, this process of fostering movement solidarity through buycotting was not free of tension. The yellow economy faced constant criticism not only from various state actors but also from within the ranks of the protest camp. A prevalent issue was the perceived level of a yellow business's commitment to the movement – whether it was 'yellow' enough. This was measured by their contributions to the movement through donations, resource offerings, or the hiring of protesters. Despite receiving support from protesters, some yellow businesses were criticized for 'not doing enough' for the movement. Conversely, others were accused of feigning 'yellow' solely to capitalize on the buycotting trend. While our focus is not to scrutinize these allegations, it is important to highlight that such conflicts are inherent in the process of building solidarity under a leaderful structure. Yellow businesses lack the traditional legitimacy that SMOs enjoy. As their primary objective remains profit-making, maintaining the trust of ordinary protest supporters presents a significant challenge. These tensions, although manageable to some degree, are unlikely to be completely eradicated.

CONCLUSION

This chapter has traced the rise of political consumption as a tactical repertoire in the Anti-Extradition Movement, highlighting the role of peer collaboration in making it a viable and popular protest strategy within a remarkably short timeframe. As illustrated, protesters initially started by boycotting pro-government businesses but soon broadened their scope to include the buycotting of pro-movement businesses. This expansion led to a series of collective actions that leveraged market logic, eventually culminating in the emergence of what came to be known as the yellow economy.

There was a marked difference between boycotting and buycotting. Boycotting successfully posed a threat to many pro-government elites, pressuring them to avoid supporting the government openly during the protests. However, it fell short of fundamentally altering the statist-corporatist nature of Hong Kong's political system. This was not only due to the relatively small scale of the boycotts, but also because of Hong Kong's entrenched corporatist system. It was simply not possible to dismantle the pervasive influence of local conglomerates and state-owned firms within a short period of time. In contrast, the more proactive act of buycotting facilitated mutual assistance and networking among protesters through market interactions. By providing resources to protesters in need, it converted pro-movement businesses into nodes of mutual assistance and resource provision, bolstering the movement's logistical support in the absence of centralized leadership. This repertoire helped facilitate a more sustained mobilization effort.

10

Radicalization with Solidarity

Despite the ethical appeal and strategic advantages of non-violence (Chenoweth and Stephan 2011), violence often surfaces in the midst of contentious struggles. Even the iconic US Civil Rights Movement, often heralded for its doctrine of nonviolent civil disobedience, witnessed bouts of violent protest, occasionally manifesting in the form of urban riots (Wasow 2020). Similarly, in Northern Ireland during the 1960s, the Catholic minority initially pursued nonviolent demonstrations to oppose Unionism's discriminatory policies and demand equal rights and full enfranchisement; but violent tactics soon took hold and ignited a thirty-year-long conflict known as the Troubles (De Fazio 2013). Recent spontaneous movements in places such as Chile and the United States have also seen protesters using violence in response to state repression, bracing against tear gas, rubber bullets, water cannons, and live ammunition.

Violence also beset the Anti-Extradition Movement. Despite a peaceful start, the movement gradually embraced more radical and disruptive tactics. On 12 June, just three days after the inaugural million-strong protest, clashes between protesters and the police already erupted. In subsequent weeks, as the government deployed riot police, protesters escalated their actions. Instances of protesters physically assaulting police officers with sticks, bricks, and umbrellas occurred in July. By early August, protesters began hurling Molotov cocktails at police defence lines and erecting road barricades. In September, some protesters vandalized pro-government shops and restaurants, whereas others physically confronted counter-protesters who were attacking or harassing fellow demonstrators. However, protesters were not the sole perpetrators of violence. Their adoption of violent strategies unfolded in tandem with escalating police responses, including the increasing use of tear gas, bean bag rounds, and rubber bullets. In late August, crowd management vehicles equipped with water cannons were introduced. During the siege of two university campuses in mid-November, more than 7,000 canisters of tear gas were fired over two days.

Hong Kong has a tradition of peaceful protests emphasizing non-violence and adherence to public order (Ho 2019; Ku 2007; Lee and Chan 2010). Although this doctrine has been challenged since the early 2010s, militant tactics in protests largely remained marginal. However, the Anti-Extradition Movement saw a growing reliance on such tactics. In addition to a trend of tactical radicalization, there was a surprising level of tolerance for protest-related violence among moderate participants and the wider public. Figure 10.1 illustrates this phenomenon based on protest surveys conducted by the authors. Over 80 per cent of respondents in peaceful rallies in July 2019, and over 90 per cent from August to October 2019, expressed sympathy for radical actions. Similarly, opinion polls in September and October 2019 revealed that 55 and 59 per cent of respondents, respectively, displayed similar sentiments. A survey conducted in November and December 2019, after the chaotic university campus clashes, found that 62 per cent of the public continued to support the movement, whereas only 18 per cent opposed it. Given that militant protests often erode public support and alienate moderate backers (Chenoweth 2021; Edwards and Arnon 2021; Muñoz and Anduiza 2019), the Anti-Extradition Movement poses a counterintuitive puzzle.

What contributed to tactical radicalization as the movement progressed? How did protesters maintain solidarity and public support in the face of

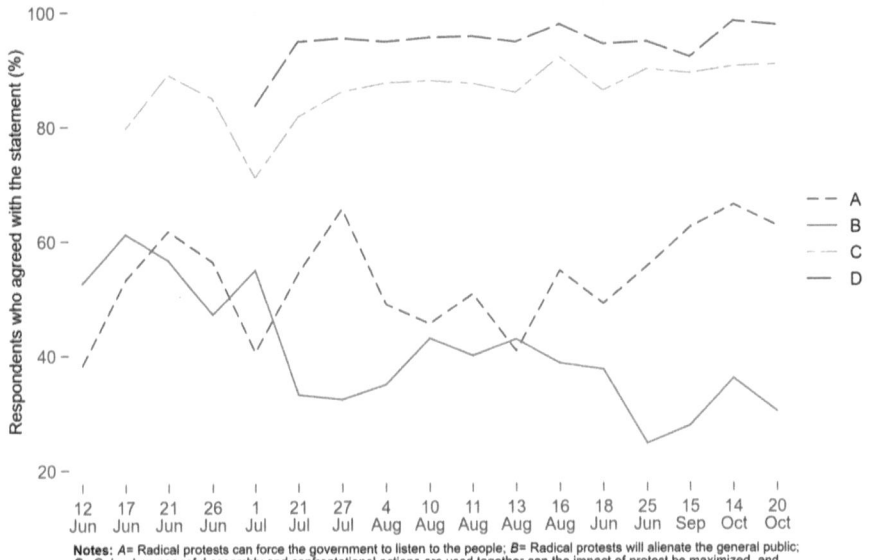

FIGURE 10.1 Approval of radical protests.
Source: Authors' onsite surveys.

increasing radicalization? While the theory of mediated threat helps to explain the rise of the movement's leaderful dynamics, it does not account for why and how it would tactically radicalize. In this chapter, we argue that radicalization was a contingent but highly probable outcome of leaderful mobilization, particularly as levels of repression escalated. Using a relational framework that views radicalization as a product of interactions across various arenas (Alimi 2011; de Fazio 2013; della Porta 2008), we illustrate how anti-extradition protesters radicalized in response to contingent threats emerging from their interactions with the police, counter-protesters, and the broader environment. Furthermore, we argue that this radicalization process was simultaneously moderated by discursive negotiations among the protesters themselves, which enabled them to preserve solidarity and prevent extremes despite the absence of centralized leadership. Even as moderate protesters tacitly endorsed the use of violent tactics, they simultaneously applied internal brakes on their militant peers to curtail excessive measures.

A RELATIONAL APPROACH

Sociologist Colin Beck (2015: 18) defines radicalism as a departure from society's 'common routines of politics', with the aim of bringing about significant extra-institutional transformations across socioeconomic, cultural, and political structures. In the context of social movements, radicalization denotes the process or tendency towards embracing more radical ideologies or methods of action (Alimi, Bosi and Demetriou 2012). By benchmarking against society's prevailing 'common routines', Beck's formulation of the radical is contingent on context. What constitutes radicalism can thus vary across different settings: ideologies deemed radical in one context may not be regarded as such in another (Accornero 2013). Additionally, while radicalization within social movements often encompasses both ideological and tactical escalation, these two dimensions can be seen as distinct. Individuals and organizations inclined towards more radical ideologies typically – but not exclusively – adopt more radical tactics (Yaziji and Doh 2013).

This chapter focuses solely on tactical radicalization. The existing literature tends to examine protest radicalization through two approaches: one looks at the individual-level factors that make people more positively disposed towards radical or violent tactics (Bosi and della Porta 2012; Goodwin, Jasper, and Polletta 2001; Maguire et al. 2018; McCauley and Moskalenko 2008; Stekelenburg and Klandermans 2013; Vergani, Barton, and Iqbal 2017; Zaidise, Canetti-Nisim, and Pedahzur 2007); another views the use of violence as a strategic tool for advancing protest objectives (Gamson 1990; Piven 2012; Piven and Cloward 1977). However, neither approach shed light on the social mechanisms that transform violence into a sustained and widely adopted tactic. Charles Tilly (2003) thus proposes a relational approach that focuses on the 'ways that variable patterns of social interaction constitute and cause different varieties of collective violence' (Tilly 2003: 18). As such, tactical radicalization can be seen as a group phenomenon that hinges on a complex interplay of interactions among individuals, groups, and institutional actors (della Porta 2018: 463).

This approach sees radicalization as a process involving a multitude of actors and various forms of action, with participants shifting between different modes of action as movements evolve. Building on this approach, Eitan Alimi, Lorenzo Bosi, and Chares Demetriou (2012) proposes a framework for explaining the process of tactical radicalization through four mechanisms. First, interactions between the movement and its political context create 'opportunity and threat spirals' that help movement actors justify adopting radical tactics based on their perceptions of opportunities and threats. Second, the interplay between the movement and oppressive state forces creates the phenomenon of 'outbidding', in which both sides one-up each other with escalating actions and rising stakes. Third, interactions between movements and counter-movements lead to 'object shift', whereby new arenas of contention emerge to exert significant influence on the dynamics of radicalization. Finally, activist groups within the movement often '[compete] for power', in part by advocating radical tactics and ideologies. This framework provides a useful lens to unpack the radicalization process during the Anti-Extradition Movement. Without a centralized leadership, the movement was largely driven by spontaneous and decentralized interactions among protesters, counter-protesters, and the state. To understand its tactical radicalization, it is thus important to unravel these relational interplays.

While relational dynamics are crucial it is important to also highlight the role of meaning-making and discursive negotiation. Generally, meaning-making plays a pivotal role in social movements (Snow and Benford 1988). Since protest actions are considered 'culturally learned creations' (Tilly 1995: 42), novel tactics often require activists to engage in discursive efforts to persuade supporters and the public to accept them (Hayes 2006). Such endeavours may necessitate justifications and negotiations, especially if the tactics are contentious. As a movement radicalizes, protesters are likely to rationalize the use of increasingly confrontational and violent tactics, in order to maintain the movement's legitimacy and internal solidarity. They are also likely to establish norms to govern and limit these tactics' application (Weisburd and Lernau 2006). This process can both fuel and mitigate radicalization: it can radicalize moderate participants and public segments by providing justifications for supporting radical tactics, while simultaneously de-radicalizing the most fervent participants by introducing norms to guide and confine actions.

PROTEST DYNAMICS AND TACTICAL RADICALIZATION

As outlined in previous chapters, support for and participation in the Anti-Extradition Movement was partially driven by the perceived threats presented by the extradition bill. Early protest organizers, such as Demosisto and CHRF, played an indispensable role in framing and articulating this threat. Beginning in April 2019, political parties and activists started using the phrase *faan sung jung* – 'no extradition to China' or simply 'against sending off to China' – to highlight what they saw as the most alarming aspect of the extradition bill. As one protest organizer noted, this phrase simplified matters and played a pivotal role in raising public concern (Interview A1). The threat of extradition to China deeply resonated with protesters: according to a survey conducted on 9 June, 88.8 per cent of respondents were either very or quite concerned that pro-democracy figures and activists could be extradited if the law were enacted. The same percentage expressed concern about Hong Kong citizens being extradited for criticizing mainland political affairs, whereas 54.4 per cent were worried about the possibility of their own extradition, and that of their friends or family members.

RESPONDING TO THREATS (AND OPPORTUNITIES)

Interestingly, this profound sense of threat did not immediately incite violent protests. The June 9 protest, despite its enormous size, remained peaceful. Although some protesters stayed in the streets after the march ended, there were no clashes with the police. Protesters only began to adopt a more militant stance on June 12. Fearing that the extradition bill might be passed in the legislature that day, protesters occupied the roads surrounding the LegCo building. In response, the police used tear gas and bean bag rounds to disperse them. Facing a public backlash, the government dramatically reversed its stance, announcing the suspension of the bill's legislative process on June 15. This did not satisfy the public, who gathered in another massive protest the next day to demand a formal withdrawal of the bill. Protesters also called for the establishment of an independent commission to investigate police actions on June 12.

The massive turnout on June 16 showed that the suspension of the extradition bill did not ease the perceived threat. Paradoxically, the fact that the bill was merely suspended – rather than scrapped – fostered an 'endgame imagination' among protesters – that is, the potential end of Hong Kong's autonomous status as a Chinese city with relatively higher degrees of liberty and autonomy. This mindset was captured in the protest survey on June 16. A significant 91.8 per cent of survey respondents agreed that the extradition bill could transform Hong Kong's 'One Country Two Systems' into 'One Country One System'. A more substantial 96.4 per cent believed that the bill could dismantle Hong Kong's rule of law. This mindset arguably paved the way for escalating actions, as the movement was seen as the final chance for Hong Kong citizens to resist. As revealed in the June 16 survey, respondents who recognized the severity of the bill's potential impact tended to support the idea that it becomes necessary for some protesters to use physical force when the government ignores the people.

Ironically, for the protesters, the government's decision to suspend the bill after the June 12 clashes vindicated their militancy. This was reflected in a growing number of those surveyed who agreed that radical protests can compel the government to listen to the people, and a declining proportion who felt that radical protests would alienate the public. By early July, support for violence more widespread among the protesters. This support only accelerated as the movement progressed. Many protesters, even those of moderate disposition, considered the use of violence both necessary and effective. For instance, during the July 1 protest, a significant 83.5 per cent agreed that 'radical tactics by protesters become understandable when the government fails to listen to the people'.

Remarkably, the rationale for supporting radical tactics shifted at this point. As the contingent, generalized threat that had fuelled the endgame imagination gradually subsided following the bill's suspension, it was replaced by the perceived particularistic threat of escalating repression that target protesters, a concern that had been hinted at on June 12. From late July, the police intensified their crackdown on the protests with even greater force. In mid-August, rumours circulated that the Chinese government would mobilize the PLA to quell the protests. In response to this looming threat, the discourse of "laam chaau", which literally means 'burning together', emerged within the movement. This term is borrowed from poker to mean making your opponent suffer as much as you do (*Quartz*, 30 June 2020). Some saw it as scorched earth philosophy for raising the stakes of the protests. The discourse posited that if the Chinese government resorted to extreme measures to suppress the protests, there would be immense consequences as China would face international sanctions. Since the movement were likely to fail anyway, it would better bring down the opponents. The "laam chaau" discourse thus provided an ideological basis for the movement to escalate its tactics.

The discourse embodied the movement's display of confidence and determination in the face of increasing repression. It provided a clear example of how a shifting perception of threats could justify a progressively radical approach. In the August 31 protest survey, a striking 82.1 per cent of respondents concurred that 'if extreme scenarios were to occur in Hong Kong, Beijing would incur greater losses than Hong Kong', whereas 74.7 per cent agreed that 'under the international spotlight, the movement would benefit if Hong Kong's situation were to deteriorate'. Respondents who agreed with these statements particularly supported radical tactics, such as road-blocking, police station sieges, and physical attacks on police officers.

VIOLENCE OUTBIDDING

Studies of social movements have repeatedly shown that police violence can radicalize protesters (della Porta 1995; della Porta and Reiter 1998). From a relational perspective, an alternating use of force by protesters and law enforcement can push both parties to intensify their actions, resulting in a cycle of violence. As mentioned earlier, the increase in protester violence coincided with tactical escalation from the police. In Hong Kong's case, this cycle became more pronounced from the beginning of July 2019. As protesters increasingly resorted to disruptive and violent tactics, the police became more repressive.

In July, anti-extradition protesters built roadblocks, threw bricks, and breached the LegCo building, while police countered with more intense use of tear gas and bean bag rounds. In August, protesters began using Molotov cocktails, lighting bonfires, and vandalizing metro stations. In response, the police deployed water cannons and crowd control vehicles. They also shut down metro stations both to curb vandalism and block protesters' escape routes. Rhetorically, the government began in early August to emphasize the policy of *zhibao zhiluan* (stop the violence and chaos), echoing a phrase that appeared widely in state-controlled newspapers. This effectively gave a high-level policy endorsement of the police's tactical escalation.

From September onwards, instances of protesters directly attacking police with Molotov cocktails became more frequent. On October 1, China's National Day, the police fired nearly 1,700 tear gas canisters, and an officer shot a protester. In an attempt to regain control, the government implemented an emergency law on October 4 banning face masks at public gatherings, since masks were commonly among militant protesters for hiding their identity. This action led to further escalation of violent protests. On the very day the law took effect, protesters took over major thoroughfares on Hong Kong Island, causing significant disruptions in the city's busiest district. In mid-November, escalation further intensified as protesters occupied two university campuses – those of the Hong Kong Polytechnic University and the Chinese University of Hong Kong – and paralyzed two key highways. The police responded by encircling the campuses and attempting to disperse protesters with riot vehicles, tear gas, and bean bag rounds. The Chinese University of Hong Kong saw some of the most intense clashes, with some 2,000 tear gas canisters fired by the police (*Apple Daily*, 13 November 2019).

Protesters' tactical radicalization was a product of this spiral of escalating violence. In theory, this could have reduced public sympathy for the protests. However, opinion polls conducted in September and October revealed that approximately 70 per cent of respondents deemed the police to have used excessive force, compared to only 40 per cent for the protesters. The lack of strong public condemnation for protester violence arguably encouraged the more militant protester factions to continue their actions.

One reason behind the absence of a strong public backlash has to do with the fluidity of the protests. Initially, most protests took place in commercial areas like Admiralty and Central, where key political institutions are located. However, as militant protesters moved around the city to confront riot police, the protests shifted into residential neighbourhoods. As the movement progressed, an increasing number of protest actions took place in unconventional

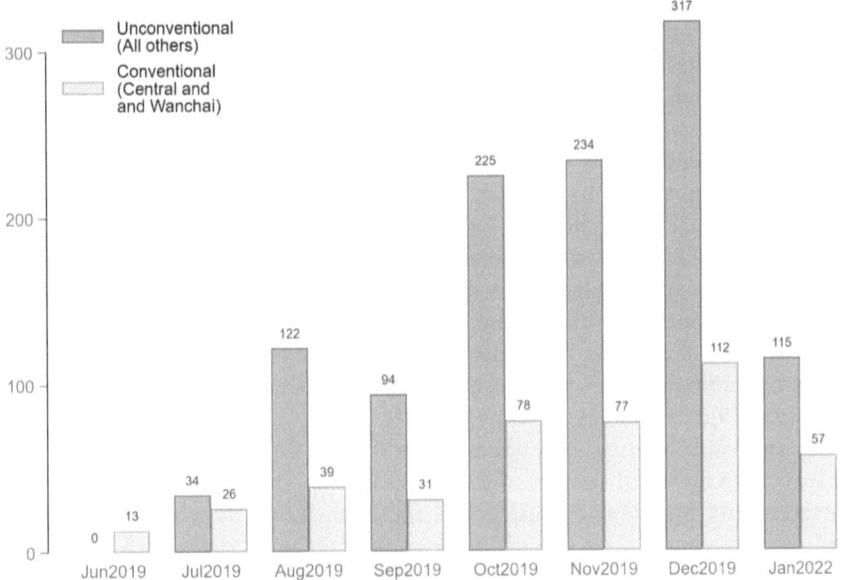

FIGURE 10.2 Protest events by location.
Source: Data obtained from HKU JMSC, Mobilization Map.

locales, including residential areas, as suggested by Figure 10.2. When protests occurred in residential areas, it was not uncommon to see local residents joining in support. This dynamic made it challenging for the police to distinguish between militants, moderates, and local residents as the demographics at protest sites became increasingly mixed. Moderates and residents often became unintended victims of the police's use of physical force. Such incidents bolstered the perception and experience of indiscriminate police violence. This fostered the prevailing sense of contingent threat and generated greater sympathy for radical actions. In the December 8 survey, only 13.5 per cent of respondents reported having attempted to halt the police's advances on frontlines, indicating that a small fraction of respondents had directly engaged in 'frontline actions'. However, 52.2 per cent of respondents recounted experiences of police firing tear gas near their residences, whereas 69 per cent had encountered tear gas at protest sites. Although people could have underreported their engagement in 'frontline actions', the discrepancy between taking actions and being repressed remained substantial.

MOVEMENT–COUNTERMOVEMENT DYNAMICS

Globally, pro-democracy protests within non-democratic contexts often contended with counter-mobilization efforts led by pro-government forces (Ekiert, Perry, and Yan 2020; Hellmeier and Weidmann 2020; Robertson 2010).

Hong Kong was no exception. Since the early 2010s, pro-government groups has consistently staged protests to counter the pro-democracy movement (Yuen 2023). An example was the 2014 Umbrella Movement, when pro-government groups mobilized aggrieved citizens against the disruption and inconvenience caused by the continual occupation of public spaces (Varese and Wong 2018). This effort aligned closely with the state's tactic of undermining the Umbrella Movement's legitimacy by framing it as a 'public nuisance' (Lee and Chan 2018: 161–165). During the Anti-Extradition Movement, counter-mobilization efforts similarly focused on supporting the police and opposing protester violence. Between early July and December 2019, numerous pro-government rallies showed support for the police and condemnation of the violence linked to the protests. Still, due to public distrust of the police and perceptions of their indiscriminate use of force, the counter-mobilization efforts failed to turn majority public opinion against the protests.

Counter-mobilization engendered new threats and fuelled radicalization. On July 21, a group of suspected gangsters launched a brutal assault on both protesters and innocent bystanders at the Yuen Long metro station. While solid evidence regarding the ultimate orchestrator of the attack remained elusive, footage emerged showing a pro-government legislator congratulating the attackers shortly after the incident.[1] The media reported that citizens had alerted the police upon seeing suspected gang members, dressed in white, congregating on the street during the early evening. Despite these reports, it took nearly forty minutes for the first police officers to arrive at the scene after the attack began, by which point most assailants had already fled. Astonishingly, the mobs returned for a second wave of attacks after the police had left (*South China Morning Post*, 23 July 2019). These facts fed growing suspicions that the attack might have been orchestrated by pro-government forces.

Viewing the vicious attack as a significant escalation, protesters responded with more radical tactics. On July 27, the following weekend, protesters convened in Yuen Long to protest against the previous week's attack. This marked the first large-scale rally that was not authorized by the police, making attendance illegal. The protest quickly descended into violence as police used tear gas to disperse the crowd. Regardless of who orchestrated the July 21 attack, the Yuen Long assault marked a pivotal juncture in the movement's trajectory. In an onsite survey conducted on 20 October, a significant 79.5 per cent of respondents singled out the Yuen Long assault as the event that most eroded their trust in the police. Furthermore, the surveys revealed a shift in protester demands. Starting from July, addressing police abuses of power overtook the extradition bill withdrawal as the primary focus of the protests. The suspected involvement of gang members in the Yuen Long assault

---

[1] The film was shown in programs such as an episode of Radio Television Hong Kong's Hong Kong Connection, titled 'Who governs the truth of 21 July,' aired on 13 July 2020.

unequivocally positioned the protesters as victims, thereby weakening the credibility and legitimacy of counter-protests.

Several incidents further reinforced the perceived ties between counter-protesters and gangsters. On August 5, a group wielding long poles attacked protesters in the North Point district, while at least four protesters were assaulted by alleged gang members with knives in the Tsuen Wan district (*Hong Kong Free Press*, 6 August 2019). Instances of severe violence perpetrated by counter-protesters, whether linked to suspected gang activity or not, were also documented. In one case, a man armed with two knives attacked three movement supporters near a Lennon Wall, which are physical display of pro-movement messages written on post-its and printed posters (*Hong Kong Free Press*, 20 August 2019).

These incidents of counter-protester violence significantly eroded protesters' prior sense of public order. Protesters began to feel increasingly unsafe and distrustful of the police force. The increasing feeling of insecurity and growing distrust of the police among the protesters led to a shift in sentiment towards using physical force as a means of self-defence. This context is vital for understanding the escalation of protester-driven vandalism and vigilantism after August. During a protest in Tsuen Wan in late August, militant protesters vandalized two mah-jong parlours believed to be owned by gangsters involved in the August 5 attack (*South China Morning Post*, 31 August 2019). This initial act of vandalism set a precedent, leading to an increase in similar acts. In some instances, they even got into physical confrontations with pro-government citizens. An opinion poll conducted in October 2019 offered insightful findings: 52.6 per cent of respondents agreed that protesters have the right to self-defence, but only to the extent of stopping the attacker when conflicts arise. On the other hand, 18.2 per cent believed that protesters have the right to physically retaliate. Only 25.8 per cent believed that protesters should call the police to handle their conflicts with counter-protesters.

INTRA-MOVEMENT DYNAMICS

Radicalization can also arise from a movement's internal dynamics, especially when a centralized leadership is absent. However, in contrast to movements plagued by a power struggle between different groups, the Anti-Extradition Movement displayed remarkable solidarity between its moderate and radical factions. This unity was reflected in the prevalence of slogans such as 'no severing of ties and no splitting' (*bugexi, bufenhua; bat-got-jik, bat-fun-fa*), 'going up and down together' (*qishang qiluo; chai-seung-chai-lok*) and 'brothers climbing mountains, each offering one's own efforts' (*xiongdi pashan gezi nuli; hing-dai-pa-saan, gok-ji-nou-lik*). As the movement evolved, protesters increasingly referred to each other as 'hands and feet' (*shouzu; sau-juk*), signifying a deep bond of comradeship. As depicted in Figure 10.3, our on-site

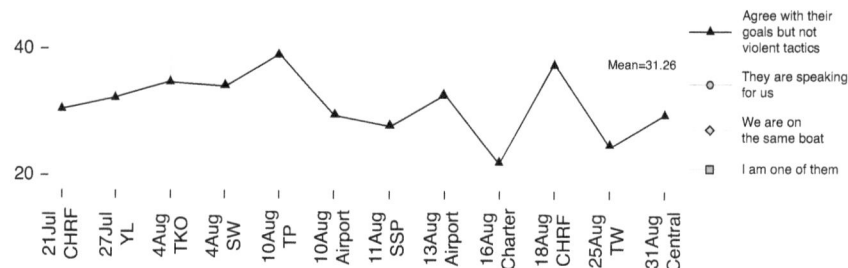

FIGURE 10.3 Degree of solidarity among protesters.
Source: Authors' onsite surveys.

survey conducted during a peaceful protest march on August 18 illustrated this
sense of solidarity. When asked about their views towards militant protesters,
95.0 per cent of respondents felt that they were being represented by these
protestors, whereas 97.4 per cent saw themselves as being 'in the same boat'
with the militants.

Francis Lee (2020) identified several factors contributing to intra-movement
cohesion in this movement. Unlike the Umbrella Movement, where tensions
between the radical and moderate factions were salient, there was a trend of
reconciliation between these factions from late 2016 to early 2019. The threat
posed by the extradition bill and escalating state repression further united the
two factions. Furthermore, the Anti-Extradition Movement also attracted
many young participants with limited exposure to past conflicts within the
pro-democracy movement. Shared protest experiences, especially encounters
with police violence, played a crucial role in nurturing camaraderie.

The consensus over protest claims also fostered intra-movement cohesion. In
many social movements, disputes over protest claims often sow discord (Zald
and Ash 1966). But this was not the case in the Anti-Extradition Movement.
Early on in the movement, protesters had collectively formulated 'five demands'
as their core claims. These demands originated not from any movement organizations but from a decentralized process involving peer collaboration across
online and offline spaces, which was detailed in Chapter 5. Despite tactical

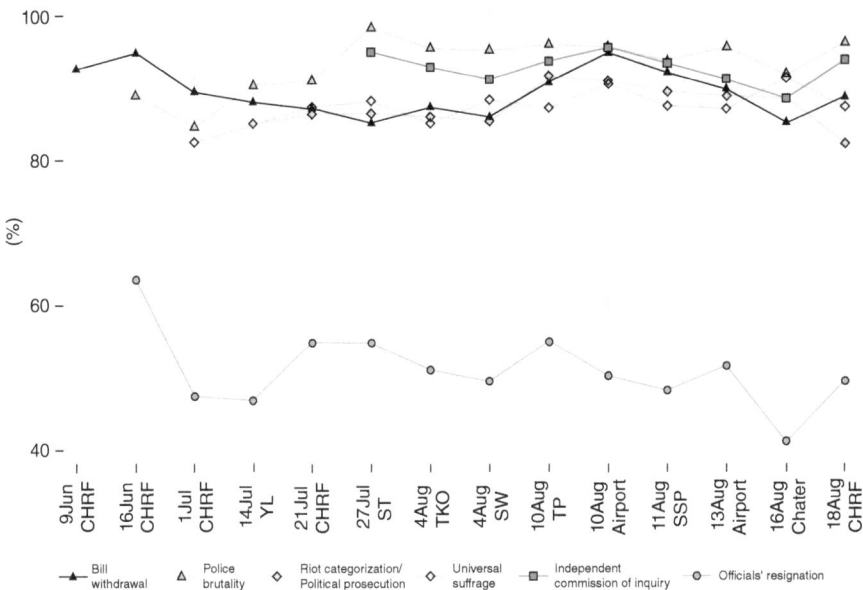

FIGURE 10.4 Support for protest demands.
Source: Authors' onsite surveys.

differences, protesters generally rallied behind these five demands. This sentiment was encapsulated by a frequently echoed slogan: 'five demands, not one
less' (*wuda suqiu, queyi buke; ng-daai-sou-kau, kyut-yat-bat-ho*). Our on-site
surveys from June to August 2019, as illustrated in Figure 10.4, consistently
indicated high support for these five demands. Given the government's refusal
to meet all these demands, their non-fulfilment served as a compelling reason
for protesters to persist and set aside their differences.

Still, tensions did exist between the moderate and radical factions, with
online debates about movement tactics and norms intensifying over time.
However, until December 2019, the prevailing solidarity remained largely
unshaken.[2] Additionally, as more protesters were arrested or injured, the
shared sense of solidarity became intertwined with a growing sense of guilt
among many moderate protesters, who believed that their militant counterparts had faced the most severe consequences on their behalf (Tang
and Cheng 2021). In our December 8 survey, a remarkable 96.9 per cent
of respondents shared the sentiment that the militant protesters had made
sacrifices for the peaceful protesters. Additionally, 79.5 per cent felt that
peaceful protesters owed something to the militants. Both solidarity and guilt

---

[2] In the onsite survey on December 8, 95.8 per cent agreed that the militants were acting and
speaking on their behalf, 97.4 per cent felt that they were in the same boat and 84.4 per cent felt
that they were 'one of them'.

could motivate individuals to maintain sympathy, if not outright support, for radical actions. The same December 8 survey also revealed a significant correlation between a solidarity index (derived from the solidarity-related statements) and the acceptance of radical tactics ($r = 0.53$, $p < 0.001$, $n = 901$). This suggests that solidarity plays a crucial role in encouraging moderates to accept radicalization.

DISCURSIVE NEGOTIATION

The preceding section illustrated the interactive dynamics leading to tactical radicalization. However, this analysis only partially explains public receptiveness to protest violence. Radicalism, by definition, involves acts deviating from mainstream social norms and routines. Without a concerted effort to justify these actions, ordinary citizens are unlikely to understand or find these tactics acceptable. Moreover, it is also important to moderate the pace of radicalization, allowing time for moderates and the general public to 'catch up'. Collective restraints must be established for this purpose.

Throughout the movement, the articulation of justifications and constraints for radical actions – which we call *discursive negotiation* – was prevalent in the public domain. Consider, for instance, a fifteen-page pamphlet written by a group of Hong Kong university students. This pamphlet expounded upon the Hong Kong protests and addressed queries such as: 'What is the extradition bill?' 'Why do Hong Kong people oppose the bill?' and so forth. It also elucidated the reasons behind protesters setting bonfires and addressed incidents of vandalism at metro stations, while justifying acts of vandalizing shops. In the context of setting fires, the pamphlet commenced with a reference to the Yuen Long attack and subsequently highlighted instances of ongoing police actions. The pamphlet noted:

There are protesters who set fires in front of police stations or damaged government buildings in order to protest against police violence. There are also protesters setting fires in the middle of the road when confronting the police in order to obstruct the police. It aims at gaining time for the frontline protesters to retreat. Protesters do not set fire to residential buildings and do not attack innocent citizens.

While the accuracy of this statement is debatable, it indicates that even movement supporters understood how certain controversial actions were justified and the constraints militant protesters followed when using radical tactics.

Examining online discussions in LIHKG can offer insights into discursive negotiation as a micro-mechanism of action organization. As previously discussed, LIHKG served as a centralized communication platform where protesters and supporters discussed all aspects of the protests. Due to its public nature, LIHKG also became an important arena for discursive negotiation among protesters. To illustrate LIHKG's role in the radicalization process, we identified the moments when keywords associated with or indicative of

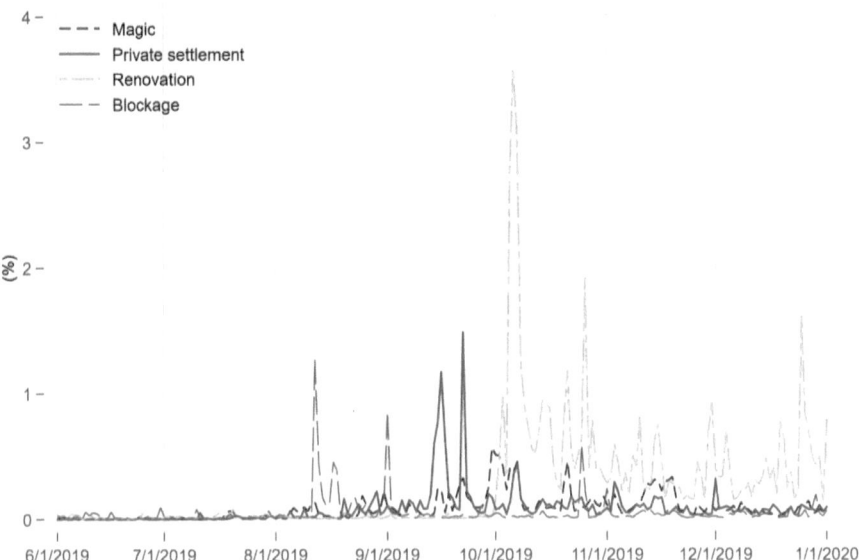

FIGURE 10.5 Frequency of radical tactics-related keywords on LIHKG, 2019.
Source: Authors' LIHKG data.

various radical tactics appeared in online discussions. Figure 10.5 shows the proportions of threads and comments in the public affairs and chit-chat channels of LIHKG that contained: (1) magic (*mofa; mo-faat*), a euphemism for arson and petrol bombs; (2) private settlement (*siliao; si-liu*), a euphemism for vigilantism; (3) renovation (*zhuangxiu; jong-sau*), another euphemism for vandalism; and (4) blockage (*saibao; sak-baau*), a term for obstructing metro stations. These keywords emerged at different times. They were not used extensively in June and July 2019 but appeared around the time when the actions they represented started to manifest on the streets: in August, protesters began using petrol bombs and blocking metro stations; in mid-September, they began the practice of vigilantism; and in early October, they began vandalizing targeted shops.

Using euphemisms for radical tactics indicates protesters' efforts to justify their actions and protect themselves from potential legal repercussions. In some cases, the introduction of these terms was linked to specific events during distinct protest events. For instance, the term 'blockage' gained prominence in late August after several metro stations were closed along a protest route just hours before its scheduled start. This event was perceived as an attempt by the metro company to side with the government. It catalyzed the emergence of the term in online discussions and subsequently gave rise to incidents of vandalism at metro stations.

If LIHKG served as a platform for tactical negotiation among protesters, one would expect to see a simultaneous increase in discussions about maintaining

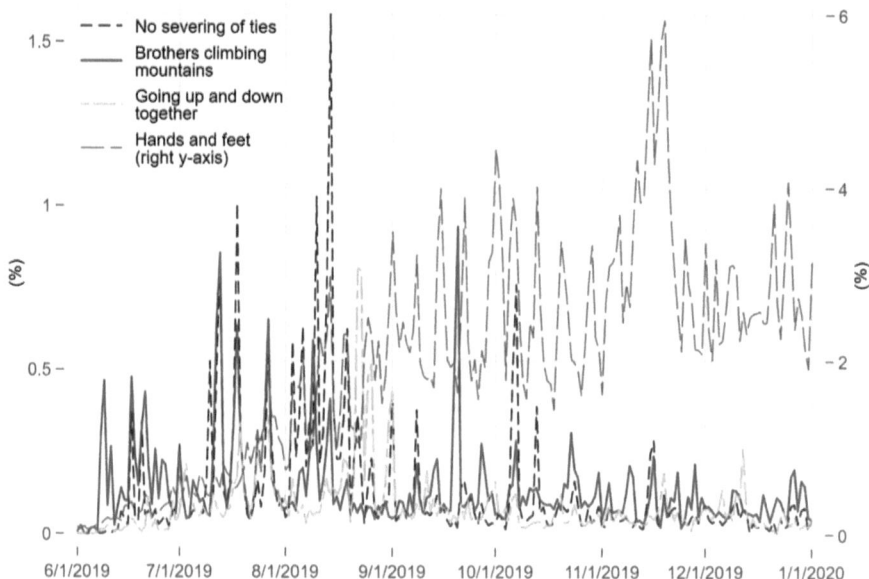

FIGURE 10.6 Frequency of solidarity keywords on LIHKG, 2019.
Note: The y-axis on the left indicates percentages of posts containing the keywords
sau-juk (hands and feet). The y-axis on the right indicates percentages of posts
containing bat-got-jik (no severing of ties), hing-dai-pa-saan (brothers climbing
mountains), chai-seung-chai-lok (going up and down together).
Source: Authors' LIHKG data.

solidarity as discussions about militant tactics intensified. Figure 10.6 shows
the frequency of four solidarity-related terms often used within the movement:
'hands and feet' (*shouzu; sau-juk*), 'no severing of ties' (*bugexi; bat-got-jik*),
'brothers climbing mountains' (*xiongdi pashan; hing-dai-pa-saan*), and 'going
up and down together' (*qishang qiluo; chai-seung-chai-lok*). The data shows
that while solidarity-related keywords were present in June and July when
protest violence was minimal, their frequency, particularly that of 'no severing of ties', significantly increased in mid-August, coinciding with the onset
of violence. Some of these keywords saw subsequent increases after August,
such as in late September and early October, aligning with corresponding rises
in keywords associated with radical tactics. Despite a gradual decrease in the
frequency of three of these keywords after September, 'hands and feet' consistently saw heightened usage. Notably, its surge in mid-November coincided
with the most intense conflicts, namely the occupation of two university campuses. Overall, a positive and statistically significant correlation exists between
keywords linked to radical tactics and those related to solidarity (Pearson *r* =
0.53, *p* < 0.0001, *n* = 215), indicating a frequent co-occurrence of discussions
surrounding both subjects.

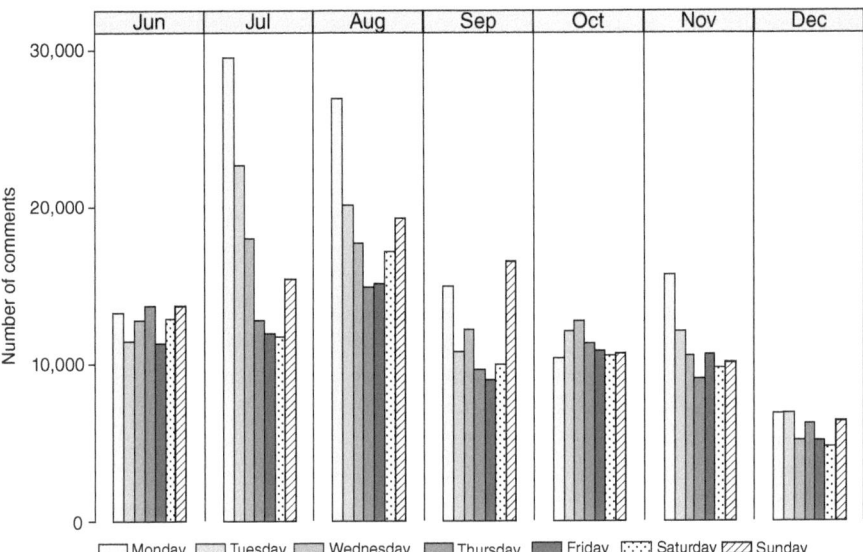

FIGURE 10.7 Average number of LIHKG comments by day of the week, 2019.
Source: Authors' LIHKG data.

Generally, the rhythm of online discussions mirrored the ebb and flow of protest actions. Figure 10.7 shows the average number of comments on LIHKG's public affairs channel for each day of the week from June to November 2019. In June, comment counts showed little variation across the days of the week. However, a noticeable weekly pattern emerged in July and August. Mondays saw the most comment activity, followed by Tuesdays and Wednesdays. Comment volumes dipped on Thursdays and Fridays, only to surge again over the weekends. This pattern stemmed from the movement's intense protest actions during July and August, primarily occurring on Saturdays and Sundays. These protests often led to unexpected events that both movement participants and the public sought to understand, leading to robust online discussions, particularly on Mondays. A similar weekly pattern persisted through September. However, in October, the rhythm of protest actions shifted. With metro services suspended in response to clashes and the police rejecting most protest applications, protesters adopted a strategy of organizing numerous small-scale protests across the city on different days, deviating from the previous focus on large weekend gatherings. Consequently, the pattern of online discussions also shifted in October before reverting to the previous pattern in November.

This rhythmic pattern suggests that tactical negotiation often unfolded in response to specific events and that movement participants showed a strong interest in post-event evaluations. Intense debates arose when certain actions were perceived as crossing the threshold of justifiability. An example of this occurred during the airport sign-in on August 13. Initially, protesters had staged airport sit-ins in late July to amplify their message on the global stage. Peaceful and non-disruptive to start, these actions involved protesters sitting in the arrival hall and engaging with international media and visitors. However, on August 13, some protesters obstructed restricted airport areas, preventing travellers from boarding flights. In addition, a group of protesters detained and assaulted a mainland journalist who was deemed suspicious (*Hong Kong Free Press*, 14 August 2019).

This incident sparked intense debates about whether preventing travellers from boarding their flights could undermine the movement's public support and whether protesters had the right to detain individuals under suspicion at protest sites. On LIHKG, some users attempted to articulate the norms governing the use of physical force. A notable post, written by a group identifying themselves as 'lawyers, bankers, software developers, political scientists, and historians' compared protest sites to battlefields. Although it acknowledged the need for pre-emptive self-defence, the post presented nine principles, encompassing guidelines such as 'force must not exceed what is necessary for the situation', 'force cannot be directed at non-combatants or citizens', 'ensure humanitarian aid for all affected individuals', 'no theft or looting of opponents' property, except weapons', and others.

Interestingly, some of these negotiations gave rise to concrete actions. In the wake of the airport controversy, some movement supporters visited the airport on August 14 to apologize to international visitors. This was not the only time moderate protesters publicly apologized to citizens who had been inconvenienced due to protest actions. On June 25, a small group of protesters apologized at the entrance of the Inland Revenue Department Building for the previous day's 'occupation action' (*Hong Kong Free Press*, 26 June 2019). At times, protesters also deliberately organized peaceful protests to counterbalance instances of violent confrontation. Following the airport incident, the CHRF called for a peaceful 'be water' march on August 18, urging participants to refrain from all forms of violence during the protest. The organizer reported that over 1.7 million citizens participated, though the figure was disputed.

However, discussions about the norms governing actions were often tense. Not all militant protesters supported the idea of public apologies. Those who did were sometimes criticized as 'air-con strategists' – people who opined on movement strategies while staying safely in air-conditioned spaces, avoiding active participation. Some even fundamentally resisted the idea of imposing moral constraints on actions. Nevertheless, these discursive negotiations continued amid such tensions. As incidents of vigilantism increased in September, online discussions advocated for employing violence proportionately and only against those who physically attacked protesters. When protesters began vandalizing shops, discussions gave rise to the principle of proportionate retribution: 'vandalize black [shops run by gangsters], decorate red [shops owned by mainland Chinese capital], boycott blue [shops supporting the government],

and shop at yellow [shops supporting the movement]'. In other words, protesters should differentiate between different types of shops. The creation of such
norms effectively served as a call for restraint.

Despite these discussions, there were noticeable discrepancies between
the norms proposed online and the actual frontline actions. There were clear
instances of 'disproportionate' vigilantism, such as the severe burning of a fifty-
seven-year-old man who confronted protesters vandalizing a metro station
on November 11. This horrific act was widely condemned within the movement. Furthermore, regarding vandalism, protesters indiscriminately attacked
'black', 'red', and some 'blue' shops, without making clear distinctions. This
divergence between online norms and real-world actions became more apparent as the movement continued its radicalization.

However, the occurrence of such extreme actions did not mean that the
normative discussions were meaningless. The fact that the discussions were
held was itself significant. While militant protesters may not have strictly
adhered to the exact norms delineated online, they were at least reminded
of the necessity to contemplate public reactions and the moral defensibility
of their actions. They were aware that the latitude they had for using militant tactics depended on the support of moderate protesters and the general
public, which could be withdrawn at any point. This resulted in continuous
efforts to find a normative balance, even though the balance point constantly
shifted as the movement developed (Weisburd and Lernau 2006). Indeed,
militant protesters demonstrated some restraint in their actions. Up until late
January 2020, vandalism was limited to specific types of shops. There were no
instances of looting, and fires were primarily kindled using street rubbish or at
the entrances of metro stations and targeted shops. Notably, a public opinion
poll conducted in November and early December revealed that 71.1 per cent
of respondents saw that the police had employed excessive force, whereas only
32.8 per cent believed the same of the protesters. Arguably, public tolerance of
protester violence was contingent upon these restraints; and discursive negotiations played a crucial role in establishing and communicating both justifications and limits.

CONCLUSION

This chapter has examined the process of tactical radicalization within the
Anti-Extradition Movement. Using a relational perspective, we have shown
that tactical radicalization emerged not as a deliberate strategy but rather as
a contingent outcome of the interactions between protesters, various actors,
and the wider political context. Through these interactions, protesters were
exposed to new threats and increasingly turned to or supported more radical
and violent tactics. We have also highlighted the vital role of discursive negotiation in shaping the justifications and norms related to radical tactics. This
mechanism not only fostered unity between the moderates and the radicals but

also urged the radicals to exercise restraint. While militant protesters did not always conform to established norms, the attempts to negotiate represented a search for a normative balance.

Our analysis of discursive negotiation highlights a distinct mechanism parallel to the process of peer collaboration, which serves to regulate the speed and intensity of radicalization. In leaderful mobilizations, the lack of a centralized authority left protesters free to act on their individual judgments about what they believed to be best for the movement, which makes them prone to radicalization and violent excesses. Discursive negotiation provides a way for protesters to construct shared protest norms and regulate protest actions. Although it is difficult to measure the effectiveness of this mechanism, it enables some degree of consensus-making among protesters despite the absence of leadership.

11

Conclusion

The year 2019 will leave its imprint on the history of contentious politics. Much like the iconic years of 1848, 1968, and 1989, this year also witnessed a tsunami of protests that swept across the world and engulfed both democratic and authoritarian regimes. Other than in Hong Kong, citizens in various countries have similarly taken to the streets to express their discontent on issues ranging from political freedom to socioeconomic inequality and environmental concerns. In Chile, a rise in metro fare sparked widespread, sometimes violent, demonstrations against unemployment and economic inequity. In Belarus, contested election results spurred sustained protests against the long-serving president Alexander Lukashenko, exposing vulnerabilities of a seemingly stable authoritarian regime. In the United States, the death of George Floyd under a police officer's knee galvanized the Black Lives Matter Movement, underscoring racial inequalities and sparking nationwide protests, some of which escalated into violent clashes. In Thailand, young protesters mobilized against the pro-military government in early 2020, demanding reform of the monarchy and the resignation of the government leader. In Spain, Catalan protesters took to the streets demanding the release of detained pro-independence leaders. Echoing the tactics used in Hong Kong, they even attempted to block Barcelona's main airport in October 2019 – replicating a strategy used by Hong Kong protesters two months earlier (*Quartz*, 16 October 2019).

Similar to the Arab Spring uprisings and the global Occupy movement in the early 2010s, these protests have been described by scholars and observers as 'leaderless'. This term refers to the manner in which ordinary citizens, feeling unrepresented, mobilized spontaneously without the structure of traditional SMOs. The prevailing view is that social media and digital technologies were crucial in facilitating their leaderlessness. For instance, a *Financial Times* editorial (25 October 2019) observed that '[these mass protests] are usually leaderless rebellions, whose organisation and principles are not set out in a little red book or thrashed out in party meetings, but instead emerge on *social media*. These are revolts that are convened by smartphone and inspired by hashtags, rather than guided by party leaders and slogans drafted by central committees'. Similarly, an essay in *The Atlantic* (Serhan 2019) remarked that '[t]he success of these protests can be attributed in large part to social media, which has enabled participants to communicate and organize in a more decentralized way'.

These perspectives have offered valuable insights; and describing such protests as 'leaderless' certainly distinguishes them from past movements that prominently featured traditional organizational structures and charismatic leaders. However, by defining these protests by what they *lack* and overly emphasizing the role of digital technologies, these viewpoints overlook a crucial discussion about the actual organizational dynamics of these protests. If these movements truly had no leaders, then how were demands, strategies and tactics conceived? How did protesters organize and coordinate actions on the ground? More fundamentally, why *would* individuals mobilize without traditional organizations and leaders, even when such entities were accessible on the eve of protests? Besides, in the absence of conventional leadership, how did protesters forge the collective identity and mobilizing structures necessary for them to assemble as a cohesive force? These are questions that remain inadequately addressed by simply labelling these movements as 'leaderless'. Neither can the role of digital technologies, regardless of their undeniable utility, provide an adequate explanation.

LEADERFUL MOBILIZATIONS

The Making of Leaderful Mobilization presents a novel perspective for understanding the wave of protests that have swept across the globe since the early 2010s. We describe these mass mobilizations as *leaderful*, not leaderless, to encapsulate how a multitude of protesters collectively and simultaneously exercise leadership in a decentralized manner. In leaderful mobilizations, leadership exists even in the absence of prominent leaders. Rather than being defined by a title, a position or a set of attributes, leadership emerges through actions distributed and shared among a diverse array of actors, including ordinary citizens, latent networks, and established organizations. Digital communication technologies certainly play a pivotal role in enabling these actors to distribute and exercise leadership tasks, but they are useful *only* because they are strategically utilized by individuals to facilitate protest organizing and are superimposed into existing social relationships. At the heart of these movements are still the ordinary citizens, who are driven by a desire to assert their agency as political subjects, not merely as passive figures to be mobilized.

Certainly, not all of these mass protests are *leaderful* to the same extent. In some of them, conventional organizations and charismatic leaders continued to play a prominent role. For instance, the Tunisian Revolution in 2011 was partly led by established trade unions and human rights organizations, which formed the Tunisian National Dialogue Quartet that later received the Nobel Peace Prize. Similarly, the 2019–2020 pro-democracy protests in Thailand were symbolically led by a group of student activists who became the movement's public faces. This is why we do not consider leaderful mobilizations as a binary concept. It is better viewed as a *spectrum* within which some movements can be more leaderful than others, particularly when ordinary citizens take a more active role in steering the movement. The purpose of categorizing these protests as leaderful is not to deny the existence or emergence of some form of hierarchical leadership structure, but rather to emphasize the participatory role of ordinary citizens within the mobilization process. A movement's leaderfulness depends greatly on the extent to which ordinary citizens independently initiate and carry out mobilization efforts.

This book does not aim to explore the full spectrum of leaderful mobilizations. Instead, it seeks to offer a theoretically grounded explanation for the emergence and dynamics of an exemplary leaderful mobilization within a single case. Post-handover Hong Kong, a protest-ridden territory on the edge of China, presents a compelling case for exploration. The city's evolution of contention spanning decades exemplifies how mass mobilizations arise and evolve as a result of state-society interactions. These shifting forms of mobilizations – from brokered to leaderful ones – provide a unique opportunity to examine temporal and within-unit variations, even within a single case (Gerring 2017).

Using a mixed-method approach, this book highlights the role of perceived threats in the evolution of mass mobilizations in post-handover Hong Kong, where the institutionalized opposition was gradually marginalized under an advancing state, and where structural political opportunities for democratic reforms were increasingly scarce. We present a theory of mediated threat that emphasizes how perceived threats can mobilize political challengers while simultaneously shaping their actions and relational dynamics. Our core argument posits that these threats do not directly and automatically trigger mass mobilizations. Instead, they are perceived and mediated through the opposition's relational dynamics, which are determined by the strength of the institutionalized opposition and the level of fractionalization within the opposition. This mediation process significantly influences the resulting form of mobilizations. Furthermore, these threats can alter the opposition's relational dynamics, thereby influencing the perception and response to future threats.

This book also aims to unpack the organizational dynamics of leaderful mobilizations through the lens of Hong Kong's 2019 Anti-Extradition Movement. Our analysis has revealed the mechanisms that sparked and sustained this phenomenal movement. It demonstrates how ordinary citizens – professionals, churchgoers, students, netizens, and so on – organized and coordinated protest actions through digital communication technologies and various latent and spontaneous networks. These networks offered shared identities and social capital, such as trust, knowledge, and expertise, to facilitate peer collaboration amongst protesters. They also provided the relational infrastructures for team formation, enabling the translation of ideas into actions. The symbiotic interplay between digital and social networks was key to what facilitated and sustained leaderful mobilizations.

To what extent can our findings from Hong Kong travel to other political contexts? Surely, post-handover Hong Kong has a unique political system in many ways, as outlined in Chapter 1. Despite being classified as a hybrid regime, Hong Kong has enjoyed a notable degree of civil and political liberties, along with a multifaceted state structure that includes the local government, the PRC's central government, and economic elites. It may be challenging to find a case elsewhere in the world that mirrors these specific attributes. However, it is precisely Hong Kong's unique situation and its transformation that have allowed us to witness the rapid evolution of contentious politics over two decades and the emergence of leaderful mobilization. Without an increasingly assertive state aiming to expand its reach, we might not have observed a weakening institutionalized opposition that was losing popular support as leaders of mobilization. Similarly, without the political and civic freedoms that permitted opposition groups and networks to sustain and expand, we might not have observed the pattern of evolving mobilizations. In other words, Hong Kong's distinctiveness makes it a valuable case for *inductive theory building*.

What, then, can be extrapolated from the case of Hong Kong? While we do not expect our theory of mediated threat to be generalizable to every context, we believe in its potential to illuminate three key aspects of contemporary social movements, particularly in non-democracies with some degree of openness: the influence of perceived threats in shaping the dynamics of contention, the origins and mechanisms of leaderful mobilizations, and the impact of mass mobilizations on regime structure.

THE POLITICS OF PERCEIVED THREATS

The book's first major contribution is to have presented a nuanced theorization of threats in contentious politics. Instead of echoing existing research that focuses on how threats ignite contention, our framework underscores the mediated nature of threats. Our findings reveal how perceived threats may modify the mobilizing structure of challengers, stimulating the growth of civil society groups and networks beyond traditional opposition organizations. This process reshapes the relational dynamics of the opposition and influences how future threats will be perceived. By viewing threats as perceived realities rather than objective facts, our findings also highlight how variations in perceived threats among diverse groups and networks can lead to differing ideological and tactical preferences. Such variations can instigate internal conflicts among these potential challengers, despite facing the same overarching threats. For collective mobilization to achieve greater cohesion, perceived threats must align relatively consistently among disparate citizen groups and networks, as well as with self-mobilizing citizens who participate on a spontaneous basis.

Deepening our understanding of the role threats play in contentious politics is important, especially given that threats often serve as a primary catalyst for mobilization in authoritarian or hybrid contexts where political opportunities are scarce and elusive. While some scholarly work has examined the role of threats in such contexts, the research typically centres on the effects of repression on mobilization – the particularistic threats that target individuals as conceptualized in our book – which has so far yielded inconclusive results on whether it bolsters or deters protests (Lichbach 1987; Rasler 1996; Steinert-Threlkeld, Chan, and Joo 2022). In contrast, there has been limited focus on the effects of threats targeted at political institutions – the generalized threats as defined in this book. Such threats are neither immediately repressive nor overtly visible; but they may unfold over an extended period and gradually undermine institutions that people often take for granted. These can include elements such as freedom of expression, due process, judicial independence, and the rule of law, among others.

Generalized threats – those that target institutions – are particularly prominent in hybrid regimes and democratic regimes experiencing backsliding or autocratization (Hellmeier et al. 2021; Lührmann and Lindberg 2019; Maerz et al. 2020). In these contexts, governments and the ruling elites are generally not repressive – or not as repressive as classic authoritarian regimes. Instead, they employ democratic institutions – such as legislature, regular elections, and free media – to represent citizens' interests, protect their rights, and impose checks and balances to limit the incumbent's power. However, in practice, incumbents can easily manipulate, weaken, or circumvent these political institutions. For instance, in Turkey, there has been an increasing consolidation of power by the ruling party – the Justice and Development Party – after it came to power in the early 2000s, pushing the country towards electoral authoritarianism. Under the leadership of Recep Tayyip Erdoğan, the government has faced widespread criticisms for interfering with elections, eroding judicial independence, suppressing journalistic freedoms, and curtailing civil liberties (Yilmaz and Bashirov 2018). In Indonesia and the Philippines, both nominally democratic countries, governments have been accused of 'executive aggrandizement'. Elected rulers are said to have weakened democracy from within by eroding institutional checks on the exercise of executive power (Bermeo 2016; Croissant and Haynes 2021). This includes the weakening or dismantling of independent state agencies, the stifling of opposition activity within formal representative institutions, and the restriction of criticisms of the government (Power 2020). These institutions-targeting threats may not seem immediately repressive to the ordinary citizen. Sometimes, they even garner some level of popular support as the rulers introducing them are elected democratically. However, over time, such manoeuvres can significantly undermine a society's democratic fabric.

Generalized but contingent threats played an important role in sparking some of the leaderful mobilizations seen after 2019. For example, in Indonesia, thousands of students across the country protested in 2019 against a new criminal code that would have criminalized extramarital sex and insulted the president's dignity, as well as legislative changes that would weaken the anti-corruption agency. This marked the biggest protest since the fall of the former president Suharto in 1998. In Israel, judicial reforms that would curb the power of the Supreme Court sparked nationwide protests in 2023 and brought together a diverse array of groups who saw the reform as a constitutional coup. More recently, in Kenya, a finance bill proposed by the government that planned to increase taxes on fuel and commodities sparked nationwide protests in mid-2024, which were "led" in a decentralized fashion by tech-savvy Gen Z protesters. Around the same time in Bangladesh, the government's proposal to reform the quota system in public service recruitment triggered massive youth-led protests, eventually leading to the resignation of the Prime Minister Sheikh Hasina. Our study on Hong Kong offers an extended view on the evolution of threat perceptions, thereby enriching our understanding of why and how such mobilizations may emerge when states expand their power and weaken the opposition. Moreover, by exploring the varied effects of perceived threats on the organizational form of mobilization, our study bridges the gap between the motivations for mobilization and the strategies employed in the process. This under-theorized connection in the current literature provides a more comprehensive understanding of the mechanisms at work in contentious politics.

ORIGINS AND MECHANISMS OF LEADERFUL MOBILIZATIONS

Our book also provides unique insights into both the origins and mechanisms of leaderful mobilizations. Existing research that labels them as 'leaderless' has produced several impressions about such kind of mobilization. First, leaderful mobilizations are often viewed as events that would emerge in contexts lacking pre-existing organizational structure. A prime example was Syria during the Arab Spring, in which protesters mobilized 'from scratch' (Pearlman 2021). Second, in the absence of centralized leadership, leaderful mobilizations are presumed to be structureless and entirely spontaneous: nothing can be planned, and actions are always improvised. Third, it is assumed that leaderful mobilizations are often short-lived. Because of their lack of organizational structure, they are likely to encounter 'tactical freeze' (Tufekci 2017) after the initial stages of mobilization.

These impressions are not entirely inaccurate as they do capture the essence of some of these mobilizations, particularly those in the early 2010s. However, our analysis of Hong Kong's Anti-Extradition Movement shows that they are oversimplified. First, this leaderful mobilization emerged *even* when a pre-existing political opposition was available as a mobilizing structure. But even though it played a crucial role as the 'early risers', protesters did not rely on them as leaders after the early stages of mobilization. Instead, they began to mobilize leaderfully, organizing and coordinating actions on their own. Second, this leaderful mobilization was not structureless or entirely spontaneous. Pre-existing, latent social networks – such as students, alumni, professions, hobby groups, residential communities – played a pivotal role in serving as the mobilizing structure, bringing together ordinary citizens who did not necessarily identify as activists. Even though not all of these networks were well-organized and resource-rich, the social identities they cultivated helped to unite individuals around common meanings, values, and norms. Furthermore, new hierarchies might arise within leaderful mobilizations. Such structures could develop informal chains of command primarily to facilitate the division of labour, but they are unlikely to evolve into centralized leadership.

Third, this leaderful mobilization was able to sustain and maintain cohesion for a significant period of time, even without a centralized leadership. Contrary to existing research that focuses on the initial stages of such mobilizations (Abrams 2023; Castells 2012; Pearlman 2021), our book shed lights on their backstage labour and organizational dynamics. Our findings underscore the interplay between digital technologies and relational infrastructures in enabling what 'peer collaboration', a key process in sustaining leaderful mobilizations. Digital technologies certainly played a crucial role in coordinating actions and disseminating information among protestors. However, without the pre-existing social networks and face-to-face interactions that physically brought individuals together, it would be difficult for protesters to build trust in a high-risk environment and access resources. Meanwhile, our findings also shed light on how leaderful mobilizations are conducive to tactical radicalization, given the absence of a central authority to moderate actions. We demonstrate that tactical radicalization was not a linear process; it involved discursive negotiations among protesters that simultaneously provided justifications for escalation and imposed collective restraints on radical excesses. While these negotiations did not entirely prevent the use of extreme violence, they managed to slow down the radicalization process. This shows that while the dynamics of leaderful mobilizations are inherently unpredictable, protestors may develop endogenous routines to regulate their progression.

Collectively, these findings spotlight the prominent and proactive role of ordinary citizens in leaderful mobilizations, challenging our conventional understanding of what it means to participate in protests. In the context of this movement, while conventional organizations played a significant role as early risers of mobilization, ordinary citizens felt a strong urge to mobilize on their own, while viewing these organizations not as leaders but as logistical support hubs. These citizens did far more than simply attending protests or contributing to overall turnout. They were deeply engaged in the mobilization process, dedicating their time, effort, skills, and expertise. They also brought in their personal social networks and leveraged various forms of social capital to facilitate the organizing process. Beyond attending protests, some even took the initiative to devise, plan, and coordinate actions, actively collaborating with their peers. In this regard, these protesters were not simply attendees. They acted as informal leaders who guided the course of the mobilization.

It is therefore not accurate to label these mobilizations as leaderless. Despite the absence of centralized leadership, many informal leaders exist and play important roles in the process, rendering such mobilizations as leaderful rather than leaderless. This leaderful dynamic leads to a form of distributed leadership, where power is not consolidated in the hands of a few individuals but dispersed among various informal leaders who emerge and fade throughout the course of mobilization. These informal leaders act as the nodes and facilitators of leaderful mobilizations, enabling protesters to remain organized without the need for centralized leaders.

However, it is important to note that these informal leaders do not fit the conventional mould of movement leaders who derive their authority from charisma or control over bureaucratic organizations (Weber 1964). Instead of deriving from pre-existing qualities, their 'leadership' emerges organically from their contributions to various stages and facets of the movement, combined with their capacity to influence and manage the organizational process. Every participant has the potential to ascend to the role of informal leaders by assuming key positions capable of shaping the course of the movement, such as a thread leader in a discussion forum or a social media channel administrator, even though their influence may not necessarily be enduring. These informal positions enable informal leaders to exercise two types of power as conceptualized by Steven Lukes (1974): (1) decision-making power, or the ability to make a choice among alternative modes of action and (2) agenda-setting power, or the ability to control what is being discussed and what is not. Take the example of a channel administrator: on the one hand, they can wield decision-making power by deciding to schedule a protest at a specific location and time, among various proposals; on the other hand, they can exert agenda-setting power by pinpointing particular issues or ideas in the chat group for further discussion or suppressing the attention on others.

Leaderful mobilizations are enabled not only by the interplay between digital and physical networks. For informal leaders to exercise their decision-making and agenda-setting power, they must command some form of legitimacy among the masses. This legitimacy can stem from their collective identities or shared movement goals. Alternatively, it can arise from the shared norms and values ingrained in their social identities, which drive their participation in the movement. These shared meanings foster trust among strangers, allowing them to collaborate effectively in high-risk, fluid environments. Importantly, they also give rise to protesters' compliance with the agenda and decisions set forth by the informal leaders. It is crucial to note that unlike networks or connections, shared meanings within a society – whether they are norms, values, or beliefs – cannot be created spontaneously. They are often deeply rooted in its historical and cultural fabric of a society, evolving through generations and nurtured by different communities. They also serve as the social adhesive that bonds individuals together. It is the activation and articulation of these shared meanings, combined with the mobilization of pre-existing networks, that make leaderful mobilizations work. In this sense, spontaneity is not entirely unscripted. It is enabled, at least partially, by what has been socially embedded.

RESILIENCE AND FRAGILITY OF HYBRID REGIMES

Lastly, our book enriches the literature on hybrid regimes by exploring how mass mobilizations can alter the power dynamics within these systems. Existing scholarship on hybrid regimes has three main areas of focus: how autocrats maintain their power by selectively adopt institutional features of liberal democracies – such as elections and legislatures (Brownlee 2007; Diamond 2002; Gandhi 2008; Levitsky and Way 2010; Magaloni 2008; Svolik 2012); how rulers erode institutional constraints, contributing to democratic backsliding (Croissant and Haynes 2021; Haggard and Kaufman 2021; Lorch 2021); and how opposition actors challenge incumbents through limited political competition and mass mobilizations (Bellin 2012; Bunce and Wolchik 2010; Chang 2015; Gamboa 2022). The findings of this book resonate most with the latter two. However, rather than analysing solely from a state or societal perspective, we examine sociopolitical changes through the relational interactions between state and societal actors over an extended period of time (Goldstone 2004). Moreover, contrary to studies that emphasize the power of protests in undermining incumbents, our findings, echoing some recent research (Gamboa 2022; Rhodes-Purdy and Rosenblatt 2023), suggest that mass mobilizations can either check or intensify backsliding, depending on the nature of mobilizations.

Our temporal examination of Hong Kong's contentious politics reveals multiple pathways through which mass protests can reshape hybrid regimes in the contemporary era. One prevalent pathway involves a regulated form of autocratization following a moderate opposition pushback. Here, being regulated does not mean eventual transition to liberal democracy, but the putting in place of checks and balances in hybrid regimes. By effectively combining electoral politics and street protests, opposition actors were essentially establishing a framework to constrain autocrats. This approach was exemplified by the Colombian opposition during the Álvaro Uribe and Iván Duque administrations (Gamboa 2023), and the Malaysian opposition's challenges to the domination of the National Front government (Gandhi and Ong 2019; Weiss 2006). It was also seen in the Tunisia coalition building that preserved the only stable electoral democracy after the Arab Spring (Williamson 2021). In the context of Hong Kong, the opposition's strategy to combine institutional bargaining with brokered mobilizations in the 2000s echoed these approaches.

This 'boundary-spanning contention' provided both political challengers and their supporters with the space and protection to engage in dissent

(O'Brien 2003). By revealing the strength of the opposition and the demands of the most proactive citizens, mass protests are more likely to be tolerated by rulers (Cai and Chen 2022; Yuen and Cheng 2017). On the other hand, rulers are also constrained by the institutions that preserve their interests and power, such as the rule of law, competitive elections, media scrutiny, bureaucratic norms, business interests, or international recognition. Even when rulers intend to expand their control, they will have to consider the potential backlash caused by their actions. Their intention to prevent such uncertainties thus increases the chances of preserving the 'status quo'. From Southeast Asia to Latin America, although clientelism or populism remains salient, political power has been regulated by social forces. Regular elections and mass protests often enable the rise of new parties and politicians, some even lead to government alternation. In this sense, this prevalent pathway suggests that mass protests can express grievances and mediate threats from both the incumbent and the opposition, thereby prolonging the resilience of hybrid regimes (Levitsky and Way 2023; Merkel and Lührmann 2021).

Another prevalent pathway involves further autocratization in the wake of strong opposition pushback. This scenario typically unfolds when the state tightens control in hybrid regimes, thereby shrinking the space for institutional bargaining. As a result, established politicians and organizations find themselves stripped of their authority to lead opposition movements. Emergent groups and networks then come into prominence, often finding themselves either barred from participating in elections or disillusioned by the perceived lack of trustworthiness of the institutions. Consequently, they may start to advocate for more radical means of resistance. Historically, such exclusion from formal institutions often led to a contraction of organizational resources, which hampered the effective recruitment of supporters. However, the contemporary generation of activists find themselves in more favourable circumstances. The advent of digital technologies, together with the presence of supportive urban infrastructure (Beissinger 2022), has made spontaneous and 'leaderless' mobilizations easier than ever before. The eruption of such mobilization often takes hybrid regimes undergoing autocratization by surprise (Abrams 2023). In response to these bottom-up threats, such regimes may resort to violent repression, while also seeking to increase control over society to pre-empt the emergence of future political opportunities. This pathway towards autocratization was amply demonstrated in the aftermath of the violent waves of protest challenging Nicolás Maduro's rule in Venezuela in 2014 and 2019 (Somer, McCoy, and Luke 2021), and that of the 2013 Gezi Park Protests and the 2016 coup in Turkey (Draege 2022). Similarly, in the more authoritarian Belarus, mass protests against alleged election frauds in 2020 were met with lethal repression, mass arrests, restrictions on assembly, and the suspension of elections (De Vogel 2022). In the case of Hong Kong, this pathway could be observed in the late 2010s, as increasingly spontaneous and decentralized mobilizations were met with stronger state reprisals that eventually ended the era of liberal oligarchy.

Our analysis also highlights the unintended consequences that emerge from leaderful mobilizations (Bosi, Giugni and Uba 2016). In such mobilizations, leadership is distributed and decentralized, making it difficult to reach compromises at the movement level since no one could make binding decisions for all protesters. Moreover, despite their initially non-violent resistance, these mobilizations are often susceptible to a shift towards tactical radicalization. Both factors pose significant threats to the incumbent because of the uncertainties stemming from intensified conflicts (Chenoweth 2023). However, perhaps the most substantial threat comes from the extensive participation on the streets. This sends a powerful signal to incumbents that mass mobilization can translate into protest votes and that they are likely to lose in the upcoming elections. Faced with the threat of losing their grip on power, incumbents may resort to intensified repression and institutional overhauls to mitigate the risk of their power being undermined. This imperative for political elites to retain power frequently becomes a decisive factor that weakens the structural constraints preventing outright autocratization in hybrid regimes.

Taking a longer historical view to understand hybrid regimes thus enables us to see both its resilience and fragility. Our findings reveal that despite the existence of institutional constraints, strategic interactions between the incumbent and the opposition can continue to unfold and intensify. Paradoxically, the policies and measures aimed at strengthening the state's control can serve to intensify mass protests and deepen the mistrust of the institutionalized opposition and their supporters, thereby destabilizing the status quo. Even when elite and opposition political actors do not consciously intend to alter the existing balance, their potential to outbid one another can lead to unforeseen and unintended consequences.

MOVEMENT CONSEQUENCES

The 2019 Anti-Extradition Movement did not achieve most of its stated goals: only one of the five demands – the withdrawal of the extradition bill – was met. However, it achieved something that had seemed unattainable in the past for the pro-democracy movement. In November 2019, after the two university campus clashes, the democratic opposition won a landslide victory over the pro-government camp in the District Council. With a record turnout of 71 per cent of eligible voters, the pro-democracy camp tripled its seats from 124 to 388, whereas the pro-government camp held onto only sixty-two seats (Registration and Electoral Office 2019). This unprecedented victory bolstered the opposition. It also encouraged the veteran democrats, the neo-democrats and the localists to collaborate on planning an unofficial primary that aimed to select candidates in order to optimize their chances of securing a majority in the upcoming 2020 LegCo elections. Achieving a majority control of the LegCo would provide them with the leverage necessary to compel the authorities to concede to all the remaining movement goals. The Beijing central government, however, interpreted the opposition's plan as a provocative attempt to seize power (*Wenweipo*, 7 January 2021). Although the movement subsided with the onset of COVID-19, the democrats, emboldened by public sentiments, decided to proceed with their plan to secure a legislative majority.

The introduction of the National Security Law (NSL) by the Chinese central government in May 2020 occurred in this context. The NSL, consisting of sixty-six articles, primarily criminalizes four types of acts: secession, subversion, terrorism, and collusion with foreign or external forces. The law grants extensive powers to the executive branch to handle national security-related offences and mandates the creation of its own national security commission and police force to enforce these laws. Cases of the most serious nature can be tried in mainland China. This means that offenders can be legally extradited. The legislation of the NSL was an unprecedented move by Beijing – not only because of the severe nature of the laws but also because it was directly incorporated into the Basic Law framework (Chen 2021). Many local elites had little knowledge about it before it was officially announced.

The enactment of the NSL brought an end to the liberal oligarchy era. The provisions of the law encompass a wide array of activities, including both action and speech (Chopra and Pils 2022). The boundaries are pervasive and vague: many forms of political expression could potentially fall within the scope of the punishable offences. In conjunction with the NSL provisions, numerous ordinances related to incitement and sedition, which had been dormant since the 1967 riots, were also reactivated (*Hong Kong Free Press*, 3 July 2022). The new legal framework and newly established state apparatuses have made national security a political imperative, limiting the autonomy previously enjoyed by the Hong Kong government and its courts (Petersen 2020).

The political repercussions of the NSL were felt immediately. On 1 July 2020, which marked the anniversary of Hong Kong's handover and the first full day the NSL was in effect, a twenty-three-year-old protester was arrested and subsequently sentenced to nine years in prison under the NSL, for driving a motorbike decorated with a pro-movement flag into a group of police officers. In January 2021, forty-seven opposition activists were detained and charged with conspiracy to commit subversion for organizing a primary ahead of the LegCo election. In total, by July 2023, 260 individuals had been arrested on national security grounds (*South China Morning Post*, 4 July 2023). At the same time, utilizing the extensive pandemic control measures during the COVID-19 pandemic, the government banned almost all opposition protest gatherings, including the June 4 vigils and July 1 rallies (Lo 2021). Mass protests, once a common sight in Hong Kong, has become extinct.

Beijing's long-term policy of cautious state and nation-building became significantly much more direct and explicit over time. The first institution to undergo transformation was the LegCo. In March 2021, the National People's Congress declared that the rules of LegCo elections would be altered to ensure that only 'patriots govern Hong Kong' (*aiguozhe zhigang*). While the total number of LegCo seats would rise from 70 to 90, the seats returned by popular vote would decrease from 35 to 20. The remaining seats would be returned by functional constituencies and electoral committees – the former were reorganized, and the latter were reinstated after their abolition in 2004. This electoral overhaul also introduced a vetting mechanism, which would be guarded by members appointed by the government, to preselect the candidates. Ultimately, when the postponed LegCo election was held in 2021, no major pro-democracy candidate participated.

These dramatic institutional and societal changes brought a detrimental impact on the democratic opposition. Dozens of leading pro-democracy politicians and activists involved in the 2019 protests and the 2020 primaries were prosecuted, imprisoned, or forced into self-exile. Over 200 popularly elected district councillors resigned from their positions due to worries of failing the patriotic screening and facing increasing political pressure if they continued their duties. *Apple Daily*, Hong Kong's most widely read media outlet and most vocal government critic, was forced to cease operations on 24 June 2021, after the police froze the company's assets using the NSL (*The New York Times*, 23 June 2021). Its downfall instilled a sense of fear and unease among other critical media. Other smaller independent media outlets, such as Stand News and Citizen News, disbanded one after another in the following months.

Civil society organizations once serving as backbone of the pro-democracy movement suffered a similar fate. The Hong Kong Professional Teachers' Union and the Hong Kong Confederation of Trade Unions announced their dissolution shortly afterwards. Another defining moment came when the CHRF and Hong Kong Alliance, the organizers for the July 1 rallies and the June 4 candlelight vigils, announced their decisions to disband immediately on 14 August and 25 September 2021, respectively. Over fifty unions, churches, media outlets, political parties, and community groups – many of which had been active for several decades – were reported to have disbanded in 2021 (*Hong Kong Free Press*, 30 June 2022). By the end of 2022, most of the organizational strongholds of Hong Kong's pro-democracy movement had been dismantled. As the organizational nodes that once served as catalysts and logistical support hubs for mass mobilization have vanished, both brokered and leaderful mobilizations now seem like distant dreams. In the foreseeable future, the recurrence of mass mobilizations that marked the 2000s and 2010s appears unlikely. This may not mean that activism will completely disappear, but it is likely to take a more individualized, hidden, or transnational form (Fu 2018; Moss 2022).

State responses to mass protests can have unintended consequences extending beyond national borders. In borderlands like Hong Kong, the likelihood of sparking international reactions is particularly heightened. Borderlands are situated on the edges of empires, nations and world systems where exchanges and interactions frequently occurred and where the cohabitation of powers is being acknowledged (Hämäläinen and Truet 2011). However, their exceptions and ambiguities can be suddenly disrupted by contingencies and state responses to political contestations (Hung 2022). Indeed, western powers have responded strongly to the Hong Kong situation by imposing sanctions, issuing travel alerts, enacting technology bans, and preparing for economic withdrawal. This trajectory of bilateral securitization has intensified the US-China rivalry since 2019, described by Avery Goldstein as a 'irreversible turn for the worse' (Goldstein 2020: 48). Barry Buzan even suggested that the reinterpretation of the OCTS shifted public perception of China in the western world, initiating what he claims 'the beginning of the Second Cold War' (Buzan 2024: 250).

EXIT, VOICE, LOYALTY, AND ADAPTATION

In response to these momentous changes in state-society relations, many Hong Kong citizens have left the city, either temporarily or permanently. From mid-2019 to the end of 2022, the city saw the departure of over 200,000 residents, amounting to around 2.6 per cent of the resident population (Hong Kong Census and Statistical Department 2023). Although the population bounced back to the 2019 level in 2023, the rebound is likely due to new immigration schemes and some residents returning after the COVID-19 pandemic, with the biggest growth happening among residents aged over sixty (Hong Kong Census and Statistical Department 2023). Indeed, many middle class households with talent, capital, and children have emigrated via programs introduced by countries such as Britain and Canada (Ho 2023). For example, Britain's British National (Overseas) (BN(O)) scheme, which enables Hong Kong's BN(O) passport holders and their dependents to settle and gain citizenship, has attracted over 180,000 applicants by 2023, with more than 80 per cent already settled in the country (*South China Morning Post*, 24 August 2023).

More citizens, despite having easier emigration options, have chosen to remain. However, they have become more disengaged from politics. With the NSL in effect and the overhaul in the LegCo elections, many citizens, especially pro-democracy supporters, saw little room to promote substantial changes through political participation. The significant drop in election turnout was indicative. In the 2016 LegCo election, geographical constituencies had a turnout of 59.3 per cent of eligible voters. However, under the newly revised rules, the turnout for the 2021 LegCo election and 2023 District Council elections dwindled to 30.2 per cent and 27.6 per cent, respectively. These figures approximately equalled the total vote share of the pro-establishment parties in 2016. A rising trend of self-censorship has also been observed among citizens, especially among pro-democracy supporters (Kobayashi and Chan 2022) and journalists (Koo 2022; Lee, Tang, and Chan 2023).

These developments remind us of Albert Hirschman's (1970) framework of exit, voice, and loyalty. Originally conceived within an economic context, this framework has been widely applied to the political setting (Dowding et al. 2000; Pfaff and Kim 2003). In the face of unpalatable social or political conditions, individuals have two primary choices according to the framework: to voice by protesting against the status quo or to exit by migrating to another country. Loyalty influences whether individuals are inclined to voice or exit. If an individual has a high allegiance to a place or country, she may be less likely to exit and more inclined to exercise voice to effect change. This framework appears particularly relevant to the situation in post-NSL Hong Kong, where many have chosen to exit when their ability to voice their discontent has been curtailed. However, Hirschman's framework prompts questions regarding those who opt not to leave. Is it loyalty that makes them stay? When individuals choose to stay, how do they make themselves heard? And what actions do they undertake to better their well-being?

Post-NSL Hong Kong offers an active laboratory for examining and expanding upon Hirschman's framework. Predicting the future is undoubtedly difficult, but it is possible to identify at least two trends. First, intensified state and nation-building efforts are expected to broaden the reach of the state and reinforce the loyalty of certain citizen groups to the nation. This process is likely to promote the return of 'hearts and minds', an agenda which was not fully achieved in the first two post-handover decades. Whether this process will produce more loyalists or more 'patriotic dissenters' in the new era, however, remains to be seen.

Second, a significant number of those who stayed on have developed ways to adapt to the new realities – for example, by managing and minimizing risks associated with the legal boundaries and political uncertainties (Koopmans 2004; Lee 2023). These practices can be considered a form of *adaptation* – an alternative type of response in addition to exit and voice. From the state's perspective, adaption may not signify a change of mind but is sufficient to demonstrate compliance with behaviour. For citizens, however, adaptation can serve as a coping strategy to protect individual beliefs and collective well-being in the wake of trauma.

There are other more proactive ways of adaption. A sizeable portion of the population may hold on to their views, even if they do not explicitly discuss politics or engage in activism. For example, some supporters of the 2019 Anti-Extradition Movement have sustained their practice of political consumption, albeit on a smaller scale and less visible practices. Newly established media within the city have tried to provide professional and alternative journalism, maintaining communication and ties with the diaspora. New civil society initiatives, such as community newspapers, independent bookshops, walking tours, and fan clubs, have emerged, fostering civic practices through a localized, grassroots, and cultural approach. These might not manifest as voices in the classic Hirschmanian sense, but the resilience of such practices has disrupted an otherwise prevailing silence.

Appendices

Code		Date
B3	Medical doctor, first aid team	February 2020
B4	Psychologist, voluntary counselling service	February 2020
B5	Nurse, voluntary judicial team	March 2020
B6	Nurse, voluntary judicial team	April 2020
B7	Lawyer, voluntary judicial team	March 2020
B8	Lawyer, Occupy Central legal team	July 2015
B9	Medical doctor, first aid team	March 2020
B10	Barrister voluntary judicial team	March 2020
B11	Convenor, community mobilization	August 2019
B12	Convenor, community mobilization	September 2019
B13	Chinese medicine practitioner, medical treatment team	May 2020
B14	Chinese medicine practitioner, medical treatment team	June 2020
B15	Lawyer, voluntary judicial team	August 2019#
B16	Psychologist, voluntary counselling service	August 2019
B17	Nurse, member of voluntary physiotherapy	November 2019
B18	Priest, Roman Catholic Church	November 2019
B19	Pastor, Baptist Church	December 2019
B20	Pastor, Methodist Church	December 2019
B21	Pastor, Anglican Church	May 2020
B22	Academic, broker of the student–government dialogue	July 2018
B23	Convenor, social workers	August 2018

Code		Date
C1	Volunteer, recycling station, Admiralty occupied site, 2014	October 2014
C2	Militant protester, Mongkok occupied site, 2014	November 2016
C3	Petition initiator, 2019	May 2020
C4	Petition initiator, 2019	June 2020
C5	Campaign organizer, 2019	September 2022
C6	Campaign organizer, 2019	August 2022
C7	Campaign organizer, 2019	August 2022
C8	Administrator of a publicity channel, 2019	August 2022
C9	Founder of NeoGuideHK, 2019	August 2020
C10	Founder of YellowBlue Map, 2109	September 2020
C11	Owner of a yellow restaurant	May 2020
C12	Owner of yellow business Call-A-Van	May 2020
C13	Volunteer, defence team, Admiralty occupied site, 2014	October 2014
C14	Volunteer, supply station, Admiralty occupied site, 2014	September 2014
C15	Volunteer, supply station, Admiralty occupied site, 2014	September 2014

Code	Number of interviewees	Date
D1	1 graduate from a Band 2 girls' school	October 2019
D2	4 Form 6 students from a Band 1 boys' School	October 2019
D3	2 Form 6 students from a Band 1 girls' school	October 2019
D4	4 Form 4–6 students from a Band 3 co-educational school	November 2019

Code	Number of interviewees	Date
D5	2 Form 4–6 students from a Band 1 girls' school	November 2019
D6	3 Form 4–6 students from a Band 2 co-educational school	November 2019
D7	4 Form 4–6 students from a Band 2 girls' school	November 2019
D8	2 Form 5–6 students from a Band 1 boys' school	November 2019
D9	3 Form 4–6 students from a Band 1 boys' school	November 2019
D10	1 Form 4 student from a Band 2 co-educational school	January 2020
D11	1 student SMO activist	January 2020
D12	1 Form 5 student from a Band 1 boys' school	January 2020
D13	1 graduate from a girls' school	March 2020
D14	1 Form 1 student from a Band 3 co-educational school	June 2020
D15	3 Form 3–5 students from a Band 3 co-educational school	June 2020

\# Follow up interviews.
* Follow up conservations.

APPENDIX 2: TIMELINE OF IMPORTANT PROTEST EVENTS

Date	Major events	#Arrest*	#Round*
9-Jun	Mass demonstration participated by 1 million people	0	0
12-Jun	Second reading of the bill. Besieging of government headquarters. Police-protester clash	33	295
14-Jun	Mothers' gathering for young protesters	0	0
15-Jun	Suspension of the bill. Accidental death of the 'raincoat man' Marco Leung Ling-kit	0	0
16-Jun	Mass demonstration participated by 2 million people	0	0
21-Jun	Besieging of police headquarters	0	0
26-Jun	G20 mass rally	0	0
1-Jul	Mass demonstration. Besieging of and breaking into the Legislative Council by militant protesters	19	33
5-Jul	2nd mothers' gathering for young protesters	0	0
6-Jul	Reclaim Tuen Mun march, which started the regular reclaim marches in different districts during weekends	0	0
7-Jul	Mass demonstration in Kowloon	4	0
13-Jul	Reclaim Sheung Shui march	4	0
14-Jul	Mass demonstration in Shatin. Police-protester clash	47	0
16-Jul	Silver-hair march for young protesters	1	0
20-Jul	Pro-government 'Safeguard Hong Kong' rally	9	0

Date	Major events	#Arrest*	#Round*
21-Jul	Mass demonstration. Defacing the national emblem. Attack of protesters and citizens by suspected gangsters in Yuen Long	2	89
26-Jul	First airport sit-in demonstration	2	0
27-Jul	Reclaim Yuen Long	10	182
28-Jul	Rally against Yuen Long Attacks	58	555
2-Aug	Rally by civil servants	12	0
3-Aug	Mong Kok march	24	107
4-Aug	Tseung Kwan O march	57	147
5-Aug	General strike and citywide non-cooperation movement	165	1,211
9–11 Aug	Airport sit-in	0	0
11-Aug	Sham Shui Po march. A first aider's eye shot by the bean bag round fired by the police amidst police-protester clash	101	402
13-Aug	Airport sit-in against police brutality. Surrounding of a Global Times journalist	5	0
18-Aug	Mass demonstration participated by 1.7 million people	0	0
23-Aug	Citywide human chain actions	6	0
31-Aug	Police-protester clash in Kowloon. Attack of protesters and citizens by the riot police in the Prince Edward station	88	428
2-Sep	Class boycott by university and secondary students. General strike	37	1
3-Sep	General strike (2nd day)	38	7
6-Sep	'No White Terror, No Chinazi' rally. Besieging of the Mong Kok police station	9	42
8-Sep	Mass rally to U.S. Consulate General to support the Hong Kong Human Rights and Democracy Act	88	43
9–12 Sep	Beginning of 'Glory to Hong Kong' sing along protests	0	0
15-Sep	Mass demonstration on Hong Kong Island. Death of Christy Chan Yin-lam	57	97
21-Sep	Tuen Mun march. Protests in front of police stations.	31	61
27-Sep	Rally against San Uk Ling detentions	2	0
28-Sep	Mass rally to commemorate the 5th anniversary of the Umbrella Movement	11	21
1-Oct	National Day protests in different districts	299	3,344
4-Oct	Activation of the Emergency Regulations Ordinance. Enactment of the anti-mask law	13	485
6-Oct	Mass rallies in Hong Kong Island and Kowloon	121	233

Date	Major events	#Arrest*	#Round*
13-Oct	Protests at shopping malls across the city, followed by police-protester clashes in several districts	178	39
14-Oct	HK Human Rights & Democracy Act rally	9	0
20-Oct	Mass rally in Kowloon	60	468
23-Oct	Formal withdrawal of the bill	3	0
31-Oct	Police-protester clashes in Central and Mongkok	53	166
2-Nov	'Fight for Autonomy' rally. Police-protester clash	262	579
8-Nov	Death of Alex Chow Tsz-lok	39	176
11-Nov	Beginning of daily 'lunch with you' protests. Citywide general strike	296	1,046
11–15 Nov	Police siege of CUHK	762	7,552
17–29 Nov	Police siege of PolyU	1,529	10,977
28-Nov	Thanksgiving for HKHRDA	6	0
1-Dec	'Lest We Forget' march	42	30
6-Dec	'Say No to Tear Gas' rally	2	0
8-Dec	Mass demonstration participated by 0.8 million people	21	0
12-Dec	'United We Stand' rally to commemorate six months of the protests. Memorial ceremony for Alex Chow Tsz-lok	0	0
15-Dec	Beginning of daily 'shop with you' protests at shopping malls	23	30

*We report the total numbers of arrests and crowd-control agents deployed by the police in the annotated time period. They are not necessarily due to the major events we highlight in the second column.

References

Abdelrahman, Maha. 2013. 'In Praise of Organization: Egypt between Activism and Revolution'. *Development and Change* 44(3): 569–585.

Abrams, Benjamin. 2023. *The Rise of the Masses: Spontaneous Mobilization and Contentious Politics*. University of Chicago Press.

Accornero, Guya. 2013. 'Contentious Politics and Student Dissent in the Twilight of the Portuguese Dictatorship: Analysis of a Protest Cycle'. *Democratization* 20(6): 1036–1055.

Adams, Vincanne. 1998. *Doctors for Democracy: Health Professionals in the Nepal Revolution*. Cambridge: Cambridge University Press.

Agur, Colin, and Nicholas Frisch. 2019. 'Digital Disobedience and the Limits of Persuasion: Social Media Activism in Hong Kong's 2014 Umbrella Movement'. *Social Media + Society* 5(1): 2056305119827002.

Alderman, Derek H., Paul Kingsbury, and Owen J. Dwyer. 2013. 'Reexamining the Montgomery Bus Boycott: Toward an Empathetic Pedagogy of the Civil Rights Movement'. *The Professional Geographer* 65(1): 171–186.

Alimi, Eitan Y. 2011. 'Relational Dynamics in Factional Adoption of Terrorist Tactics: A Comparative Perspective'. *Theory and Society* 40(1): 95–118.

Alimi, Eitan Y., Lorenzo Bosi, and Chares Demetriou. 2012. 'Relational Dynamics and Processes of Radicalization: A Comparative Framework'. *Mobilization* 17(1): 7–26.

Alimi, Eitan Y., Lorenzo Bosi, and Chares Demetriou. 2015. *The Dynamics of Radicalization: A Relational and Comparative Perspective*. New York: Oxford University Press.

Almeida, Paul D. 2003. 'Opportunity Organizations and Threat-Induced Contention: Protest Waves in Authoritarian Settings'. *American Journal of Sociology* 109(2): 345–400.

Almeida, Paul D. 2008. *Waves of Protest: Popular Struggle in El Salvador, 1925–2005*. Minneapolis, MN: University of Minnesota Press.

Almeida, Paul D. 2019. 'The Role of Threat in Collective Action'. In *The Wiley Blackwell Companion to Social Movements*, eds. David A. Snow, Sarah A. Soul, Hanspeter Kriesi, and Holly J. McCammon, 43–62. Chichester: John Wiley & Sons.

Altheide, David L., and John M. Johnson. 1994. 'Criteria for Assessing Interpretive Validity in Qualitative Research'. In *Handbook of Qualitative Research*, eds. Norman K. Denzin, and Yvonna S. Lincoln, 485–499. Thousand Oaks, CA: SAGE Publications.

Andretta, Massimiliano, and Donatella della Porta. 2014. 'Surveying Protestors: Why and How'. In *Methodological Practices in Social Movement Research*, ed. Donatella della Porta, 308–334. Oxford: Oxford University Press.

Andrews, Kenneth T. 1997. 'The Impacts of Social Movements on the Political Process: The Civil Rights Movement and Black Electoral Politics in Mississippi'. *American Sociological Review* 62(5): 800–819.

Andrews, Kenneth T., and Charles Seguin. 2015. 'Group Threat and Policy Change: The Spatial Dynamics of Prohibition Politics, 1890–1919'. *American Journal of Sociology* 121(2): 475–510.

Apple Daily. 2019. '2356 Pieces of Tear Gas Grenades Were Found in the Chinese University of Hong Kong after a Night of Police Violence'. 13 November. https://web.archive.org/web/20220903023135/https://www.appledaily.com.tw/international/20191113/INGAOFTHT53OEWRZQTMAFBMLV4/ (Accessed on 4 October 2021).

Armstrong, David, Ora John Reuter, and Graeme B. Robertson. 2020. 'Getting the Opposition Together: Protest Coordination in Authoritarian Regimes'. *Post-Soviet Affairs* 36(1): 1–19.

Arriola, Leonardo R., Jed Devaro, and Anne Meng. 2021. 'Democratic Subversion: Elite Cooptation and Opposition Fragmentation'. *American Political Science Review* 115(4): 1358–1372.

Ash, Konstantin. 2015. 'The Election Trap: The Cycle of Post-electoral Repression and Opposition Fragmentation in Lukashenko's Belarus'. *Democratization* 22(6): 1030–1053.

Baek, Young Min. 2010. 'To Buy or Not to Buy: Who Are Political Consumers? What Do They Think and How Do They Participate?' *Political Studies* 58(5): 1065–1086.

Balsiger, Philip. 2010. 'Making Political Consumers: The Tactical Action Repertoire of a Campaign for Clean Clothes'. *Social Movement Studies* 9(3): 311–329.

Baumann, Shyon, Athena Engman, and Josée Johnston. 2015. 'Political Consumption, Conventional Politics, and High Cultural Capital'. *International Journal of Consumer Studies* 39(5): 413–421.

Bawden, David, and Lyn Robinson. 2020. 'Information Overload: An Introduction'. In *Oxford Research Encyclopedia of Politics*. Oxford University Press. https://doi.org/10.1093/acrefore/9780190228637.013.1360.

Bayat, Asef. 1997a. *Street Politics: Poor People's Movements in Iran*. New York: Columbia University Press.

Bayat, Asef. 1997b. 'Cairo's Poor: Dilemmas of Survival and Solidarity'. *Middle East Report* 202: 7–12. https://merip.org/1997/03/cairos-poor/ (Accessed on 12 April 2024).

Bayat, Asef. 2013. *Life as Politics: How Ordinary People Change the Middle East*. Stanford, CA: Stanford University Press.

BBC. 2014. 'Xianggang fanminjiu zhenggai timing fangan neihong' [Hong Kong Pro-Democracy Camp Divided Over Political Reform Nomination Plan]. 10 January.

www.bbc.com/zhongwen/trad/china/2014/01/140110_hk_democrats_election_ reform (Accessed on 22 October 2022).

BBC. 2016. 'Liang Zhenying: Xianggang Wangjiao chongtu shijian wei "bao luan"' [Leung Chun-ying: Hong Kong Mong Kok Clash Classified as 'Riot']. 9 February. www.bbc.com/zhongwen/trad/china/2016/02/160209_hk_riot_rex (Accessed on 10 October 2023).

BBC. 2019. 'How Apps Power Hong Kong's "Leaderless" Protests'. 30 June. www.bbc .com/news/technology-48802125. (Accessed on 1 September 2022).

Beck, Colin J. 2015. *Radicals, Revolutionaries, and Terrorists*. Cambridge: Polity.

Beissinger, Mark R. 2011. 'Mechanisms of Maidan: The Structure of Contingency in the Making of the Orange Revolution'. *Mobilization* 16(1): 25–43.

Beissinger, Mark R. 2022. *The Revolutionary City: Urbanization and the Global Transformation of Rebellion*. Princeton: Princeton University Press.

Beissinger, Mark R., Amaney A. Jamal, and Kevin Mazur. 2015. 'Explaining Divergent Revolutionary Coalitions: Regime Strategies and the Structuring of Participation in the Tunisian and Egyptian Revolutions'. *Comparative Politics* 48(1): 1–24.

Béja, Jean-Philippe. 2009. 'China since Tiananmen: The Massacre's Long Shadow'. *Journal of Democracy* 20(3): 5–16.

Béja, Jean-Philippe, Fu Hualing, and Eva Pils. eds. 2012. *Liu Xiaobo, Charter 08 and the Challenges of Political Reform in China*. Hong Kong: Hong Kong University Press.

Bellin, Eva. 2012. 'Reconsidering the Robustness of Authoritarianism in the Middle East: Lessons from the Arab Spring'. *Comparative Politics* 44(2): 127–149.

Benford, Robert D., and David A. Snow. 2000. 'Framing Processes and Social Movements: An Overview and Assessment'. *Annual Review of Sociology* 26: 611–639.

Bennett, W. Lance, and Alexandra Segerberg. 2013. *The Logic of Connective Action: Digital Media and the Personalization of Contentious Politics*. Cambridge: Cambridge University Press.

Bennett, W. Lance, Alexandra Segerberg, and Shawn Walker. 2014. 'Organization in the Crowd: Peer Production in Large-scale Networked Protests'. *Information, Communication & Society* 17(2): 232–260.

Bermeo, Nancy. 2016. 'On Democratic Backsliding'. *Journal of Democracy* 27: 5.

Best Mart 360 Holdings Ltd. 2020. Announcement: Profit Warning. *HKEXnews*. 7 May. www1.hkexnews.hk/listedco/listconews/sehk/2020/0507/2020050701525.pdf (Accessed on 5 October 2023).

Bickers, Robert, and Ray Yep. 2009. *May Days in Hong Kong: Riot and Emergency in 1967*. Hong Kong: Hong Kong University Press.

Biggs, Michael. 2003. 'Positive Feedback in Collective Mobilization: The American Strike Wave Of 1886'. *Theory and Society* 32(2): 217–254.

Bimber, Bruce, Andrew Flanagin, and Cynthia Stohl. 2012. *Collective Action in Organizations: Interaction and Engagement in an Era of Technological Change*. Cambridge: Cambridge University Press.

Blee, Kathleen. 2013. 'Interviewing Activists'. In *Wiley-Blackwell Encyclopedia of Social and Political Movements*, eds. David Snow, Donatella della Porta, Bert Klandermans, and Doug McAdam. London: Blackwell

Bonilla, Yarimar, and Jonathan Rosa. 2015. '#Ferguson: Digital Protest, Hashtag Ethnography, and the Racial Politics of Social Media in the United States'. *American Ethnologist* 42(1): 4–17.

Bosi, Lorenzo, and Donatella Della Porta. 2012. 'Micro-mobilization into Armed Groups: Ideological, Instrumental and Solidaristic Paths'. *Qualitative Sociology* 35(4): 361–383.

Bosi, Lorenzo, Marco Giugni, and Katrin Uba, eds. 2016. *The Consequences of Social Movements*. New York: Cambridge University Press.

Boström, Magnus, Michele Micheletti, and Peter Oosterveer. 2019. 'Studying Political Consumerism'. In *The Oxford Handbook of Political Consumerism*, eds. Magnus Boström, Michele Micheletti, and Peter Oosterveer, 1–26. Oxford: Oxford University Press.

Bourdieu, Pierre. 1986. 'The Forms of Capital'. In *Handbook of Theory and Research for the Sociology of Education*, ed. John Richardson, 241–258. Westport, CT: Greenwood.

Brownlee, Jason. 2007. *Authoritarianism in an Age of Democratization*. Cambridge: Cambridge University Press.

Buechler, Steven M. 2011. *Understanding Social Movements Theories from the Classical Era to the Present*. New York: Routledge.

Bunce, Valerie J., and Sharon L. Wolchik. 2010. 'Defeating Dictators: Electoral Change and Stability in Competitive Authoritarian Regimes'. *World Politics* 62(1): 43–86.

Burns, John P. 2004. *Government Capacity and the Hong Kong Civil Service*. London: Oxford University Press.

Bush, Richard C. 2016. *Hong Kong in the Shadow of China: Living with the Leviathan*. Washington, DC: Brookings Institution Press.

Buzan, Barry. 2024. 'A New Cold War?: The Case for a General Concept'. *International Politics* 61(2): 239–257.

Cable TV. 2014, December 22. Interview with Alex Chow. Hong Kong.

Cai, Yongshun. 2010. *Collective Resistance in China: Why Popular Protests Succeed or Fail*. Stanford, CA: Stanford University Press.

Cai, Yongshun. 2016. *The Occupy Movement in Hong Kong: Sustaining Decentralized Protest*. London: Routledge.

Cai, Yongshun, and Chih-Jou Jay Chen. 2022. *State and Social Protests in China*. Cambridge: Cambridge University Press.

Cao, Er Bao. 2008. 'Yiguo liangzhi tiaojianxia xianggang de guanzhi liliang' [Hong Kong's Governing Power Under the Principle of One Country, Two Systems]. *Study Times: Journal of the Central Party School* 422(5).

Carothers, Christopher. 2018. 'The Surprising Instability of Competitive Authoritarianism'. *Journal of Democracy* 29: 129.

Carroll, John M. 2005. *Edge of Empires: Chinese Elites and British Colonials in Hong Kong*. Cambridge: Harvard University Press.

Case, William. 2008. 'Hybrid Politics and New Competitiveness: Hong Kong's 2007 Chief Executive Election'. *East Asia* 25(4): 365–388.

Castells, Manuel. 2012. *Networks of Outrage and Hope: Social Movements in the Internet Age*. Cambridge: Polity.

Cavatorta, Francesco, and Vincent Durac. 2010. *Civil Society and Democratization in the Arab World: The Dynamics of Activism*. Routledge.

Central Government Liaison Office. 2020. 'Xianggang zhonglianban fayan ren: Yanli qianze jiduan jijin fenzi wushi minsheng jiku zaiqi baoli lanchao' [Liaison Office Spokesman: Serious Condemnation on Extreme Radicals' Restarting of Violent Mutual Destruction, regardless of people's livelihood]. 2 May. www.locpg.gov.cn/jsdt/2020-05/02/c_1210601685.htm (Accessed on 9 September 2023).

Central Policy Unit. 2024. *The Study of the Third Sector Landscape in Hong Kong*. Hong Kong: Government Information Service.

Chan, Chris King-Chi, Sophia Shuk-Ying Chan, and Lynn Tang. 2019. 'Reflecting on Social Movement Unionism in Hong Kong: The Case of the Dockworkers' Strike in 2013'. *Journal of Contemporary Asia* 49(1): 54–77.

Chan, Chung-hong, Cassius Siu-lun Chow, and King-wa Fu. 2019. 'Echoslamming: How Incivility Interacts with Cyberbalkanization on the Social Media in Hong Kong'. *Asian Journal of Communication* 29(4): 307–327.

Chan, Debby Sze Wan. 2022. 'The Consumption Power of the Politically Powerless: The Yellow Economy in Hong Kong'. *Journal of Civil Society* 18(1): 69–86.

Chan, Debby Sze Wan, and Ngai Pun. 2020. 'Economic Power of the Politically Powerless in the 2019 Hong Kong Pro-democracy Movement'. *Critical Asian Studies* 52(1): 33–43.

Chan, Elaine, and Joseph Chan. 2014. 'Liberal Patriotism in Hong Kong'. *Journal of Contemporary China* 23(89): 952–970.

Chan, Elaine, and Joseph Chan. 2017. 'Hong Kong 2007–2017: A Backlash in Civil Society'. *Asia Pacific Journal of Public Administration* 39(2): 135–152.

Chan, Shun-hing. 2015. 'The Protestant Community and the Umbrella Movement in Hong Kong'. *Inter-Asia Cultural Studies* 16(3): 380–395.

Chang, Paul. 2015. *Protest Dialectics: State Repression and South Korea's Democracy Movement, 1970–1979*. Stanford University Press.

Chen, Albert H. Y. 2021. 'The National Security Law of the HKSAR: A Contextual and Legal Study'. Available at SSRN: https://ssrn.com/abstract=3958261 or http://dx.doi.org/10.2139/ssrn.3958261.

Chen, Yun-Chung, and Mirana M. Szeto. 2015. 'The Forgotten Road of Progressive Localism: New Preservation Movement in Hong Kong'. *Inter-Asia Cultural Studies* 16(3): 436–453.

Chen, Xi. 2012. *Social Protest and Contentious Authoritarianism in China*. Cambridge and New York: Cambridge University Press.

Cheng, Edmund W. 2016. 'Street Politics in a Hybrid Regime: The Diffusion of Political Activism in Post-colonial Hong Kong'. *The China Quarterly* 226: 383–406.

Cheng, Edmund W. 2020. 'United Front Work and Mechanisms of Counter-mobilization in Hong Kong'. *The China Journal* 83: 1–33.

Cheng, Edmund W., and Ngok Ma, eds. 2020. *The Umbrella Movement: Civil Resistance and Contentious Space in Hong Kong*. Amsterdam: Amsterdam University Press.

Cheng, Edmund W., and Wai-Yin Chan. 2017. 'Explaining Spontaneous Occupation: Antecedents, Contingencies and Spaces in the Umbrella Movement'. *Social Movement Studies* 16(2): 222–239.

Cheng, Edmund W., and Samson Yuen. 2019. 'Memory in Movement: Collective Identity and Memory Contestation in Hong Kong's Tiananmen Vigils'. *Mobilization* 24(4): 419–437.

Cheng, Edmund W., Elizabeth Lui, and King-wa Fu. 2023. 'The Power of Digital Activism for Transnational Advocacy: Leadership, Engagement, and Affordance'. *New Media & Society*. https://doi.org/10.1177/14614448231155376.

Cheng, Edmund W., Francis L. F. Lee, Samson Yuen, and Gary Tang. 2022. 'Total Mobilization from Below: Hong Kong's Freedom Summer'. *The China Quarterly* 251: 629–659.

Cheng, Edmund W., Hiu-Fung Chung, and Ho-wai Cheng. 2022. 'Life Satisfaction and the Conventionality of Political Participation: The Moderation Effect of Post-Material Values'. *International Political Science Review* 44(2): 157–177.

Cheng, Jie. 2009. 'The Story of a New Policy'. *Hong Kong Journal* (Fall), www.hkbasiclaw.com/Hong%20Kong%20Journal/Cheng%20Jie%20article.htm (Accessed on 4 April 2021).

Cheng, Roger H. M. 2004. 'Moral Education in Hong Kong: Confucian-parental, Christian-Religious and Liberal-civic Influences'. *Journal of Moral Education* 33(4): 533–551.

Chenoweth, Erica. 2021. *Civil Resistance: What Everyone Needs to Know*. Oxford: Oxford University Press.

Chenoweth, Erica, and Maria J. Stephan. 2011. *Why Civil Resistance Works: The Strategic Logic of Nonviolent Conflict*. New York: Columbia University Press.

Cheung, Anthony B. L. 1996. 'Efficiency as the Rhetoric: Public-Sector Reform in Hong Kong Explained'. *International Review of Administrative Sciences* 62(1): 31–47.

Chenoweth, Erica. 2023. 'The Role of Violence in Nonviolent Resistance'. *Annual Review of Political Science* 26: 55–77.

Cheung, Anthony B. L. 2010. 'In Search of Trust and Legitimacy: The Political Trajectory of Hong Kong as Part of China'. *International Public Management Review* 11(2): 38–63.

Cheung, Anthony B. L. 2012. 'One Country, Two Experiences: Administrative Reforms in China and Hong Kong'. *International Review of Administrative Sciences* 78(2): 261–283.

Cheung, Gary Ka Wai. 2009. *Hong Kong's Watershed: The 1967 Riots*. Hong Kong: Hong Kong University Press.

Cheung, Peter T. Y. 2015. 'Toward Collaborative Governance between Hong Kong and Mainland China'. *Urban Studies* 52(10): 1915–1933.

Ching, Frank. 2005, June 7. 'Divided Loyalties at the Top'. *South China Morning Post*, www.scmp.com/article/503468/divided-loyalties-top (Accessed on 5 April 2021).

Chiu, Stephen Wing Kai, and Tai Lok Lui, eds. 2000. *The Dynamics of Social Movement in Hong Kong*. Hong Kong: Hong Kong University Press.

Chiu, Stephen Wing Kai, and Tai Lok Lui. 2004. 'Testing the Global City-Social Polarisation Thesis: Hong Kong since the 1990s'. *Urban Studies* 41(10): 1863–1888.

Choi, Chi Keung, Ngok Ma, and Chan Chun Man. 2021. *The Electoral System and Voting Behaviour in the Hong Kong Special Administrative Region*. Hong Kong: City Univeristy Press. (In Chinese).

Choi, Susanne Y. P. 2020. 'When Protests and Daily Life Converge: The Spaces and People of Hong Kong's Anti-Extradition Movement'. *Critique of Anthropology* 40(2): 277–282.

Choi, Susanne Y. P. 2022. 'Doing and Undoing Gender: Women on the Frontline of Hong Kong's Anti-Extradition Bill Movement'. *Social Movement Studies* (2022): 1–16. http://dx.doi.org/10.1080/14742837.2022.2086114.

Chopra, Surabhi, and Eva Pils. 2022. 'The Hong Kong National Security Law and the Struggle over Rule of Law and Democracy in Hong Kong'. *Federal Law Review* 50(3): 292–313.

Chu, Donna S. C. 2018. 'Media Use and Protest Mobilization: A Case Study of Umbrella Movement within Hong Kong Schools'. *Social Media + Society* 4(1): 2056305118763350.

Chu, Donna S. C. 2021. 'Remembering 1989: A Case Study of Anniversary Journalism in Hong Kong'. *Memory Studies* 14(4): 819–833.

Chu, Yiu Wai. 2013. *Lost in Transition: Hong Kong Culture in the Age of China.* New York: State University of New York Press.

Chung, Vincent C. H., Sheila Hillier, Chun Hong Lau, Samuel Y. S. Wong et al. 2011. 'Referral to and Attitude towards Traditional Chinese Medicine amongst Western Medical Doctors in Postcolonial Hong Kong'. *Social Science & Medicine* 72(2): 247–255.

Chupryna, Oleg. 2021. 'Ukraine's Euromaidan Revolution: A Final Breakaway from Russia'. *Geopolitical Monitor*, November 25. www.geopoliticalmonitor.com/ukraines-euromaidan-revolution-a-final-breakaway-from-russia/ (Accessed on 5 August 2021).

Citizen News. 2017. 'The Difficult Dialogue during the Occupation'. 28 September.

Civic Party. 2010. 'One Person, One Vote, Demolish Functional Constituency: A Joint Statement by Higher Education 2012 and Joint Committee of the 5 District Referendum Movement'. 20 April.

Clarke, Killian. 2014. 'Unexpected Brokers of Mobilization: Contingency and Networks in the 2011 Egyptian Uprising'. *Comparative Politics* 46(4): 379–397.

Clarke, Killian. 2011. 'Saying "Enough": Authoritarianism and Egypt's Kefaya Movement'. *Mobilization: An International Quarterly* 16(4): 397–416.

Clarke, Killian, and Korhan Kocak. 2020. 'Launching Revolution: Social Media and the Egyptian Uprising's First Movers'. *British Journal of Political Science* 50(3): 1025–1045.

Coleman, James S. 1988. 'Social Capital in the Creation of Human Capital'. *American Journal of Sociology* 94: 95–120.

Collins, Randall. 2004. *Interaction Ritual Chains.* Princeton: Princeton University Press.

Copeland, Lauren. 2014. 'Conceptualizing Political Consumerism: How Citizenship Norms Differentiate Boycotting from Buycotting'. *Political Studies* 62: 172–186.

Costain, Anne N. 1992. *Inviting Women's Rebellion: A Political Process Interpretation of the Women's Movement.* Baltimore, MD: Johns Hopkins University Press.

Costanza-Chock, Sasha. 2012. 'Mic Check! Media Cultures and the Occupy Movement'. *Social Movement Studies*, 11(3–4): 375–385.

Croissant, Aurel, and Jeffrey Haynes. 2021. 'Democratic Regression in Asia: Introduction'. *Democratization* 28(1): 1–21.

Cunningham, David, and Benjamin T. Phillips. 2007. 'Contexts for Mobilization: Spatial Settings and Klan Presence in North Carolina, 1964–1966'. *American Journal of Sociology* 113(3): 781–814.

Dahl, Robert A. 1971. *Polyarchy: Participation and Opposition.* New Haven: Yale University Press.

Dahlum, Sirianne, and Tore Wig. 2021. 'Chaos on Campus: Universities and Mass Political Protest'. *Comparative Political Studies* 54(1): 3–32.

Dapiran, Anthony. 2017. *City of Protest: A Recent History of Dissent in Hong Kong.* Hong Kong: Penguin.

Davenport, Christian. 2007. 'State Repression and Political Order'. *Annual Review of Political Science* 10: 1–23.

Davis, Jenny L., and James B. Chouinard. 2016. 'Theorizing Affordances: From Request to Refuse'. *Bulletin of Science, Technology & Society* 36(4): 241–248.

De Fazio, Gianluca. 2013. 'The Radicalization of Contention in Northern Ireland, 1968–1972: A Relational Perspective'. *Mobilization* 18(4): 475–496.

De Vogel, Sasha. 2022. 'Anti-opposition Crackdowns and Protest: The Case of Belarus, 2000–2019'. *Post-Soviet Affairs* 38(1–2): 9–25.

Della Porta, Donatella. 1988. 'Recruitment Processes in Clandestine Political Organizations'. *International Social Movement Research* 1: 155–169.

Della Porta, Donatella. 1995. *Social Movements, Political Violence, and the State: A Comparative Analysis of Italy and Germany*. Cambridge: Cambridge University Press.

Della Porta, Donatella, and Herbert Reiter, eds. 1998. *Policing Protest: The Control of Mass Demonstrations in Western Democracies*. Minneapolis, MN: University of Minnesota Press.

Della Porta, Donatella. 2008. 'Research on Social Movements and Political Violence'. *Qualitative Sociology* 31(3): 221–230.

Della Porta, Donatella. 2018. 'Radicalization: A Relational Perspective'. *Annual Review of Political Science* 21: 461–474.

Deng, Xiaoping. 1987. *Selected Work of Dengxiaoping*. Beijing: People's Publishers.

Diamond, Larry. 2002. 'Elections without Democracy: Thinking about Hybrid Regimes'. *Journal of Democracy* 13(2): 21–35.

Diani, Mario. 1992. 'The Concept of Social Movement'. *The Sociological Review* 40(1): 1–25.

Diani, Mario. 1997. 'Social Movements and Social Capital: A Network Perspective on Movement Outcomes'. *Mobilization* 2(2): 129–147.

Diani, Mario. 2003. 'Leaders or Brokers? Positions and Influence in Social Movement Networks'. In *Social Movements and Networks: Relational Approaches to Collective Action*, eds. Mario Diani, and Doug McAdam, 105–122. Oxford: Oxford University Press.

Diani, Mario. 2015. *The Cement of Civil Society*. Cambridge: Cambridge University Press.

Dickson, Roger A., and Mary L. Carsky. 2005. 'The Consumer as Economic Voter'. In *The Ethical Consumer*, eds. Rob Harrison, Terry Newholm, and Deirdre Shaw, 25–36. London: SAGE Publications.

Dimbleby, Jonathan. 1997. *The Last Governor: Chris Patten and the Handover of Hong Kong*. London: Pen and Sword.

Dittmer, John. 2009. *The Good Doctors: The Medical Committee for Human Rights and the Struggle for Social Justice in Health Care*. New York: Bloomsbury.

Dodson, Kyle. 2016. 'Economic Threat and Protest Behavior in Comparative Perspective'. *Sociological Perspectives* 59(4): 873–891.

Della Porta, Donatella, Lorenzo Cini, and Cesar Guzman-Concha. 2020. *Contesting Higher Education: Student Movements against Neoliberal Universities*. Bristol: Bristol University Press.

Doug, McAdam, Sidney Tarrow, and Charles Tilly. 2005. *Contentious Politics*. New York: Oxford University Press.

Dowding, Keith, Peter John, Thanos Mergoupis, and Mark Van Vugt. 2000. 'Exit, Voice and Loyalty: Analytic and Empirical Developments'. *European Journal of Political Research* 37(4): 469–495.

Draege, Jonas Bergan. 2022. 'Narrow Responses to Social Movements: Evidence from Turkey's Gezi Protests'. *Representation*. http://dx.doi.org/10.1080/00344893.2022.2111596.

Dresden, Jennifer Raymond, and Marc Morjé Howard. 2016. 'Authoritarian Backsliding and the Concentration of Political Power'. *Democratization* 23(7): 1122–1143.

Du, Ming, and Qingjiang Kong. 2020. 'Explaining the Limits of the WTO in Shaping the Rule of Law in China'. *Journal of International Economic Law* 23(4): 885–905.

Durkheim, Emilie. 1984. *The Division of Labour in Society*. London: Macmillan.

Earl, Jennifer. 2003. 'Tanks, Tear Gas, and Taxes: Toward a Theory of Movement Repression'. *Sociological Theory* 21(1): 44–68.

Earl, Jennifer. 2007. 'Leading Tasks in a Leaderless Movement: The Case of Strategic Voting'. *American Behavioral Scientist* 50(10): 1327–1349.

Earl, Jennifer. 2015. 'The Future of Social Movement Organizations: The Waning Dominance of SMOs Online'. *American Behavioral Scientist* 59(1): 35–52.

Earl, Jennifer, and Katrina Kimport. 2011. *Digitally Enabled Social Change: Activism in the Internet Age*. Cambridge: MIT Press.

Earl, Jennifer, and R. Kelly Garrett. 2017. 'The New Information Frontier: Toward a More Nuanced View of Social Movement Communication'. *Social Movement Studies* 16(4): 479–493.

Economy, Elizabeth. 2022. 'Xi Jinping's New World Order: Can China Remake the International System?' *Foreign Affairs* 101(1): 52.

Edwards, Pearce, and Daniel Arnon. 2021. 'Violence on Many Sides: Framing Effects on Protest and Support for Repression'. *British Journal of Political Science* 51(2): 488–506.

Einwohner, Rachel, and Thomas Maher. 2011. 'Threat Assessment and Collective-action Emergence: Death-camp and Ghetto Resistance during the Holocaust'. *Mobilization* 16(2): 127–146.

Eisinger, Peter K. 1973. 'The Conditions of Protest Behavior in American Cities'. *American Political Science Review* 67(1): 11–28.

Ekiert, Grzegorz, Elizabeth J. Perry, and Xiaojun Yan, eds. 2020. *Ruling by Other Means: State-mobilized Movements*. Cambridge: Cambridge University Press.

Endres, Kyle, and Costas Panagopoulos. 2017. 'Boycotts, Buycotts, and Political Consumerism in America'. *Research & Politics* 4(4): 1–9.

Episcopal. 2019. 'Pastoral Letter of Archbishop Paul Kwong'. 11 June. https://echo .hkskh.org/news_article_details.aspx?lang=1&nid=6257 (Accessed on 15 June 2023).

Esherick, Joseph W., and Jeffrey N. Wasserstrom. 1990. 'Acting Out Democracy: Political Theater in Modern China'. *The Journal of Asian Studies* 49(4): 835–865.

Faure, David. 2003. *Colonialism and the Hong Kong Mentality*. Hong Kong: Centre of Asia Studies, Hong Kong University Press.

Fewsmith, Joseph. 2021. *Rethinking Chinese Politics*. New York: Cambridge University Press.

Financial Times. 2019a. 'Hong Kong Protesters Play Dangerous Endgame with China'. 15 August. www.ft.com/content/5ec723e0-bfd0-11e9-b350-db00d509634e (Accessed 5 September 2023).

Financial Times. 2019b. 'Leaderless Rebellion: How Social Media Enables Global Protests'. 26 October. www.ft.com/content/19dc5dfe-f67b-11e9-a79c-bc9aca e3b654. (Accessed 5 September 2023).

Fisher, Dana R. 2019. *American Resistance: From the Women's March to the Blue Wave*. New York: Columbia University Press.

Fisher, Dana R., Kenneth T. Andrews, Neal Caren, Erica Chenoweth, Michael T. Heaney, Tommy Leung, L. Nathan Perkins, and Jeremy Pressman. 2019. 'The Science of Contemporary Street Protest: New efforts in the United States'. *Science Advances* 5(10): eaaw5461.

Flesher Fominaya, Cristina. 2020. *Democracy Reloaded: Inside Spain's Political Laboratory from 15-M to Podemos*. New York: Oxford University Press.

Fong, Brian C. 2014. 'The Partnership between the Chinese Government and Hong Kong's Capitalist Class: Implications for HKSAR Governance, 1997–2012'. *The China Quarterly* 217: 195–220.

Fong, Brian C. 2017. 'In-between Liberal Authoritarianism and Electoral Authoritarianism: Hong Kong's Democratization under Chinese Sovereignty, 1997–2016'. *Democratization* 24(4): 724–750.

Forrest, Ray, Adrienne La Grange, and Ngai-ming Yip. 2004. 'Hong Kong as a Global City? Social Distance and Spatial Differentiation'. *Urban Studies* 41(1): 207–227.

Foust, Christina R., and Kate Drazner Hoyt. 2018. 'Social Movement 2.0: Integrating and Assessing Scholarship on Social Media and Movement'. *Review of Communication* 18(1): 37–55.

Francisco, Ronald A. 1995. 'The Relationship between Coercion and Protest: An Empirical Evaluation in Three Coercive States'. *Journal of Conflict Resolution* 39(2): 263–282.

Francisco, Ronald A. 1996. 'Coercion and Protest: An Empirical Test in Two Democratic States'. *American Journal of Political Science* 40(4): 1179–1204.

Freeman, Jo. 1972. 'The Tyranny of Structurelessness'. *Berkeley Journal of Sociology* 17: 151–164.

Friedman, Milton. 1998. 'The Hong Kong Experiment'. Hoover Digest. www.hoover.org/research/hong-kong-experiment (Accessed on 30 September 2022).

Fu, Diana. 2018. *Mobilizing without the Masses: Control and Contention in China*. Cambridge: Cambridge University Press.

Fu, Diana, and Erica S. Simmons. 2021. 'Ethnographic Approaches to Contentious Politics: The What, How, and Why'. *Comparative Political Studies* 54(10): 1695–1721.

Fu, King-wa. 2023. 'Digital Mobilization via Attention Building: The Logic of Cross-boundary Actions in the 2019 Hong Kong Social Movement'. *The Information Society* 39(3): 158–170.

Fukuyama, Francis. 2004. 'The Imperative of State-Building'. *Journal of Democracy* 15(2): 17–31.

Fulum Group Holdings Ltd. 2020. '2020 Interim Report'. https://media-fulum.todayir.com/20191220164802132491043 59_en.pdf (Accessed on 1 September 2023).

Fung, Dennis, and Angie Su. 2016. 'The Influence of Liberal Studies on Students' Participation in Socio-political Activities: The Case of the Umbrella Movement in Hong Kong'. *Oxford Review of Education* 42(1): 89–107.

Fung, Frederick Kin-kee. 2002. *Shibu xiangman* [*Honestly Speaking*]. Hong Kong: Sense Creative House.

Gamboa, Laura. 2022. *Resisting Backsliding: Opposition Strategies against the Erosion of Democracy*. New York: Cambridge University Press.

Gamboa, Laura. 2023. 'How Oppositions Fight Back'. *Journal of Democracy* 34(3): 90–104.

Gamson, William A. 1990. *The Strategy of Social Protest*. Belmont, CA: Wadsworth.

Gamson, William A. 1991. 'Commitment and Agency in Social Movements'. *Sociological Forum* 6(1): 27–50.

Gamson, William A. 1992. 'The Social Psychology of Collective Action'. In *Frontiers in Social Movement Theory*, eds. Aldon D. Morris and Carol McClurg Mueller, 53–76. New Haven: Yale University Press.

Gamson, William A., and David S. Meyer. 1996. 'Framing Political Opportunity'. In *Comparative Perspectives on Social Movements: Political Opportunities, Mobilizing Structures, and Cultural Framings*, eds. Doug McAdam, John D. McCarthy, and Mayer N. Zald, 275–290. Cambridge: Cambridge University Press.

Gandhi, Jennifer. 2008. 'Dictatorial Institutions and Their Impact on Economic Growth'. *European Journal of Sociology* 49(1): 3–30.

Gandhi, Jennifer, and Adam Przeworski. 2007. 'Authoritarian Institutions and the Survival of Autocrats'. *Comparative Political Studies* 40(11): 1279–1301.

Gandhi, Jennifer, and Elvin Ong. 2019. 'Committed or Conditional Democrats? Opposition Dynamics in Electoral Autocracies'. *American Journal of Political Science* 63(4): 948–963.

Ganz, Marshall. 2000. 'Resources and Resourcefulness: Strategic Capacity in the Unionization of California Agriculture, 1959–1966'. *American Journal of Sociology* 105(4): 1003–1062.

Garcia, Roger. 1989. 'Xianggang gongwuyuan de bendihua' [The Localization of Hong Kong Civil Services]. *Administration* 2(6): 801–803.

Geha, Carmen. 2019. 'Politics of a Garbage Crisis: Social Networks, Narratives, and Frames of Lebanon's 2015 Protests and Their Aftermath'. *Social Movement Studies* 18(1): 78–92.

George, Alexander L., and Andrew Bennett. 2005. *Case Studies and Theory Development in the Social Sciences*. Cambridge: MIT Press.

Gerbaudo, Paolo. 2012. *Tweets and the Streets: Social Media and Contemporary Activism*. London: Pluto Press.

Gerbaudo, Pablo. 2017. 'Social Media Teams as Digital Vanguards: The Question of Leadership in the Management of Key Facebook and Twitter Accounts of Occupy Wall Street, Indignados and UK Uncut'. *Information, Communication & Society* 20(2): 185–202.

Gerbaudo, Paolo, and Emiliano Treré. 2015. 'In Search of the "We" of Social Media Activism: Introduction to the Special Issue on Social Media and Protest Identities'. *Information, Communication & Society* 18(8): 865–871.

Gerring, John. 2017. *Case Study Research: Principles and Practices*. Cambridge: Cambridge University Press.

Gillan, Kevin. 2009. 'The UK Anti-war Movement Online: Uses and Limitations of Internet Technologies for Contemporary Activism'. *Information, Communication & Society* 12(1): 25–43.

Glenn, John K. 1999. 'Competing Challengers and Contested Outcomes to State Breakdown: The Velvet Revolution in Czechoslovakia'. *Social Forces* 78(1): 187–211.

Goh, Daniel P. S. 2016. 'Secular Space, Spiritual Community and the Hybrid Urbanisms of Christianity in Hong Kong and Singapore'. *International Sociology* 31(4): 432–449.

Gold, Thomas, and Sebastian Veg. eds. 2020. *Sunflowers and Umbrellas: Social Movements, Expressive Practices, and Political Culture in Taiwan and Hong Kong*. Berkeley, CA: Institute of East Asian Studies, University of California.

Goldstein, Avery. 2020. 'US–China Rivalry in the twenty-first century: Déjà vu and Cold War II'. *China International Strategy Review* 2(1): 48–62.

Goldstone, Jack A. 2004. 'More Social Movements or Fewer? Beyond Political Opportunity Structures to Relational Fields'. *Theory and Society* 33: 333–365.

Goldstone, Jack A., and Charles Tilly. 2001. 'Threat and Opportunity: Popular Action and State Response in the Dynamics of Contentious Action'. In *Silence and Voice in the Study of Contentious Politics*, eds. Ronald R. Aminzade, Jack A. Goldstone, Doug McAdam, Elizabeth Perry, William H. Sewell, Sidney Tarrow, and Charles Tilly, 179–194. Cambridge: Cambridge University Press.

Goodstadt, Leo F. 2000. 'China and the Selection of Hong Kong's Post-colonial Political Elite'. *The China Quarterly* 163: 721–741.

Goodwin, Jeff, and James M. Jasper. 1999. 'Caught in a Winding, Snarling Vine: The Structural Bias of Political Process Theory'. *Sociological Forum* 14(1): 27–54.

Goodwin, Jeff, James M. Jasper, and Francesca Polletta. 2001. 'Introduction: Why Emotions Matter'. In *Passionate Politics: Emotions and Social Movements*, eds. Jeff Goodwin, James M. Jasper, and Francesca Polletta, 1–25. Chicago: The University of Chicago Press.

Gordon, Hava R., and Jessica K. Taft. 2011. 'Rethinking Youth Political Socialization: Teenage Activists Talk Back'. *Youth & Society* 43(4): 1499–1527.

Gospel Herald. 2019. 'Jidujiao tuanti fa lianshusheng' [Christianity Groups Release a Joint Statement]. 23 May. https://bit.ly/3CPCkIh (Accessed on 1 June 2023).

Gould, Roger V. 1995. *Insurgent Identities: Class, Community, and Protest in Paris from 1848 to the Commune*. Chicago: University of Chicago Press.

Graham, Jesse, and Jonathan Haidt. 2010. 'Beyond Beliefs: Religions Bind Individuals into Moral Communities'. *Personality and Social Psychology Review* 14(1): 140–150.

Guardian. 2022. 'A Year on from Apple Daily's Closure, What's Left of Hong Kong's Free Press?' 24 June. www.theguardian.com/global-development/2022/jun/24/year-on-from-pro-democracy-apple-daily-closure-whats-left-of-hong-kongs-free-press (Accessed on 23 September 2023).

Haenfler, Ross, Brett Johnson, and Ellis Jones. 2012. 'Lifestyle Movements: Exploring the Intersection of Lifestyle and Social Movements'. *Social Movement Studies* 11(1): 1–20.

Haggard, Stephan. 1990. *Pathways from the Periphery: The Politics of Growth in the Newly Industrializing Countries*. Ithaca, NY: Cornell University Press.

Haggard, Stephan, and Robert R. Kaufman. 2021. 'The Anatomy of Democratic Backsliding'. *Journal of Democracy* 32(4): 27–41.

Hall, Sarah. 2010. 'Educational Ties, Social Capital and the Translocal (Re) Production of MBA Alumni Networks'. *Global Networks* 11(1): 118–138. https://doi.org/10.1111/j.1471-0374.2011.00310.x

Hamashita, Takeshi. 2008. *China, East Asia and the Global Economy: Regional and Historical Perspectives*. New York: Routledge.

Hayes, Graeme. 2006. 'Vulnerability and Disobedience: New Repertoires in French Environmental Protests'. *Environmental Politics* 15: 821–838.

Heaney, Michael T. 2022. 'Who Are Black Lives Matter Activists? Niche Realization in a Multimovement Environment'. *Perspectives on Politics* 20: 1–24.

Heaney, Michael T., and Fabio Rojas. 2015. *Party in the Street: The Antiwar Movement and the Democratic Party after 9/11*. Cambridge: Cambridge University Press.

Hellmeier, Sebastian, and Nils B. Weidmann. 2020. 'Pulling the Strings? The Strategic Use of Pro-government Mobilization in Authoritarian Regimes'. *Comparative Political Studies* 53(1): 71–108.

Hellmeier, Sebastian, Rowan Cole, Sandra Grahn, and Palina Kolvani et al. 2021. 'State of the World 2020: Autocratization Turns Viral'. *Democratization* 28(6): 1053–1074.

Helms, Ludger. 2004. 'Five Ways of Institutionalizing Political Opposition: Lessons from the Advanced Democracies'. *Government and Opposition* 39(1): 22–54.

Hess, David, and Brian Martin. 2006. 'Repression, Backfire, and the Theory of Transformative Events'. *Mobilization* 11(2): 249–267.

Hewison, Kevin, and Veerayooth Kanchoochat, eds. 2018. *Military, Monarchy and Repression: Assessing Thailand's Authoritarian Turn*. Routledge.

Hine, Christine. 2020. *Ethnography for the Internet: Embedded, Embodied and Everyday*. London: Routledge.

Hirschman, Albert O. 1970. *Exit, Voice, and Loyalty: Responses to Decline in Firms, Organizations, and States*. Cambridge: Harvard University Press.

HK01. 2019a. '01 baike: Xianggang zongjiao shili bipin' [01 Encyclopedia: The Comparison of Different Religious Groups in Hong Kong]. 17 February. https://bit.ly/491QLak (Accessed 17 September 2023).

HK01. 2019b. 'He zhuguo jiepi xiuli cun Linzheng: you pengyou you birenla qu zuojian' [Charles Ho Criticizes the Amendments to Carrie Lam: His Friend Was Worried being Imprisoned]. 26 March. https://bit.ly/2FBEYnk (Accessed 17 September 2023).

HKNet. 2020. 'Meixin qunian yingli die 22% yuebing xiaoshou jixu zeng' [Profits of Maxim Drops 22% Last Year, While Sales of Mooncakes Continues to Rise]. 5 March. https://bit.ly/3FprWYa (Accessed 18 September 2023).

HKUJMSC (Hong Kong University Journalism and Media Studies Centre). 2020. https://datahub.hku.hk/articles/dataset/ANTIELAB_Research_Data_Archive_-_Mobilization_Map_Data/13711540 (Accessed 1 October 2023).

HKUPOP (Hong Kong University Public Opinion Program). 2019a. 'People's Categorical Ethnic Identity'. www.pori.hk/pop-poll/ethnic-identity-en/q001.html?lang=en (Accessed 2 October 2023).

HKUPOP (Hong Kong University Public Opinion Program). 2019b. 'People's Trust in the HKSAR Government'. www.pori.hk/pop-poll/government-en/k001.html?lang=en (Accessed 2 October 2023).

HKUPOP (Hong Kong University Public Opinion Program). 2019c. 'People's Satisfaction with the HKSAR Government'. www.pori.hk/pop-poll/government-en/h001.html?lang=en (Accessed 2 October 2023).

Ho, Chun-yan Albert. 2010. *Qianbei de fendou [Humble Struggle]*. Hong Kong: Hong Kong University Press.

Ho, Ming-Sho. 2018. 'From Mobilization to Improvisation: The Lessons from Taiwan's 2014 Sunflower Movement'. *Social Movement Studies* 17(2): 189–202.

Ho, Ming-sho. 2019. *Challenging Beijing's Mandate of Heaven: Taiwan's Sunflower Movement and Hong Kong's Umbrella Movement*. Philadelphia: Temple University Press.

Ho, Ming-sho. 2020. 'How Protests Evolve: Hong Kong's Anti-Extradition Movement and Lessons Learned from the Umbrella Movement'. *Mobilization* 25(5): 711–728.

Ho, Ming-sho. 2023. 'Relational Tactics and Trust in High-risk Activism: Anonymity, Preexisting Ties, and Bonding in Hong Kong's 2019–2020 Protest'. *International Journal of Comparative Sociology* (2023): 00207152231220524.

Ho, Ming-Sho, and Wai Ki Wan. 2023. 'Universities as an Arena of Contentious Politics: Mobilization and Control in Hong Kong's Anti-Extradition Movement of 2019'. *International Studies in Sociology of Education* 32(2): 313–336.

Ho, Wing Chung. 2023. 'The Settling Experience of Hongkongers in London'. *China Review* 23(3): 245–272.

Holliday, Ian, and Linda Wong. 2003. 'Social Policy under One Country, Two Systems: Institutional Dynamics in China and Hong Kong since 1997'. *Public Administration Review* 63(3): 269–282.

Hong Kong Bar Association. 2019. 'Summary of the Observations of the Hong Kong Bar Association ("HKBA") on the Security Bureau's Proposal to Amend the Mutual Legal Assistance in Criminal Matters Ordinance, Cap. 525 ("MLAO") and the Fugitive Offenders Ordinance, Cap.503 ("FOO")'. https://blackdotresearch.sg/wp-content/uploads/2019/07/Summary-of-HKBAs-Observations-Eng-Final.pdf (Accessed 23 October 2023).

Hong Kong Census and Statistical Department. 2022. 'Mid-year Population for 2022'. www.info.gov.hk/gia/general/202208/11/P2022081100393.htm?fontSize=1 (Accessed on 4 October 2023).

Hong Kong Census and Statistical Department. 2023. 'Mid-year Population for 2023'. www.info.gov.hk/gia/general/202308/15/P2023081500251.htm (Accessed on 4 October 2023).

Hong Kong Federations of Students (HKFS). 2014a. 'Xuelian jiu jintian Wangjiao he Tongluowan dengdi chuxian de youzuzhide baotu xingwei he jingfang zhi fa shengming' [Statement of HKFS on mob attack and police law enforcement in Mong Kok and Causeway Bay]. Facebook. 3 October. www.facebook.com/hkfs1958/photos/a.433111302 871/10152478720577872 (Accessed 18 September 2023).

Hong Kong Federations of Students (HKFS) and Scholarism. 2014b. 'Zhanling yundong biandi kaihua'. [The Occupation is Blossoming Everywhere]. Facebook. 29 September. www.facebook.com/hkfs1958/photos/a.433111302871/10152470384422872 (Accessed 18 September 2023).

Hong Kong Free Press. 2019a. '26-year-old Woman in Critical Condition after Knife Attack at Hong Kong "Lennon Wall"'. 20 August. https://hongkongfp.com/2019/08/20/26-year-old-hong-kong-woman-critical-condition-knife-attack-lennon-wall-tseung-kwan-o/ (Accessed on 4 October 2023).

Hong Kong Free Press. 2019b. 'Hong Kong Police Fire 800 Tear Gas Rounds, Arrest 148 People during City-wide Chaos on Monday'. 6 August. https://hongkongfp.com/2019/08/06/hong-kong-police-fire-800-tear-gas-rounds-arrest-148-people-mass-protest/ (Accessed on 4 October 2023).

Hong Kong Free Press. 2019c. 'Hong Kong Watchdog Urges Mainland Chinese Reporters to Show Credentials Clearly, after Journalist Accosted'. 14 August. https://hongkongfp.com/2019/08/14/hong-kong-watchdog-urges-mainland-chinese-reporters-show-credentials-clearly-journalist-accosted/ (Accessed on 4 October 2023).

Hong Kong Free Press. 2019d. 'Hong Kong's End Game: Why the Extradition Bill Is an Infinity Stone That Could Decimate Half of Society'. 9 June. https://hongkongfp.com/2019/06/09/hong-kongs-end-game-extradition-bill-infinity-stone-decimate-half-society/ (Accessed on 4 October 2023).

Hong Kong Free Press. 2022a. 'Explainer: Hong Kong's Sedition Law – A Colonial Relic Revived after Half a Century'. 30 July. https://hongkongfp.com/2022/07/30/explainer-hong-kongs-sedition-law-a-colonial-relic-revived-after-half-a-century/ (Accessed on 4 October 2023).

Hong Kong Free Press. 2022b. 'Timeline: 58 Hong Kong Civil Society Groups Disband Following the Onset of the Security Law'. 30 June. https://hongkongfp .com/2022/06/30/explainer-over-50-groups-gone-in-11-months-how-hong-kongs-pro-democracy -forces-crumbled/ (Accessed on 4 October 2023).

Hong Kong Government. 1991. 'Hong Kong Year Book. Hong Kong: Government Information Service'.

Hong Kong Government. 2019. 'Government Response to Procession'. 9 June. www .info.gov.hk/gia/general/201906/09/P2019060900587.htm (Accessed on 6 August 2023).

Hong Kong Public Opinion Research Institute. 2021. 'Anti-Extradition Bill Movement Public Sentiment Report'. www.pori.hk/research-reports-en/anti-extradition-bill-movement-2019.html?lang=en (Accessed 2 October 2023).

Hong Kong Trade and Development Council. 2022. 'Legal Services Industry in Hong Kong'. 9 June. https://research.hktdc.com/en/article/MzEzODc5NTk5 (Accessed on 5 April 2023).

Hong Kong Yearbook. 2019. www.yearbook.gov.hk/2019/tc/index.html (5 October 2023).

Hostrup Haugbølle, Rikke, and Francesco Cavatorta. 2011. 'Will the Real Tunisian Opposition Please Stand Up? Opposition Coordination Failures under Authoritarian Constraints'. *British Journal of Middle Eastern Studies* 38(3): 323–341.

Howard, Philip N., and Muzammil M. Hussain. 2013. *Democracy's Fourth Wave? Digital Media and the Arab Spring*. Oxford: Oxford University Press. https:// onlinelibrary.wiley.com/doi/abs/10.1002/9780470674871.wbespm111. www.legco .gov.hk/yr01-02/english/panels/se/papers/ajlsse0926cb2-2640-1e.pdf (Accessed 15 October 2023). www.legco.gov.hk/yr92-93/english/lc_sitg/hansard/h921007.pdf (Accessed 15 October 2023).

Huang, Yasheng. 2023. *The Rise and Fall of the East: How Exams, Autocracy, Stability, and Technology brought China Success, and Why They Might Lead to Its Decline*. New Haven: Yale University Press.

Hung, Ho Fung. 2022. *City on the Edge: Hong Kong under Chinese Rule*. Cambridge: Cambridge University Press.

Inclán, María de la Luz. 2009. 'Repressive Threats, Procedural Concessions, and the Zapatista Cycle of Protests, 1994–2003'. *Journal of Conflict Resolution* 53(5): 794–819.

InmediaHK. 2007. 'Huanghou gaoji: Zuishao liangren beibu, jinwan qishi tianxing yizhi jihui' [Queen's Pier Emergency: At Least Two Arrested, Gathering at Tsim Sha Tsui Star Ferry Pier Scheduled for 7 PM Tonight]. 1 August. https://bit.ly/471WlYk (Accessed 6 October 2023).

InmediaHK. 2014. 'Duihua zhi lu suijin, minzhu zhixin busi: Zhi quan gang shimin shu' [Though the Road of Dialogue Is Over, the Heart of Democracy Never Dies – To All Hong Kong Citizens]. 31 August. https://bit.ly/3PUPZDi (Accessed 6 October 2023).

InmediaHK. 2015. 'Zhou Yongkang: Yundong shangceng lingdao shi xiao' [Alex Chow: The Defunction of Movement Leadership]. 3 September. www.inmediahk .net/node/1037169 (Accessed on 23 October 2023).

Ivankova, Nataliya, and Nancy Wingo. 2018. 'Applying Mixed Methods in Action Research: Methodological Potentials and Advantages'. *American Behavioral Scientist* 62(7): 978–997.

Jenkins, J. Craig, and Charles Perrow. 1977. 'Insurgency of the Powerless: Farm Worker Movements (1946–1972)'. *American Sociological Review* 42(2): 249–268.

Jiang, Shigong. 2017. *China's Hong Kong: A Political and Cultural Perspective.* Singapore: Springer Singapore.

Jiang, Zemin. 1997. 'Shoudu gejie qingzhu xianggang huigui zuguo dahui shang de jianghua' [Speech at the Capital's Celebration Ceremony of Hong Kong's Return to the Motherland], Hong Kong Basic Law Committee. 1 July. https://web.archive .org/web/20220705213807/www.npc.gov.cn/npc/c5946/200804/207d466cb28542 of85ff9fd5c259a353.shtml (Accessed on 20 October 2023).

Jiménez-Martínez, César. 2021. 'The Instrumental Mediated Visibility of Violence: The 2013 Protests in Brazil and the Limitations of the Protest Paradigm'. *The International Journal of Press/Politics* 26(3): 525–546.

Johnson, Erik W., and Scott Frickel. 2011. 'Ecological Threat and the Founding of US National Environmental Movement Organizations, 1962–1998'. *Social Problems* 58(3): 305–329.

Jung, Jai Kwan. 2023. 'The Candlelight Protests in South Korea: A Dynamics of Contention Approach'. *Social Movement Studies* 22(5–6): 767–785.

Juris, Jeffrey S. 2012. 'Reflections on #Occupy Everywhere: Social Media, Public Space, and Emerging l=Logics of Aggregation'. *American Ethnologist* 39(2): 259–279.

Kaeding, Malte Philipp. 2017. 'The Rise of Localism in Hong Kong'. *Journal of Democracy* 28(1): 157–171.

Kan, Karita. 2013. 'Occupy Central and Constitutional Reform in Hong Kong'. *China Perspectives* 3: 73–78.

Kang, Yi. 2020. 'Dispersed Domination through Patron-clientelism: The Evolution of the Local State–NGO Relationship in Post-disaster Sichuan'. *Journal of Contemporary China* 29(124): 598–613.

Karpf, David. 2012. *The MoveOn Effect: The Unexpected Transformation of American Political Advocacy.* New York: Oxford University Press.

Kaufhold, Marc-André, Alexis Gizikis, Christian Reuter, Matthias Habdank, and Margarita Grinko. 2019. 'Avoiding Chaotic Use of Social Media before, during, and after Emergencies: Design and Evaluation of Citizens' Guidelines'. *Journal of Contingencies and Crisis Management* 27(3): 198–213.

Ketchley, Neil. 2017. *Egypt in a Time of Revolution.* Cambridge: Cambridge University Press.

Khawaja, Marwan. 1993. 'Repression and Popular Collective Action: Evidence from the West Bank'. *Sociological Forum* 8(1): 47–71.

Khazraee, Emad, and Alison N. Novak. 2018. 'Digitally Mediated Protest: Social Media Affordances for Collective Identity Construction'. *Social Media + Society* 4(1): 1–14.

Kitschelt, Herbert P. 1986. 'Political Opportunity Structures and Political Protest: Anti-nuclear Movements in Four Democracies'. *British Journal of Political Science* 16(1): 57–85.

King, Ambrose Yeo-chi. 1975. 'Administrative Absorption of Politics in Hong Kong: Emphasis on the Grassroots Level'. *Asian Survey* 15(5): 422–439.

Klandermans, Bert. 2014. 'Identity Politics and Politicized Identities: Identity Processes and the Dynamics of Protest'. *Political Psychology* 35: 1–22.

Kobayashi, Tetsuro, and Polly Chan. 2022. 'Political Sensitivity Bias in Autocratizing Hong Kong'. *International Journal of Public Opinion Research* 34(4): edac028.

Kong, Karen. 2019. 'Human Rights Activist Scholars and Social Change in Hong Kong: Reflections on the Umbrella Movement and Beyond'. *The International Journal of Human Rights* 23(6): 899–914.

Koo, Alex Zhi-Xiong. 2022. 'The Evolution of Self-Censorship in Hong Kong Online Journalism: Influences from Digitalization and the State'. *The International Journal of Press/Politics*: 19401612221075553.

Koopmans, Ruud. 2004. 'Protest in Time and Space: The Evolution of Waves of Contention'. In *The Wiley Blackwell Companion to Social Movements*, eds. David A. Snow, Sarah A. Soul, Hanspeter Kriesi, and Holly J. McCammon, 43–62. Chichester: John Wiley & Sons.

Krasner, Stephen D. 2001. 'Problematic Sovereignty'. In *Problematic Sovereignty: Contested rules and Political Possibilities*, ed. Stephen D. Krasner, 1–23. New York: Columbia University Press.

Kriesi, Hanspeter, Ruud Koopmans, Jan Willem Duyvendak, and Marco G. Giugni. 1992. 'New Social Movements and Political Opportunities in Western Europe'. *European Journal of Political Research* 22(2): 219–244.

Ku, Agnes Shuk-mei. 2007. 'Constructing and Contesting the "Order" Imagery in Media Discourse: Implications for Civil Society in Hong Kong'. *Asian Journal of Communication* 17(2): 186–200.

Ku, Agnes Shuk-mei. 2012. 'Remaking Places and Fashioning an Opposition Discourse: Struggle over the Star Ferry Pier and the Queen's Pier in Hong Kong'. *Environment and Planning D: Society and Space* 30(1): 5–22.

Ku, Agnes S. 2004. 'Negotiating the Space of Civil Autonomy in Hong Kong: Power, Discourses and Dramaturgical Representations'. *The China Quarterly* 179: 647–664.

Ku, Agnes Shuk-mei. 2019. 'In Search of a New Political Subjectivity in Hong Kong: The Umbrella Movement as a Street Theater of Generational Change'. *The China Journal* 82(1): 111–132.

Kuah-Pearce, Khun Eng, and Gilles Guiheux. 2009. *Social Movements in China and Hong Kong: The Expansion of Protest Space*. Amsterdam: Amsterdam University Press.

Kuan, Hsin Chi, and Siu-Kai Lau. 2002. 'Between Liberal Autocracy and Democracy: Democratic Legitimacy in Hong Kong'. *Democratization* 9(4): 58–76.

Kuran, Timur. 1991. 'Now Out of Never: The Element of Surprise in the East European Revolution of 1989'. *World Politics* 44(1): 7–48.

Kurzman, Charles. 1996. 'Structural Opportunity and Perceived Opportunity in Social-Movement Theory: The Iranian Revolution of 1979'. *American Sociological Review* 61(1): 153–170.

Kwong, Yin-ho. 2016. 'The Growth of "Localism" in Hong Kong: A New Path for the Democracy Movement?' *China Perspectives* 3: 63–68.

Kwok, Chi, and Ngai Keung Chan. "Human automated collectives: Automating communication for social movement mobilization." *New Media & Society* 26.9 (2024): 4992–5012.

Laato, Samuli, A. K. M. Najmul Islam, Muhammad Nazrul Islam, and Eoin Whelan. 2020. 'What Drives Unverified Information Sharing and Cyberchondria during the COVID-19 Pandemic?' *European Journal of Information Systems* 29(3): 288–305.

Lai, Yan-ho, and Ming Sing. 2020. 'Solidarity and Implications of a Leaderless Movement in Hong Kong: Its Strengths and Limitations'. *Communist and Post-Communist Studies* 53(4): 41–67.

Lam-Knott, Sonia. 2020. 'Contesting Brandscapes in Hong Kong: Exploring Youth Activist Experiences of the Contemporary Consumerist Landscape'. *Urban Studies* 57(5): 1087–1104.

Lam, Wai Man. 2004. *Understanding the Political Culture of Hong Kong: The Paradox of Activism and Depoliticization*. New York: Routledge.

Lau Chan, Kit Ching. 1999. *From Nothing to Nothing: The Chinese Communist Movement and Hong Kong 1921–1936*. Hong Kong: Hong Kong University Press.

Lau, Siu Kai. 2015. *Yiguo liangzhi zai Xianggang de shijian* [*The Practice of the One Country Two Systems in Hong Kong*]. Hong Kong: Commercial Press.

Lau, Siu Kai, and Kuan, Hsin Chi. 1988. *The Ethos of the Hong Kong Chinese*. Hong Kong: Chinese University Press.

Law, Wing Sang. 2009. *Collaborative Colonial Power: The Making of the Hong Kong Chinese*. Hong Kong: Hong Kong University Press.

Law, Wing Sang. 2017. 'Why Reunion in Democracy Fails? The Past and the Future of a Colonial City'. *Cultural Studies* 31(6): 802–819.

Le Bon, Gustave. 1896. *The Crowd: A Study of the Popular Mind*. New York: Macmillan.

Leach, Darcy K. 2013. 'Culture and the Structure of Tyrannylessness'. *The Sociological Quarterly* 54(2): 181–191.

Lee, Ching Kwan, and Ming Sing, eds. 2019. *Take Back Our Future: An Eventful Sociology of the Hong Kong Umbrella Movement*. Ithaca, NY: Cornell University Press.

Lee, Eliza W. Y. 2005. 'Nonprofit Development in Hong Kong: The Case of a Statist–Corporatist Regime'. *Voluntas: International Journal of Voluntary and Nonprofit Organizations* 16: 51–68.

Lee, Eliza W. Y. 2020. 'United Front, Clientelism, and Indirect Rule: Theorizing the Role of the "Liaison Office" in Hong Kong'. *Journal of Contemporary China* 29(125): 763–775.

Lee, Eliza W. Y., and Ahmed Shafiqul Huque. 2006. 'The New Public Management Reform and Governance in Asian NICs: A Comparison of Hong Kong and Singapore'. *Governance* 19(4): 605–626.

Lee, Francis L. F. 2020. 'Solidarity in the Anti-Extradition Bill Movement in Hong Kong'. *Critical Asian Studies* 52(1): 18–32.

Lee, Francis. 2023. 'Beyond Self-Censorship: Hong Kong's Journalistic Risk Culture Under the National Security Law'. *The China Journal* 90(1): 129–153.

Lee, Francis L. F. 2025, Pro-Democracy Contention in Hong Kong Relational Dynamics between the Umbrella Movement and the Anti-Extradition Protests. New York. SUNY Press.

Lee, Francis L. F., and Joseph M. Chan. 2010. *Media, Social Mobilisation and Mass Protests in Post-colonial Hong Kong: The Power of a Critical Event*. New York: Routledge.

Lee, Francis L. F., and Joseph M. Chan. 2018. *Media and Protest Logics in the Digital Era: The Umbrella Movement in Hong Kong*. Oxford: Oxford University Press.

Lee, Francis L. F., Gary K. Y. Tang, and Chi-Kit Chan. 2023. 'Media Self-Censorship in a Self-Censoring Society: Transformation of Journalist-Source Relationships in Hong Kong'. *Journalism Studies* 24(12): 1539–1556.

Lee, Francis L. F., Gary K. Y. Tang, Samson Yuen, Edmund W. Cheng. 2020. 'Five Demands and (Not Quite) Beyond: Claim Making and Ideology in Hong Kong's Anti-Extradition Bill Movement'. *Communist and Post-Communist Studies* 53(4): 22–40.

Lee, Francis L. F., Edmund W. Cheng, Hai Liang, Gary K. Y. Tang, and Samson Yuen. 2022a. 'Dynamics of Tactical Radicalisation and Public Receptiveness in Hong Kong's Anti-Extradition Bill Movement'. *Journal of Contemporary Asia* 52(3): 429–451.

Lee, Francis L. F., Hai Liang, Edmund W. Cheng, Gary K. Y. Tang, and Samson Yuen. 2022b. 'Affordances, Movement Dynamics, and a Centralized Digital

Communication Platform in a Networked Movement'. *Information, Communication & Society* 25(12): 1699–1716.

Lee, Francis L. F., Samson Yuen, Gary Tang, and Edmund W. Cheng. 2019. 'Hong Kong's Summer of Uprising: From Anti-extradition to Anti-authoritarian Protests'. *China Review* 19(4): 1–32.

Lee, Grace OM, and Ahmed Shafiqul Huque. 1995. 'Transition and the Localization of the Civil Service in Hong Kong'. *International Review of Administrative Sciences* 61(1): 107–120.

Lee, Joseph Tse-Hei. 2021. 'Christian Witness and Resistance in Hong Kong: Faith-based Activism from the Umbrella Movement to the Anti-Extradition Struggle'. *Tamkang Journal of International Affairs* 24(3): 95–139.

Leenders, Reinoud, and Steven Heydemann. 2012. 'Popular Mobilization in Syria: Opportunity and Threat, and the Social Networks of the Early Risers'. *Mediterranean Politics* 17(2): 139–159.

LegCo (Hong Kong Legislative Council). 1992. 'Official Record of Proceedings'. October 7.

LegCo (Hong Kong Legislative Council). 2003. LC Paper No. CB (2)2640/01-02(01),

LegCo (Hong Kong Legislative Council). 2019. 'Security Cooperation between Hong Kong and Other Places on Juridical Assistance in Criminal Matters'. 15 February. LC Paper No. CB (2)767/18-19(03), www.legco.gov.hk/yr18-19/english/panels/se/papers/se20190215cb2-767-3-e.pdf (Accessed 15 October 2023).

Lertchoosakul, Kanokrat. 2021. 'The White Ribbon Movement: High School Students in the 2020 Thai Youth Protests'. *Critical Asian Studies* 53(2): 206–218.

Leung, Beatrice, and Shun Hing Chan. 2003. *Changing Church and State Relations in Hong Kong, 1950–2000*. Hong Kong: Hong Kong University Press.

Leung, Benjamin, and Stephen Chiu. 1991. *A Social History of Industrial Strike and the Labour Movement in Hong Kong, 1946–1989*. Hong Kong: Social Science Research Center.

Leung, Yan Wing, and Hoi Yu Ng. 2014. 'Delivering Civic Education in Hong Kong: Why Is It Not an Independent Subject?' *Citizenship, Social and Economics Education* 13(1): 2–13.

Levitsky, Steven, and Lucan A. Way. 2010. *Competitive Authoritarianism: Hybrid Regimes after the Cold War*. New York: Cambridge University Press.

Levitsky, Steven, and Lucan A. Way. 2023. 'Democracy's Surprising Resilience'. *Journal of Democracy* 34(4): 5–20.

Lewis, David. 2013. 'Civil Society and the Authoritarian State: Cooperation, Contestation and Discourse'. *Journal of Civil Society* 9(3): 325–340.

Li, Yao-Tai, and Katherine Whitworth. 2022. 'Reclaiming Hong Kong through Neighbourhood Making: A Study of the 2019 Anti-ELAB Movement'. *Urban Studies* 59(7): 1372–1388.

Li, Yao-Tai, and Katherine Whitworth. 2023. 'Redefining Consumer Nationalism: The Ambiguities of Shopping Yellow during the 2019 Hong Kong Anti-ELAB Movement'. *Journal of Consumer Culture* 23(3): 517–535.

Liang, Hai, and Francis L. F. Lee. 2023. 'Opinion Leadership in a Leaderless Movement: Discussion of the Anti-extradition Bill Movement in the LIHKG Web Forum'. *Social Movement Studies* 22(5–6): 670–668.

Lichbach, Mark Irving. 1987. 'Deterrence or Escalation? The Puzzle of Aggregate Studies of Repression and Dissent'. *Journal of Conflict Resolution* 31(2): 266–297.

Lim, Merlyna. 2013. 'Framing Bouazizi: "White Lies," Hybrid Network, and Collective/connective Action in the 2010–11 Tunisian Uprising'. *Journalism* 14(7): 921–941.

Lin, Holin, and Chuen-Tsai Sun. 2022. 'Game-Assisted Social Activism: Game Literacy in Hong Kong's Anti-Extradition Movement'. *Games and Culture* 17(7–8): 954–976.

Lindenmeier, Jörg, Christoph Schleer, and Denise Pricl. 2012. 'Consumer Outrage: Emotional Reactions to Unethical Corporate Behavior'. *Journal of Business Research* 65(9): 1364–1373.

Ling, Peter. 2006. 'Social Capital, Resource Mobilization and Origins of the Civil Rights Movement'. *Journal of Historical Sociology* 19(2): 202–214.

Link, Perry. 2010. 'June Fourth: Memory and Ethics'. In *The Impact of China's 1989 Tiananmen Massacre*, ed. Jean-Phillippe Beja, 25–44. New York: Routledge.

Linz, Juan J. 1993. 'State Building and Nation Building'. *European Review* 1(4): 355–369.

Linz, Juan J., and Alfred Stepan. 1996. *Problems of Democratic Transition and Consolidation: Southern Europe, South America, and Post-Communist Europe*. Baltimore, MD: Johns Hopkins University Press.

Liu, Tik-sang. 2003. 'A Nameless but Active Religion: An Anthropologist's View of Local Religion in Hong Kong and Macau'. *The China Quarterly* 174: 373–394.

Lo, Sonny. 2021. 'Hong Kong in 2020: National Security Law and Truncated Autonomy'. *Asian Survey* 61(1): 34–42.

Lo, Sonny Shiu-Hing, Steven Chung-Fun Hung, and Jeff Hai-Chi Loo. 2019. *China's New United Front Work in Hong Kong: Penetrative Politics and Its Implications*. Springer.

Loh, Christine. 2010. *Underground Front: The Chinese Communist Party in Hong Kong*. Hong Kong: Hong Kong University Press.

Lohmann, Susanne. 1994. 'The Dynamics of Informational Cascades: The Monday Demonstrations in Leipzig, East Germany, 1989–91'. *World Politics* 47(1): 42–101.

Loken, Meredith. 2022. 'Noncombat Participation in Rebellion: A Gendered Typology'. *International Security* 47(1): 139–170.

Lorch, Jasmin. 2021. 'Elite Capture, Civil Society and Democratic Backsliding in Bangladesh, Thailand and the Philippines'. *Democratization* 28(1): 81–102.

Lu, Tracy L. D. 2009. 'Heritage Conservation in Post-colonial Hong Kong'. *International Journal of Heritage Studies* 15(2–3): 258–272.

Lührmann, Anna, and Staffan I. Lindberg. 2019. 'A Third Wave of Autocratization Is Here: What Is New about It?' *Democratization* 26(7): 1095–1113.

Lui, Tai-lok. 2015. 'A Missing Page in the Grand Plan of "One Country, Two Systems": Regional Integration and Its Challenges to Post-1997 Hong Kong'. *Inter-Asia Cultural Studies* 16(3): 396–409.

Lui, Tai Lok. 2018. *Ganga [Embarrassment]*. Hong Kong: Oxford University Press.

Lui, Tai Lok, and James K. S. Kung. 1985. *Chengshi zongheng: Xianggang jumin yundong ji chengshi zhengzhi yanjiu [City Unlimited: Housing Protests and Urban Politics in Hong Kong]*. Hong Kong: Wide Angle Press.

Luk, Bernard Hung Kay. 2016. *Zuokan yunqi shi: Yiben Xianggangren de Jiaoxie shi [A People's History of the Hong Kong Professional Trade Unions]*. Hong Kong: City University of Hong Kong Press.

Lukes, Steven. 1974. *Power: A Radical View*. London: Macmillan.

Luo, Jar-Der. 2005. 'Particularistic Trust and General Trust: A Network Analysis in Chinese Organizations'. *Management and Organization Review* 1(3): 437–458.

Luqiu, Luwei Rose, and Shuning Lu. 2021. 'Bounded or Boundless: A Case Study of Foreign Correspondents' Use of Twitter during the 2019 Hong Kong Protests'. *Social Media + Society* 7(1): 1–10.

Lust-Okar, Ellen. 2005. *Structuring Conflict in the Arab World: Incumbents, Opponents, and Institutions.* Cambridge: Cambridge University Press.

Lust, Ellen. 2009. 'Democratization by Elections? Competitive Clientelism in the Middle East'. *Journal of Democracy* 20(3): 122–135.

Ma, E. K. W., and Anthony Y. H. Fung. 2007. 'Negotiating Local and National Identifications: Hong Kong Identity Surveys 1996–2006'. *Asian Journal of Communication* 17(2): 172–185.

Ma, Ngok. 2005. 'Civil Society in Self-defense: The Struggle Against National Security Legislation in Hong Kong'. *Journal of Contemporary China* 14(44): 465–482.

Ma, Ngok. 2007. *Political Development in Hong Kong: State, Political Society, and Civil Society.* Hong Kong: Hong Kong University Press.

Ma, Ngok. 2009. 'Reinventing the Hong Kong State or Rediscovering It? From Low Interventionism to Eclectic Corporatism'. *Economy and Society* 38(3): 492–519.

Ma, Ngok. 2011a. 'Value Changes and Legitimacy Crisis in Post-industrial Hong Kong'. *Asian Survey* 51(4): 683–712.

Ma, Ngok. 2016. 'The Making of a Corporatist State in Hong Kong: The Road to Sectoral Intervention'. *Journal of Contemporary Asia* 46(2): 247–266.

Ma, Ngok. 2020. 'The Plebeian Moment and Its Traces: Post-Umbrella Movement Professional Groups in Hong Kong'. In *Sunflowers and Umbrellas Social Movements, Expressive Practices, and Political Culture in Taiwan and Hong Kong*, eds. Thomas Gold, and Sebastian Veg, 228–252. Berkeley, CA: University of California Press.

Ma, Ngok, and Chi Keung Choy. 2003. 'The Impact of Electoral Rule Change on Party Campaign Strategy: Hong Kong as a Case Study'. *Party Politics* 9(3): 347–367.

Maerz, Seraphine F., Anna Lührmann, Sebastian Hellmeier, and Sandra Grahn. 2020. 'State of the World 2019: Autocratization Surges–Resistance Grows'. *Democratization* 27(6): 909–927.

Magaloni, Beatriz. 2008. 'Credible Power-Sharing and the Longevity of Authoritarian Rule'. *Comparative Political Studies* 41(4–5): 715–741.

Maguire, Edward R., Maya Barak, Karie Cross, and Kris Lugo. 2018. 'Attitudes among Occupy DC Participants about the Use of Violence against Police'. *Policing & Society* 28(5): 526–540.

Maher, Thomas V. 2010. 'Threat, Resistance, and Collective Action: The Cases of Sobibór, Treblinka, and Auschwitz'. *American Sociological Review* 75(2): 252–272.

Martin, Andrew W., and Marc Dixon. 2010. 'Changing to Win? Threat, Resistance, and the Role of Unions in Strikes, 1984–2002'. *American Journal of Sociology* 116(1): 93–129.

Mateo, Emma. 2022. 'All of Belarus Has Come out onto the Streets: Exploring Nationwide Protest and the Role of Pre-existing Social Networks'. *Post-Soviet Affairs* 38(1–2): 26–42.

Mathews, Gordon, Eric Ma, and Tai-lok Lui. 2007. *Hong Kong, China: Learning to Belong to a Nation.* Routledge.

McAdam, Doug. 1982. *Political Process and the Development of Black Insurgency, 1930–1970.* Chicago: University of Chicago Press.

McAdam, Doug. 1983. 'Tactical Innovation and the Pace of Insurgency'. *American Sociological Review* 48(6): 735–754.

McAdam, Doug. 1986. 'Recruitment to High-risk Activism: The Case of Freedom Summer'. *American Journal of Sociology* 92(1): 64–90.

McAdam, Doug. 1996. 'Political Opportunities: Conceptual Origins, Current Problems, Future Directions'. In *Comparative Perspectives on Social Movements: Political Opportunities, Mobilizing Structures, and Cultural Framings*, eds. Doug McAdam, John D. McCarthy, and Mayer N. Zald, 23–40. Cambridge: Cambridge University Press.

McAdam, Doug. 2000. 'Culture and Social Movements'. In *Culture and Politics: A Reader*, eds. Lane Crothers, and Charles Lockhart, 253–268. New York: St. Martin's Press.

McAdam, Doug, and Sidney Tarrow. 2019. 'The Political Context of Social Movements'. In *The Wiley Blackwell Companion to Social Movements*, eds. David A. Snow, Sarah A. Soul, Hanspeter Kriesi, and Holly J. McCammon, 17–42. Chichester: John Wiley & Sons.

McAdam, Doug, John D. McCarthy, and Mayer N. Zald. 1996. 'Introduction: Opportunities, Mobilizing Structures and Framing Processes – Toward a Synthetic, Comparative Perspective on Social Movements'. In *Comparative Perspectives on Social Movements*, eds. Doug McAdam, John D. McCarthy, and Mayer N. Zald, 1–20. Cambridge: Cambridge University Press.

McAdam, Doug, Sidney Tarrow, and Charles Tilly. 1997. 'Toward an Integrated Perspective on Social Movements and Revolution'. In *Comparative Politics: Rationality, Culture, and Structure*, eds. Mark Irving Lichbach, and Alan S. Zuckerman, 142–173. New York: Cambridge University Press.

McAdam, Doug, Sidney Tarrow, and Charles Tilly. 2001. *Dynamics of Contention*. Cambridge and New York: Cambridge University Press.

McCammon, Holly J. 2012. *The U.S. Women's Jury Movements and Strategic Adaptation a More Just Verdict*. Cambridge: Cambridge University Press.

McCarthy, John D., and Mayer N. Zald. 1973. *The Trend of Social Movements*. Morristown, NJ: General Learning.

McCarthy, John D., and Mayer N. Zald. 1977. 'Resource Mobilization and Social Movements: A Partial Theory'. *American Journal of Sociology* 82(6): 1212–1241.

McCauley, Clark, and Sophia Moskalenko. 2008. 'Mechanisms of Political Radicalization: Pathways toward Terrorism'. *Terrorism and Political Violence* 20(3): 415–433.

Mekouar, Merouan. 2014. 'No Political Agents, No Diffusion: Evidence from North Africa'. *International Studies Review* 16(2): 206–216.

Melucci, Alberto. 1995. 'The Process of Collective Identity'. In *Social Movements and Culture*, eds. Hank Johnston, and Bert Klandermans, 41–63. Minneapolis, MN: University of Minnesota Press.

Melucci, Alberto. 1989. *Nomads of the Present: Social Movements and Individual Needs in Contemporary Society*. London: Hutchinson Radius.

Melucci, Alberto. 1996. *Challenging Codes: Collective Action in the Information Age*. Cambridge: Cambridge University Press.

Merkel, Wolfgang, and Anna Lührmann. 2021. 'Resilience of Democracies: Responses to Illiberal and Authoritarian Challenges'. *Democratization* 28(5): 869–884.

Meyer, David S. 2004. 'Protest and Political Opportunities'. *Annual Review Sociology* 30: 125–145.

Micheletti, Michele. 2003. *Political Virtue and Shopping*. New York: Palgrave Macmillan.

Michels, Robert. 1962. *Political Parties: A Sociological Study of the Oligarchical Tendencies of Modern Democracy*. New York: Free Press.

Milan, Stefania. 2015. 'From Social Movements to Cloud Protesting: The Evolution of Collective Identity'. *Information, Communication & Society* 18(8): 887–900.

Miners, Norman J. 1986. 'Plans for Constitutional Reform in Hong Kong, 1946–52'. *The China Quarterly* 107: 463–482.

Ming Pao. 2011. 'Caiyuancun zuzhu weiban, erbai jing taizou cunmin' [200 Police Officers Removed Villagers in Choi Yuen Village Who Were Blocking the Construction of a Fence'. 25 January. http://news.mingpao.com/20110125/gma1.htm. (Accessed 6 May 2015).

Ming Pao. 2019. 'Huangdian shengyi budiefansheng: Xiang zhengming gangren neng chengqi Xianggang jingji' [*The Rising Turn of Yellow Shops' Business: A Desire to Prove the Capability of Hong Kong People to Support Hong Kong Economy*]. 10 October. https://bit.ly/3S83K46 (Accessed 23 October 2023).

Minkoff, Debra C. 1997. 'The Sequencing of Social Movements'. *American Sociological Review* 62(5): 779–799.

Mok, Chit Wai John. 2020. 'Why and How Umbrella Movement Participants Ran in the Authoritarian Elections in Hong Kong: Bringing Umbrellas Indoors'. *Asian Survey* 60(6): 1142–1171.

Mok, Florence. 2019. 'Public Opinion Polls and Covert Colonialism in British Hong Kong'. *China Information* 33(1): 66–87.

Moore, Alan W. 2000. *Collectivities: Protest, Counter-culture and Political Postmodernism in New York City Artists' Organizations, 1969–1985*. New York: City University of New York.

Morris, Aldon D. 1986. *The Origins of the Civil Rights Movement: Black Communities Organizing for Change*. New York: Free Press.

Morris, Aldon D. 1999. 'A Retrospective on the Civil Rights Movement: Political and Intellectual Landmarks'. *Annual Review of Sociology* 25: 517–539.

Morris, Aldon D., and Suzanne Staggenborg. 2004. 'Leadership in Social Movements'. In *The Blackwell Companion to Social Movements*, eds. David A. Snow, Sarah Anne Soule, and Hanspeter Kriesi, 171–196. Malden, MA: Blackwell.

Morris, Paul, and Edward Vickers. 2015. 'Schooling, Politics and the Construction of Identity in Hong Kong: The 2012 Moral and National Education Crisis in Historical Context'. *Comparative Education* 51(3): 305–326.

Moss, Dana M. 2022. *The Arab Spring Abroad: Diaspora Activism against Authoritarian Regimes*. New York: Cambridge University Press.

Muñoz, Jordi, and Eva Anduiza. 2019. '"If a Fight Starts, Watch the Crowd": The Effect of Violence on Popular Support for Social Movements'. *Journal of Peace Research* 56(4): 485–498.

Nathan, Andrew J., and Andrew Scobell. 2015. *China's Search for Security*. New York: Columbia University Press.

Neilson, Lisa A., and Pamela Paxton. 2010. 'Social Capital and Political Consumerism: A Multilevel Analysis'. *Social Problems* 57(1): 5–24.

New York Times. 2019a. 'The Infinity War in the Streets of Hong Kong'. 27 December. www.nytimes.com/2019/12/27/opinion/hong-kong-protests.html (Accessed 5 October 2023).

New York Times. 2019b. 'With Hymns and Prayers, Christians Help Drive Hong Kong's Protests'. 19 June. www.nytimes.com/2019/06/19/world/asia/hong-kong-extradition-protests-christians.html (Accessed 5 October 2023).

New York Times. 2021. "Forbidden Fruit": Apple Daily, Pro-Democracy Newspaper in Hong Kong, Is Forced to Close'. 23 June. www.nytimes.com/2021/06/23/world/asia/apple-daily-hong-kong.html (Accessed 5 October 2023).

Newman, Benjamin J., and Brandon L. Bartels. 2011. 'Politics at the Checkout Line: Explaining Political Consumerism in the United States'. *Political Research Quarterly* 64(4): 803–817.

Next Film. 2019, June, 5, 6 and 7. www.youtube.com/watch?v=lBjtVCv8xSY&list=PLun3UI73pC_odkLKHRj9LPfcb21yyNGD7, www.youtube.com/watch?v=cUG_4UX6L5s&list=PLun3UI73pC_odkLKHRj9LPfcb21yyNGD7, www.youtube.com/watch?v=RDoaZw3a_Lo&list=PLun3UI73pC_odkLKHRj9LPfcb21yyNGD7 (Accessed on 23 October 2023).

Ng, Mee Kam. 2020. 'The making of 'violent' Hong Kong: A centennial dream? A fight for democracy? A challenge to humanity?' *Planning Theory & Practice* 21(3): 483–494.

Ng, Michael. 2022. *Political Censorship in British Hong Kong: Freedom of Expression and the Law (1842–1997)*. Cambridge: Cambridge University Press.

Ngo, Tak Wing. ed. 1999. *Hong Kong's History: State and Society under Colonial Rule*. London: Routledge.

Ngo, Tak Wing. 2018. 'A Genealogy of Business and Politics in Hong Kong'. In *Routledge Handbook of Contemporary Hong Kong*, eds. Tai Lok Lui, Stephen W. K. Chiu, and Ray Yep, 324–341. Boca Raton, FL: Routledge.

North, Douglass C. 1990. *Institutions, Institutional Change and Economic Performance*. Cambridge: Cambridge University Press.

Nugent, Elizabeth R. 2020. *After Repression: How Polarization Derails Democratic Transition*. Princeton: Princeton University Press.

O'Brien, Kevin. 2003. 'Neither Transgressive nor Contained: Boundary-spanning Contention in China'. *Mobilization* 8(1): 51–64.

O'Brien, Kevin J., and Lianjiang Li. 2006. *Rightful Resistance in Rural China*. Cambridge: Cambridge University Press.

Oberschall, Anthony. 1973. *Social Conflict and Social Movements*. Englewood Cliffs, NJ: Prentice-Hall.

Oliver, Pamela E., and Gerald Marwell. 1988. 'The Paradox of Group Size in Collective Action: A Theory of the Critical Mass. II'. *American Sociological Review* 53(1): 1–8.

Oliver, Pamela. 1980. 'Rewards and Punishments as Selective Incentives for Collective Action: Theoretical Investigations'. *American Journal of Sociology* 85(6): 1356–1375.

Olivier, Johan L. 1990. 'Causes of Ethnic Collective Action in the Pretoria-Witwatersrand Triangle, 1970 to 1984'. *South African Sociological Review* 2(2): 89–108.

Olson, Mancur. 1971. *The Logic of Collective Action*. Cambridge, MA: Harvard University Press.

Ong, Elvin. 2022. 'What Are We Voting For? Opposition Alliance Joint Campaigns in Electoral Autocracies'. *Party Politics* 28(5): 954–967.

Ong, Lynette H. 2022. *Outsourcing Repression: Everyday State Power in Contemporary China*. New York: Oxford University Press.

Onuch, Olga. 2015. 'EuroMaidan Protests in Ukraine: Social Media versus Social Networks'. *Problems of Post-Communism* 62(4): 217–235.

Opp, Karl-Dieter. 2001. 'Social Networks and the Emergence of Protest Norms'. In *Social Norms*, eds. Michael Hechter, and Karl-Dieter Opp, 234–273. New York: Russell Sage Foundation.

Opp, Karl-Dieter, and Christiane Gern. 1993. 'Dissident Groups, Personal Networks, and Spontaneous Cooperation: The East German Revolution of 1989'. *American Sociological Review* 58(5): 659–680.

Opp, Karl-Dieter, and Wolfgang Roehl. 1990. 'Repression, Micromobilization, and Political Protest'. *Social Forces* 69(2): 521–547.

Ortmann, Stephan. 2015. 'The Umbrella Movement and Hong Kong's Protracted Democratization Process'. *Asian Affairs* 46(1): 32–50.

Overholt, William H. 2001. 'Hong Kong: The Perils of Semidemocracy'. *Journal of Democracy* 12(4): 5–18.

Pang, Lai Kwan. 2020. *The Appearing Demos: Hong Kong during and after the Umbrella Movement*. Ann Arbor, MI: University of Michigan Press.

Parkinson, Sarah E. 2013. 'Organizing Rebellion: Rethinking High-risk Mobilization and Social Networks in War'. *American Political Science Review* 107(3): 418–432.

Parkinson, Sarah E. 2022. *Beyond the Lines: Social Networks and Palestinian Militant Organizations in Wartime Lebanon*. Ithaca, NY: Cornell University Press.

Pearlman, Wendy. 2018. 'Moral Identity and Protest Cascades in Syria'. *British Journal of Political Science* 48(4): 877–901.

Pearlman, Wendy. 2021. 'Mobilizing from Scratch: Large-Scale Collective Action Without Pre-existing Organization in The Syrian Uprising'. *Comparative Political Studies* 54(10): 1786–1817.

People's Daily. 2020. 'Huangse jingjiquan shi Xianggang jingji wenming zhichi' [*Yellow is a Shame of Hong Kong Economic Civilization*]. 3 January.

Pepinsky, Thomas B. 2019. 'The Return of the Single-Country Study'. *Annual Review of Political Science* 22: 187–203.

Pepper, Suzanne. 2008. *Keeping Democracy at Bay: Hong Kong and the Challenge of Chinese Political Reform*. Lanham, MD: Rowman & Littlefield.

Petersen, Carole J. 2020. 'The Disappearing Firewall: International Consequences of Beijing's Decision to Impose a National Security Law and Operate National Security Institutions in Hong Kong'. *Hong Kong Law Journal* 50: 633–656.

Pfaff, Steven. 1996. 'Collective Identity and Informal Groups in Revolutionary Mobilization: East Germany in 1989'. *Social Forces* 75(1): 91–117.

Pfaff, Steven, and Hyojoung Kim. 2003. 'Exit-voice Dynamics in Collective Action: An Analysis of Emigration and Protest in the East German Revolution'. *American Journal of Sociology* 109(2): 401–444.

Piketty, Thomas, and Li Yang. 2021. 'Income and Wealth Inequality in Hong Kong, 1981–2020: The Rise of Pluto-Communism?' SSRN, http://dx.doi.org/10.2139/ssrn.3888118.

Pilati, Katia, Giuseppe Acconcia, David Leone Suber, and Henda Chennaoui. 2019. 'Between Organization and Spontaneity of Protests: The 2010–2011 Tunisian and Egyptian Uprisings'. *Social Movement Studies* 18(4): 463–481.

Pinard, Maurice. 2011. *Motivational Dimensions in Social Movements and Contentious Collective Action*. Montreal: McGill-Queen's University Press.

Piven, Frances Fox. 2012. 'Protest Movements and Violence'. In *Violent Protest, Contentious Politics, and the Neoliberal State*, eds. Seraphim Seferiades, and Hank Johnston, 37–46. London: Routledge.

Piven, Frances Fox, and Richard A. Cloward. 1977. *Poor People's Movements: Why They Succeed, How They Fail.* New York: Vintage.

Plattner, Marc F. 1998. 'Liberalism and Democracy: Can't Have One without the Other'. *Foreign Affairs* 77(2): 171–180.

Polletta, Francesca. 2006. *It Was Like a Fever: Storytelling in Protest and Politics.* Chicago: University of Chicago Press.

Poon, Hannah, and Tommy Tse. 2022. 'Enacting Cross-platform (Buy/Boy) Cotts: Yellow Economic Circle and the New Citizen-consumer Politics in Hong Kong'. *New Media & Society*: 14614448221097305.

Power, Thomas P. 2020. 'Assailing Accountability: Law Enforcement Politicisation, Partisan Coercion and Executive Aggrandisement under the Jokowi Administration'. In *Democracy in Indonesia: From Stagnation to Regression?* eds. Thomas Power, and Eve Warburton, 277–302. Singapore: ISEAS-Yusof Ishak Institute.

Prestor, Katarina. 2014, September 28. 'Erlingyisi nian jiuyue nianbari, wozai zuo shenme?' [What Was I Doing on 28 September 2014?]. Local Press, http://web.archive .org/web/20150423114530/www.localpresshk.com/2014/10/1hand-record-928/ (Accessed 4 October 2023).

Pringle, Tim. 2021. 'The Unionisation Wave in Hong Kong: The Noise before Defeat or the Route to Victory?' *Global Labour Journal* 12(2): 1–8.

Progressive Lawyers Group. 2019. 'Hong Kong's End Game: Why the Extradition Bill is an "Infinity Stone" that Could Decimate Half of Society'. Hong Kong Free Press. 9 June. https://hongkongfp.com/2019/06/09/hong-kongs-end-game-extradition-bill-infinity-stone-decimate-half-society/ (Accessed 20 October 2023).

Putnam, Robert D. 1993. 'The Prosperous Community: Social Capital and Public Life'. *The American Prospect* 13: 35–42.

Putnam, Robert D. 1995. 'Bowling Alone: America's Declining Social Capital'. *Journal of Democracy* 6(1): 65–78.

Quartz. 2019, October 16. 'Hong Kong Is Exporting Its Protest Techniques around the World'. https://qz.com/1728078/be-water-catalonia-protesters-learn-from-hong-kong. (Accessed 10 September 2023).

Quartz. 2020, June 30. '"Laam Caau" The High-stakes Game that Hong Kong Protesters are Waging with China'. https://qz.com/1873189/hong-kong-protesters-gamble-national-security-law-will-backfire-on-china. (Accessed 10 September 2023).

Raelin, Joe. 2011. 'From Leadership-as-Practice to Leaderful Practice'. *Leadership* 7(2): 195–211.

Raelin, Joseph A. 2003. *Creating Leaderful Organizations: How to Bring Out Leadership in Everyone.* Berrett-Koehler Publishers.

Rasler, Karen. 1996. 'Concessions, Repression, and Political Protest in the Iranian Revolution'. *American Sociological Review* 61(1): 132–152.

Registration and Electoral Office, Hong Kong. 2019. 'District Council Election Results'. www.elections.gov.hk/dc2019/eng/results.html (Accessed 5 October 2023).

Reuters. 2019. 'Medic Shot in Eye during Hong Kong Protests'. 12 August. www .reuters.com/news/picture/medic-shot-in-eye-during-hong-kong-prote-idUSRTS2MBDL (Accessed on 5 October 2023).

Rhodes-Purdy, Matthew, and Fernando Rosenblatt. 2023. 'Raising the Red Flag: Democratic Elitism and the Protests in Chile'. *Perspectives on Politics* 21(1): 241–253.

Rigger, Shelley. 1999. *Politics in Taiwan: Voting for Democracy.* London: Routledge.

Rigger, Shelley. 2001. *From Opposition to Power: Taiwan's Democratic Progressive Party*. London: Lynne Rienner Publishers.

Robertson, Graeme B. 2010. *The Politics of Protest in Hybrid Regimes: Managing Dissent in Post-communist Russia*. New York: Cambridge University Press.

Rössel, Jörg, and Patrick Henri Schenk. 2018. 'How Political Is Political Consumption? The Case of Activism for the Global South and Fair Trade'. *Social Problems* 65(2): 266–284.

Sato, Yuko, and Michael Wahman. 2019. 'Elite Coordination and Popular Protest: The Joint Effect on Democratic Change'. *Democratization* 26(8): 1419–1438.

Saunders, Clare. 2009. 'It's Not Just Structural: Social Movements Are Not Homogenous Responses to Structural Features, but Networks Shaped by Organisational Strategies and Status'. *Sociological Research Online* 14(1): 26–41.

Schmitter, Philippe C. 2015. 'Crisis and Transition, But Not Decline'. *Journal of Democracy* 26(1): 32–44.

Schock, Kurt. 1999, 'People Power and Political Opportunities: Social Movement Mobilization and Outcomes in the Philippines and Burma'. *Social Problems* 46(3): 355–375.

Schudson, Michael. 2007. 'Citizens, Consumers, and the Good Society'. *The ANNALS of the American Academy of Political and Social Science* 611(1): 236–249.

SCMP. 2018. 'In tomorrow's world, Hong Kong's leader sees a massive HK$500 billion artificial island in middle of the sea, home to 1.1 million people'. www .scmp.com/news/hong-kong/hong-kong-economy/article/2167936/tomorrows-world-hong-kongs-leader-sees-massive.

Scott, Ian. 1989. *Political Change and the Crisis of Legitimacy in Hong Kong*. Honolulu, HI: University of Hawaii Press.

Scott, Ian. 2022. *The Public Sector in Hong Kong*, 2nd edition. Hong Kong: Hong Kong University Press.

Seferiades, Seraphim, and Hank Johnston. 2016. 'The Dynamics of Violent Protest: Emotions, Repression and Disruptive Deficit'. In *Violent Protest, Contentious Politics, and the Neoliberal State*, eds. Seraphim Seferiades, and Hank Johnston, 21–36. Routledge.

Selçuk, Orçun, and Dilara Hekimci. 2020. 'The Rise of the Democracy–Authoritarianism Cleavage and Opposition Coordination in Turkey (2014–2019)'. *Democratization* 27(8): 1496–1514.

Serhan, Yasmeen. 2019. 'The Common Element Uniting Worldwide Protests'. 19 November. *The Atlantic*.

Sewell, William H. 2005. *Logics of History: Social Theory and Social Transformation*. Chicago: University of Chicago Press.

Shah, Dhavan V., Douglas M. McLeod, Eunkyung Kim, Sun Young Lee, Melissa R. Gotlieb, Shirley S. Ho, and Hilde Breivik. 2007. 'Political Consumerism: How Communication and Consumption Orientations Drive "Lifestyle Politics"'. *The ANNALS of the American Academy of Political and Social Science* 611(1): 217–235.

Shen, Fei, Chuanli Xia, and Marko Skoric. 2020. 'Examining the Roles of Social Media and Alternative Media in Social Movement Participation: A Study of Hong Kong's Umbrella Movement'. *Telematics and Informatics* 47: 101303.

Shesterinina, Anastasia. 2016. 'Collective Threat Framing and Mobilization in Civil War'. *American Political Science Review* 110(3): 411–427.

Shin, Hyun Bang, Loretta Lees, and Ernesto López-Morales. 2016. 'Introduction: Locating Gentrification in the Global East'. *Urban Studies* 53(3): 455–470.

Shirky, Clay. 2008. *Here Comes Everybody: The Power of Organizing without Organizations*. New York: Penguin.

Shriver, Thomas E., Alison E. Adams, and Stefano B. Longo. 2015. 'Environmental Threats and Political Opportunities: Citizen Activism in the North Bohemian Coal Basin'. *Social Forces* 94(2): 699–722.

Sidel, John T. 2021. *Republicanism, Communism, Islam: Cosmopolitan Origins of Revolution in Southeast Asia*. Cornell University Press.

Sika, Nadine. 2019. 'Repression, Cooptation, and Movement Fragmentation in Authoritarian Regimes: Evidence from the Youth Movement in Egypt'. *Political Studies* 67(3): 676–692.

Sika, Nadine. 2023. 'Mobilization, Repression and Policy Concessions in Authoritarian Regimes: The Cases of Egypt and Jordan'. *Political Studies*: 00323217221141426.

Simmons, Erica. 2014. 'Grievances Do Matter in Mobilization'. *Theory and Society* 43(5): 513–546.

Simmons, Erica S. 2016. *Meaningful Resistance: Market Reforms and the Roots of Social Protest in Latin America*. Cambridge: Cambridge University Press.

Sing, Ming. 2010. 'Explaining Mass Support for Democracy in Hong Kong'. *Democratization* 17(1): 175–205.

Skitka, Linda J., Christopher W. Bauman, and Elizabeth Mullen. 2004. 'Political Tolerance and Coming to Psychological Closure Following the September 11, 2001, Terrorist Attacks: An Integrative Approach'. *Personality and Social Psychology Bulletin* 30(6): 743–756.

Slater, Dan, and Nicholas Rush Smith. 2016. 'The Power of Counterrevolution: Elitist Origins of Political Order in Postcolonial Asia and Africa'. *American Journal of Sociology* 121(5): 1472–1516.

Smelser, Neil J. 1962. *Theory of Collective Behavior*. London: Routledge & Kegan Paul.

Smith, Jackie. 2001. 'Globalizing Resistance: The Battle of Seattle and the Future of Social Movements'. *Mobilization* 6(1): 1–19.

Smith, Jackie, and Bob Glidden. 2012. 'Occupy Pittsburgh and the Challenges of Participatory Democracy'. *Social Movement Studies* 11(3–4): 288–294.

Snow, David A. 2001. 'Collective Identity and Expressive Forms'. *UC Irvine CSD Working Papers*. https://escholarship.org/uc/item/2zn1t7bj.

Snow, David A., and Catherine Corrigall-Brown. 2015. 'Collective Identity'. In *International Encyclopedia of the Social & Behavioral Sciences*, ed. James Wright, 174–180. Oxford: Elsevier.

Snow, David A., and Dana M. Moss. 2014. 'Protest on the Fly: Toward a Theory of Spontaneity in the Dynamics of Protest and Social Movements'. *American Sociological Review* 79(6): 1122–1143.

Snow, David A., and Robert D. Benford. 1988. 'Ideology, Frame Resonance, and Participant Mobilization'. *International Social Movement Research* 1: 197–218.

Snow, David A., Louis A. Zurcher Jr, and Sheldon Ekland-Olson. 1980. 'Social Networks and Social Movements: A Microstructural Approach to Differential Recruitment'. *American Sociological Review* 45(5): 787–801.

Snow, David, and Doug McAdam. 2000. 'Identity Work Processes in the Context of Social Movements: Clarifying the Identity/movement Nexus'. In *Self, Identity, and*

Social Movements, eds. Sheldon Stryker, Timothy J. Owens, and Robert W. White, 41–67. Minneapolis, MN: University of Minnesota Press.

Snow, David, Daniel Cress, Liam Downey, and Andrew Jones. 1998. 'Disrupting the "Quotidian": Reconceptualizing the Relationship between Breakdown and the Emergence of Collective Action'. *Mobilization* 3(1): 1–22.

So, Alvin Y. 1999. *Hong Kong's Embattled Democracy: A Societal Analysis*. Baltimore, MD: John Hopkins University Press.

So, Alvin Y., and Ludmilla Kwitko. 1990. 'The New Middle Class and the Democratic Movement in Hong Kong'. *Journal of Contemporary Asia* 20(3): 384–398.

Somer, Murat, Jennifer L. McCoy, and Russell E. Luke. 2021. 'Pernicious Polarization, Autocratization and Opposition Strategies'. *Democratization* 28(5): 929–948.

South China Morning Post. 2007. 'Protest Voyagers Sail from Pier'. 23 April. www.scmp.com/article/590096/protest-voyagers-sail-pier (Accessed on 23 October 2023).

South China Morning Post. 2019a. 'Best Mart 360 Shuns "War Zone" Hong Kong for Mainland China in Growth Plan after Protesters Trash 75 of Its 102 Store'. 28 November. www.scmp.com/business/companies/article/3039803/best-mart-360-flees-war-zone-hong-kong-mainland-china-after (Accessed on 23 October 2023).

South China Morning Post. 2019b. 'Fugitive Tycoon Joseph Lau Launches Legal Challenge against Hong Kong Government Proposal to Change Extradition Law'. 1 April. www.scmp.com/news/hong-kong/law-and-crime/article/3004094/fugitive-tycoon-joseph-lau-launches-legal-challenge (Accessed on 23 October 2023).

South China Morning Post. 2019c. 'Hong Kong Protesters Apologise after Storming Government Building'. 25 June. www.scmp.com/video/hong-kong/3016092/hong-kong-protesters-apologise-after-storming-government-building (Accessed on 23 October 2023).

South China Morning Post. 2019d. 'Hong Kong Protests: How the City's Reddit-Like Forum LIHKG Has become the Leading Platform for Organising Demonstrations'. 3 August. www.scmp.com/news/hong-kong/society/article/3021224/hong-kong-protests-how-citys-reddit-forum-lihkg-has-become (Accessed on 23 October 2023).

South China Morning Post. 2019e. 'How Marauding Gang Struck Fear into Yuen Long, Leaving Dozens of Protesters and Passengers Injured, and Hong Kong Police Defending Their Response'. 23 July. www.scmp.com/news/hong-kong/politics/article/3019669/how-marauding-gang-struck-fear-yuen-long-leaving-pregnant (Accessed on 23 October 2023).

South China Morning Post. 2019f. 'Mahjong Parlours and "Fujian Gangsters": How the Peaceful New Territories Town of Tsuen Wan Became a Flashpoint in Hong Kong's Protests'. 31 August. www.scmp.com/news/hong-kong/society/article/3025147/mahjong-parlours-and-fujian-gangsters-how-peaceful-new (Accessed on 23 October 2023).

South China Morning Post. 2023g. '"Dozens of Hong Kong Residents" on Police National Security "Wanted" List, Including for Crowdfunding Drives'. 4 July. www.scmp.com/news/hong-kong/law-and-crime/article/3226559/dozens-hong-kong-residents-police-national-security-wanted-list-including-crowdfunding-drives-post (Accessed on 23 October 2023).

South China Morning Post. 2023h. 'Applications for Hong Kong Path to UK Citizenship Show No Signs of Slowing, British Figures Show'. 24 August. www.scmp.com/news/hong-kong/society/article/3232190/applications-hong-kong-path-uk-citizenship-show-no-signs-slowing-british-figures-show (Accessed on 23 October 2023).

Spires, Anthony J. 2011. 'Contingent Symbiosis and Civil Society in an Authoritarian State: Understanding the Survival of China's Grassroots NGOs'. *American Journal of Sociology* 117(1): 1–45.

State Council of the People's Republic of China. 2014. 'The Practice of the "One Country, Two Systems" Policy in the Hong Kong Special Administrative Region'. http://english.www.gov.cn/archive/white_paper/2014/08/23/content_281474982986578.htm (Accessed on 23 October 2023).

Steinert-Threlkeld, Zachary C. 2017. 'Spontaneous Collective Action: Peripheral Mobilization during the Arab Spring'. *American Political Science Review* 111(2): 379–403.

Steinert-Threlkeld, Zachary C., Alexander M. Chan, and Jungseock Joo. 2022. 'How State and Protester Violence Affect Protest Dynamics'. *The Journal of Politics* 84(2): 798–813.

Steinhardt, H. Christoph, Linda Chelan Li, and Yihong Jiang. 2018. 'The Identity Shift in Hong Kong since 1997: Measurement and Explanation'. *Journal of Contemporary China* 27(110): 261–276.

Stolle, Dietlind, and Micheletti, Michele. 2006. 'The Gender Gap Reversed: Political Consumerism as a Women-friendly Form of Civic and Political Engagement'. In *Gender and Social Capital*, eds. Brenda O'Neil, and Elisabeth Gidengil, 45–77. New York: Routledge.

Stolle, Dietlind, Marc Hooghe, and Michele Micheletti. 2005. 'Politics in the Supermarket: Political Consumerism as a Form of Political Participation'. *International Political Science Review* 26(3): 245–269.

Su, Chris Chao, Michael Chan, and Sejin Paik. 2022. 'Telegram and the Anti-ELAB Movement in Hong Kong: Reshaping Networked Social Movements through Symbolic Participation and Spontaneous Interaction'. *Chinese Journal of Communication* 15(3): 431–448.

Sutherland, Neil, Christopher Land, and Steffen Böhm. 2014. 'Anti-leaders (hip) in Social Movement Organizations: The Case of Autonomous Grassroots Groups'. *Organization* 21(6): 759–781.

Svolik, Milan W. 2012. *The Politics of Authoritarian Rule*. Cambridge: Cambridge University Press.

Szeto, Wah. 2011. *Dajiang dongqu: Si Tu Hua huiyilu* [*The River of No Return: A Memoir of Szeto Wah*]. Hong Kong: Oxford University Press.

Tai, Benny Y. T. 2013. 'Gongmin kangming de zuida shashangli wuqi' [The Most Lethal Weapon of Civil Disobedience]. *Hong Kong Economic Journal*, 16 January. https://bennytai.github.io/HongKongReflections/%E6%80%9D%E8%80%83%E9%A6%99%E6%B8%AF6/2--The%20Most%20Lethal%20Weapon%20of%20Civil%20Disobedience.html (Accessed on 6 October 2023).

Tajfel, Henri. 1978. *Differentiation between Social Groups: Studies in the Social Psychology of Intergroup Relations*. London: Academic Press.

Takungpao. 2019. 'Wanzi liang jiaotang zhuangong baotu chadian' [*Two Churches in Wanchai Shelter Rioters*]. 7 October. www.takungpao.com.hk/news/232109/2019/1007/358299.html (Accessed 2 October 2023).

Tam, Wai Keung. 2012. *Legal Mobilization under Authoritarianism: The Case of Post-Colonial Hong Kong*. Cambridge: Cambridge University Press.

Tang, Gary. 2015. 'Mobilization by Images: TV Screen and Mediated Instant Grievances in the Umbrella Movement'. *Chinese Journal of Communication* 8(4): 338–355.

Tang, Gary, and Francis L. F. Lee. 2013. 'Facebook Use and Political Participation: The Impact of Exposure to Shared Political Information, Connections with Public Political Actors, and Network Structural Heterogeneity'. *Social Science Computer Review* 31(6): 763–773.

Tang, Gary, and Edmund W. Cheng. 2021. 'Affective Solidarity: How Guilt Enables Cross-generational Support for Political Radicalization in Hong Kong'. *Japanese Journal of Political Science* 22(4): 198–214.

Tarrow, Sidney. 1989. *Democracy and Disorder*. Oxford: Oxford University Press.

Tarrow, Sidney. 1993. 'Cycles of Collective Action: Between Moments of Madness and The Repertoire of Contention'. *Social Science History* 17(2): 281–307.

Tarrow, Sidney. 1998. *Power in Movement*. Cambridge: Cambridge University Press.

Tarrow, Sidney. 2008. 'Charles Tilly and the Practice of Contentious Politics'. *Social Movement Studies* 7(3): 225–246.

Tarrow, Sidney. 2021. Movements and Parties Critical Connections in American Political Development. New York: Cambridge University Press.

Tarrow, Sidney. 2022. *Power in Movement: Social Movements and Contentious Politics*. 4th edition. Cambridge: Cambridge University Press.

Taylor, Verta. 1989. 'Social Movement Continuity: The Women's Movement in Abeyance'. *American Sociological Review* 54(5): 761–775.

Teets, Jessica C. 2013. 'Let Many Civil Societies Bloom: The Rise of Consultative Authoritarianism in China'. *The China Quarterly* 213: 19–38.

Thompson, Mark R. 2021. 'Pushback after Backsliding? Unconstrained Executive Aggrandizement in the Philippines Versus Contested Military-Monarchical Rule in Thailand'. *Democratization* 28(1): 124–141.

Thompson., Mark R., and Stephan Ortmann. 2020. *China's 'Singapore Model' and Authoritarian Learning*. London: Routledge.

Tilly, Charles. 1978. *From Mobilization to Revolution*. Reading, MA: Addison-Wesley.

Tilly, Charles. 1986. *The Contentious French: Four Centuries of Popular Struggle*. Cambridge: Belknap.

Tilly, Charles. 1995. *Popular Contention in Great Britain, 1758–1834*. Cambridge, MA: Harvard University Press.

Tilly, Charles. 1999. 'From Interactions to Outcomes in Social Movements'. In *How Social Movements Matter*, eds. Marco Giugni, Doug McAdam, and Charles Tilly, 253–270. Minneapolis, MN: University of Minnesota Press.

Tilly, Charles. 2002. 'Event Catalogs as Theories'. *Sociological Theory* 20(2): 248–254.

Tilly, Charles. 2003. *The Politics of Collective Violence*. New York: Cambridge University Press.

Tilly, Charles. 2008. *Contentious Performance*. New York: Cambridge University Press.

Tilly, Charles, and Sidney Tarrow. 2007. *Contentious Politics*. Boulder, CO: Paradigm Publishers.

Trejo, Guillermo. 2012. *Popular Movements in Autocracies: Religion, Repression, and Indigenous Collective Action in Mexico*. Cambridge: Cambridge University Press.

Tsai, Kellee S. 2018. 'Rescaling State-Society Relations in China and India'. In *Beyond Regimes: China and India Compared*, eds. Prasenjit Duara, and Elizabeth J. Perry, 255–293. Cambridge, MA: Harvard University Asia Center.

Tsang, Steve. 1997. 'Strategy for Survival: The Cold War and Hong Kong's Policy Towards Kuomintang and Chinese Communist activities in the 1950s'. *The Journal of Imperial and Commonwealth History* 25(2): 294–317.

Tsang, Steve. 2003. *A Modern History of Hong Kong: 1841–1997*. London: Bloomsbury.

Tsang, Steve. 2004. *A Modern history of Hong Kong*. London: I.B. Tauris.

Tsao, Jack, Ian Hardy, and Bob Lingard. 2018. 'Aspirational Ambivalence of Middle-Class Secondary Students in Hong Kong'. *British Journal of Sociology of Education* 39(8): 1094–1110.

Tsatsou, Panayiota. 2018. 'Social Media and Informal Organisation of Citizen Activism: Lessons from the Use of Facebook in the Sunflower Movement'. *Social Media + Society* 4(1). http://dx.doi.org/10.1177/2056305117775138.

Tufekci, Zeynep. 2017. *Twitter and Tear Gas: The Power and Fragility of Networked Protest*. London: Yale University Press.

Tufekci, Zeynep, and Christopher Wilson. 2012. 'Social Media and the Decision to Participate in Political Protest: Observations from Tahrir Square'. *Journal of Communication* 62(2): 363–379.

Turner, Ralph H., and Lewis M. Killian. 1987. *Collective Behavior*. London: Prentice-Hall International.

United Nations Development Programme. 2018. *Human Development Report*. New York: United Nations Development Programme.

Urman, Aleksandra, and Stefan Katz. 2022. 'Online Publicity and Outcomes of Individual Politically Salient Criminal Cases in an Authoritarian Regime: Evidence from Russia'. *Political Research Exchange* 4(1). http://dx.doi.org/10.1080/24747 36X.2022.2095920.

Urman, Aleksandra, Justin Chun-ting Ho, and Stefan Katz. 2021. 'Analyzing Protest Mobilization on Telegram: The Case of 2019 Anti-Extradition Bill Movement in Hong Kong'. *PloS One* 16(10). http://dx.doi.org/10.1371/journal.pone.0256675.

Van Dyke, Nella. 1998. 'Hotbeds of Activism: Locations of Student Protest'. *Social Problems* 45(2): 205–220.

Van Dyke, Nella. 2013. 'Threat'. In *The Wiley-Blackwell Encyclopedia of Social and Political Movements*. https://doi.org/10.1002/9780470674871.wbespm213.

Van Dyke, Nella, and Sarah A. Soule. 2002. 'Structural Social Change and the Mobilizing Effect of Threat: Explaining Levels of Patriot and Militia Organizing in the United States'. *Social Problems* 49(4): 497–520.

Van Stekelenburg, Jacquelien, and Bert Klandermans. 2013. 'The Social Psychology of Protest'. *Current Sociology* 61(5–6): 886–905.

Varese, Federico, and Rebecca W. Y. Wong. 2018. 'Resurgent Triads? Democratic Mobilization and Organized Crime in Hong Kong'. *Journal of Criminology* 51(1): 23–39.

Veg, Sebastian. 2016. 'Creating a Textual Public Space: Slogans and Texts from Hong Kong's Umbrella Movement'. *The Journal of Asian Studies* 75(3): 673–702.

Veg, Sebastian. 2017. 'The Rise of "Localism" and Civic Identity in Post-handover Hong Kong: Questioning the Chinese Nation-state'. *The China Quarterly* 230: 323–347.

Vergani, Matteo, Greg Barton, and Muhammad Iqbal. 2017. 'Beyond Social Relationships: Investigating Positive and Negative Attitudes towards Violent Protest within the Same Social Movement'. *Journal of Sociology* 53(2): 445–460.

Wackenhut, Arne F. 2020. 'Revisiting the Egyptian Uprising of 2011: Exploring the Role of Relational Networks within the Cairo-based Political Opposition'. *Social Problems* 67(2): 342–357.

Walgrave, Stefaan, and Joris Verhulst. 2011. 'Selection and Response Bias in Protest Surveys'. *Mobilization* 16(2): 203–222.

Wang, Dan J., and Sarah A. Soule. 2016. 'Tactical Innovation in Social Movements: The Effects of Peripheral and Multi-issue Protest'. *American Sociological Review* 81(3): 517–548.

Wasow, Omar. 2020. 'Agenda Seeding: How 1960s Black Protests Moved Elites, Public Opinion and Voting'. *American Political Science Review* 114(3): 638–659.

Wasserstrom, Jeffrey N. 2020. *Vigil: Hong Kong on the Brink*. New York: Columbia Global Reports.

Weber, Max. 1964. *The Theory of Social and Economic Organization*. New York: Free Press.

Weisburd, David, and Hagit Lernau. 2006. 'What Prevented Violence in Jewish Settlements in the Withdrawal from the Gaza Strip?' *Ohio State Journal of Dispute Resolution* 22(1): 37–81.

Weiss, Meredith Leigh. 2006. *Protest and Possibilities: Civil Society and Coalitions for Political Change in Malaysia*. Stanford University Press.

Weiss, Meredith Leigh, and Edward Aspinall, eds. 2012. *Student Activism in Asia: between Protest and Powerlessness*. Minneapolis, MN: University of Minnesota Press.

Wenweipo. 2014. '"Occupy Central" is the Hong Kong's Version of the Color Revolution. This Hat Cannot Be Taken off'. 13 October. http://paper.wenweipo.com/2014/10/13/PL1410130001.htm. (Accessed on 22 October 2023).

Wenweipo. 2019. 'Shengtang yi cangwu, xiaoxue bi baotu2' [Churches Were Suspected to Hide Dirt, Primary School Accommodated Rioters]. 20 September. http://paper.wenweipo.com/2019/09/20/HK1909200011.htm. (Accessed on 22 October 2023).

Wenweipo. 2021. 'Duoquan zhaoshu: shibu zhubu tuijin, juzhong mou duo zhengquan' [Power Grab Countdown | Ten-Step Plan Progressing Gradually, Plotting to Seize Power]. 7 January. www.tkww.hk/a/202101/07/AP5ff6624be4b060b720362350.html (Accessed 22 October 2023).

Western, Simon. 2014. 'Autonomist Leadership in Leaderless Movements: Anarchists Leading the Way'. *Ephemera: Theory & Politics in Organization* 14(4): 673–698.

Wijermars, Mariëlle, and Tetyana Lokot. 2022. 'Is Telegram a "Harbinger of Freedom"? The Performance, Practices, and Perception of Platforms as Political Actors in Authoritarian States'. *Post-Soviet Affairs* 38(1–2): 125–145.

Wiktorowicz, Quintan. 2000. *The Management of Islamic Activism: Salafis, the Muslim Brotherhood, and State Power in Jordan*. New York: State University of New York Press.

Williamson, Scott. 2021. 'Elections, Legitimacy, and Compliance in Authoritarian Regimes: Evidence from the Arab World'. *Democratization* 28(8): 1483–1504.

Willis, Margaret M., and Juliet B. Schor. 2012. 'Does Changing a Light Bulb Lead to Changing the World? Political Action and the Conscious Consumer'. *The ANNALS of the American Academy of Political and Social Science* 644(1): 160–190.

Woneifei. 2019, August 12. 'Flying with You. We Are Hongkonger'. YouTube. www.youtube.com/watch?v=2UltvQ1nkuM (Accessed 22 October 2023).

Wong, John D. 2022. 'Constructing the Legitimacy of Governance in Hong Kong: Prosperity and Stability Meets Democracy and Freedom'. *The Journal of Asian Studies* 81(1): 43–61.

Wong, Stan Hok-Wui. 2019. 'Gerrymandering in Electoral Autocracies: Evidence from Hong Kong'. *British Journal of Political Science* 49(2): 579–610.

Woo-Cumings, Meredith. ed. 1999. *The Developmental State*. London: Cornell University Press.

Wood, Elisabeth Jean. 2003. *Insurgent Collective Action and Civil War in El Salvador*. Cambridge: Cambridge University Press.

Wood, Richard L. 2002. *Faith in Action: Religion, Race, and Democratic Organizing in America*. Chicago: University of Chicago Press.

World Bank. 1991. *World Development Report*. New York: World Bank.

Wu, Fulong. 2016. 'China's Emergent City-Region Governance: A New Form of State Spatial Selectivity through State-Orchestrated Rescaling'. *International Journal of Urban and Regional Research* 40(6): 1134–1151.

Xu, Bin. 2014. 'Consensus Crisis and Civil Society: The Sichuan Earthquake Response and State–Society Relations'. *The China Journal* 71(1): 91–108.

Xu, Jiatun. 1993. *Xu Jiatun Xianggang huiyilu* [*Xu Jiatun's Hong Kong Memoir*]. Taipei: Linking Publishing.

Yahuda, Michael. 1993. 'Hong Kong's Future: Sino-British Negotiations, Perceptions, Organization and Political Culture'. *International Affairs* 69(2): 245–266.

Yang, Shen. 2020. 'Enclave Deliberation and Social Movement Mobilization: The DDays in Occupy Central'. *Social Movement Studies* 19(2): 144–159.

Yang, Mundo, and Sigrid Baringhors. 2019. 'Studying Media within Political Consumerism'. In *The Oxford Handbook of Political Consumerism*, eds. Magnus Boström, Michele Micheletti, and Peter Oosterveer, 181–204. Oxford: Oxford University Press.

Yaziji, Michael, and Jonathan P. Doh. 2013. 'The Role of Ideological Radicalism and Resource Homogeneity in Social Movement Organization Campaigns against Corporations'. *Organization Studies* 34(5–6): 755–780.

Yep, Ray. 2008. 'The 1967 Riots in Hong Kong: The Diplomatic and Domestic Fronts of the Colonial Governor'. *The China Quarterly* 193: 122–139.

Yep, Ray. 2018. 'Confrontation, state repression and the autonomy of metropolitan Hong Kong: The Umbrella Movement and the 1967 Riots compared'. In *Routledge Handbook of Contemporary Hong Kong*, eds. Tai-lok Lui, Stephen WK Chiu, and Ray Yep, 227–244. London: Routledge.

Yep, Ray, and Tai-Lok Lui. 2010. 'Revisiting the Golden Era of MacLehose and the Dynamics of Social Reforms'. *China Information* 24(3): 249–272.

Yilmaz, Ihsan, and Galib Bashirov. 2018. 'The AKP after 15 Years: Emergence of Erdoganism in Turkey'. *Third World Quarterly* 39(9): 1812–1830.

Ying, Fuk-tsang. 2021. 'The Entanglement between Religion and Politics: Hong Kong Christianity in the Anti-Extradition Bill Movement'. *Review of Religion and Chinese Society* 8: 111–142.

Yuen, Samson. 2018. 'Contesting Middle-Class Civility: Place-Based Collective Identity in Hong Kong's Occupy Mongkok'. *Social Movement Studies* 17(4): 393–407.

Yuen, Samson. 2023. 'The Institutional Foundation of Countermobilization: Elites and Pro-regime Grassroots Organizations in Post-handover Hong Kong'. *Government and Opposition* 58(2): 316–337.

Yuen, Samson, and Edmund W. Cheng. 2017. 'Neither Repression nor Concession? A Regime's Attrition against Mass Protests'. *Political Studies* 65(3): 611–630.

Yuen, Samson, and Edmund W. Cheng. 2020. 'Deepening the State: The Dynamics of China's United Front Work in Post-Handover Hong Kong'. *Communist and Post-Communist Studies* 53(4): 136–154.

Yuen, Samson, and Chit Wai John Mok. 2023. 'Groundwork for Democracy? Community Abeyance and Lived Citizenship in Hong Kong'. *The China Journal* 90(1): 78–105.

Yuen, Samson, and Sanho Chung. 2018. 'Explaining Localism in Post-handover Hong Kong: An Eventful Approach'. *China Perspectives* 3: 19–29.

Yuen, Samson, Gary Tang, Francis L. F. Lee, and Edmund W. Cheng. 2022. 'Surveying Spontaneous Mass Protests: Mixed-mode Sampling and Field Methods'. *Sociological Methodology* 52(1): 75–102.

Yukawa, Taku, Kaoru Hidaka, Kaori Kushima, and Masafumi Fujita. 2022. 'Coup d'état and a Democratic Signal: The Connection between Protests and Coups after the Cold War'. *Journal of Peace Research* 59(6): 828–843.

Zaidise, Eran, Daphna Canetti-Nisim, and Ami Pedahzur. 2007. 'Politics of God or Politics of Man? The Role of Religion and Deprivation in Predicting Support for Political Violence in Israel'. *Political Studies* 55(3): 499–521.

Zald, Mayer N., and Roberta Ash. 1966. 'Social Movement Organizations: Growth, Decay and Change'. *Social Forces* 44(3): 327–341.

Zelizer, Viviana A. The social meaning of money: Pin money, paychecks, poor relief, and other currencies. Princeton University Press, 2017.

Zen, Joseph. 2019. 'Youshi "dongla xiche"' [*Waffle on East and West*]. 1 April. https://oldyosef.hkdavc.com/?p=1193 (Accessed on 22 October 2023).

Zhao, Dingxin. 2001. *The Power of Tiananmen: State-society Relations and the 1989 Beijing Student Movement*. Chicago: University of Chicago Press.

Zheng, Yongnian. 2022. *Civilization and the Chinese Body Politic*. London: Taylor & Francis.

Zhu, Yuner, Edmund W. Cheng, Fei Shen, and Richard Walker. 2022. 'An Eye for an Eye? An Integrated Model of Attitude Change toward Protest Violence'. *Political Communication* 39(4): 539–563.

Index

For EU product safety concerns, contact us at Calle de José Abascal, 56–1°,
28003 Madrid, Spain or eugpsr@cambridge.org.

www.ingramcontent.com/pod-product-compliance
Ingram Content Group UK Ltd.
Pitfield, Milton Keynes, MK11 3LW, UK
UKHW040620240426
470322UK00011B/241